Parent–
Child
Relations
Throughout
Life

*P*arent-*C*hild *R*elations *T*hroughout *L*ife

Edited by

Karl *P*illemer
Cornell University

Kathleen *M*cCartney
University of New Hampshire

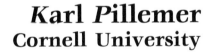 LAWRENCE ERLBAUM ASSOCIATES, PUBLISHERS
1991 Hillsdale, New Jersey   Hove and London

Lawrence Erlbaum Associates, Inc., Publishers
365 Broadway
Hillsdale, New Jersey 07642

Library of Congress Cataloging-in-Publication Data

Parent-child relations throughout life / edited by Karl Pillemer,
    Kathleen McCartney.
        p.   cm.
    Includes the papers of a conference held in May of 1989 in Durham,
New Hampshire.
    Includes bibliographical references and indexes.
    ISBN 0-8058-0822-1
    1. Parent and child—Congresses.   2. Developmental psychology—
Congresses.   3. Family—Congresses.   I. Pillemer, Karl A.
II. McCartney, Kathleen.
    BF723.P25P271991   91-8539
                                                                      CIP

Printed in the United States of America
10   9   8   7   6   5   4   3   2   1

To our parents,
   Jean Burrell and *Louis Pillemer*
   Rose and *George McCartney*

and to our children,
   Hannah and *Sarah Pillemer*
   Kaitlin and *Kimberly McCartney Strovink*

Contents

Contributors

Vern L. Bengtson is AARP/University chair in gerontology and professor of sociology as well as director of the Andrus Gerontology Center's Gerontology Research Institute at the University of Southern California.

Zeynep Biringen is a postdoctoral fellow (sponsored by the MacArthur Research Network on Early Childhood Transitions) in the Department of Psychiatry at the University of Colorado Health Sciences Center.

Andrew M. Boxer is director of the Center for the Study of Adolescence, in the Department of Psychiatry, at Michael Reese Hospital and Medical Center, Chicago, Illinois.

Inge Bretherton is professor in the Department of Child and Family Studies at the University of Wisconsin–Madison.

Victor G. Cicirelli is professor of developmental and aging psychology in the Department of Psychological Sciences at Purdue University, West Lafayette, Indiana.

Judith A. Cook is director of the National Research and Training Center on Rehabilitation of Long-Term Mental Illness at Thresholds Psychiatric Rehabilitation Agency, Chicago, Illinois.

Mihaly Csikszentmihalyi is professor of human development and education at the University of Chicago.

Judy Dunn is distinguished professor of human development at the Pennsylvania State University.

Gilbert Herdt is associate professor in the Committee on Human Development, Department of Psychology, and the College, at the University of Chicago.

Elizabeth Jordan is a doctoral student in psychology at the University of New Hampshire at Durham.

Gerardo Marti is a doctoral student in sociology at the University of Southern California and a research trainee on the Longitudinal Study of Generations.

Kathleen McCartney is associate professor of psychology at the University of New Hampshire at Durham.

Carolyn Mebert is associate professor of psychology at the University of New Hampshire at Durham.

Elizabeth G. Menaghan is associate professor of sociology at the Ohio State University.

Vera Mouradian is a doctoral student in psychology at the University of North Carolina at Greensboro.

Corinne Nydegger is professor of medical anthropology at the University of California, San Francisco.

Toby L. Parcel is associate professor of sociology at the Ohio State University.

Karl Pillemer is assistant professor, Department of Human Development and Family Studies, Cornell University.

Kevin Rathunde is a research associate in the Department of Psychology, University of Chicago.

Doreen Ridgeway is affiliated with the Department of Psychology at the State University of New York at Stony Brook.

Robert E. L. Roberts is a research associate in the Andrus Gerontology Center at the University of Southern California.

Wendy Wagner Robeson is a research associate at the Center for Research on Women at Wellesley College.

Alice S. Rossi is Harriet Martineau Professor of Sociology, University of Massachusetts at Amherst.

Peter H. Rossi is Stuart A. Rice Professor of Sociology and Acting Director, Social and Demographic Research Institute, University of Massachusetts at Amherst.

Sandra Scarr is Commonwealth Professor of Psychology at the University of Virginia.

J. Jill Suitor is associate professor in the Department of Sociology at the Louisiana State University.

Foreword

Sandra Scarr

Chicken Littles have told us repeatedly that the sky is falling on our families. The idealized two-parent family with 2.2 children is a small minority of today's families. Divorced, unmarried, and surrogate mothers seem to have taken a toll on the vitality of the "Traditional American Family." Alternative family forms abound: single parents and children, adolescents rearing children alone, gay couples with children, older adults living together, and so forth.

Born in the idealized 1950s, the imaginary family ideal even today is of two married, heterosexual parents and their young children. However, there are millions of families made up of middle-aged parents with adult children still in the household, of grandparents caring for grandchildren, of middle-aged children caring for their aged parents. In this volume, research is presented on the varied family forms encountered today. The research shows that the contemporary American family has amazing variety and resilience.

Whether families "work" to nurture and protect participants depends on both external and internal systems. External economic conditions, social networks, extended family systems, and other societal supports (or more commonly the lack thereof) all bear on how well family members can function in each others' best interests.

Thus, parents without jobs or adequate income are less able to function as parents and role models for their children than the more fortunately employed. Elderly adults without adequate retirement and medical protection can become abused dependents of resentful adult children. Internal to the family, many personal and relational strains can interfere with the family's functioning. By temperament, some children are easier for parents to like and get along with than others. Children with disabilities place additional strains on parents' relationships and on the family system as a whole. Yet, most families "work" reasonably well to support members' development. Some "work" better than others, a matter that is described in many of the chapters.

Families are both affectional and obligatory systems. Love and obligation characterize all enduring human relationships. Parents not only love their children, they are obligated to provide care and support for them to maturity. Obligations of adult children to their elderly parents require them to provide care and nurturance, reciprocating for their earlier receipt of such benefits. In some cases, physically and mentally disabled adults are perpetual burdens to their aging parents. In other cases, adult children are caring for aging parents with dementia. Obligations continue in many varieties of parent–child relationships across the life span.

Understanding the affectional and obligatory systems of families today requires the perspectives of parents, as well as children, and of variation as well as norms. In this book, the authors address both aspects of parent–child relationships, which is a rare occurrence. Even rarer is the study that investigates individual differences among relationships between parents and their children at any age. In this volume, we find chapters on individual differences in early interactions between infant and preschool siblings and their parents, on daughters' and sons' relationships with mothers and fathers, and on age changes in relational obligations and affection. This is a rich array of variations on the parent–child theme.

Relationships between parents and their children undergo profound changes as children develop and as parents enter new life stages. Developmental psychology has too often ignored the developing adult, whose parenting role changes dramatically from young adulthood and young children, to older adulthood and the children's own maturity. Grandparenthood is yet another life stage: Affectional relations and familial obligations shift from one-sided giving by parents when children are small, to reciprocity in the middle years. This book succeeds in presenting this array of changes in parent–child relations across the life span.

Preface

Karl Pillemer
Kathleen McCartney

One of us is a sociologist who studies aging; the other is a psychologist who studies early childhood. Several years ago, we began to have conversations about our own research. Despite differences in our backgrounds, we quickly realized that we shared a common interest: understanding the nature and dynamics of parent–child relations.

However, because we study parent–child relations at different points in the life course, communication was initially difficult. We found that we read different journals, used different methods, and consulted with different sets of colleagues. This situation was further complicated by the differences in discipline: We had to overcome some of our biases regarding which questions were even worthy of investigation.

Over time, we discovered that by sharing questions and ideas our own research lives were enriched. As we found our own interaction to be beneficial, we became convinced that others in our respective fields would also benefit from greater communication.

One way to achieve this goal is interdisciplinary contact. We therefore planned a conference in which researchers interested in parent–child relations at different points in the life span could come together and discuss common themes. In May 1989 the conference brought together a group of researchers in Durham, New Hampshire to discuss these general themes with respect to young children, adolescents, and adult children of elderly parents. The group was intentionally diverse, and included representatives from psychology, sociology, and anthropology. This volume is comprised of 13 of the papers presented at the conference.

STATEMENT OF THE PROBLEM

As we found in our own experience, a review of the literature reveals a curious phenomenon in the study of parent–child relations: Several parallel lines of research are being conducted with surprisingly little interaction among participants in each group. Most obvious are disciplinary boundaries; to date, communication between psychologists and sociologists investigating parent–child relations is still limited. As Mortimer (1984) has noted, sociologists tend to emphasize social-structural determinants of parent–child relations, such as position in the class structure. Psychologists, on the other hand, are more likely to focus on such factors as individual differences, the child's developmental status, and ongoing parent and child behaviors. However, some progress has recently been made, as indicated by several volumes on parent–child relations that have included members of both disciplines (Hinde & Stevenson-Hinde, 1988; Kreppner & Lerner, 1989; Perlmutter, 1984).

In our view, more striking is the gap that exists between researchers in child development and researchers in aging. This difference has been highlighted by Hagestad (1984), who characterized the two lines of research as *alpha*—research on young children and their parents—and *omega*—research on elderly parents and adult children. Numerous exhortations to bring the alpha and omega research traditions together have met with little success. As Hagestad asserted, "Past work has taken two distinct directions, representing two separate traditions and focusing on two extremes of the human life span" (p. 130).

To be sure, obvious differences exist between the early stages of the family life cycle and the later ones. In early childhood, parent–child relations are more intense, and the influence of parents on children is undoubtedly greater. Essentially, family members cannot easily escape one another's influence. In later life, relations between parents and children assume a more voluntary character (Foner, 1986; Hess & Waring, 1978; Suitor & Pillemer, 1987). This difference is best reflected in the fact that young children almost always live with their parents, whereas adult offspring most often do not.

Given such life-course variations, it is often assumed that issues affecting parents in the early child-rearing years will be very different from those affecting middle-aged and elderly parents. In fact, two vigorous areas of inquiry now exist, divided by the gulf of the life span. Researchers on child development and social gerontologists have worked in isolation from one another, using different types of methods and publishing in different journals. We believe that the contributions to this volume demonstrate one fact: Researchers on young children and their parents and those who study parent–child relations in the middle and later years have much to learn from one another.

PLAN OF THE VOLUME

A review of the literature indicates that despite the differences in the nature
and structure of parent–child relations at different points in the life course,
several overarching themes exist. These major themes, which are reflected in
the outline of this book, are as follows: (a) parent–child attachment, (b) transitions and their impact on parent–child relationships, (c) relationships between
and within families, and (d) the influence of social-structural factors on relations between parents and children. Here, we briefly trace these common
themes, as they appear in the contributions to this book.

Parent–Child Attachment

According to Freud (1962), Erikson (1963), and others, the first psychosocial
task of the infant is *attachment*. Although the term is often used to describe a
relationship between parent and child, social scientists also speak of the child
as "being attached" to the parent. Freud originally hypothesized that the relationship with the mother served as the prototype for future relationships; indeed, this idea can be found in more recent writings by Bowlby (1969), Ainsworth, Blehar, Waters, and Wall (1978), and others. A healthy parent–child
attachment is critical for the individual's emotional adjustment.

Parent–child attachment is also a particularly promising area in which to
examine variations at different life-course stages. In the present volume, two
new perspectives on parent–child attachment are offered. Bretherton, Biring-
ton, and Ridgeway (chapter 1) examine the parental side of attachment, a perspective that has in general been neglected. Cicirelli (chapter 2) extends the
attachment perspective to parent–child relations in later life.

Bretherton et al. explore the inner experience of mothers' attachment relationships. Through interviews, they assessed mothers' thoughts and feelings
regarding their attachment relationships with one of their children. In so doing, they attempted to ascertain the "internal working model" mothers held
of the attached figure and of their own selves. Bretherton et al. find strong
correlations between mothers' sensitivity and insight and the quality of children's attachment to them.

Cicirelli examines adult children's attachment to aging parents in the context of caregiving. This stands in contrast to prior efforts to explain adult children's caregiving, such as those based on obligation or equity theory. Cicirelli
argues that theories based on cultural conditioning or exchange alone are inadequate, because they cannot sufficiently explain children's motivation. Attachment theory, however, can account for motivation. Thus, Cicirelli's explanation for why adult children continue to invest heavily in their parents
is developmental in nature and draws on the notion of internal working models.

In this regard, Cicirelli's logic is quite consistent with that of Bretherton and her colleagues. It also follows that there will be individual differences in adult children's motivation to care for aging parents as a function of the children's internal working models with respect to security.

Life-Course Transitions

Major life transitions are another clear area of overlap between researchers on younger and later life families. As Parke (1988) has observed, interest in stressful normative and non-normative life transitions and their impact on the family has been growing rapidly since the 1970s. He argues that taking a life-span perspective in understanding transitions is of critical importance, in that the impact of transitions depends on the specific developmental status of the individuals affected. There is thus much to be gained by examining transitions that occur at different points in the life span and by considering differences and similarities in their nature and outcomes.

This volume includes three chapters that address the topic of transitions and parent–child relations. Two of these chapters deal with normative transitions: Mebert (chapter 3) on the transition to parenthood and Nydegger (chapter 5) on the development of maturity in intergenerational relations. In contrast, Boxer and his colleagues (chapter 4) treat a non-normative transition: the impact on the family of the revelation that an adolescent is gay or is a lesbian.

Mebert begins by noting that the transition to parenthood was originally viewed as an abrupt ''crisis,'' but that this interpretation has been called into question. She argues that the transition does not occur suddenly with the birth of the first child, but instead begins gradually before the child is born. First, Mebert determines whether the level of motivation for pregnancy is related to several psychological variables. Second, she addresses the question of whether parents who differ in motivation also vary in their mode of approaching parenthood (''assimilative'' vs. ''accommodative''). Her results demonstrate that the timing of the transition to parenthood, as indicated by original motivation and planning for pregnancy, affects such factors as mothers' depression and locus of control. Further, mothers with high motivation are better able to integrate the new baby into their lives.

Nydegger attempts to merge psychological concepts of maturity with research on intergenerational relations. Taking Blenkner's often cited, but largely un-researched, concept of ''filial maturity'' as a springboard, Nydegger explores the degree to which relationships with aging parents are in fact a path to maturity. Filial and parental maturity emerge from her research as matched concepts, which develop in parallel courses. Further, Nydegger is able to refine and revise Blenkner's view by rejecting the notion that filial maturity must follow a crisis and that it only occurs in middle age. Instead, Nydegger demonstrates that maturity in children develops gradually throughout their relationships with their parents. She also notes that within-family diversity exists; different children within the same family may have widely varying filial maturity experiences.

Boxer, Cook, and Herdt examine the process of "coming out" as gay or lesbian and its impact on the quality of parent–child relationships. Based on an extensive research project that involved interviews with adolescents and parents, Boxer et al. establish that alterations in parent–child relations are a critical dimension of this identity transition. They are able to specify ways in which parents are affected by the disclosure that their child is gay or lesbian and how parents and children subsequently alter their relationships. The transition to a publicly gay or lesbian identity becomes a family event or, in the authors' words, a "family coming out process," in which parents restructure their expectations and goals for the future life course of their children.

Between-Family and Within-Family Approaches

Until relatively recently, researchers conceived of parent–child relations in a somewhat limited way. Traditionally, investigators focused on parents' effects on children and paid scant attention to children's effects on parents. In fact, family systems theory suggests that family dynamics consist of more than just parent effects and child effects (Sameroff, 1982; Steinglass, 1987). In addition, between-family designs, in which comparisons are made among individuals from different kinds of families, are much more typical than within-family designs, in which comparisons are made within the family.

Although the between-family approach can be useful, it is limited when variations within families moderate or obscure between-family effects. For example, birth order has most often been studied using between-family analyses; however, it is likely that birth-order effects can only be understood by considering conditions within the family, such as spacing of siblings, gender of siblings, or even personality of siblings (Plomin & Daniels, 1987).

This volume includes five empirical chapters in which between-family and within-family analyses are presented. What unites these five chapters is their departure from traditional socialization research that has focused on parent effects on children using between-family comparisons. The first two chapters are by developmental psychologists. Both chapters advocate the need for within-family studies. The data presented by Dunn (chapter 6) show evidence for similar treatment of children by parents, whereas McCartney and colleagues (chapter 7) show that treatment is more similar when the children are more similar— at least with respect to language use. Rathunde and Csikszentmihalyi (chapter 8) conduct between-family analyses on the dimension of complexity, and relate it to adolescent happiness. Pillemer and Suitor (chapter 9) consider children's effects on elderly parents' well-being, and Suitor and Pillemer (chapter 10) examine the impact of coresidence on various dyads within the family.

Dunn demonstrates convincingly the importance of differences in siblings' experiences from a developmental perspective. Her argument is easily made based on data from her Cambridge Sibling Study and from collaborative work with Robert Plomin on the Colorado Adoption Project. Dunn suggests that the origin of individual differences lies primarily with differential parental treatment. Although mothers are relatively consistent in their behavior toward their different children when the children are the same age, their behavior toward each child is not stable. Thus, at any given time, a mother behaves differently toward her different children.

McCartney, Robeson, Jordan, and Mouradian examine differential parental treatment directly within the context of language use. McCartney and her colleagues studied mothers and their first-born and second-born children when each child was 21 months old. Mothers were consistent in their language use to their two children, especially with respect to syntax. Mothers also adapted their language to their two children, especially with respect to certain language functions. The chapter concludes with a taxonomy of potential sources of differential parental treatment of siblings that will help to guide future research.

Rathunde and Csikszentmihalyi studied adolescents' perceptions of their happiness at home. Using the Experience Sampling Method, individuals assessed their subjective experience at random intervals. Based on questionnaire data, families were categorized as *complex* if they were both integrated and differentiated; that is, if they were flexible. The researchers found that children need more complex environments so that they can engage in activities that promote their development. Rathunde and Csikszentmihalyi link the ideas of integration and differentiation with attachment and autonomy, and discuss the implications of these dimensions for healthy parent–child relationships.

Pillemer and Suitor's chapter examines the issue of reciprocal influences between parents and children in later life. They begin by arguing that gerontological research has overemphasized the influence of elderly parents on their adult children. In particular, the literature focuses on declines in health of elderly parents and resulting dependency on children as the major dynamic in late-life families. However, based on recent research in child development, Pillemer and Suitor argue that adult children are equally likely to have a significant impact on their *parents*, even into later life. They focus on adult children who have serious problems with mental and physical health. Using data from a random sample survey, they provide evidence that having a troubled adult child is negatively related to parental well-being.

Suitor and Pillemer's chapter examines elderly parent–adult child relationships when the generations share a residence. The focus of this chapter is the impact of residence-sharing on parents' marital relationships and on relationships with their adult children. Contrary to previous speculation, simply shar-

ing a residence with an adult child was not found to have an impact on elderly parents' marriages. Further, surprisingly low levels of parent–child conflict were found in shared households regardless of whether children lived in
their parents' homes, or the reverse. The authors argue that the voluntary nature of parent–child relationships in later life allows elderly parents to choose
whether to live with their children. Thus, elderly persons do not involve
themselves in shared living situations with children that are conflictual and
distressing.

Social-Structural Influences on Parent–Child Relations

There is a long-standing tendency to view parent–child relations strictly in an
intrafamilial context. However, a number of social scientists have attempted
to move beyond this more limited perspective. Sociologists often quote C.
Wright Mills (1959) in this context, who asserted that ''the individual can understand his own experience and gauge his own fate only by locating himself
within his period, [and] he can know his own chances in life only by becoming
aware of those of all individuals in his circumstances'' (p. 5). The argument
is made that social science in general should focus on larger social processes
that influence the lives of individuals (for a recent review of this perspective,
see House & Mortimer, 1990). Psychologists, too, have embraced such a view
(Bronfenbrenner, 1979; Cochran, Lerner, Riley, Gunnarson, & Henderson,
1990; Kessen, 1978; Parke, 1988).

   This perspective has led to analyses of parent–child relations that include
structural variables. The goal is to examine how factors like economic conditions, race, or group norms and values affect such diverse family characteristics as child-rearing practices (Kohn, 1969), family conflict and violence (Straus
& Gelles, 1990), or intergenerational support in later life (Mutran, 1985).

   The three chapters in this section reflect a concern with understanding ex-
trafamilial influences on parent–child relations, although the authors approach
this topic in different ways. Three different aspects of social structure are
represented in these articles: Rossi and Rossi (chapter 11), the power of social
norms; Menaghan and Parcel (chapter 12), the economic system; and Bengtson, Marti, and Roberts (chapter 13), the political system.

   Rossi and Rossi undertake a systematic analysis of the structure of social
norms regarding relationships with kin. In particular, they examine the ways
in which these general rules regarding obligations toward kin are translated
into specific guides for behavior. Their findings indicate that normative obligations toward kin are highly patterned by the structure of the relationship
and are not greatly affected by situational factors. Parents and children evoke
the greatest obligation, followed by more distant relatives. Norms regarding
helping parents and children are so strong that factors such as gender and mar-

ital status do not affect levels of obligation. Norms regarding helping appear to translate into actual behavior, as well: Individuals who report higher levels of kin obligation also report greater exchange of help with parents and children.

Menaghan and Parcel employ social-structural variables to understand parent–child relations. They focus on mothers who are employed, asking what effects the occupational and economic experiences of those mothers have on their children's lives. By examining the influence of structural factors on the relationship between maternal employment and child outcomes, they attempt to understand the ways in which social structure shapes family structure and thereby human development. Menaghan and Parcel assert that mothers' employment experience affects both parental values and maternal well-being, which in turn influence children's cognitive, social, and emotional outcomes. Further, they hold that a similar relationship exists between mothers' employment experiences and *non*-family child care. Both mothers' economic situation and their values help determine the type and quality of day care their children receive and thereby also the outcomes for the children.

Bengtson, Marti, and Roberts tackle the complex and controversial debate over "generational equity," which centers around the distribution of resources among cohorts in society. Increases in resources to the elderly are seen by some critics as resulting in decreases in resources to needy children. Concern over generational equity has led to the founding of national organizations that lobby for a reallocation of resources from programs for the elderly to those for children. The authors argue that the generational equity debate can be illuminated by examining three family issues that characterize intergenerational interaction: autonomy, solidarity, and affirmation. Within families, the generations struggle with the contradictions between autonomy and dependency, solidarity and individuality, and affirmation and conflict. Much of what occurs at the societal level, they assert, reflects these basic conflicts. Throughout the chapter, Bengtson et al. move back and forth between the macro- and microlevels, using family-level data to illuminate the larger social policy issue.

SOME FINAL THOUGHTS

It is apparent that the contributions to this volume address a wide range of substantive issues and use a variety of theoretical perspectives and methods. Thus, it is appropriate to consider the question: What is the value of bringing together a diverse group of researchers who seem to study parent–child relations differently?

The most obvious answer to this question are the common themes around which the chapters are organized. They make clear the considerable community of interests among these scholars that transcends disciplinary and life-span boundaries. Beyond these themes that have been explicitly identified, a careful reading of the chapters shows numerous other areas of agreement. For example, a number of the authors reject the notion that parent–child relations are characterized by crises. Other authors demonstrate the need to examine different gender combinations in parent–child relations. Many also discuss the need to examine the family more closely, by looking within it, by studying both fathers and mothers, or by considering bidirectional influence.

We believe that the most important benefit to be gained from this volume is the generation of new ideas for research. Beyond the specific suggestions for future research given in each chapter, we hope that the volume inspires scholars to reach across disciplines and across different points in the life span in designing their research. To give only one example, with a few notable exceptions, gerontologists have not examined questions that are burning issues in child development: Children's influence on parents and differences among siblings within the same family are only two possible avenues for exploration.

Our conviction that it is of critical importance to look for common themes in parent–child relations throughout life stems in part from our experience in preparing this volume and in organizing the conference that led to it. We hope that readers will share our enthusiasm for weakening the barriers that divide researchers and for devising a broader view of relationships between parents and children throughout life.

ACKNOWLEDGMENTS

We are grateful to a number of individuals for their assistance in bringing this volume into being. The Elliot Fund of the University of New Hampshire generously sponsored the project. Several administrators and faculty at the University of New Hampshire provided support and advice at various points, including Peter Dodge, Richard Hersh, David Leary, Dennis Meadows, Stuart Palmer, and Murray Straus. Angele Cook and Amanda Diggins deserve special mention for ably assisting with administrative tasks. Elizabeth Howley provided assistance in planning the conference on which the volume was based. We are most grateful to the participants, whose intellectual contributions made this volume possible.

REFERENCES

Ainsworth, M. D. S., Blehar, M. C., Waters, E., & Wall, S. (1978). *Patterns of attachment*. Hillsdale, NJ: Lawrence Erlbaum Associates.

Bowlby, J. (1969). *Attachment and loss, Vol. 1: Attachment*. New York: Basic Books.

Bronfenbrenner, U. (1979). *The ecology of human development: Experiments by nature and design*. Cambridge, MA: Harvard University Press.

Cochran, M., Lerner, M., Riley, D., Gunnarson, L., & Henderson, C. R. (1990). *Extending families: The social networks of parents and their children*. Cambridge: Cambridge University Press.

Erikson, E. (1963). *Childhood and society*. New York: Norton.

Foner, A. (1986). *Aging and old age*. Englewood Cliffs, NJ: Prentice-Hall.

Freud, S. (1962). *Three contributions to the theory of sex*. New York: E. P. Dutton.

Hagestad, G. O. (1984). The continuous bond: A dynamic, multigenerational perspective on parent–child relations between adults: In M. Perlmutter (Ed.), *Parent–child interaction and parent–child relations in child development. Minnesota Symposium on Child Psychology* (Vol. 17, pp. 129–158). Hillsdale, NJ: Lawrence Erlbaum Associates.

Hess, B. B., & Waring, J. M. (1978). Changing patterns of aging and family bonds in later life. *Family Coordinator, 27*, 303–314.

Hinde, R. A., & Stevenson-Hinde, J. (1988). *Relationships within families*. Oxford, England: Oxford University Press.

House, J. S., & Mortimer, J. T. (1990). Social structure and the individual: Emerging themes and new directions. *Social Psychology Quarterly, 53*, 71–80.

Kessen, W. (1978). The American child and other cultural inventions. *American Psychologist, 34*, 815–820.

Kohn, M. L. (1969). *Class and conformity: A study in values*. Homewood, IL: Dorsey Press.

Kreppner, K., & Lerner, R. M. (1989). *Family systems and life-span development*. Hillsdale, NJ: Lawrence Erlbaum Associates.

Mills, C. W., (1959). *The sociological imagination*. New York: Oxford.

Mortimer, J. T. (1984). Commentary: Psychological and sociological perspectives on parent–child relations. In M. Perlmutter (Ed.), *Parent–child interaction and parent–child relations in child development. Minnesota Symposium on Child Psychology* (Vol. 17, pp. 159–165). Hillsdale, NJ: Lawrence Erlbaum Associates.

Mutran, E. (1985). Intergenerational family support among Blacks and Whites: Response to culture or to socioeconomic differences? *Journal of Gerontology, 40*, 382–389.

Parke, R. D. (1988). Families in life-span perspective: A multilevel developmental approach. In E. M. Hetherington, R. M. Lerner, & M. Perlmutter (Eds.), *Child development in life-span perspective*. (pp. 159–190). Hillsdale, NJ: Lawrence Erlbaum Associates.

Perlmutter, M. (Ed.). (1984). *Parent–child interaction and parent–child relations in child development. Minnesota Symposium on Child Psychology* (vol. 17). Hillsdale, NJ: Lawrence Erlbaum Associates.

Plomin, R., & Daniels, D. (1987). Why are children in the same family so different from one another? *Behavioral and Brain Sciences, 10*, 1–59.

Sameroff, A. J. (1982). Development and dialectic: The need for a systems approach. In W. A. Collins (Ed.), *Minnesota Symposium on Child Psychology* (Vol. 15, pp. 187–244). Hillsdale, NJ: Lawrence Erlbaum Associates.

Steinglass, P. (1987). *The alcoholic family*. New York: Basic Books.

Straus, M., & Gelles, R. J. (1990). *Physical violence in American families: Risk factors and adaptations to violence in 8,145 families*. New Brunswick, NJ: Transaction.

Suitor, J. J., & Pillemer, K. (1987). The presence of adult children: A source of stress for elderly couples' marriages? *Journal of Marriage and the Family, 49*, 717–725.

I

ATTACHMENT

The Parental Side of Attachment

Inge Bretherton
University of Wisconsin-Madison
Zeynep Biringen
University of Colorado Health Sciences Center
Doreen Ridgeway
State University of New York at Stony Brook

Until quite recently, attachment theorists and researchers paid rather little heed to the parental experience of attachment relationships. Following Bowlby's (1958, 1969) theoretical formulations, empirical studies emphasized the infant's need for a special figure who is emotionally and physically available and thereby facilitates exploration of the environment (secure base), whose sensitive responsiveness in stressful or alarming situations provides reassurance, comfort, and protection (secure haven), whose departure arouses anxiety and whose return is generally welcomed with relief and pleasure (Ainsworth, Blehar, Waters, & Wall, 1978). Even when investigators began to explore attachment experiences beyond infancy (Bretherton, Ridgeway, & Cassidy, in press; Cassidy, 1988; Kaplan, 1984; Main, Kaplan, & Cassidy, 1985; Marvin, 1977), the focus remained on attachment from the filial point of view, whether the assessments were of children or adults.

This neglect of the parental side of attachment is surprising for two reasons. First, findings by Ainsworth and her colleagues (summarized in Ainsworth, Bell, & Stayton 1974) had strongly suggested that parental sensitivity and responsiveness are a strong causal factor in the quality of developing attachment relationships. It would therefore seem a natural next step to also probe individual differences in parents' inner experience of the attachment relationship. Second, spontaneous expressions of parental attachment behavior (watching, warning, retrieving, protecting) are easy to observe in everyday life. Indeed, there have been studies of maternal separation anxiety (Hock, 1984), but these were not guided by attachment theory.

Some investigators (e.g., Stevenson-Hinde, personal communication, July 1987) prefer to use the term parent–child bond or caregiving relationship rather

1

than parent–child attachment. These researchers contend that *attachment* as defined by Bowlby (1969) refers to a relationship in which the attachment figure
is stronger and wiser than the attached person. Under this definition, a child
can be attached to a parent, but the converse cannot obtain. However, we believe that a strong case can be made for using the term *attachment* in both senses.
True, the provision of protection and security is complementary (not equal)
to the seeking of protection and security, but there are striking emotional
parallels. It is not only the infant who keeps tabs on the parent, and who becomes distressed upon separation; parents also keep a watchful eye on their
infant, become alarmed when the infant's whereabouts are not known or the
infant's well-being is endangered, and feel relieved when the infant is found
or the danger past. These feelings are so compelling that the label *caregiving
relationship* (suggested by Bowlby) seems somehow too pale. As one father
remarked to us as he rescued his 2-year-old from the vicinity of a swimming
pool: "Before we had a child, I didn't know what fear was." A statement by
a mother belonging to the !Kung hunter-gatherer society of the Kalahari desert
(Shostak, 1981) attests to the universality of such feelings:

> When I sit in the village and my children are playing around me, I don't worry.
> I just watch what they do. When I leave them behind and go gathering, I worry
> that they won't be well taken care of, especially if the only person in the village
> is there because she isn't well. (p. 106)

Although the parental side of attachment was not the primary focus of his
interest, Bowlby did not neglect this topic altogether. In a brief section in his
1969 volume, he considers it in the context of discussing maternal retrieving
behavior in mammals:

> Whilst maternal retrieving behavior is to be seen in its most elementary forms
> in non-human species, it is evident also in human mothers. In primitive societies
> a mother is likely to remain very near her infant, and almost always within eye-
> shot or earshot of him. The mother's alarm or the infant's distress will at once
> elicit action. In more developed communities the scene becomes more complex,
> partly because not infrequently a mother appoints someone to deputize for her
> for a shorter or longer part of the day. Even so, most mothers experience a strong
> pull to be close to their babies and young children. Whether they submit to the
> pull, or stand out against it depends on a hundred variables, personal, cultural
> and economic. (p. 241)

Bowlby further argued that, beyond infancy, the attachment relationship
could best be characterized as a goal-corrected partnership between parent and
child. In such a partnership, each member is able to see the world from the
perspective of the other and to take that perspective into account in the negotiation of joint goals. This idea is supported by recent evidence that even tod-

dlers have some rudimentary role-taking ability (Bretherton & Beeghly, 1982). By 4 years of age the ability to negotiate plans regarding maternal departures is sufficiently well developed to have a significant influence on child behavior (Marvin & Greenberg, 1982). However, the parents' equally important contribution to the goal-corrected partnership has not yet been examined, although it is clear that individual differences in parental perspective taking must play a crucial role in the developing relationship.

In the study reported in this chapter we begin to explore the parental side of attachment through interviews in which we asked mothers to discuss their thoughts and feelings about their attachment relationship with a specific child. The theoretical basis for our investigation was Bowlby's account of the internationalization of attachment relations in infancy (Bowlby, 1969, 1973, 1980).

PARENTAL ATTACHMENT AND THE CONCEPT OF "INTERNAL WORKING MODELS"

In discussing the *infant's* experience and representation of attachment relations, Bowlby (1969, 1973, 1980) proposed the concept of "internal working model." Internal working models of the environment and of the significant people in it are dynamic representations constructed through transactions with the world (for reviews and further development of these ideas see Bretherton, 1985, 1987, 1990).

An especially important *component* of an individual's working model of the world are working models of the attachment figure and the self. To quote Bowlby (1969):

> Starting, we may suppose, toward the end of the first year, and probably especially actively during his second and third year when he acquires the powerful and extraordinary gift of language, a child is busy constructing working models of how his mother and other significant persons may be expected to behave, how he himself may be expected to behave, and of how each interacts with all the others. Within the framework of these working models he evaluates his situation and makes his plans. And within the framework of the working models of his mother and himself he evaluates special aspects of his situation and makes his attachment plans. (p. 354)

According to Bowlby (1973, 1980), internal working models provide the basic framework for experiencing, interpreting and anticipating events in the world, including attachment-related events. For this reason, the healthy functioning of attachment relationships is crucially dependent on how valid and accessible to conscious awareness (vs. distorted and inaccessible) a child's internal models of self and attachment figure are (Bowlby, 1969). It is equally important that the child's developing working models of self and attachment figure(s) mesh well with the parents' internal working models of self and child (Bretherton, 1987, in press). Yet so far, parents' internal working models of self as attachment figure in relation to a specific child have been assessed only indirectly, that is in relation to the parents' family of origin.

In a seminal study, Main, Kaplan, and Cassidy (1985) discovered that the quality of children's attachment to parents, as observed at 1 and 6 years of age, is impressively correlated with specific patterns of parental responses to a semistructured interview, the Berkeley Adult Attachment Interview (Main & Goldwyn, in press). This interview consists of a series of open-ended questions regarding parental recollections of childhood attachment figures, and the influence of these early attachment on the parents' own development and relationships. To analyze the interview, Main and Goldwyn (in press; see also Main et al., 1985) eschewed the more usual procedure of analyzing separate responses to each question. Instead, they carefully read and reread each interview transcript, and then evaluated the text as a whole. Their analysis revealed three major patterns of responding. First, parents of 6-year-olds classified as secure with them in infancy valued both attachment and autonomy, and seemed at ease when discussing the influence of attachment-related issues on their own development (whether or not they recalled a secure childhood). Second, parents of children who were classified as insecure-avoidant with them in infancy, dismissed and devalued attachment. They appeared to believe that early attachment experiences had little effect on their own development, and frequently claimed not to remember any incidents from childhood. Specific memories that emerged despite this denial were likely not to support the generalized (often highly idealized) descriptions of their parents. Third, parents of children previously classified as insecure-resistant seemed preoccupied with their early attachments. They recalled many specific, often conflict-ridden incidents about childhood attachments without being able to weave them into a consistent overall picture. In summary, both the dismissing and preoccupied parents found it difficult to discuss attachment relationships in an integrated way. Recently, a fourth major classification of infant–attachment (insecure-disorganized) has been identified by Main and Solomon (1990). Data from the Adult Attachment Interview showed that parents of such infants seemed to be struggling with unresolved issues concerning the loss of an attachment figure in childhood (see Main & Solomon, 1990). These results have been replicated in two other samples (Eichberg, 1987; Grossmann, Fremmer-Bombik, Rudolph, & Grossmann, in press).

On the basis of Main's (1985) findings with the Adult Attachment Interview, we reasoned that an interview focused on parents' attachment experiences with their own child should furnish us with material suitable for an analogous qualitative analysis. We also expected that findings from such an analysis would, like those of Main et al. (1985), be systematically related to observational measures of attachment. Consequently, we designed an in-depth, structured but open-ended *Parent Attachment Interview*, in which we inquired about the relationship from an attachment-theoretical perspective. Although the primary intent was to examine the interview text in relation to individual differences in attachment quality, we decided to begin with a content analysis in order to gain some insight into the attachment-related issues that concern mothers of 2-year-olds. The subsequent qualitative analysis of individual differences among mothers relied on a scale of maternal sensitivity/insight developed by Biringen and Bretherton (elaborating on Biringen, 1988) which was applied to the transcribed interview texts as a whole. The theoretical basis of this scale derived from two sources: Findings showing (a) that a mother's ability to respond promptly and appropriately to her infant's signals is associated with the development of a secure infant–mother relationship (Ainsworth et al., 1978), and (b) that mothers of secure infants are able to discuss attachment issues with emotional openness and reflectiveness (Main et al., 1985). For validation purposes sensitivity/insight scores were compared with prior, concurrent, and later measures of attachment and with a variety of other attachment-relevant socioemotional variables.

METHOD

Sample

Participating in this research were 37 lower to upper middle-class families. Maternal education ranged from 12 to 22 years (M = 14.6 years). Most mothers were in their late 20s or early 30s (M = 29.3 years, range 20 to 36 years). The families were recruited into the study when the children were 18 months old. Names were obtained through birth announcements in the local newspaper. A letter of invitation describing the study was sent to the family, and was followed by a telephone call. Of those contacted, 80% agreed to participate.

Mothers and children (20 girls, 17 boys) were asked to take part in a two-phase longitudinal study of mastery motivation and its relation to attachment security at 18 and 25 months (Maslin, Bretherton, & Morgan, 1987). The project was later extended to include affect communication and the child's representation of attachment at 37 months (Bretherton et al., 1990). Twenty-nine families participated in this third phase of the study.

Procedure

A large body of data was collected when the children were 18, 25, and 37 months old. The centerpiece of this chapter is the parent attachment interview given to the mothers when the children were 25 months old, but other attachment-related measures were also obtained. At 18 months, the Ainsworth Strange Situation was administered during one of two laboratory sessions. At 25 months, the mothers performed the Waters and Deane Attachment Q-sort after the interview session; at 37 months they performed the same Q-sort at home. In preparation for the final sorts, the mothers were asked to do a preliminary sort in the lab and were given a list of the Q-sort items to take home. This list was to serve as a basis for observing child behavior during the ensuing week. In addition, an attachment story completion task (Bretherton et al., 1990) was administered to the children in the laboratory at 37 months. This task consisted of five story beginnings enacted with small props and family figures. Security was assessed on the basis of the child's open, coherent responding to and benign resolution of the story issues (misbehavior, pain, fear, separation and reunion in the attachment relationship). Following this task, a separation-reunion procedure was conducted. This procedure consisted of a 3-minute episode, during which the child played in the presence of the tester, followed by a second 3-minute period, during which the child was alone while the tester left ("to get your Mommy"). Security classifications based on the reunion behaviors were performed by Cassidy, using a coding system for 3- to 5-year-olds developed by Cassidy, Marvin, and the MacArthur Attachment Work Group (1987).

The mother also filled out a variety of questionnaires during the home and laboratory visits at 18, 25, and 37 months. These included two child temperament scales, a marital questionnaire, a family questionnaire, a personality inventory, a maternal attitude survey, and a family of origin parenting assessment. The Colorado child temperament inventory (Rowe & Plomin, 1977) with scales for activity level, attention span, emotionality, sociability, and shyness, and the difficultness scale from the infant characteristics questionnaire (Bates, Freeland, & Lounsbury, 1979) were given at 18 months. The Spanier dyadic adjustment scale (Spanier, 1976) was administered at 18 and 25 months to assess marital satisfaction. At 25 months, the family adaptability and cohesion evaluation scale (FACESII; Olson, Bell, & Portner, 1983) was used to obtain information on family functioning. In addition, the mother filled out the Myers-Briggs type indicator (MBTI; a Jungian personality scale) at 18 months. The MBTI (Meyers, 1962) includes scales for extraversion versus introversion, thinking versus feeling, sensing versus intuition, and perceptiveness versus judging. The SUNY temperament, attitude and activity survey (Waters & Ridgeway, 1986) was also administered at 37 months. Interspersed amongst positive items, this survey contains a depression scale (adapted from the Beck depression inventory; Beck, Ward, Mendelson, Mock, & Erbaugh, 1961), and the interfering affects scale developed by Waters and Ridgeway as part of the larger scale. The latter assesses the degree to which anxiety and defensiveness intrude into an individual's capacity for enjoyment. The depression and interfering affects scales provided information about the mother's current emotional well-being. Finally, we included the mother–father–peer scale (Epstein, 1983), with scales assessing parental acceptance–rejection and parental encouragement of independence in the mother's family of origin.

THE PARENT ATTACHMENT INTERVIEW

During the 25-months phase of the study, we invited the mothers to come to our laboratory for an interview to help us "find out what it is like to be a parent to your 2-year-old." Questions concentrated on a number of attachment-related issues, although other aspects of the relationship were also examined. An attempt was made to create a relaxed atmosphere by offering light refreshments in a comfortable living-room setting. The session lasted from 45 to 90 minutes (normally about 1 hour) and was audiotaped.

A standard sequence of questions with optional probes was used. Mothers were encouraged to describe one or more specific situations in answer to each question, not just to reply in general terms. No specific response categories were suggested. This was accomplished by phrasing the questions in terms of "Tell me about what happens when . . . ," "What do you do when X happens," "How is X different from or similar to Y."

First, by way of introduction, we asked about the mother's expectations of the baby during pregnancy, and from whom she had sought advice. Because the mother's bond to the infant predates the infant's attachment to the mother (Glogger-Tippelt, 1989), we asked about her thoughts and feelings at the baby's birth, and what the baby was like as a person during the first 2 months or so. We then inquired about her experiences with the 2-year-old toddler. This part of the interview began with a request to describe the toddler with five adjectives and then to elaborate on the reasons for choosing them. In further questions, we focused on emotional experiences that the dyad had shared, asking about enjoyable times, as well as situations that aroused anger, sadness, fear, pain, and empathy. These questions on emotion and emotion communication were included because of observational and interview findings linking open affect communication with secure attachment relationships (Escher-Graeub & Grossmann, 1983; Grossmann & Grossmann, 1984; Grossmann, Grossmann, & Schwan, 1986).

Direct questions about attachment issues focused on separations (bedtime, nighttime, and maternal absences) and on autonomy-related negotiations. Regarding the latter, we asked how the mother responded when the child was trying to do something she judged him or her unable to do and, conversely, how the mother responded when the child asked her to do something that he or she had already mastered.

In addition, we requested that the mother compare and contrast the child's relationships to mother and father. This was followed by a second comparison question regarding similarities and differences between the mother's relationship with her own mother in childhood and her current relationship to her child. Finally, we asked the mother to share her thoughts about the child as an adolescent or adult.

Data Analysis

Audiotapes of the interviews were transcribed verbatim. Pauses were marked by dashes. The content analysis focused on maternal thoughts regarding particular attachment issues. It was primarily based on responses to specific questions, but whenever additional material pertinent to a topic was mentioned elsewhere in the interview, it was also taken into account. For example, bedtime issues were not only discussed during the bedtime question, but also tended to come up during earlier questions about emotional experiences. The first step of this analysis was carried out by two research assistants. It consisted of breaking the information down into grosser categories (e.g., what the mother said regarding positive and negative similarities in the cross-generational mother–child relationship, and what she said about positive and negative differences). The second step consisted in tabulating the response categories used by the mother herself. This tabulation was performed by the first author.

The global analysis was aimed at detecting individual differences in the quality of the relationship as seen from the mother's perspective. As previously noted, parents' ability to give coherent descriptions of their own attachment relations in childhood, as well as parental sensitivity in parent–infant interactions have been excellent discriminators between secure and insecure relationships (Ainsworth et al., 1978; Main et al., 1985). Building on these findings, we created a nine-point rating scale was created to assess the mother's sensitivity/insight concerning her relationship with the child.

High scores (6 or above) on the sensitivity/insight scale are awarded if the interview vividly conveys a mother's sensitive and appropriate responses to her child's communications (where sensitive and appropriate are defined within the framework of attachment theory), and documents her ability to reflect on her relationship with the child, as well as on her own and her child's behavior and personality. In applying the scale, it is important to assess whether the mother's general statements about child rearing and about the child's relationship with her and other family members are consistent with her specific descriptions of what actually happens.

Low scores (less than 5) are given if a mother talks about the "right" things to do, but then describes her own behavior in terms that are at variance with her general statements about child rearing (i.e., the interview documents low sensitivity as well as low insight). A mother may also fail to make obvious connections between her own and her child's behavior, or repeatedly express her puzzlement or perplexity at why the child behaves as he or she does. Alternatively, she may describe overcontrolling or undercontrolling behavior by herself or the child, but given the impression that she is helpless to do much about it. Low scores are also awarded if the mother consistently speaks of the child as if he or she were a possession. If the mother describes insensitive behavior in relationship to the child, but can pinpoint what is wrong she receives a less extreme low score than if she demonstrates little or no insight.

The second author who had no other knowledge about the subjects, applied the sensitivity/insight scale to the interview text. To test for reliability, an independent rater—also blind to other data from the study—received training in using the scale, and then independently rated 10 interviews. The product moment correlation coefficient for both sets of ratings was .81.

RESULTS AND DISCUSSION

The results are reported and discussed in two parts. First we present findings from the content analysis of those interview questions that are especially pertinent to attachment from the maternal perspective. Next, we focus on the sensitivity/insight scale that was designed to capture individual differences in maternal working models of self and child in the attachment relationship. In this connection, we consider two sets of findings: (a) correlations of the sensitivity/insight scale from the interview with other measures of attachment obtained at 18, 25, and 37 months, and (b) correlations between the interview scale and maternal information (derived from questionnaires) regarding child temperament, family functioning, maternal personality, and family of origin.

Content Analysis of the Parental Attachment Interview

We have chosen to report maternal responses to the following questions: (a) the mothers' thoughts and feelings during the baby's birth, (b) the baby's personality during the first 2 months, (c) the mother's statements regarding separations (nighttime, maternal absence), (d) maternal coping with autonomy issues, and (e) intergenerational comparison in which the mother describes herself as a child and as a mother.

Feelings at the Child's Birth. According to attachment theory (Bowlby, 1969), an infant's attachment to the mother develops during the second half of the first year of life. The maternal bond to the child, by contrast, begins at birth (see Table 1.1a), if not before (Zeanah, Keener, Stewart, & Anders, 1985; Glogger-Tippelt, 1989). A question about the mother's feelings and thoughts at the birth was therefore highly relevant to assessing attachment from the parental perspective. To describe their feelings, many mothers used very

TABLE 1.1
Maternal Responses to Specific Interview Topics*

1a. *Mothers' Feelings at the Infant's Birth*	
Intense Happiness	21
Baby look beautiful	7
Love for baby	7
Pleased with baby's gender	15
Disappointed, depressed about baby's gender	4
Alarmed about baby's condition	4

1b. *The Baby as a Person During the First 2 Months*	
Happy, content, not fussy	20
Calm, good sleeper	19
Easy, easygoing	12
Alert, playful	11
Active	8
Cuddly	3
Fussy, colicky	8
Demanding	3

1c. *Parental and Child Responses to Nighttime Waking*	
Child climbs into parental bed unnoticed	5
Child climbs into parental bed (parents sometimes discourage)	7
Mother brings child to parental bed	3
Child habitually sleeps in same bed as sibling	4
Mother or sometimes father, go to child	18
Child falls back to sleep without help	4
Child has not woken at night for a long time	5

1d. *Maternal Feelings About Separation*	
Mother not worried if child well cared for	14
Mother enjoys being away	8
Mother puts child out of mind, shifts gears	5
Mother misses child, thinks about what child might be doing	18
Mother worries	
about child missing her	4
about child feeling bad	11
about child's safety, care	12
about correct discipline	1
about child behavior to sitter	8
Mother feels guilty about working	6

1f. *Child Wants to Perform an Activity Unaided That He or She Has Not Mastered*	
Mother distinguishes danger from nondanger situations	16
Mother monitors child closely	
in danger situations	8
in mess situations	2
in breakage situations	2

(Continued)

TABLE 1.1

(Continued)

1f. Child Wants to Perform an Activity Unaided That He or She Has Not Mastered

---

Child resists unwanted help	18
Child requests or accepts help when stuck	16
Child accepts partial help, demonstration, or substitute activity	15
Mother mentions time as nuisance factor	10
Mother accepts possibility of mishaps	
(not in danger situations)	5

1g. Similarities Between the Mother's Relationship With Her Own Mother and to Her Child

---

Affection, loving	8
Comforting, soothing	6
Doing joint activities	9
Understanding, explaining, encouragement, respect	7
Discipline	4
Maternal personality	7

1h. Differences Between Mother's Relationship to Her Mother and the Relationship Her Own Child

---

More closeness, affection	11
More communication	5
More activities together	11
Different discipline	13
Other	10

Note: Figures refer to the number of moters who gave a response in each category. They could give more than one response, or have no response in that category. Hence totals do not necessarily add up to 37.

strong emotional words: "ecstatic," "elated," "excited," "thrilled," "extreme peace." Many commented on how beautiful the baby looked to them, and on the love they felt: "It's hard to explain, but you feel super close. Even though you don't know him (the baby) it's like you *do* know him. It's just so warm, and you're kind of scared too. This little baby is going to depend on you, but you feel really warm and all this love pours out into this little kid."

Of the seven mothers who did not use any positive descriptions, three were alarmed about the baby's condition (one was slightly burnt on the arm by a cauterizer), and the other four were disappointed about the baby's gender. As one mother said, "For 2 months I mourned the daughter I will never have." Other mothers also dwelt on the baby's gender, by expressing their pleasure or satisfaction at having a daughter (N = 9) or son (N = 6). We found it remarkable, however, that in a community where fathers are usually present at the birth of child, only two mothers mentioned closeness with the father in connection with the birth experience: "I felt extreme closeness with my husband. It was just like we were one. The look on his face and in his eyes was real special."

The Early Relationship. In describing their baby as a person during the first 2 months or so (see Table 1.1b), altogether 25 mothers mentioned that he or she was easy to take care of, either explicitly (12) or implicitly (13). Mothers used words like "content," "happy," "not fussy," slept and ate," "alert," "playful," and "calm" (meaning didn't cry). A minority of mothers described their babies as fussy or colicky, or demanding. The word "difficult" was not used. Rather, the mothers talked about how tired they themselves felt, how hard it was on them.

Adjectives Describing the 2-Year-Old. We were not surprised that many mothers commented on aspects of the proverbial "terrible two's." 16 mentioned assertiveness ("determined," "independent," "strongheaded," and "strongwilled"), and 16 focused on difficulties with discipline and control ("ornery," "brat," "stinker," "full of piss and vinegar," "wild child," and "little devil"). It was therefore all the more noteworthy that 16 mothers commented on their toddlers' affectionateness ("loving," "caring," "warm") and that 11 talked about their children's capacity to elicit affection ("lovable," "adorable," "huggable," "sweetheart"). These qualities do not generally figure in the folk description of 2-year-olds. The following comments illustrate what the mothers meant by "loving" and "lovable": "When Johnny comes up to me, wrapping his arms around me and saying 'I love you' "; "He takes care of his babies—all of his stuffed animals have names, they all have to be tucked into bed, they all have to be covered with a blanket."; "Because she wants to give you hugs and kisses"; "Because she gets the blanket and crawls into your lap."

Nighttime. The question on nighttime waking was included in the interview because it represents a mild separation experience for toddlers (see Table 1.1c). 14 of the children frequently or occasionally ended up in their parents' bed after waking in the middle of the night. In a few instances the mother brought the child to bed, but more often the child took the initiative, climbing into the parental bed in the small hours of the morning. In some of these cases, the mothers tried (often in vain) to persuade the child to return to his or her own bed. Often mothers first noticed the child in their bed only upon waking up in the morning. In other words, a lot of the children had discovered their own way of seeking reassurance, and many parents accepted this as the least bothersome solution. In addition, three of the children slept in the same bed as a sibling, and one tried to do so frequently, but was discouraged.

If mothers went to the child at night, they offered a drink or verbal reassurance, and sometimes affection. A few did nothing, saying the child usually fell back to sleep without intervention.

Mothers' Feelings About Separations. Almost half of the mothers said they did *not* worry about being away from the child, provided they could be sure that the child was well cared for (see Table 1.1d). Fewer said they enjoyed being away, and some said that they tried to put the child out of their mind. Altogether, 18 mothers mentioned that they missed the child or thought about what he or she might be doing during their absence. When mothers worried, it was primarily about whether the child would be missing them or feeling bad, and whether the child was safe and well cared for. Only 1 mother worried about the child being disciplined in the way she wanted, and several worried about the child's behavior toward the sitter (especially if the sitter was a grandparent). Six of the mothers spontaneously mentioned guilt, in connection with having a job outside the home.

How the mother felt often depended on the situation (had the child protested as she left; was the sitter new; did the child not like the setting, such as the church nursery): "If he's not unhappy, then I'm not unhappy." According to maternal report, about half the children sometimes cried during the mother's departure, especially when they were left with someone new. Some mothers used very strong words to describe their feelings during separations, especially if they were away overnight or for several days: "I can't stand it. I can't be without her. I'm worried she might get scared at night," "I feel empty even though she is with her brother," "it bothers me tremendously," "I miss them terribly when I go back to work after the summer. I sit and wonder what they're doing," "I'm now at the point where I don't have to call at least once (meaning during the evening), but I normally do." There is the other extreme, too: "I don't get homesick. I'm doing what I want to, and I'll be back. I put it out of my mind."

Overall, 20 of the 37 mothers worried about separation in some way on some occasions, but felt more positive about others. These mothers usually qualified positive statements with "because I know he's well cared for." About one third of the mothers expressed only negative feelings about separation. Overall, leaving the child with a substitute caregiver was not a completely carefree situation for most mothers of 25-month-olds. Those who mentioned only positive feelings with respect to separation were in a small minority (N = 4).

Negotiations About Autonomy. Inspired by work on the goal-corrected partnership (Marvin, 1977; Marvin & Greenberg, 1982), we wanted to know how the mothers dealt with the child's self-assertion in situations where they felt that the child needed help or support to engage in the proposed activity. Almost half the mothers (see Table 1.1f) immediately distinguished danger from nondanger situations. For these mothers, there were no mini-bargains when potential harm was involved. Other mothers did not immediately intervene even then. These mothers stood close by, ready for a potential mishap "I would be there in case he slipped."

In potential mess or breakage situations a few mothers also reported monitoring every second rather than actually interfering, although just turning away is another solution for dealing with messy feedings: "I look away and let the dog clean it up." Many mothers mentioned the child's resistance to maternal intervention if it came too soon: "If I help, she will undo it and dress again." These mothers learned to keep out of the way until the child gave up. However, many of the children were reported to ask for help or at least accept it once they found out that they could not do the activity unaided. As one mother said: "I ask her if she needs help. When she finally says 'yes' I'll help her." Some children accepted partial help (demonstrations, explanations, or substitutions): "We let her paint the board so she wouldn't paint the dresser"; "he likes to dump his potty in the big potty after he is done, I hold his wrist, and help him pour it where it is supposed to go." 10 mothers mentioned the time factor: how long things take with a toddler who insists on dressing herself, or that they have to intervene if time is short "and then I have to listen to the screams." Some mothers develop sneaky procedures, "he takes things off the shelf in the supermarket, and screams if I put them back, so I get rid of them a few aisles later."

The mothers' responses to assertive child behaviors attest to their considerable respect for the child's desire to be self-reliant, although explicit reasons for postponing help until asked for were also "to let him find out he can't do it"; "because he throws a tantrum if I do"; "because it's easier than fighting."

Intergenerational Similarities and Differences. The comparison between the mother–child relationship across generations is a good index of those relationship qualities that were especially salient to the mothers (see Tables 1.1g and 1.1h). We had the impression that posing the question about intergenerational continuity/discontinuity in this way enabled the mothers to pinpoint intergenerational differences without having to criticize parents directly.

With regard to similarities between generations, mothers mentioned affection and closeness, being available and comforting to the child when needed, doing things together, maternal understandingness, encouragement, and willingness to explain things to the child, disciplining, and maternal personality. Altogether, 19 mothers mentioned one or more positive aspects about their family of origin that they wanted to carry over into the relationship with their own child. Only in speaking about personality traits did the mothers mention negative aspects that were similar across generations, such as their own and mother's short temper, being easily upset, and lack of self-esteem.

Interestingly, the mothers who described the mother–child relationship as different across generations seemed to share the values of the mothers who described it as similar. These mothers told us that they were trying to provide more affection (especially physical affection), to have better communication, to do more things together, and to use different discipline than had been the case in their family of origin. Only one mother claimed to be enforcing stricter discipline. The remaining mothers described themselves as more lenient or "mellow" than their own mothers. Other issues that came up less frequently were differences in level of concern for the child's appearance, less parental discord, less emphasis on finishing food, less demand on an older child's responsibility for younger siblings, less criticism, and different values than those in the family of origin. Altogether, 28 of the 37 mothers mentioned one or more aspects of the parent-child relationship that differed from their own early experiences. Only in one case was this difference self-critical: "I pay less attention to them."

The number of mothers who talked exclusively about positive similarities across generations was relatively small (N = 7). Of the 37 mothers, 15 discussed both similarities *and* differences (i.e., positive aspects of the early relationships in the family of origin that they wanted recreate in their own families, and negative aspects of early relationships that they did not want to repeat). Fourteen mothers mentioned negative aspects of their early relationships without talking about any positive similarities. Interestingly, however, only one mother dwelt exclusively on negative similarities (angry reactions) without also mentioning a desire for change.

When asked how the relationship with parents had changed now that the mothers were parents and adults themselves, 11 of the mothers reported good relationships, often after difficulties in adolescence, using expressions like "supergood friends," "more like good friends," "good friends—wish she lived closer," "more a parent-to-parent relationship now." These included almost all the mothers who wanted their own families to be like their family of origin.

Other mothers felt that the relationship had changed for the better since childhood: "My father never even hugged me until I had my child." Eleven of these reported an improvement in the relationship after adolescence, but with qualifications: "because I left home, "because she has finally accepted me as adult," "because she can't intimidate me anymore." Three mothers had experienced no amelioration in a trying relationship (in one case the mother felt she had been the caregiver of her own mother and siblings ever since childhood). Seven mothers said that they now understood better why their mothers behaved as they did, although the present relationship was still not good. Four mothers could not answer this question because they had lost their own mothers in early adulthood, and in one case this question was not asked.

In summary, most mothers wanted either to achieve a better relationship (as defined by them) with their own child than the relationship they remembered from childhood or they wanted to recreate the same good relationship. In either case, the mothers wanted to same things: closeness and affection, to be there when needed, to communicate well, to do things together as a family. Moreover, both sets of mothers considered discipline important (whether lenient or strict). It is noteworthy, however, that a substantial number of these mothers were still struggling with the problem of how to relate comfortably to their own mothers.

One mother spoke eloquently and poignantly about intergenerational transmission:

I know that the things that I've identified about my Mom that I want to change, I have only partially changed. I can still see so much of myself in her. When I get angry or when . . . in some negative things with my husband or my children, it's exactly what my mother would have said, and I wonder in the next generation, if my kids can get rid of some of those same negatives and just take the good from the parent. . . . The way that she (grandmother) is afraid that (child) is going to be self-centered and conceited, and some undesirable, boastful little girl, then in fact I realize why I've had a hard time with self-esteem, because I was told all those things over and over again.

Other mothers showed less insight. One who claimed that she was just like her own mother, described her as extremely responsive: "she was always right there when I woke from a bad dream." Elsewhere in the interview, however, this mother mentioned that she did not go to check on her child when he woke up from a bad dream because he normally cried himself back to sleep. She also told of several other instances where she was not responsive to her child's distress. Such individual differences in sensitivity and insight played an important role in our evaluations of the interview text as a whole. Findings regarding these evaluations are presented in the next section of this chapter.

Individual Differences in Responding to the Interview

In the first part of this section we discuss correlations between the sensitivity/insight scale and other attachment measures obtained at 18, 25 and 37 months. In the second part, we report on relationships between the interview scale and questionnaires concerning child temperament as well as family and maternal functioning that the mother had filled out.

The Parent Attachment Interview as Related to Other Attachment Measures. Five attachment measures were available for comparison with the sensitivity/insight scale (see Table 1.2): Strange Situation classification at 18 months, the Waters and Deane (1985) Attachment Q-sort at 25 and 37 months, the attachment story completion task at 37 months and a separation–reunion procedure, also administered at 37 months. Strange Situation classifications were converted into security scores, using the following system: B3 = 5, B1,B2,B4 = 4, A2, C1 = 3, A1, C2 = 2, D = 1. That is, B3 children were regarded as more secure than the other B-classifications, A2 and C1 as less insecure than A1 and C2. This system is based on findings reported in Ainsworth et al. (1978), showing that the mothers of infants classified as B3 in the strange situation have the most sensitive mothers. Maternal sensitivity ratings for the remainder of the B group were somewhat lower, followed by those for the A2/C1 and finally the A1/C2 groups. This procedure for converting classifications into security scores has been used in other publications (Brether-

TABLE 1.2
Intercorrelations Among Attachment Measures at 18, 25, and 36 Months

	1.	2.	3.	4.	5.
1. Strange Situation, 18 months	1.00				
2. Attachment Q-Sort Security, 25 months	.40**	1.00			
3. Interview (Sensitivity/ Insight Scale) 25 months	.44**	.60***	1.00		
4. Attachment Q-Sort Security, 37 months	.14	.39*	.38*	1.00	
Attachment Story Completions, 37 months	.33*	.61***	.44**	.26 +	1.00
6. Separation–Reunion Security, 37 months	.31*	.19	.16	– .18	.49**

N at 18 months = 36 (1 Strange Situation missing)
N at 25 months = 37
N at 37 months 29 (ASC) or 28 (SR)
+ p < .10; *p < .05; **p < .01; ***p < .001.

ton, Bates, Benigni, Camaioni, & Volterra, 1979; Bretherton et al., 1990). The new D classification (see Main & Hesse, 1990) was given the lowest rating because it tends to be most common in at-risk samples, implying that the disorganized children may be even more insecure than A1 and C2 (e.g., Radke-Yarrow, Cummings, Kuczynsky, & Chapman, 1985).

It is particularly noteworthy that the sensitivity/insight scale was significantly correlated with the Strange Situation at 18 months and the attachment story completion task at 37 months because shared method variance played no role in this correlation: The Strange Situation is based on direct observation of mother and child, and the attachment story completion task is an assessment administered to the child alone. There is shared method variance between the interview scales and security scores derived from the Attachment Q-Sorts at 25 and 37 months. Both assessments are based on maternal report. Note, however, that the overlap in specific content addressed by the interview and the Q-sort was not particularly great even though both were organized around attachment issues. In contrast to the interview, the Q-sort items probed neither the mother's feelings regarding separation nor her perceptions about her family of origin. Rather, it focused exclusively on descriptions of attachment-relevant child behavior, especially as regards the secure base phenomenon. Shared method variance alone is thus unlikely to explain the positive correlations between the interview scales and the Q-sort security scores.

With regard to the intercorrelations amongst all attachment measures, there was notable consistency, but Table 1.2 also illustrates that different ways of assessing the quality of attachment relationships cannot simply be taken as substitutes for each other. None of the correlations were in the range of .70–.90, nor were all possible intercorrelations significant. It is particularly puzzling that the reunion patterns at 37-months were not correlated with the interview scale. These ratings were significantly related only to the 37-months attachment story completion task [r (27) = .49, p < .01], in contrast to the other attachment measures that showed more consistent patterns of intercorrelation across ages.

The Parent Attachment Interview as Related to Other Questionnaire Findings. It was also of interest to relate the sensitivity/insight scores derived from the parent attachment interview to relevant questionnaire information provided by the mother at 18, 25, and 37 months (see Table 1.3). Of the five temperament scales from the Colorado child temperament inventory, only activity level was *not* correlated with the interview scales.

Maternal descriptions of children's attention span and sociability were positively, and emotionality was negatively correlated with the sensitivity/insight scores. Correlations with shyness and difficultness did not reach conventional levels of significance, but were in the expected (negative) direction. Although past reports have shown that temperament assessed at birth or during the first few months of life is not consistently related to attachment classifications (Sroufe, 1985), there was reason to expect such associations during the toddler period.

TABLE 1.3
Correlations of Sensitivity/Insight Interview Scales
with Other Maternal Questionnaire Measures

Maternal Questionnaire Measures	*Correlations With Interview Sensitivity/Insight Scale*
Child Temperament	
Attention span, 18 months	.42**
Emotionality, 18 months	−.57***
Sociability, 18 months	.37*
Shyness, 18 months	−.23
Difficultness, 18 months	−.25 +
Family Evaluation	
Cohesion, 25 months	.35*
Adaptability, 25 months	.33*
Maternal Personality	
Extraversion, 18 months	.40**
Depression scale, 37 months	−.27 +
Interfering affect, 37 months	−.29 +
Intergenerational Assessment	
Parental acceptance	.37*
Parental encouragement of Independence	.27 +

N at 18, 25 months = 37; N at 37 months = 29
+p < .10; *p < .05; **p < .01; ***p < .001.

As noted by Stevenson-Hinde (1988), a mother's perception of child temperament beyond the first year is likely to reflect well-established patterns of mother–child interaction. If this view is correct, we should not be surprised at significant associations between maternal reports of emotionality (i.e., emotional over-reactiveness) and insecurity. Significant correlations with maternal ratings of the child's attention span, sociability, and shyness were likewise expectable within the framework of attachment theory (Bowlby, 1969). A secure attachment with the mother should facilitate exploration of the environment (attention span) and the capacity for social engagement with unfamiliar people (sociability).

The correlations between measures of family functioning (from FACESII) and the sensitivity/insight scale from the interview also make theoretical sense. In the context of a satisfying (close and adaptable) family climate, the mother's role as an effective secure base and haven should be significantly enhanced. Indeed, prior studies have revealed such associations between family variables and attachment (Belsky, Rovine, & Fish, in press; Bretherton, Ridgeway, & Cassidy, 1990; Goldberg & Easterbrooks, 1984; Howes & Markman, 1989; Isabella & Belsky, 1985). In some of these studies marital satisfaction was also related to attachment. In the present study only measures assessing family cohesion and adaptability (not the marital assessments) were positively related to the sensitivity/insight scale.

Questionnaire-based self-report measures of maternal personality and emotional state also showed associations with the sensitivity/insight scale. The extraversion dimension of the Meyers–Briggs type indicator was significantly correlated with the interview scale in a positive direction, whereas the depression and interfering affect scales showed a trend in the (expected) negative direction.

Correlations of the sensitivity/insight scores with the parental acceptance scale from the Epstein Mother–Father–Peer scale (1983) were significant, although the correlations with each parent taken separately were significant only for the father [$r(28) = .45$]. Correlations of the sensitivity/insight scores with parental encouragement of independence did not reach conventional significance levels, but again, the separate correlation for father was significant [$r(28) = .31$, $p < .05$]. In light of other studies reporting correlations between the Mother–Father–Peer scale and assessments of the current mother–child relationship (Biringen, in press; Ricks, 1985) it is noteworthy that, in our study, this relationship was indirect. The mother's assessment of parental acceptance in childhood was related to her discussion of the current mother–child relationship (i.e., the sensitivity/insight scores). The sensitivity/insight scores, in turn, were related to independent assessments of the *current* relationship (see Table 1.3). However, there was no significant *direct* correlation between intergenerational measures and observed quality of child–mother attachment.

Finally, we examined correlations between the interview scale and maternal education and age. That we found no significant correlations lends credence to the view that the interview was not just a reflection of the mother's verbal articulateness. Furthermore, the sensitivity/insight scale was also not correlated with the child's Bayley MDI at 18 and 25 months, and with child gender.

CONCLUSIONS

The parent attachment interview has considerable promise as a tool for probing mothers' thoughts and feelings about attachment-related issues in relation to a specific child. The content analysis of the interview showed that issues of attachment, mother–child separation, and child autonomy are of great relevance to mothers of 25-month-olds. Overall, the mothers were engaged in a sometimes difficult balancing act between their role as an autonomy-fostering secure base and as an emotionally supportive safe haven. They felt much respect for and some exasperation with their children's need for self-assertion, but they also appreciated the children's affectionate behavior, and need for support. Their tolerance for inconvenient attachment behavior at night was quite high. Most experienced mild unease in the face of separation. What they valued in the maternal role was to provide emotional support, to give physical affection, and to engage in joint activities. Many had not yet worked out a truly comfortable relationship to their own mothers.

With respect to the Sensitivity/Insight scale designed to assess the quality of the mother's working model of a specific mother–child relationship, our data show that how a mother speaks about her child in an open-ended interview can provide relevant information about the quality of the relationship. We need to reiterate here, however, that the other attachment measures used in this study were not so highly correlated with the sensitivity/insight scores that these different attachment measures could be recommended as substitutes for one another. In other words, assessing the relationship from the maternal perspective yields somewhat different information than, say, Strange Situation classifications. It is also of interest that the Sensitivity/Insight scale was meaningfully related to questionnaire-based material about family adaptability and cohesiveness, child temperament, and maternal emotional well-being. Note further that intergenerational measures of attachment relations in the mother's family of origin were only indirectly related to other assessments of attachment quality (i.e., via the Sensitivity/Insight scale).

Directions for Future Research

If the Parent Attachment Interview continues to live up to its early promise, a number of further applications suggest themselves. First, we plan to use it with a larger sample of mothers whose children were classified as insecure with them, in order to detect patterns of responding associated with avoidant, resistant and disorganized patterns of attachment. Our present data suggest that this may be as feasible with the parent attachment interview as with the Berkeley adult attachment interview (Main, 1985), in which patterns of secure-autonomous, preoccupied and dismissing responses were identified. Indeed, we intend to compare parental responses to both interviews in a future study.

Further improvements of the parent attachment interview will include more questions about the parental inner experience, in addition to questions about "What happens when. . . . " However, even as currently worded and with our present tools (i.e., the Sensitivity/Insight scale), the interview will allow us to conduct a number of interesting additional studies. First, we will be able to contrast paternal and maternal perspectives on the same child. Second, we will be able to tap the same parent's view of attachment relationships with different children. Third, and perhaps most important from an attachment-theoretical point of view, we hope that this interview will allow us to track stability and change in attachment relationships across time. One of the drawbacks of administering the same interview on repeated occasions is that it may become a stale or tedious experience for the parent. Fortunately young children's rapid development makes this much less likely with the Parent Attachment Interview. Were we to conduct such repeated interviews we might discover that changes in the observed child–parent attachment relationship are accompanied by changes in the quality of parental representations. Alternatively, we might find that parental interviews provide a more stable picture of the relationship than observational assessments that may be more influenced by temporary perturbations occasioned by the arrival of a sibling, a family member's illness, parental job loss, divorce, or other stressful life events. In the present study (see Table 1.2), the sensitivity/insight scale derived from the Parent Attachment Interview was consistently related to prior, concurrent and subsequent assessments of attachment quality, suggesting that it may be fruitful to test this working hypothesis more intensively.

ACKNOWLEDGMENTS

This is an expanded version of a paper published in the *Infant Mental Health Journal*, September, 1989. We would like to thank the John D. and Catherine T. MacArthur Foundation Research Network for Childhood Transitions for supporting this research. We are also grateful to the mothers who provided the information on which this chapter is based, and to Cynthia Brody and Brenda Edwards who coded the content of the interviews.

REFERENCES

Ainsworth, M. D. S., Bell, S. M., & Stayton, D. (1974). Infant-mother attachment and social development: "Socialization" as a product of reciprocal responsiveness to signals. In M. P. M. Richards (Ed.), *The integration of the child into a social world* (pp. 99–135). London: Cambridge University Press.

Ainsworth, M. D. S., Blehar, M. C., Waters, E., & Wall, S. (1978). *Patterns of attachment: A psychological study of the strange situation.* Hillsdale, NJ: Lawrence Erlbaum Associates.

Bates, J. E., Freeland, C. A. B., & Lounsbury, M. L. (1979). Measurement of infant difficultness, *Child Development, 50,* 794–803.

Beck, A. T., Ward, C. H., Mendelson, M., Mock, J. E., & Erbaugh, J. (1961). An inventory for measuring depression. *Archives of General Psychiatry, 4,* 561–571.

Belsky, J., Rovine, M., & Fish, M. (in press). The developing family system. In M. Gunnar (Ed.). *Systems and development: Minnesota symposium on child psychology* (Vol. 22). Hillsdale, NJ: Lawrence Erlbaum Associates.

Biringen, Z. (in press). Direct observation of maternal sensitivity and mother–infant interaction in the home: Relations to maternal representations. *Developmental Psychology.*

Bowlby, J. (1958). The nature of the child's tie to his mother. *International Journal of Psychoanalysis, 39,* 350–373.

Bowlby, J. (1969). *Attachment and loss. Vol. 1: Attachment.* New York: Basic Books.

Bowlby, J. (1973). *Attachment and loss. Vol. 2: Separation.* New York: Basic Books.

Bowlby, J. (1980). *Attachment and loss, Vol. 3: Loss, sadness and depression.* New York: Basic Books.

Bretherton, I. (1985). Attachment theory: Retrospect and prospect. In I. Bretherton & E. Waters (Eds.), Growing points of attachment theory and research. *Monographs of the society for research in child development, 55* (1–2, Serial No. 209).

Bretherton, I. (1987). New perspectives on attachment relations: Security, communication and internal working models. In J. Osofsky (Ed.). *Handbook of infant development* (2nd ed. pp. 1061–1100). New York: Wiley.

Bretherton, I. (1990). Open communication and internal working models: Their role in attachment relationships. In R. Thompson (Ed.), *Socioemotional development* (Nebraska Symposium 1987) (pp. 57–113). Lincoln, NE: University of Nebraska Press.

Bretherton, I., Bates, E., Benigni, L., Camaioni, L., & Volterra, V. (1979). Relationships between cognition, communication and attachment. In E. Bates (Ed.), *The emergence of symbols* (pp. 223–269). New York: Academic Press.

Bretherton, I., & Beeghly, M. (1982). Talking about internal states: The acquisition of an explicit theory of mind. *Developmental Psychology, 18,* 906–921.

Bretherton, I., Ridgeway, D., & Cassidy, J. (1990). The role of internal working models in attachment relations as assessed in a story-completion task for 3-year-olds. In M. Greenberg, M. Cummings, & D. Cicchetti (Eds.), *Attachment beyond the preschool years* (pp. 273–308). Chicago: University of Chicago Press.

Cassidy, J. (1988). The self as related to child–mother attachment at six. *Child Development, 59,* 121–134.

Cassidy, J., Marvin, R. S., & the MacArthur Attachment Work Group. (1987). *Attachment organization in 3- and 4-year-olds: Coding guidelines.* Unpublished manuscript, University of Virginia, Charlottesville, VA.

Eichberg, D. (1987). *Quality of infant–parent attachment: Related to mother's representation of her own relationship history.* Paper presented at the biennial meetings of the Society for Research in Child Development, Baltimore, MD.

Epstein, S. (1983). *The mother-father-peer scale.* Unpublished manuscript, University of Massachusetts, Amherst, MA.

Escher-Graeub, D., & Grossmann, K. E. (1983). *Bindungssicherheit im zweiten Lebensjahr— die Regensburger Querschnittuntersuchung* [Attachment security in the second year of life: The Regensburg cross-sectional study]. Research Report, University of Regensburg, Germany.

Glogger-Tippelt, G. (1989, July). *Mothers' conception of their child during the transition to parenthood.* Paper presented at the 10th biennial meetings of the International Society for the Study of Behavioral Development, Jyvaskyla, Finland.

Goldberg, W. A., & Easterbrooks, M. A. (1984). The role of marital quality in toddler development. *Developmental Psychology, 20*, 504–514.

Grossmann, K., Fremmer-Bombik, E., Rudolph, J., & Grossmann, K. E. (in press). Maternal attachment representations as related to patterns of infant–mother attachment and maternal care during the first year. In R. A. Hinde & J. Stevenson-Hinde (Eds.), *Relationships within families.* Oxford: Oxford University Press.

Grossmann, K. E., & Grossmann, K. (1984, September). *The development of conversational styles in the first year of life and its relationship to maternal sensitivity and attachment quality between mother and child.* Paper presented at the congress of the German Society for Psychology, Vienna, Austria.

Grossmann, K. E., Grossmann, K., & Schwan, A. (1986). Capturing the wider view of attachment: A reanalysis of Ainsworth's Strange Situation. In C. E. Izard & P. B. Read (Eds.), *Measuring emotions in infants and children* (Vol. 2, pp. 124–171). New York: Cambridge University Press.

Hock, E. (1984). The transition to daycare: Effects of maternal separation anxiety on infant attachment. In R. Ainslie (Ed.), *The child and the day care setting: Qualitative variations and development* (pp. 183–206). New York: Praeger.

Howes, P., & Markman, H. J. (1989). Marital quality and child functioning: A longitudinal investigation. *Child Development, 60*, 1044–1051.

Isabella, R., & Belsky, J. (1985). Marital consensus during the transition to parenthood and security of infant–parent attachment. *Journal of Family Issues, 6*, 505–522.

Kaplan, N. (1984). *Internal representations of separation experiences in 6-year-olds: Related to actual experiences of separation.* Unpublished master's thesis, University of California, Berkeley, CA.

Main, M. (1985, April). *Adult mental organization with respect to attachment: Related to infant strange situation attachment status.* Paper presented at the biennial meeting of the Society for Research in Child Development, Toronto, Canada.

Main, M., & Goldwyn, R. (in press). Interview-based attachment classifications: Related to infant–mother and infant–father attachment. *Developmental Psychology.*

Main, M., & Hesse, E. (1990). The insecure disorganized/disoriented attachment pattern in infancy: Precursors and sequelae. In M. Greenberg, D. Cicchetti, & E. M. Cummings (Eds.), *Attachment during the preschool years: Theory, research, and intervention* (pp. 161–182). Chicago: University of Chicago Press.

Main, M., Kaplan, K., & Cassidy, J. (1985). Security in infancy, childhood and adulthood: A move to the level of representation. In I. Bretherton & E. Waters (Eds.), Growing points of attachment theory and research. *Monographs of the society for research in child development, 50*, (1–2, Serial No., 209)

Main, M., & Solomon, J. (1990). Procedure for identifying infants as disorganized/disoriented during the Ainsworth Strange situation. In M. Greenberg, D. Cicchetti, & E. M. Cummings (Eds.), *Attachment during the preschool years: theory, research, and intervention* (pp. 121–160). Chicago: University of Chicago Press.

Marvin, R. S. (1977). An ethological-cognitive model for mother–child attachment behavior. In T. M. Alloway & L. Kramer (Eds.), *Advances in the study of communication and affect. Vol. 1: The development of social attachments.* New York: Plenum.

Marvin, R. S., & Greenberg, M. T. (1982). Preschoolers' changing conceptions of their mothers: A social cognitive study of mother-child attachment. In D. Forbes & M. T. Greenberg (Eds.), *Children's planning strategies* (pp. 47–60). San Francisco: Jossey-Bass.

Maslin, C., Bretherton, I., & Morgan, G. A. (1987, June). *Attachment security and maternal scaffolding as related to mastery motivation.* Paper presented at the Summer Institute of the MacArthur Research Network on the Transition from Infancy to Childhood. Durango, CO.

Meyers, I. B. (1962). *The Myers-Briggs type indicator manual.* Palo Alto, CA: Consulting Psychologists Press.

Olson, D. H., Bell, R., & Portner, J. (1983). *FACES II (Family Adaptability and Cohesion Evaluation Scales).* Unpublished Manuscript, Department of Family Social Science, University of Minnesota, Saint-Paul, MN.

Rowe, D. C., & Plomin, R. (1977). Temperament in early childhood. *Journal of Personality Assessment, 41,* 150–156.

Radke-Yarrow, M., Cummings, E. M., Kuczynsky, L., & Chapman, M. (1985). Patterns of attachment in two- and three-year-olds in normal families and families with parental depression. *Child Development, 56,* 884–893.

Ricks, M. (1985). The social transmission of parental behavior: Attachment across generations. In I. Bretherton & E. Waters (Eds.), Growing points of attachment theory and research. *Monographs of the Society for Research in Child Development, 50,* (1–2, Serial No. 206)

Shostak, M. (1981). *Nisa: The life and words of a !Kung woman.* Cambridge: Harvard University Press.

Spanier, G. B. (1976). Measuring dyadic adjustment: New scales for assessing the quality of marriage and similar dyads. *Journal of Marriage and the Family, 38,* 15–28.

Sroufe, L. A. (1985). Attachment classification from the perspective of infant-caregiver relationships and infant temperament. *Child Development, 56,* 1–14.

Stevenson-Hinde, J. (1988). Individuals in relationships. In R. A. Hinde & J. Stevenson-Hinde (Eds.), *Relationships within families: Mutual influences* (pp. 68–80). Oxford: Clarendon Press.

Waters, E., & Deane, K. E. (1985). Defining and assessing individual differences in attachment relationships: Q-methodology and the organization of behavior in infancy and early childhood. In I. Bretherton & E. Waters (Eds.), Growing points in attachment theory and research. *Monographs of the Society for Research in Child Development, 50*(1–2), Serial No. 209, 41–65.

Waters, E., & Ridgeway, D. (1986). *The SUNY temperament, attitude and activity survey.* Unpublished manuscript, State University of New York at Stony Brook.

Zeanah, C. H., Keener, M. A., Stewart, L., & Anders, T. F. (1985). Prenatal perception of infant personality: A preliminary investigation. *Journal of the American Academy of Child Psychiatry, 24,* 204–210.

Attachment Theory in Old Age: Protection of the Attached Figure

Victor G. Cicirelli
Purdue University

Although attachment has been much studied as a theoretical concept explaining the child's relationship to its parent or caregiver, only in recent years has there been interest in the concept as applied to relationships in adulthood and old age. There are questions regarding the relationships of adult children with their parents that need answers: What accounts for the continuation of the relationship of adult children and their parents into the years beyond adolescence, even across separations of distance and time? More important, what explains the motivations of adult children to provide support and care to aging parents? As yet, other theoretical formulations have been only partially successful in answering these questions.

In this chapter, attachment theory is examined as it applies to the relationship of the adult child to the parent and to the adult child's provision of help to the aging parent, especially to the frail elderly mother. In doing so, four basic questions are answered: What is attachment? Does attachment continue into adulthood and old age? Does attachment lead to protective behavior in regard to the attached figure, that is, does attachment explain the child's persistent motivation to give care to an aging parent? What are the implications of attachment theory for a public policy regarding care of the elderly?

Before proceeding further, it should be noted that this chapter is somewhat speculative in nature as well as limited in focus. First, the chapter does not deal with reciprocal interactions between parent and child, although they are of obvious importance. Second, the chapter does not deal with multiple attachments, although their existence and importance is recognized. Third, the chapter does not deal with contextual variables to any great extent, although the importance of context is obvious. Employment of adult daughters, normative obligations, generational equity, and so on, all have their influence on attachment and on provision of help to the elderly. Fourth, the chapter does not deal with individual differences in attachment and protective behaviors to any great degree, although the importance of accounting for intra- and interindividual differences over time is recognized as a goal of developmental research. Finally, the chapter does not deal with the long-range effects of infant attachment on the individual's emotional-social development, as important as that question may be.

Basically, the chapter pertains to the continuation of infant attachment to the parent through adulthood, and the relationship of such attachment to the provision of help to frail elderly parents.

What Is Attachment?

The concept of attachment was originally formulated in the attempt to explain the failure of infants to thrive when separated from their mother (or principal caregivers) for extended periods of time (Bowlby, 1969, 1973, 1980). Attachment refers to the bond or tie that an infant forms with the mother; it is an internal state within the individual that is inferred from the propensity of the infant to seek proximity and contact with the mother. The mother (or other attachment figure) is seen as stronger and/or wiser and is associated with feelings of security. A system of attachment behaviors develops with regard to the mother that includes observation to monitor the mother's whereabouts, approaching the mother, clinging, calling or crying out to avoid separation from the mother, distress upon separation from the mother, and joy, comfort, or lessened anxiety upon reunion with the mother. In a familiar situation where no threat is perceived in the presence of the mother, the infant feels confident in exploring the environment within a certain protective range of the mother. However, if this range is exceeded, or if there is a strange person or element in the situation, or if the mother is separated from the infant, the infant is likely to manifest distress and anxiety, and attempt to reach a closer proximity to the mother. (In cases of a prolonged separation from the mother, the infant may exhibit despair and detachment.) Over a period of time, based on experience with the mother in a variety of situations and brief separations, the child develops a "working model" or inner representation of the mother as a reliable source of security and protection. That is, if the parent gives comfort and help when the infant needs it, the infant develops a secure attachment to the mother. On the other hand, if the mother is not reliably responsive, the infant may develop an anxious or insecure attachment.

Ainsworth (Ainsworth, Blehar, Waters, & Wall, 1978) used the infant's response to a standardized strange situation as the measure of the strength and nature of the attachment bond. On the basis of their behavior in the strange situation, infants were classified as securely attached (the majority of cases) or as showing anxious or insecure attachment; this latter group was further classified as avoidant or ambivalent. In addition, a "disorganized/detached" attachment pattern has been reported among children who had been maltreated (Carlson, Cicchetti, Barnett, & Braunwald, 1989; Main & Solomon, 1986).

More than a decade of research into the nature of infant attachment has provided some evidence for the stability of secure attachment, at least among middle-class infants. However, findings of other studies using the strange situation technique have indicated that secure attachment among the majority of children may not be a universal phenomenon observed in all cultures (e.g., a majority of infants in a German sample did not exhibit secure attachment; (Grossman, Grossman, Huber, & Wartner, 1981; Thompson & Lamb, 1986). Also, response to the strange situation may be at least partially dependent on the basic temperament of the infant, and the best indication of secure attachment in infants is whether they are able to find solace and be soothed by the mother after becoming upset (rather than whether they become anxious when confronted by a stranger). Observations of the interactions between infants and their mothers in the home over the first year of life (Isabella, Belsky, & von Eye, 1989) led to the conclusion that infants who could be easily soothed by a mother who was highly responsive to them were secure in the strange situation, whereas infants with insecure attachments tended to be temperamentally high strung and to have mothers who appeared indifferent to the baby's needs in the home observations. Thus, a classification of insecure attachment depends partially on the infant's temperament and the mother's responsiveness (see also Belsky & Rovine, 1988). Additionally, studies of the stability of attachment over time (Thompson & Lamb, 1986) indicate that attachment is not immutable, once formed, but is sensitive to changes in the home environment and the interactions with the parent.

However, the essential nature of the attachment relationship (Bretherton, 1985) is concerned with the child's seeking and the attachment figure's provision of feelings of security, protection, soothing, comfort, and help. What is universal about attachment is the child's innate predisposition to form a secure attachment, not whether the actual patterning of the attachment behavior in a given situation indicates a secure attachment. According to Bowlby, the maintenance of the infant's closeness to the mother offers protection and survival for the infant and survival of the family gene pool, when viewed from an evolutionary standpoint. The same evolutionary argument can be applied to the child's attachment to the parent and the parent's nurturance and protection of the child as the child continues to grow and develop.

Distinctions Between Attachment and Related Concepts. The term *attachment* has frequently been used in ways that suggest it is synonymous with such terms as *bond, affectional bond, love,* or *relationship.* Thus, it is important to clarify the distinctions between these terms. Bowlby (1969, 1973, 1980) variously referred to attachment as a bond, an attachment bond, or an affectional bond. He (Bowlby, 1979) regarded the essential feature of affectional bonding as the desire to remain in proximity with the object of bonding, with maintenance of the bond experienced as a source of security, threat of disruption or loss experienced as anxiety, and reunion or renewal of the bond experienced as a source of joy. Maintaining the bond is described as loving the object of bonding. However, the meaning of love does not in itself include the essential features of attachment enumerated earlier. Further, the particular kind of bond termed attachment is a special case of the term bond, which can apply to many sorts of ties between individuals.

Ainsworth (1989) has attempted to clarify the confusion between terms by first distinguishing between relationships and affectional bonds. Whereas affectional bonds are long-lasting, relationships may be brief. Relationships are dyadic in nature, whereas attachment bonds are properties of the individual. (This is not to deny that reciprocal attachment can occur; e.g., Ainsworth, 1985; Bretherton, 1985; Freud & Dann, 1951.) Finally, a relationship involves the total history of the interaction between two individuals and includes much content that is not relevant to the concept of attachment. Ainsworth defined an affectional bond as any kind of long-lasting tie, in which the partner is important as a unique individual; the attachment bond is a special case of the affectional bond that includes the ability to experience security and comfort in relation to the attachment figure. The function of attachment as a security-based bond is perhaps its most central criterion.

Because attachment in infancy seems to involve behaviors that may be classified as dependent and other behaviors regarded as autonomous, a clarification of these terms in relation to attachment is needed. Such behaviors as remaining in the proximity of the attachment figure, clinging, calling, and so on may be regarded as dependent. However, dependency is generally regarded as a personality trait, whereas attachment is a characteristic deriving from an individual's relationship to another person. Further, attachment is considered to be part of a behavioral system with the function of protecting the individual from harm, that is, maintaining homeostasis with the environment (Bowlby, 1973; Bretherton, 1985). Autonomous behaviors, in which the individual acts independently to explore the environment, appear to be indicators of an opposing behavioral system because exploration takes the child away from the attachment figure. However, the two systems act together to actually facilitate exploration under safe conditions (Bowlby, 1973; Bretherton, 1985). When no apparent danger threatens, the child can explore the environment at some distance from the attachment figure, but can return for protection should any danger threaten. Children who have developed a secure attachment, with a working model of the mother as available and responsive at times of stress, have been found to spend more time in exploration of the environment than those with insecure attachment (Ainsworth, 1979; Ainsworth et al., 1978). In this sense, attachment might be said to actually facilitate autonomy.

Does Infant Attachment to the Caregiver (Mother) Continue into Adulthood and Old Age?

Waning of Attachment With Growing Maturity.   One position with respect to the development of attachment is that it is a motivational system that functions to provide safety and security for the young developing child, but as the child grows in knowledge and autonomy, the attachment to the parent gradually fades as the individual passes through adolescence into adulthood (Weiss, 1982). If it exists at all, attachment in adulthood is weak, perhaps dormant, and rarely activated. Certainly the adult child does not need to be attached to a mother for day-to-day protection or nurturance, when that adult child has developed coping skills to be able to handle his or her own life problems autonomously. In adulthood, novelty in life continues to activate the individual's exploratory behavior system; the adult child may travel great distances, take a job thousands of miles from the parental home, and so on. Other events in life (e.g., working mothers, other interests of the mother) may also act to disrupt or weaken the child's attachment. Finally, and most important, the adult child develops strong ties (which may become attachments) to other figures (spouse and/or peers) who form a substitute support system to provide any needed feelings of security. The argument that attachment wanes by adulthood is buttressed by the fact that most adults move away from the parent home (often far away) and develop new affectional bonds.

Continuation of Attachment to Parents Throughout Life.   In contrast to the position that attachment to parents wanes in adulthood, the alternative position is that such attachment continues throughout life, albeit in a somewhat modified form. Bowlby (1979) maintained that attachment "characterizes human beings from the cradle to the grave," and that attachment behaviors continue to be displayed throughout life, especially at times when the adult child is distressed, ill, or threatened in some way. The notion of attachment as a construct underlying changing attachment behaviors over time is an example of what Kagan (1980) called heterotypic continuity. Certainly, older children and young adults continue to rely on their parents in times of stress, and throughout adulthood, adult children continue to have periodic communications and reunions with parents and to turn to them at times of stress (Adams, 1968; Cicirelli, 1983a; Troll, 1986; Troll, Miller, & Atchley, 1979). Obviously there must be changes in the nature of attachment and attachment behaviors from the simple proximity-seeking model of infancy in order to account for the continuation of attachment into adulthood.

Differences Between Infant and Adult Attachment.   As the child grows beyond infancy, the attachment system gradually changes so that attachment behaviors include communication with the mother and gaining an understanding of her viewpoint and plans. According to Ainsworth (1985), such changes may begin to take place as early as age 2 or 3. When the mother is able to communicate the reasons for an impending brief separation, the child is typically able to accept the separation without protest and to quickly resume ordinary interaction with her upon return. As the child grows older, verbal communication behavior assumes increasing importance, with earlier childhood behaviors such as crying, clinging to the mother, and frequent proximity-seeking fading out. Instead, the adult child may visit home, write letters, or telephone the parent, thereby maintaining attachment in spite of greater time and distance between actual reunions with the parent than in childhood.

Symbolic Attachment.   I have theorized elsewhere (Cicirelli, 1983b) that to maintain attachment to the parent under conditions of separation over great distances and long periods of time, the mechanism of symbolic attachment emerges in adulthood. The notion of symbolic attachment derives from the notion of the working model, but is slightly different. The working model is more broadly concerned with cognitive/affective assumptions regarding the self and attachment figure and the relationship between them. In symbolic attachment, the individual formulates a mental representation of the attachment figure (at least partially based on the working model) and achieves feelings of psychological closeness and security when considering this symbolic representation. The adult child who is away from the parent can evoke the symbolic representation of the parent, engage in "mental conversation" with the representation (e.g., thinking about what the parent would say or advise in a stressful situation), and gain some feelings of security by so doing. The symbolic image itself can involve varying degrees of complexity and can involve both cognitive and affective components. By such a mechanism, the attachment can be sustained over long time periods. Symbolic attachment with the internal representation of the attachment figure bears great similarity to the process of identification, in which a representation of the traits of a loved person is internalized. Although Bowlby (1969, 1973, 1980) spoke of inner representations, he sought to keep attachment theory separate from any Freudian concepts. However, more recent followers of Bowlby (Klass, 1987–1988) have acknowledged the connection between identification and attachment theory.

In symbolic attachment, the adult child is able to use covert thoughts to symbolize or represent the attachment figure and thereby experience closeness and imagined communication on a psychological level (Bank & Kahn, 1982; Ross & Milgram, 1982). The symbolic attachment behavior might involve the adult child's review of the close relationship to the attachment figure, but it could involve such other dimensions as the adult child's preoccupation with thoughts about the parent, a yearning to be with the parent, and feelings of anxiety or concern about being away from the parent. Thus, symbolic attachment is an important concept to explain continued attachment in adulthood when that attachment cannot be maintained by overt attachment behaviors.

Purpose of Adult Attachment.   It has been argued that the child's attachment to the mother offers protection and survival for the infant as well as for the survival of the family gene pool, and thus has utility from an evolutionary perspective. However, parents continue to live and nurture the child's growth for an extended period that may continue into late adulthood, as long as the parent is reasonably healthy and resourceful. Under stress, the adult child may still come to an elderly parent for help, advice, understanding, emotional support, and subsequent feelings of security and comfort. Certainly parents continue to provide aid to their children throughout life (even when children may reciprocate such aid), and when adult children have problems (e.g., job loss, financial difficulties, divorce) they come home to parents for help and reassurance; they may even return home to live again. Such continued parental nurturance and child attachment can be viewed as leading to optimum adaptation of the adult child to the environment, thus contributing to the long-range survival of the family gene pool. Certainly the availability of the adult child's parents for support can contribute to the survival of the adult child's own children; this is particularly the case when the adult child is a single parent (Weiss, 1982).

Measurement of Adult Attachment.   Although attachment in early childhood has typically been measured by Ainsworth's strange situation methodology (Ainsworth et al., 1978), such an approach is not possible with older children and adults because they no longer exhibit distress in connection with a brief separation from the parents. Unfortunately, the lack of a good measure of attachment in adulthood has hampered investigation of adult attachment. However, existing studies have made use of a variety of measurement approaches as well as clinical reports (Ainsworth, 1985, 1989). Most of these methods have been based on the concept of the working model (i.e., the mental representation that the adult child is capable of using to understand the self, the attachment figure, and his or her relationship to the attachment figure). The symbolic representation makes possible the use of self-report as a means of assessing attachment in adulthood.

The Waters and Deane (1985) Q-sort method, devised for young children but also used with older children, asks observers (family members, teachers, etc.) to rate the child's attachment to a given attachment figure. However, this method has not been extended to adults.

Probably the best developed of the measures of adult attachment is Main's adult attachment inventory (Main & Goldwyn, in press; Main, Kaplan, & Cassidy, 1985). In an interview procedure, adults are asked about their past relationship with and feelings toward both parents, and from this information a judgment is reached about the security or insecurity of the interviewee's generalized feelings about attachment relationships, rather than in relation to a specific attachment figure. Also, the measure is based largely on the interviewee's memories of childhood attachment feelings and experiences rather than with current attachment feelings. Because the internal working model represents present as well as past experiences with the parent, the instrument appears unsuitable for clearly assessing either childhood or contemporary attachment to a given parent.

Another approach has been to assess the strength of the attachment bond through self-reports about various indices of attachment. Troll and Smith (1976) devised a measure of attachment affect consisting of ratings of how well the individual knew the attachment object, the amount of influence the attachment figure had on the individual, the strength of the relationship, the quality of the relationship, and feelings of obligation and responsibility. In my own work (Cicirelli, 1983b), a measure of attachment was constructed from such indicators as closeness of feeling, value consensus, feelings of compatibility, and perceptions of the attachment figure's positive personality traits. These were considered to indicate the adult child's subjective feelings toward the parent, and thus (indirectly) the strength of the attachment bond. Although it is recognized that the attachment bond involves much more than such feelings of affection and compatibility, and that such measures do not assess the various patterns of secure and insecure attachment, they do attempt to assess what Bowlby considered to be one of the basic qualities of secure attachment: love for the attachment object. (I am now formulating an interview schedule to assess adult attachment, based on the characteristics of symbolic attachment.) Troll and Smith initially attempted to use measures of proximity and contact as additional indicators of attachment, but these indicators were poorly related to the remaining indicators of attachment affect. In my own work, proximity and contact have been considered as indicators of attachment behaviors and not as indicators of the attachment bond itself.

There are two differing philosophies underlying the assessment of attachment: the first that the type or pattern of attachment is the most important quality to assess, and the second that there are individual differences in the various indicators of the strength of the bond that are in themselves important to assess. Perhaps a fruitful approach to research would be to attempt to assess the pattern of attachment, and then within a given pattern or type attempt to assess the strength of the bond.

Evidence for the Continuation of Parent Attachment into Adulthood. There has been little systematic study of adult children's attachment to parents in adulthood and how it may change with increasing age. However, existing research indicates that adult children in general continue to make regular contact with their parents (Adams, 1968; Cicirelli, 1983a; Troll, 1986, Troll, Miller, & Atchley, 1979); only a very tiny fraction fail to contact parents in adulthood or have lost contact entirely. In addition, the preponderance of adult children report feelings of affectional closeness to their parents in adulthood (Baruch & Barnett, 1983; Cicirelli, 1983a; Johnson & Bursk, 1977; Troll, 1986), although there is some indication that affectional closeness may decline under conditions of parental illness and dependency in late life (Johnson & Bursk, 1977). In general, frequency of contact was not related to emotional closeness. However, Adams (1968) did find contact to be related to adult children's feelings of closeness when only intermediate parent–child distances, making frequent contact a matter of volition, were considered.

Another indicator of adult children's attachment to their parents is the grief experienced at the loss of a parent. Although grief at the loss of a parent in advanced old age is likely to be minimal for many adult children, the loss of a parent earlier in adulthood arouses the distress of the grief reaction (Bowlby, 1980; Jacobs et al., 1987–1988). Similarly, threat of parental loss, as in the case of serious illness, can arouse a strong emotional response. This response can occur even among adult children who have relatively little contact with the parent and appear to be completely autonomous. Recent research in cognitive neurobiology provides some support for such observations. According to Goleman's (1989) report of the work of LeDoux, emotional responses and cognitive information are stored in different portions of the brain, and an emotional memory (e.g., feelings of closeness to a parent, distress at separation) may be invoked even when the cognitive content associated with the memory (e.g., the early working model) may have undergone change or even extinction.

Secure and Insecure Attachments in Adulthood. Although there is some evidence that those individuals who were identified as being securely attached in childhood are likely to form more satisfactory relationships in adulthood, virtually nothing is known about the stability of earlier secure and insecure attachments into adulthood. Secure attachments at one age do not necessarily predict secure attachments at a later age, nor are later insecure attachments necessarily the result of earlier insecure attachments, even in childhood (Thompson & Lamb, 1986).

Does Attachment Lead to Protective Behavior of the Attached Figure (e.g., Caregiving for an Aging Parent)?

In addition to attachment and concomitant attachment behaviors, an adult model of attachment also involves the concept of protection of the attachment figure. According to Bowlby (1979, 1980), once attachment is established in the child, a complementary system of protective behavior develops in which the child desires to protect the attachment figure from loss or harm. Protective behavior is distinct from attachment behavior in that attachment behavior is concerned with maintaining or restoring proximity to the attachment figure, whereas protective behavior is concerned with preserving or restoring the threatened existence of the attachment figure. In this sense, attachment behavior and protective behavior are complementary to each other. In adulthood, when the existence of the attachment figure is threatened by the parent's illness, deprivation, or other vicissitude, the adult child will attempt to provide help and care to maintain the survival of the parent and preserve the concomitant emotional bond.

If one justification of attachment theory is the evolutionary argument that attachment contributes to the survival of the child and of the family gene pool, then one can rightfully inquire whether protection of the parent's existence in adulthood has any such value. Certainly, older parents' help and nurturance of adult children continues through middle age and into old age, as they provide advice, financial help, and various services to assist their adult children. Even in old age, parents may be seen as possessing knowledge and wisdom that is of value to the adult child. Thus, older parents may not only help the adult child get established in life but also provide help to assure the optimal development of grandchildren, and ultimately promote the survival of the family gene pool. It is in the child's self-interest to protect the existence of the parent and continue to obtain nurturance, as a Darwinian approach would predict. However, the parent's continued nurturance of the child throughout life may be genetically determined (Wilson, 1975), in that it contributes to the survival of the gene pool. Thus, the parent's responsiveness and the child's signals work in a reciprocal manner to form and maintain attachment.

There is still the question of whether the child can also be altruistically motivated to protect the elderly parent. Two concepts, kin-directed altruism (Hamilton, 1964) and reciprocal altruism (Trivers, 1971, 1983) imply that altruistic actions are more likely to be directed to close kin than to strangers, that altruism stimulates reciprocal altruism, and also that altruism is more likely to be reciprocated within close, intimate family relationships. Based on the parent's continued nurturance within a close, intimate parent–child relationship over time, the development of reciprocal altruism would seem likely. In this sense, the adult child's motivation to protect the elderly parents is not only selfish but also altruistic. (Trivers argued that altruism itself may be the result of natural selection.) An integration of theories of attachment and reciprocal altruism thus provides a possible explanation for the existence of both selfish and altruistic motives sustaining the adult child's caregiving for a frail elderly parent.

Evidence for the Relationship Between Attachment and Caregiving Behavior. There is ample evidence that elderly parents receive help and care from adult children. For example, Cantor (1975) found that about two-thirds of all elderly people received help from adult children; presumably not all the older people studied were in need of any assistance. When only those elderly who required assistance with personal care or daily activities were studied, 92% of daughters and 62% of sons interviewed were caregivers (Noelker & Townsend, 1987). Overall, immediate family members provide most of the help to older people for ordinary daily living, as well as care during illness or disability (Cicirelli, 1981; Horowitz & Dobrof, 1982; Shanas, 1979); the extent of family care far exceeds such sources of formal care as nursing homes, hospices, day care, formal home care, and so on. Thus, the question is not whether adult children exhibit caregiving behavior toward their elderly parents, but whether attachment to the parent is related to such caregiving.

In a study where feelings of attachment to the parent was included as a variable in a path model of commitment to provide future help to elderly parents (Cicirelli, 1983b), feelings of attachment were found to have both direct and indirect (through its effect on attachment behaviors) effects on commitment to provide future help. In later work, affectional closeness and trust were found to be significantly correlated with the number of hours of weekly care provided to parents when parent health and needs for care were controlled statistically (Cicirelli, 1990). Further, when divorced adult children were asked to indicate how important each of 14 reasons for helping elderly parents was to them (Cicirelli, 1986), reasons based on love for the parent and on desire to protect the parent from need were regarded as most important.

Other Motives for Caregiving.   Although most researchers in the area of family caregiving to the elderly agree that adult children do provide substantial help to elderly parents, there is considerable disagreement about just what motivates them to do so. In addition to attachment theory, equity theories and theories of family obligation are the major theories of caregiving motivation.

Obligation theorists hold that adult children have been acculturated to believe it to be their duty or responsibility to care for parents in old age, based on gratitude for parents' help earlier in life and on cultural norms that parent care is the responsibility of adult children. Jarrett (1985) has argued forcefully for obligation as the basic motivation for caregiving, with his argument based partially on a rejection of attachment theory's position that the affectional bond is the motivation for parent caregiving. His argument is that American society's overemphasis on affection has led to the expectation that closeness can form a basis for caregiving, but that any existing closeness dissipates under the strain of providing care, with resulting psychological distancing from the parent accompanied by guilt and despair. Obligation, on the other hand, is a motivation that has been recognized for most of man's past and that permits the adult child to provide care without attendant negative emotions.

Equity theory holds that in a helping situation most people strive to maintain a balance between help given and help received; if there is an imbalance, both parties become distressed and attempt to rectify the situation. However, equity theory has not been as successful at explaining help from family members as in explaining help between friends and neighbors. For example, Ingersoll-Dayton and Antonucci (1988) found that elderly parents were not distressed to receive unreciprocated instrumental care from adult children, although they were distressed by unreciprocated care from other caregivers.

Few studies have attempted to compare obligation and affection as a basis for caregiving. In an earlier study (Cicirelli, 1983b) in which both feelings of attachment and obligation were included in a path model of adult children's commitment to future parent caregiving, obligation had only an indirect effect on caregiving commitment whereas feelings of attachment had both direct and indirect effects; the overall effect of attachment was stronger than obligation. Adult children also rated attachment-related reasons for helping the parent as most important, with reasons based on reciprocity of intermediate importance, and reasons based on obligation of somewhat lower importance (Cicirelli, 1986). Walker, Pratt, Shin, and Jones (1989) reported that adult daughters' caregiving was motivated by both feelings of affection and obligation. On the other hand, Kivett (1988) found that obligation characterized adult sons' relationships with their elderly fathers. Probably the best conclusion at the present time is that adult children's help to elderly parents is universally motivated by attachment and simultaneously influenced by cultural conditioning regarding a sense of equity and/or obligation. To the extent that the latter (or other) factors operate, the combined effect of these motivational factors may be additive or interactive.

Does Attachment Wane as Parents Become More Frail and Burden Increases? Jarrett (1985) argued that feelings of attachment dissipate when adult children undergo the strain of caring for elderly parents, citing the finding of Johnson and Catalano (1981) that when there is strain, caregiving is carried out with psychological distancing and without much intimacy. However, the literature is mixed with regard to this question. Some studies found that a decline in the parent's health was associated with a decline in the adult child's positive feeling toward the parent (Baruch & Barnett, 1983; Johnson, 1978; Johnson & Bursk, 1977), whereas others found that affectional closeness to the elderly parent buffered the caregivers from strain and burden (Horowitz & Shindelman, 1983; Sheehan & Nuttall, 1988). A recent in-depth study of five adult children caring for a parent with Alzheimer's disease illustrates an important point even though the number of cases is small (Blieszner & Shifflett, 1989). In four of the five cases, the adult child's affection for the parent declined over the course of care, but in the fifth case affection remained strong. This parent was the only one who hugged the daughter and told her she loved her, regardless of how great the cognitive impairment became. Looking at the case from the perspective of attachment theory, this demented parent was nevertheless able to fulfill the daughter's need for emotional security; the other four parents apparently did not retain even this slight resource. One can speculate that if parents become too frail to offer psychological or emotional security to the child, the basis for maintaining attachment is gone. Thus, one would predict that attachment would decline under caregiving when the parent can no longer function to offer security and comfort to the child in some measure, although it is difficult to identify just when this point is reached. Such reasoning would seem to be borne out by the observations of adult children's often minimal grief reactions to the death of an advanced elderly parent, as if there had been some detachment of the emotional bond prior to the event. Or, from an evolutionary viewpoint, attachment wanes when parents are no longer helpful for adaptation (i.e., when they can no longer provide nurturance of some sort).

Further research into this issue is certainly warranted, and any such studies should consider whether the adult child exhibits secure attachment to the parent or one of the types of insecure attachment. It may be that those adult children whose affectional closeness to the parent declines during caregiving were not securely attached to begin with.

How Does Protective Behavior Develop When There are Several Siblings in a Family? When there is more than one child in the nuclear family, the children typically all develop an attachment to the parent, although these attachments may not all be of the same type or strength. In addition, the siblings all form secondary attachments to each other (Cicirelli, 1989). The result of such a family system is that each adult child is motivated by feelings of attachment to protect the parent, but also tends to coordinate efforts with those of siblings to provide care for the parent as a result of their attachment to each other. Whereas most studies of caregiving for the elderly tend to focus on the adult daughter as the primary caregiver, the few studies that have examined the contributions of other siblings (e.g., Matthews, 1987; Matthews & Rosner, 1988) have found that siblings typically also provide some degree of care or stand ready to assume the primary caregiver's role should the family situation change.

What are the Implications of Adult Children's Attachment for a Public Policy Regarding Care of the Elderly?

Understanding how adult children's continued attachment to elderly parents leads to protective behavior helps in understanding the preference of most families to provide care for aging parents. It appears that the attachment relationship between child and elderly parent and subsequent parent caregiving is important for the optimum development of both as well as maintaining the parent's survival. As independent as most older people want to be, it is of equal importance that they learn to accept help from their adult children when they become frail and dependent; similarly, it is important for adult children to be able to help protect the continued existence of the parent in some way. As a developmental phenomenon, this caregiving process leads to an increase in maturity and wisdom, and it should not be carelessly destroyed by the social forces operating today or an over-reliance on formal care.

Unfortunately, contemporary social forces threaten adult attachment and protective behavior perhaps more than at any time in the past. Such things as women's entry into the labor force, geographic mobility, differences in lifestyle between generations, increases in divorce and remarriage with more complex family relationships, and the increase in the advanced elderly population all tend to limit adult children's capability to help their parents as well as their closeness to them (Kingson, Hirshorn, & Cornman, 1986; Treas, 1977).

The question for policymakers is thus: What public policy can or should be formulated to assist adult children to maintain attachment and protective behavior toward the parent in the light of these social forces without overburdening the adult children? Instead of following policies that remove caregiving responsibilities from adult children, policies should be implemented that adapt or modify the social environment to meet the needs of adult children's caregiving activities. For example, in the workplace, sons and daughters of older people needing care should be given the options of flexible work schedules, leave periods, reduced work responsibilities, and so on, to permit the adult children to manage caregiving activities while maintaining their jobs. Although informal family care should remain the core of the long-term care system, various formal care services should be made available to supplement the family care system. When such formal care is used, the adult children should be the care managers of the parent's use of formal care services so that the services can be used to supplement and strengthen the family rather than to supplant it. Finally, one can assist adult children to anticipate future vulnerability of their elderly parents to physical and cognitive decline, and attempt to delay such decline for as long as possible as a way of protecting the continued survival of the parents. Adult children can help parents to stay involved with life, to ignore or challenge negative stereotypes about aging, to learn new skills, to take risks, and to reach out for new experiences in life. Policies directed toward educational programs could prepare adult children to protect their parents' existence in these ways.

Directions for Future Research

A consideration of the evidence leads to the conclusion that the child's bond of attachment to the parent does persist into adulthood and throughout life, although in a somewhat attenuated and qualitatively different form than early childhood attachment. Such attachment acts as a motivation for adult children's protective caregiving behaviors toward their aging parents.

However, much additional research needs to be carried out before the nature of attachment in adulthood is understood. Preliminary to any such research, further effort must be directed to the development and validation of suitable instruments to measure adult attachment, particularly easily administered paper-and-pencil measures.

The sequelae of secure and insecure attachment should be investigated in adult life, particularly in relation to feelings of affectional closeness, attachment behaviors, and degree and type of caregiving activities in old age. (It may be that when adult children do not provide adequate help to aging parents or even subject them to abuse, this behavior may be related to insecure attachment.) Gender differences in this connection are particularly worthy of study. Also, the nature and characteristics of symbolic attachment need to be explored.

Further studies should be carried out comparing equity, obligation, and attachment as motivations for parent caring, and determining how these motivations are related to the quality, quantity, level, and duration of caregiving as well as to situational factors and current social forces.

Finally, further research needs to be carried out on the entire sibling system of adult children in a family: What is the nature of their attachment to their parents and to each other? How are attachment behaviors and protective behaviors manifested in the system as a whole? If some children are more strongly attached to a parent than are others, what accounts for this? Do differences in attachment account for the frequently observed emergence of an adult daughter as a principal caregiver to an aging parent?

Only through a concerted research effort in the future can we hope to fully understand the life-span persistence of human bonding.

REFERENCES

Adams, B. (1968). *Kinship in an urban setting*. Chicago: Markham.

Ainsworth, M. D. S. (1979). Attachment as related to mother–infant interaction. *Advances in the Study of Behavior, 9*, 2-52.

Ainsworth, M. D. S. (1985). Attachments across the life span. *Bulletin of the New York Academy of Medicine, 61*, 792-812.

Ainsworth, M. D. S. (1989). Attachments beyond infancy. *American Psychologist, 44*, 709-716.

Ainsworth, M. D. S., Blehar, M. C., Waters, E., & Wall, S. (1978). *Patterns of attachment: A psychological study of the strange situation*. Hillsdale, NJ: Lawrence Erlbaum Associates.

Bank, S., & Kahn, M. D. (1982). *The sibling bond*. New York: Basic Books.

Baruch, G., & Barnett, R. C. (1983). Adult daughters' relationships with their mothers. *Journal of Marriage and the Family, 45*, 601-606.

Belsky, J., & Rovine, M. J. (1988). Nonmaternal care in the first year of life and the security of infant–parent attachment. *Child Development, 59*, 157–167.

Blieszner, R., & Shifflett, P. A. (1989). Affection, communication, and commitment in adult–child caregiving for parents with Alzheimer's disease. In J. A. Mancini (Ed.), *Aging parents and adult children* (pp. 231–243). Lexington, MA: Lexington Books.

Bowlby, J. (1969). *Attachment and loss. Vol. 1: Attachment.* New York: Basic Books.

Bowlby, J. (1973). *Attachment and loss. Vol. 2: Separation: Anxiety and anger.* New York: Basic Books.

Bowlby, J. (1979). *The making and breaking of affectional bonds.* London: Tavistock.

Bowlby, J. (1980). *Attachment and loss. Vol. 3: Loss: Sadness and depression.* New York: Basic Books.

Bretherton, I. (1985). Attachment theory: Retrospect and prospect. *Monographs of the Society for Research in Child Development, 50*(1–2, Serial No. 209).

Cantor, M. (1975). Life space and the social support system of the inner city elderly of New York. *The Gerontologist, 15*(Part I), 23–27.

Carlson, V., Cicchetti, D., Barnett, D., & Braunwald, K. (1989). Disorganized/disoriented attachment relationships in maltreated infants. *Developmental Psychology, 25*, 525–531.

Cicirelli, V. G. (1981). *Helping elderly parents: Role of adult children.* Boston: Auburn House.

Cicirelli, V. G. (1983a). Adult children and their elderly parents. In T. Brubaker (Ed.), *Family relationships in later life* (pp. 31–46). Beverly Hills, CA: Sage.

Cicirelli, V. G. (1983b). Adult children's attachment and helping behavior to elderly parents: A path model. *Journal of Marriage and the Family, 45*, 815–822.

Cicirelli, V. G. (1986). The relationship of divorced adult children with their elderly parents. *Journal of Divorce, 9*(4), 39–54.

Cicirelli, V. G. (1989). Helping relationships in later life: A reexamination. In J. Mancini (Ed.), *Aging parents and adult children* (pp. 167–180). Lexington, MA: Lexington Books.

Cicirelli, V. G. (1990). [Beliefs in autonomy and paternalism in relation to caregiving practices.] Unpublished raw data.

Freud, A., & Dann, S. (1951). An experiment in group upbringing. In R. S. Eisler (Ed.), *The psychoanalytic study of the child* (Vol. VI, pp. 127–168). New York: International Universities Press.

Goleman, D. (1989, August 15). Brain's design emerges as a key to emotion. *The New York Times*, pp. 15, 19.

Grossman, K. E., Grossman, K., Huber, F., & Wartner, U. (1981). German children's behavior towards their mothers at 12 months and their fathers at 18 months in Ainsworth's Strange Situation. *International Journal of Behavioral Development, 4*, 157–181.

Hamilton, W. D. (1964). The genetical evolution of social behavior: I & II. *Journal of Theoretical Biology, 7*, 1–52.

Horowitz, A., & Dobrof, R. (1982, May). *The role of families in providing long-term care to the frail and chronically ill elderly living in the community.* New York: Brookdale Center on Aging of Hunter College.

Horowitz, A., & Shindelman, L. (1983). Reciprocity and affection: Past influences on current caregiving. *Journal of Gerontological Social Work, 5*, 5–19.

Ingersoll-Dayton, B., & Antonucci, T. C. (1988). Reciprocal and nonreciprocal social support: Contrasting sides of intimate relationships. *Journal of Gerontology: Social Sciences, 43*, S65–S73.

Isabella, R. I., Belsky, J., & von Eye, A. (1989). Origins of infant–mother attachment: An examination of interactional synchrony during the infant's first year. *Developmental Psychology, 25*, 12–21.

Jacobs, S. C., Kosten, T. R., Kasl, S. V., Ostfeld, A. M., Berkman, L., & Charpentier, P. (1987–88). Attachment theory and multiple dimensions of grief. *Omega, 18*, 41–52.

Jarrett, W. H. (1985). Caregiving within kinship systems: Is affection really necessary? *The Gerontologist, 25*, 5–10.

Johnson, C. L., & Catalano, D. (1981). Childless elderly and their family supports. *The Gerontologist, 21*, 610–618.

Johnson, E. S. (1978). "Good" relationships between older mothers and their daughters: A causal model. *The Gerontologist, 18*, 90–96.

Johnson, E. S., & Bursk, B. (1977). Relationships between the elderly and their adult children. *The Gerontologist, 17*, 90–96.

Kagan, J. (1980). Perspectives on continuity. In O. G. Brim, Jr. & J. Kagan (Eds.), *Constancy and change in human development* (pp. 26–74). Cambridge, MA: Harvard University Press.

Kivett, V. R. (1988). Older rural fathers and sons: Patterns of association and helping. *Family Relations, 37*, 62–67.

Klass, D. (1987–1988). John Bowlby's model of grief and the problem of identification. *Omega, 18*, 13–32.

Kingson, E. R., Hirshorn, B. A., & Cornman, J. M. (1986). *Ties that bind: The interdependence of generations.* Washington, DC: Seven Locks Press.

Main, M., & Goldwyn, R. (in press). Interview-based adult attachment classifications: Related to infant–mother and infant–father attachment. *Developmental Psychology.*

Main, M., Kaplan, N., & Cassidy, J. (1985). Security in infancy, childhood, and adulthood: A move to the level of representation. *Monographs of the Society for Research in Child Development, 50*(1–2, Serial No. 209).

Main, M., & Solomon, J. (1986). Discovery of a disorganized/disoriented attachment pattern. In T. B. Brazelton & M. W. Yogman (Eds.), *Affective development in infancy* (pp. 95–124). Norwood, NJ: Ablex.

Matthews, S. H. (1987). Provision of care to old parents: Division of responsibility among adult children. *Research on Aging, 9*, 45–60.

Matthews, S. H., & Rosner, T. T. (1988). Shared filial responsibility: The family as the primary caregiver. *Journal of Marriage and the Family, 50*, 185–195.

Noelker, L. S., & Townsend, A. L. (1987). Perceived caregiving effectiveness: The impact of perceived parental impairment, community resources, and caregiver characteristics. In T. H. Brubaker (Ed.), *Aging, health, and family: Long-term care* (pp. 58–79). Newbury Park, CA: Sage.

Ross, H. G., & Milgram, J. I. (1982). Important variables in adult sibling relationships: A qualitative study. In M. E. Lamb & B. Sutton-Smith (Eds.), *Sibling relationships: Their nature and significance across the lifespan* (pp. 225–249). Hillsdale, NJ: Lawrence Erlbaum Associates.

Shanas, E. (1979). The family as a social support system in old age. *The Gerontologist, 19*, 169–174.

Sheehan, N. W., & Nuttall, P. (1988). Conflict, emotion, and personal strain among family caregivers. *Family Relations, 37*, 92–98.

Thompson, R. A., & Lamb, M. E. (1986). Infant–mother attachment: New directions for theory and research. In P. Balter, D. Featherman, & R. Lerner (Eds.), *Life span development and behavior* (Vol. 7, pp. 1–41). Hillsdale, NJ: Lawrence Erlbaum Associates.

Treas, J. (1977). Family support systems for the aged: Some demographic and social considerations. *The Gerontologist, 17*, 486–491.

Trivers, R. (1971). The evolution of reciprocal altruism. *Quarterly Review of Biology, 46*, 35–57.

Trivers, R. (1983). The evolution of cooperation. In D. L. Bridgeman (Ed.), *The nature of prosocial development* (pp. 43–60). New York: Academic Press.

Troll, L. E. (1986). Parent–adult child relations. In L. E. Troll (Ed.), *Family issues in current gerontology* (pp. 75–83). New York: Springer.

Troll, L. E., Miller, S., & Atchley, R. (1979). *Families of later life.* Belmont, CA: Wadsworth.

Troll, L. E., & Smith, J. (1976). Attachment through the life span: Some questions about dyadic bonds among adults. *Human Development, 19*, 156–170.

Walker, A. J., Pratt, C. C., Shin, H. Y., & Jones, L. L. (1989). Why daughters care: Perspectives of mothers and daughters in a caregiving situation. In J. A. Mancini (Ed.), *Aging parents and adult children* (pp. 199–212). Lexington, MA: Lexington Books.

Waters, E., & Deane, K. E. (1985). Defining and assessing individual differences in attachment relationships: Q-methodology and the organization of behavior in infancy and early childhood. *Monographs of the Society for Research in Child Development, 50*(1–2, Serial No. 209).

Weiss, R. S. (1982). Attachment in adult life. In C. M. Parkes & J. Stevenson-Hinde (Eds.), *The place of attachment in human behavior* (pp. 171–184). New York: Basic Books.

Wilson, E. O. (1975). *Sociobiology: The new synthesis.* Cambridge, MA: Harvard University Press.

II

TRANSITIONS

Variability in the Transition to Parenthood Experience

Carolyn J. Mebert
University of New Hampshire

A quote from Maureen Quilligan's (1989) review of Sara Ruddick's *Maternal Thinking* in the *N.Y. Times Book Review* provides an appropriate starting point for this chapter:

> A story often told to new parents goes like this: After a sleepless night dominated by the squalling of a colicky newborn, a young father found himself standing over the crib with a pillow inches from the baby's face, ready to murder it. "What's the matter with me?" he wails to his psychotherapist. The therapist asks, "You didn't do it, did you?" The father answers, "No, but I wanted to!" the therapist nods. "Welcome to parent[hood]." (p. 15)

Although the transition to parenthood has not been identified by researchers as a period of emerging homicidal tendencies, it has been characterized in a variety of other ways. One of the most frequently mentioned, but no longer accepted characterizations is LeMaster's (1957) concept of "parenthood as life crisis." More recent descriptions of the transition tend to emphasize the challenge or the potential for development or, simply, the nature of the changes accompanying the birth of a baby. For example, Reilly, Entwisle, and Doering (1987) wrote that "becoming a parent is one of life's more complex and challenging transitions" (p. 295). Tietjen and Bradley (1985) identified the basic categories in which changes occur during this period and state that although individuals may become parents by choice, the experiences they have during the transition are likely to be "disequilibrating" and stressful. Going a bit beyond the notion that the transition may be merely stressful, Feldman and Nash (1984) called it "profound." For women especially, they suggested, becoming a parent "represents a complete change in life approach" (p. 62). New mothers experience major role changes and they must modify their problem-solving strategies and re-evaluate their priorities, always placing their infant's needs above their own.

Finally, Roosa (1988) conceptualized the transition as "a major developmental milestone in adulthood . . . accompanied by the opportunities and demands for personal reorganization and growth that characterize such major changes" (p. 322). Roosa went on to say (and here, I suggest, he pointed out a very important but limiting assumption in the research) that this transition is "a most abrupt and total life style change." Therefore, the stresses that accompany it "may be more acute than [in] most other developmental transitions" (p. 322). [As Juliet said to Romeo in a thematically related context, "What's in a name? . . ."] It seems that although the term *crisis* is no longer used in this literature, the crisis tone remains.

In light of these somewhat dramatic descriptions, it is instructive to look at what has been found about couples' transition experience. A major focus of the research has been on changes in the marital relationship, and the usual method is a late pregnancy assessment and at least one postpartum assessment. Miller and Sollie (1980) and Belsky, Spanier, and Rovine (1983) found that the quality of the marital relationship declined from prepartum levels over the first 9 months postpartum. In Miller and Sollie's sample, the decline (or increase in marital stress) was not evident by the end of the first postpartum month, but did appear in the 1–8 month comparison. In Belsky et al.'s sample, the decline was most pronounced in the late pregnancy to 3 months postpartum comparison, leading Belsky to suggest that for at least 1 month after the baby's birth there is a "honeymoon" period that is obviously over by the time the baby is 3 months old. In both cases the changes were more pronounced for the women than for the men. Miller and Sollie also reported a decline in well-being across the postpartum assessments for both women and men and an increase in personal stress from pregnancy to the early postpartum period for both parents; however, the changes were not large. Similarly, Belsky et al. described the changes they found as "modest."

In subsequent work Isabella and Belsky (1985) found that an apparent consequence of changes in marital quality over the transition to parenthood is variation in the security of mother–infant attachment. Mothers reporting a continued decline in marital quality from 3 to 9 months postpartum had infants who were classified, at 1 year of age, as insecurely attached. In comparison, those whose reported decline leveled off at 3 months, had securely attached 1-year-olds, suggesting that less successful adjustment to parenthood can negatively affect the baby's socioemotional development. Particularly important in this study, however, is that differences between these two groups of mothers in how they evaluated their marriage were evident prior to the birth of the baby. The mothers with the less extensive decline had evaluated their marriage prenatally in terms of its positive aspects, whereas the others had focused on the negative aspects. This difference may be symptomatic of other differences between the groups and raises the possibility that it was not changes in the marital relationship per se that produced the attachment differences, but, perhaps, preexisting differences in the mothers' personality or in their orientation to their family situation.

Because a decline in marital satisfaction following the birth of a baby has been so consistently found, several researchers have begun looking into possible causes of the decline. It seems that at least part of the reason for it (especially among mothers) is the violation of expectations concerning the division of household responsibilities, particularly childcare, that many people experience following the birth of a baby. In an examination of parents' expected involvement in childcare compared to their actual involvement, Belsky, Ward, and Rovine (1986) found that fathers were less involved than expected and this had a negative effect on mothers' evaluation of their marriage. Similarly, Ruble, Fleming, Hackel, and Stangor (1988) found, in their cross-sectional sample, that women in the postpartum groups were doing more of the childcare than they had expected to do and they reported feeling less close to their husbands than did women in the prenatal groups. Furthermore, analyses of the longitudinal sample in Ruble et al.'s study indicated that women who were doing more of the household tasks than they had expected to do evaluated their husband's involvement in childcare and the effect of the child on the marriage more negatively than did mothers whose expectations and experiences were more congruent. However, the expectations-experience difference was unrelated to women's feelings of closeness with their spouse.

Ruble et al.'s (1988) results are consistent with other work on this issue (e.g., Goldberg, Michaels, & Lamb, 1985), but Miller and Sollie's (1980) cautionary note regarding the nature of the results is also applicable. The difference between the pregnant and postpartum women in feelings of closeness to spouse was .4–.6 on a 7-point scale, statistically significant but certainly not large. Perhaps even more important, there was no difference between either the pregnant or the postpartum groups when compared with the prepregnant group. Ruble et al. thus concluded "the birth of a baby has some negative implications for the [marital] relationship, but probably not as great as has been emphasized in the literature" (p. 86) and they suggested that the postpartum decline in marital satisfaction may be a return to baseline following the heightened spousal support many women experience during pregnancy.

Other research has focused on identifying the stresses and problems associated with the transition to parenthood, in a move away from ". . . researcher defined, potential change relevant variables . . ." (McKim, 1987, p. 22) that may not adequately reflect the experiences of new parents. Using an open-ended format, McKim (1987) and Ventura (1987) asked new parents to report the kinds of problems they have had since their baby was born (or, in McKim's case, in 3 month intervals over the first year). Less than half of the parents in McKim's sample reported problems and of the problems mentioned, 50–70% (depending on which 3 month interval is examined) concerned infant illness and nutrition. Up to 6 months postpartum, 10.7% of the problems listed were "parent problems," including role conflicts, marital conflicts, and anxiety. The incidence of such problems decreased to 4.7% by 12 months. In Ventura's sample role conflicts were reported by 35% of the mothers and 64% of the fathers; stresses specific to the marital relationship were reported by only 14% of mothers and 11% of fathers, and child care-related concerns were listed by 35% of mothers and 20% of fathers. These results are noteworthy for two major reasons: (a) they reveal the types of problems new parents consider worth mentioning when simply asked what kinds of problems they have had; and (b) they suggest that major problems, profound changes, or complete shifts in life approach are not inevitable concomitants of new parenthood. In fact, considering the magnitude of the marital changes reported by Ruble, Miller, Belsky, and others and the nature and incidence of the stressors reported by Ventura and McKim, it appears that the profundity of the transition exists more for researchers studying it than for many of the parents experiencing it.

Earlier it was mentioned that Roosa (1988) had, in characterizing the transition as abrupt, pointed to what is an important but limiting assumption underlying much of the research in this area. What is argued here is that for some individuals or couples the transition is not abrupt and may even occur, psychologically at least, well before the baby is born.

Many couples plan their pregnancies. According to demographers and family planning researchers (e.g., Booth & Duvall, 1981; Udry, 1983; White & Kim, 1987), "fertility is the result of rational decisions reflecting . . . the balance of perceived costs and rewards of childbearing compared to alternative activities" (White & Kim, 1987, p. 27). A number of studies have examined the nature of childbearing decisions (i.e., one-step or sequential) and the variables that influence such decisions. It is not clear whether the decisions are made in a single step or sequentially (Udry, 1983), but the variables influencing the decisions (e.g., financial and housing concerns, companionship, normative expectations, gender preferences, educational and career issues, etc.) are fairly clearly defined. An interesting example of this type of work is Crawford and Boyer's (1984) study, in which women of different parities were asked to generate lists of the advantages and disadvantages of having a child. In their list of disadvantages, subjects included those stresses and marital issues frequently found in the transition to parenthood literature. There were, in addition, informative parity differences in the frequency with which various disadvantages were listed. Marital friction was listed by 35% of the childless women, but by only 14% of the Parity 1 women. Similarly, constraints on time and freedom was mentioned by 77% of the childless and 41% of the Parity 1 women. Thus, as most of this research shows, experience has an effect on childbearing decisions and parenting experience appears to reduce expectations of, or concerns about, the negative consequences of having children. Such research also suggests that when a couple makes the decision to have a child, they are doing so with some understanding of the costs and benefits involved.

Taking this a step further, one might assume that when a pregnancy is planned, the lifestyle changes associated with adding a child to the family are being actively anticipated and adaptation to those changes may have already begun. However, not all pregnancies are planned. Couples who find themselves unintentionally pregnant, or otherwise not entirely pleased about their pregnancy, must first adjust to the pregnancy and only after that is accomplished can they begin integrating the baby and anticipated lifestyle changes into their schemes of themselves and their family.

What all of this leads to is the proposition that the transition to parenthood is not always dependent on the birth of a baby. For some couples it begins with the decision to have a baby, sometimes months before a pregnancy is achieved, and for others it will begin quite a bit later. Such variability in the onset of the transition is likely to have consequences for the parents and the baby and their relationships.

Following the birth of their baby, parents who are already well into the transition to parenthood might be expected to adopt an assimilative mode in their approach to parenting. As Block (1982) defined it, assimilation is "the invocation . . . of existing adaptive structures, schemes, or scripts to process experience" (p. 286). Or, as Zeanah and Anders (1987) put it, these parents have an "internal working model" of their baby and of themselves as parents and that provides them with at least a basic framework for handling their experiences with their baby.

On the other hand, parents who are just making the transition at around the time of the birth would be expected to adopt a more accommodative mode, involving "the formation of new (and reformation of old) adaptive structures, schemes and scripts to process experience" (Block, 1982, p. 286). Both modes, although involving different amounts of psychological "work", have the same goal, psychological comfort with the new situation. This is therefore a difference, rather than deficiency, perspective. Furthermore, the difference considered in this perspective is not in overall level or quality of adaptation to parenthood, but rather in timing of the establishment of parenting schemes. It is in this way that Block's (1982) view of assimilation and accommodation differed from Piaget's (1971). For Piaget, these processes occurred simultaneously and were, essentially, inseparable; ". . . there can be no assimilation of anything . . . without a corresponding accommodation . . ." (Piaget, 1971, p. 173). Block defined the processes as separable and sequential. Thus, parents who are assimilative following the birth of their baby must have, given Block's definition, accommodated at some earlier time because the ability to assimilate experiences presupposes the existence of adaptive structures. Parents who are accommodative following the birth of their baby should eventually become assimilative as their parenting structure becomes effective and stable.

One aim of the analyses discussed in this chapter was to identify differences in a number of psychological and social variables between parents who differed in their level of motivation for pregnancy. The second aim was to test the hypothesis that parents classified as high or low in motivation for pregnancy would differ in their approach to parenthood. The former were expected to show evidence of an assimilative mode, and the latter an accommodative mode.

The data for this study are from an ongoing 24-month longitudinal study that is focused primarily on infant temperament. There are six phases in the study, two during pregnancy and four in the first 18 months postpartum. Only the first three phases, 3.5 and 8.5 months of pregnancy and 3.5 months postpartum, are considered here, because very few families have been seen beyond the early postpartum phase.

The sample for these analyses was 87 couples out of the 123 who have completed the first two phases of the study. This sample was drawn from the total on the basis of their overall motivation for pregnancy, defined in terms of their scores on a measure of pregnancy planning (a single seven-point item, with one reflecting a fully planned pregnancy) and a measure, (Grossman, Eichler, & Winickoff, 1980) of conscious motivation for pregnancy. On the conscious motivation scale, low scores reflect higher motivation and the sample was initially divided on the basis of a median split of those scores. Finally, subjects assigned to the high motivation group were at or below the median on conscious motivation, had planning scores of three and below, and matched their spouse on those criteria. Subjects in the low motivation group had conscious motivation scores above the median, any planning score, and matched their spouse on those criteria. This is not a perfect way of grouping, but because it is based largely on a measure with good reliability, it seemed reasonable. This division of subjects resulted in 36 couples excluded from the analyses because of within couple mismatch in motivation scores. In 18 of these couples, the wife was high and the husband low and in the other 18 it was the reverse. The postpartum data reported here are from the 56 couples who had completed Phase 3 by the time this chapter was prepared. Only two couples had actually dropped out of the study (due to medical problems with the infants). Comparisons of the 56 couples who had completed Phase 3 with those who had not revealed no differences on any of the pre-partum variables.

Of the 87 couples, 24 were expecting their first child and 63 their second. All were White, middle class, and the majority had at least a college degree. Subjects were recruited through the offices of obstetricians where they were given information about the study during their first prenatal visit.

Table 3.1 lists the variables analyzed and when they were measured. Subjects were also interviewed in each of these phases. The questionnaires were

TABLE 3.1
Measures Administered in Each Phase of the Study.

Phase	Time	Measures
1	3.5 months of pregnancy	1. Conscious motivation for pregnancy (from Grossman, Eichler, & Winickoff, 1980)
		2. Planning of Pregnancy: single 7-point scale item; 1 = fully planned, 7 = not at all planned.
		3. Confidence in Caretaking Ability: single 7-point scale item; 1 = very confident, 7 = not confident
		4. Expectations of Infant Characteristics (modified version of Bates, Freeland, & Lounsbury's [1979] Infant Characteristics Questionnaire [ICQ]; four factors: difficultness, adaptability, dullness, predictability)
		5. Dyadic Adjustment Scale (DAS; Spanier, 1976)
		6. Beck Depression Inventory (Beck, Ward, Mendelson, Mock, & Erbaugh, 1961)
		7. Levenson's (1981) Multidimensional Locus of Control (LOC) Scale (internal, powerful others, chance)
2	8.5 months of pregnancy	1. Expectations of Infant Characteristics
		2. Beck Depression Inventory
		3. Steffensmeier's (1982) Transition to Parenthood (assesses concerns over marital intimacy and the restrictions and responsibilities of parenthood)
3	3.5 months postpartum	1. Infant Characteristics Questionnaire
		2. Transition to Parenthood
		3. Attachment Questionnaire (designed for this study; assesses strength of parents' attachment to baby)
		4. Activities with Baby Questionnaire (Only one item analyzed—hours of play with baby/day)
		5. Beck Depression Inventory
		6. Locus of Control

mailed to them a week before the interview and completed forms were picked up by the interviewers.

Presented in Tables 3.2 and 3.3 are the means for high and low motivation groups for each of the variables (prenatal in Table 3.2 and postpartum in Table 3.3). Parity Group x motivation level analyses of variance were performed on these variables for mothers and fathers separately. The F values in the tables are for the motivation factor, but any parity main effects are also noted. One of the interesting findings here is that only one parity difference was found in the mothers' analyses (DAS-Cohesion, primips higher) and four were found in analyses of the fathers' data. This is somewhat surprising, particularly with respect to the marriage variables. Because of the consistency that decline in marital quality has been reported in the transition literature, greater differences between couples with and those without children was expected. The majority of the differences found were between the two motivation groups. For

TABLE 3.2
Parity x Motivation ANOVA Results and Means of Variables Measured
in Pregnancy for High and Low Motivation Groups.

Variables	Mothers			Fathers		
	High	Low	F	High	Low	F
Conscious Motivation	11.63	20.52	176.79***	11.40	20.35	97.75***
Pregnancy Planning	1.40	4.29	65.43***	1.46	4.40	61.06***
Caretaking Ability	1.64	2.05	3.45*	1.41	1.76	5.80*
DAS-Consensus	50.71	46.02	12.09**	50.52	45.09	18.46***
Cohesion	16.56	14.81	2.57[a]	17.38	15.44	4.85*
Satisfaction	42.10	38.14	16.04***	42.21	38.58	15.87***
Affection	9.15	7.98	10.69**	9.00	7.77	9.05**
Total DAS Score	118.51	106.95	15.51***	119.21	106.88	21.08***
ICQ-Difficult (Ph.1)	21.61	21.12	.02	22.40	22.26	.16[a]
ICQ-Total (Phase 1)	51.75	50.74	.10	55.50	53.57	.34[a]
ICQ-Difficult (Ph.2)	20.57	21.75	2.68	22.64	21.82	.87[a]
ICQ-Total (Phase 2)	50.21	52.41	3.13+	56.62	54.72	.77
LOC-Internal	34.20	34.49	.14	36.00	35.45	2.91 +a
Powerful Others	14.30	13.35	.43	12.59	15.70	10.43**
Chance	13.70	14.49	.57	12.44	15.09	7.29*
Depression (Phase 1)	6.60	8.47	3.53*	2.50	4.57	5.19*
Depression (Phase 2)	7.38	10.58	8.17*	2.13	4.52	8.15*
Marital Intimacy	10.55	10.98	.35	9.22	10.23	2.06
Parental Restrictions	6.88	7.91	7.54*	6.39	6.49	.27

Note: F value is for the Motivation factor.
[a]Significant Parity difference in these variables.
+p < .10; *p < .05; **p <.01; ***p < .001

TABLE 3.3
Parity x Motivation ANOVA Results and Means of Postpartum Variables
for High and Low Motivation Groups

Variables	Mothers			Fathers		
	High	Low	F	High	Low	F
ICQ-Difficult	18.06	18.14	.24	20.50	20.78	.34
ICQ-Total	41.19	40.45	.03	48.93	47.45	.06
Attachment	6.19	5.95	.09	8.57	9.18	.30
Hours of Play/Day	3.65	3.23	.17	1.77	1.82	.25
Marital Intimacy	11.06	12.73	2.19	10.60	13.23	5.90*
Parental Restrictions	7.03	7.80	1.96	6.37	6.70	.35
LOC-Internal	35.72	35.75	.08	36.50	35.57	.42
Powerful Others	13.59	17.50	13.20**	14.97	15.52	.11
Chance	12.55	16.46	7.79*	13.00	14.33	.33
Depression	6.94	8.60	1.61	2.39	5.17	6.07*

Note: F value is for the Motivation factor.
*p < .05; **p < .01

the mothers, 8 out of 17 prenatally measured variables differed by motivation level; among the fathers the number was 10 out of 17. In all cases the difference favored the high motivation group. These are interesting differences, but it is not possible to identify the direction of effects. That is, a less satisfying marriage might be the cause of low motivation for a baby or the relatively unplanned pregnancy may be the cause of marital problems and depression. Few group differences were found in the postpartum variables.

Because several of the variables were measured more than once, change over time and temporal stability were examined. These results are presented in Table 3.4. On the basis of the hypothesized difference between high and low motivation groups in approach to parenthood, greater stability and less change was expected in the high motivation (assimilative) group. For the temperament scores the expectation concerning stability was confirmed but, contrary to expectations, there was also more consistent, positive change in these scores in the high motivation mothers. Mothers in the low motivation group changed over time in the two psychological measures. They became more depressed as the pregnancy progressed, but then went back down to their early pregnancy level by 3.5 months postpartum. Additionally, they became more external in their locus of control orientation from early pregnancy to the early postpartum period. It was this change that apparently produced the motivation group difference in locus of control scores shown in Table 3.2.

In Tables 3.5 and 3.6 are correlations, for mothers and fathers, respectively, reflecting the predictive relation between a number of the variables measured during pregnancy and five of the variables measured at 3.5 months post-

TABLE 3.4

Temporal Stability of Repeatedly Measured Variables for Mothers (and Fathers) in High and Low Motivation Groups

	High Motivation			Low Motivation		
	Phases Compared			Phases Compared		
Variable	1 with 2	1 with 3	2 with 3	1 with 2	1 with 3	2 with 3
Difficultness	.73[a](.66)	.46[a](.21)	.61[a](.23[a])	.80 (.59)	−.09 (.24)	−.12[a](.28)
Total ICQ	.56 (.35)	.30[a](.37[a])	.49[a](.34[a])	.65 (.56)	.16[a](.12[a])	−.19[a](.10[a])
Depression	.69 (.69)	.68 (.69)	.67 (.61)	.56[b](.62)	.47 (.81)	.48[a](.78)
Locus of Control:						
Internal		.57 (.48)			.67 (.80)	
Powerful Others		.73 (.52[b])			.58[b](.70)	
Chance		.53 (.43)			.68[b](.74)	
Marital Intimacy			.81 (.65[b])		.30 (.47[b])	
Parental Restrictions			.44 (.54)		.21 (−.04)	

[a]Scores on these variables decreased significantly across the phases compared.
[b]Scores on these variables increased significantly across the phases compared.

partum. Examination of the mothers' results reveals that the correlations are, with a few exceptions, higher in the high motivation group than in the low motivation group.

This pattern may reflect the existence, prior to the birth of their infants, of internal representations of the infant and of parenthood within the high motivation mothers. In these representations, mothers' own personal characteristics, their view of their marital relationship, their view of themselves as parents, and their expectations of what their baby is going to be like are coordinated. The covariation between these and the postpartum measures suggests that even before its birth, the infant had been psychologically integrated into these women's lives. This integration provides, or reflects the existence of, a structure into which parenting experiences can be assimilated.

The low motivation mothers, given the relative lack of association between pre- and postpartum variables, either constructed a representation (assimilative scheme) that did not match their subsequent experiences, or did not formulate working models during pregnancy. As a result, these women are entering parenthood without a sufficient framework into which they can place, interpret, and understand their experiences. They have, in effect, experienced the abrupt change to which Roosa (1988) referred, and in order to adapt to this change accommodation is necessary.

Before continuing in this vein, a word about the fathers' results is in order. Two features of these data are worth noting. There were, overall, fewer sig-

TABLE 3.5
Correlations Between Selected Pregnancy and Postpartum Measures
for High and Low Pregnancy Motivation Mothers

| | Postpartum Measures | | | | | | | | | |
| | Infant Difficultness | | Total ICQ | | Strength of Attachment | | Hrs. of Play/Day | | Marital Intimacy | |
Pregnancy Measures	High	Low	High	Low	High	Low	High	Low	High	Low
Difficultness (Phase 2)	.61	-.12	.46	.01	.34	.04			.28	-13
Total ICQ (Phase 2)	.62	-.11	.65	-.06	.41	.18			.30	-.14
DAS-Cohesion			-.27	.27	-.31	.15	.41	-.04	-.27	-.23
Consensus			-.43	-.01					-.26	-.37
Affection							.29	-.12	-.52	-.11
Satisfaction	-.52	-.07	-.50	.08	-.36	-.18	.41	-.10	-.53	-.42
Total DAS Score	-.35	-.02	-.45	.09	-.33	-.16	.44	-.00	-.46	-.42
Caretaking Ability					.32	.11	.01	.50	.38	.08
Locus of Control: Int.	.28	-.46	.20	-.33			.30	.04	.01	-.36
Powerful Others	.36	.08			.29	.19				
Chance	.32	.38	.25	.44	.32	.24	-.03	.44		
Marital Intimacy	.52	.26							.81	.30

nificant correlations between prenatal and postpartum variables than there were in the mothers' data. In addition, differences between the two groups of fathers were less consistent than those seen in the mothers' correlations. Such differences between mothers' and fathers' results are likely due, as other researchers (e.g., Belsky, Spanier, & Rovine, 1983) have suggested, to the fact that new parenthood generally has less of an impact on the lives of men than it has on women.

Returning now to the mothers, a question raised by the interpretation being offered is what consequences might follow from these differences in approach to early parenting. Keeping in mind that the difference suggested here is primarily one of timing (i.e., the mothers with assimilative structures accommodated prior to their infants' birth), it is possible that no striking long-term differences would exist between the two groups of mothers. In addition, and perhaps more importantly, both assimilation and accommodation are processes directed toward adaptation and it is reasonable to expect that most well functioning individuals would be able to adapt eventually and comfortably to species-typical situations. However, both approaches can be problematic, each in its own special way. As Block (1982) pointed out, "accommodations may be so quick and endlessly sliding as to suggest an absence of structure . . . as the individual thermoplastically conforms to the hot experience of a discomfiting situation" (p. 286). It is not difficult to imagine how new parenthood could be a discomfiting situation for some people, supplying a variety of hot experiences. One possible outcome of the absence or continuous sliding of structures is a sense of helplessness or lack of con-

TABLE 3.6

Correlations Between Selected Pregnancy and Postpartum Measures for High and Low Pregnancy Motivation Fathers

	Postpartum Measures									
	Infant Difficultness		Total ICQ		Strength of Attachment		Hrs. of Play/Day		Marital Intimacy	
Pregnancy Measures	High	Low	High	Low	High	Low	High	Low	High	Low
Difficultness (Phase 2)			.39	.39	.45	.32	-.03	-.44		
Total ICQ (Phase 2)			.44	.30	.50	.22	.01	-.46		
DAS-Cohesion							.05	.36		
Consensus	-.31	-.39	-.31	-.22					-.32	-.48
Affection	-.38	-.36	-.40	-.14	-.50	-.08	.30	-.29	-.21	-.47
Satisfaction	-.18	-.52			-.42	-.07			-.32	-.41
Total DAS Score	-.23	-.47	-.34	-.24	-.34	-.15			-.26	-.50
Caretaking Ability					.31	-.06				
LOC: Powerful Others					.16	.55				
Chance							.31	.18	-.03	.41
Marital Intimacy	.30	.06	.45	-.06	.46	.17			.65	.47

trol. In fact, the low motivation, presumably accommodating, mothers in the present sample did show an increase from early pregnancy to the post-partum phase in external locus of control scores. Those scores were also significantly higher than were the high-motivation mothers' in the postpartum assessment (see Tables 3.3 and 3.4). With no further data, however, it is impossible to know whether or not this change was just a transient perturbation.

With respect to assimilation, Block (1983) suggested that overreliance on it, or "the use of procrustean and perseverative methods to fit, shape or mold new perceptions into preexisting schema can result in a projective, distorted, perseverative, oversimplified, rigid approach to the world . . ." (p. 1346). As an example of how an oversimplified, rigid approach to parenting may cause problems, consider the correlations between the high motivation mothers' expectations and perceptions of their infants. The magnitude of these correlations was taken as evidence for the existence of assimilative structures concerning the infant. Also reflected in these results is within-group variability in the scores. Some mothers expect and perceive temperamentally optimal babies and others expect and perceive more difficult infants. Because mothers' expectations may influence their own behavior as well as that of their infant (as suggested more generally in social perceptions research; Nisbett & Ross, 1980; Schneider, Hastorf, & Ellsworth, 1979), some of these mothers are, no doubt unwittingly, contributing to the production of relatively more difficult babies (in their eyes, at least) through perseverative efforts to fit experience into preexisting schema. Therefore, a completely assimilative approach to new parenthood can, in a fairly subtle way, have effects that are not necessarily positive. Within both assimilating and accommodating groups, then, some variability in outcomes is expected, as is variability in the predominance of the characteristic mode and the exclusion of the other in parents' processing of information.

Whether parents adopt an assimilative or accommodative mode in their approach to parenting, it has been argued, will be influenced by the timing of their transition to parenthood. The timing of the transition appears to be influenced by the degree to which they are motivated to become parents. But, what is most likely to influence the overall quality of their experience (and that of their infants) is their willingness and ability to shift between assimilation and accommodation as the need arises. Parents who can recognize discrepancies between their schemes and experiences, realize that their schemes may be inadequate or inappropriate, and make the necessary adjustments, will have a different, perhaps better, parenthood experience than those who engage in perseverative assimilation. Similarly, parents who appropriately abandon accommodative efforts as they recognize the sufficiency of their schemes may find parenthood more comfortable and satisfying than those whose adaptational strategy takes the form of thermoplastic conformation.

SUGGESTIONS FOR FUTURE RESEARCH

The notion that there are differences in approach to parenting that can be characterized in terms of assimilation and accommodation is just one of several possible interpretations of the results of this study. One alternative is that the difference between high and low motivation mothers in the pattern of pregnancy—postpartum correlations may simply reflect greater psychological stability among the high motivation, happier, more maritally satisfied mothers, rather than anything particular to the transition to parenthood. Although such stability may have implications for parenting, it does not necessarily require or result in the earlier psychological transition to parenthood or the prepartum establishment of parenthood-relevant schemes discussed earlier. Differential timing of the transition is a particularly important point in the preceding discussion, but it was not directly assessed. Similarly, the evidence provided for the existence of schemes was largely circumstantial. Further research, aimed specifically at distinguishing between the physical and psychological transitions to parenthood is needed, as is a more direct examination of the nature and developmental course of parenting schemes.

The adoption of an assimilative or accommodative mode was considered here as a consequence of the timing of the psychological transition to parenthood. However, reasoning from Block's (1982) hypothesis that individual differences in the relative preponderance of assimilative and accommodative activities are basic personality characteristics, it is possible that one's characteristic mode of approach will influence the timing, as well as the experience, of a transition. The inability to specify with confidence the direction of effects from one variable to another is a problem that plagues much of the transition research. More work including "pre-pregnant" subjects, as in Ruble et al.'s (1988) study, would help alleviate this problem.

Finally, becoming a parent may indeed be profound, disequilibrating, and/ or acutely stressful for some people, but not for others. Identification of the factors that contribute to such differences among individuals who are, at least ostensibly, going through the same set of changes cannot help but contribute to a more complete understanding of the transition to parenthood experience.

ACKNOWLEDGMENTS

The research reported in this chapter was supported by a grant from the National Institute of Child Health and Human Development (HD23351). I would like to thank Karen Blass, Adrian Buchanan, Trey Buchanan, Beth Howley, and Saul Rosenthal for their help in various aspects of the research and the parents for their interest and support.

REFERENCES

Bates, J. E., Freeland, C., & Lounsbury, M. (1979). Measurement of infant difficultness. *Child Development, 50,* 794–803.

Beck, A. T., Ward, C. H., Mendelson, M., Mock, J., & Erbaugh, J. (1961). An inventory for measuring depression. *Archives of General Psychiatry, 4,* 561–569.

Belsky, J., Spanier, G. B., & Rovine, M. (1983). Stability and change in marriage across the transition to parenthood. *Journal of Marriage and the Family, 45,* 567–577.

Belsky, J., Ward, M. J., & Rovine, M. (1986). Prenatal expectations, postnatal experiences, and the transition to parenthood. In R. Ashmore & D. Brodinsky (Eds.), *Thinking about the family: Views of parents and children* (pp. 119–145). Hillsdale, NJ: Lawrence Erlbaum Associates.

Block, J. (1982). Assimilation, accommodation, and the dynamics of personality development. *Child Development, 53,* 281–295.

Block, J. H. (1983). Differential premises arising from differential socialization of the sexes: Some conjectures. *Child Development, 54,* 1335–1354.

Booth, A., & Duvall, D. (1981). Sex Roles and the link between fertility and employment. *Sex Roles, 7,* 847–856.

Crawford, T. J., & Boyer, R. (1984). Parity and the expected consequences of childbearing. *Population and Environment, 7,* 234–245.

Feldman, S. S., & Nash, S. C. (1984). The transition from expectancy to parenthood: Impact of the firstborn child on men and women. *Sex roles, 11,* 61–77.

Goldberg, W. A., Michaels, G. Y., & Lamb, M. E. (1985). Husbands' and wives' adjustment to pregnancy and first parenthood. *Journal of Family Issues, 6,* 483–503.

Grossman, F., Eichler, L., & Winickoff, S. (1980). *Pregnancy, birth, and parenthood.* San Francisco: Jossey-Bass.

Isabella, R., & Belsky, J. (1985). Marital change during the transition to parenthood and security of infant–parent attachment. *Journal of Family Issues, 6,* 505–522.

LeMasters, E. (1957). Parenthood as crisis. *Marriage and Family Living, 19,* 352–355.

Levenson, H. (1981). Differences among internality, powerful others and chance. In H. M. Lefcourt (Ed.), *Research with the locus of control construct* (Vol. 1, pp. 15–63). New York: Academic Press.

McKim, M. K. (1987). Transition to what? New parents' problems in the first year. *Family Relations, 36,* 22–25.

Miller, B. C., & Sollie, D. L. (1980). Normal stresses during the transition to parenthood. *Family Relations, 29,* 459–465.

Nisbett, R., & Ross, L. (1980). *Human inference: strategies and shortcomings of social judgment.* Englewood Cliffs, NJ: Prentice-Hall.

Piaget, J. (1971). *Biology and knowledge.* Chicago, IL: University of Chicago Press.

Quilligan, M. (1989, May 21). Review of *Maternal thinking: Toward a politics of peace. The New York Times,* p. 15.

Reilly, T. W., Entwisle, D. R., & Doering, S. G. (1987). Socialization into parenthood: A longitudinal study of the development of self-evaluations. *Journal of Marriage and the Family, 49,* 295–308.

Roosa, M. W. (1988). The effect of age in the transition to parenthood: Are delayed childbearers a unique group? *Family Relations, 37,* 322–327.

Ruble, D., Fleming, A. S., Hackel, L. S., & Stangor, C. (1988). Changes in the marital relationship during the transition to first time motherhood: Effects of violated expectations concerning division of household labor. *Journal of Personality and Social Psychology, 55*, 78–87.

Schneider, D. J., Hastorf, A. H., & Ellsworth, P. C. (1979). *Person perception* (2nd ed.). Reading, MA: Addison-Wesley.

Spanier, G. B. (1976). Measuring dyadic adjustment: New scales for assessing the quality of marriage and similar dyads. *Journal of Marriage and the Family, 38*, 15–28.

Steffensmeier, R. H. (1982). A role model of the transition to parenthood. *Journal of Marriage and the Family, 44*, 319–334.

Tietjen, A. M., & Bradley, C. F. (1985). Social support and maternal psychosocial adjustment during the transition to parenthood. *Canadian Journal of Behavioral Science, 17*, 109–121.

Udry, J. R. (1983). Do couples make fertility plans one birth at a time? *Demography, 20*, 117–128.

Ventura, J. N. (1987). The stresses of parenthood reexamined. *Family Relations, 36*, 26–29.

White, L. K., & Kim, H. (1987). The family-building process: Childbearing choices by parity. *Journal of Marriage and the Family, 49*, 271–279.

Zeanah, C. H., & Anders, T. F. (1987). Subjectivity in parent–infant relationships: A discussion of internal working models. *Infant Mental Health Journal, 8*, 237–250.

4

Double Jeopardy: Identity Transitions and Parent–Child Relations Among Gay and Lesbian Youth

Andrew M. Boxer
*Michael Reese Hospital & Medical Center
and The University of Chicago*
Judith A. Cook
*Thresholds Research Institute
and The University of Chicago*
Gilbert Herdt
The University of Chicago

GAY AND LESBIAN YOUTH

In this chapter we investigate parent–child relations among a group of 202 youth (ages 14–21) in the process of self-identification as gay or lesbian (also know as the "coming out" process). From data collected in a larger inter-disciplinary, developmental, and anthropological investigation (Herdt, Boxer, & Irvin, 1986) we examine the effects of the youth's self-disclosure of their sexual orientation to parents on their parental relations (with mothers and fathers), as reported by the youth. We also briefly examine this process from the point of view of a group of parents, based on pilot interviews with 50 parents whose young adult children had disclosed their gay or lesbian identities to them.

Background

Currently in our society we are accustomed to hearing of gays or lesbians "coming out of the closet" and living publicly as homosexual. The American cultural idiom "coming out" has emerged to refer to many psychological processes and social events (Herdt, 1991). This idiom, on a global level, indexes the act whereby someone declares their identity to be "homosexual" or "gay" or "lesbian" to family, friends, or co-workers who assumed the person to be "straight" or "heterosexual." Although the declaration may occur in public, private, or secret contexts, emphasis is on a single attribute: being "homosexual." Previously these phenomena were subsumed under the label *homosexuality*, the negative meanings of which were indexed to psychopathology and the marginality of disease discourse in psychiatry (Herdt, 1989). Inherent in that discourse were themes of stigma and prejudice. The emergence of the gay and lesbian movement (Adam, 1987) in American/European culture altered these biases (D'Emilio, 1983; Weeks, 1985). Gay is here defined by cultural and lifestyle choices, that is, identification with a cultural community (Whitney, 1989; p. 25). Thus the term *gay* indexes a cultural identity that is part of a richer and more supportive environment of gay and lesbian adults, institutions, and most recently emergent are younger generations of youth. Traditionally the term *homosexual* has been used synonymously with those of *gay/lesbian*. However, the distinctiveness of the cultural meanings surrounding *gay* and *lesbian* are obscured in this way. Herdt (1991) has argued that the *homosexual* cultural system indexes the historically older pathology/stigma discourse; whereas the *gay* cultural system incorporates emergent meanings that may still be disparaged in the mainstream heterosexual society, but not in the lesbian and gay community.

GAY AND LESBIAN YOUTH IN THE 1980s

Emerging evidence suggests that the age of self-identification as gay or lesbian has been lowering over the last 50 years (Coleman, 1982; Dank, 1971; Herdt, 1989; Troiden, 1989; Remafedi, 1987). A conservative estimate places the number of Americans living exclusively as "homosexual" at 12 million adults, teenagers comprising some 3 million homosexually inclined youth (Sladkin, 1983). Thus, the label *gay* or *lesbian adolescent* appears to represent a unique cultural category in history. This category is manifested in a newly emerging generation of gay/lesbian identified adolescents who should be distinguished from other youth who may experience homosexual desires or engage in homosexual behavior (but who may not identify as gay or lesbian). This group exemplifies the emerging distinction between being homosexual and being gay (Herdt, 1991; Whitney, 1989), or between homosexual behaviors and gay identity.

Historically, there were few opportunities for community socializing or socialization that today's youth may access in large urban areas such as New York, San Francisco, and in Chicago, where our study was conducted. Thus, this aspect of the life course, self-identification as gay or lesbian *during adolescence*, may be a unique developmental process found only in current cohorts of some homosexual youth and carry different consequences for the development of parent–child relations over the life course. Where earlier generations of same-sex attracted persons lived less openly, many of today's gay youth,

by contrast, assume the possibility of striving for and achieving unprecedented life goals and open social relationships at home, school, and work, unknown
to most persons of the earlier cohorts (Gerstel, Feraios, & Herdt, 1989). Among
these goals, our study suggests that most youth have strong desires to disclose
their identities to parents.

In consequence of an earlier identity transition to gay or lesbian, some youth
who have begun this process are "coming out" to parents during their adolescent years, posing new issues for their families and themselves to negotiate during that phase of the life course. Recent changes in family size and spacing
of children, combined with increased life expectancy have made the parent–
child relationship now typically one that lasts 40–60 years. For the greater part
of its duration it will be a relationship between adults (Hagestad, 1981). Thus,
coming out to parents in adolescence may presage the contours of the future
course of the relationship between children and parents, when children are being open with their parents about their sexual identity, and thereby share aspects
of their lives to a much greater extent than in previous generations of gays
and lesbians. Typically those who do come out to parents do so with the hope
of parental acceptance. In our Chicago study one 19-year-old White male told
us:

> I don't think my mom is very accepting of gay people at all. It is not so much
> gay people as it is anyone who's different. I don't feel that she would reject me,
> but she would have a hard time accepting it if I told her. I will tell her when
> I move out because I think that when I tell her we will need space for a while
> to think things out.

A young Black female also told us: "I haven't come out yet to my parents.
I'm sure it'll be a problem when I do."

ADOLESCENCE AND THE TRANSITION
TO GAY/LESBIAN IDENTITIES

Findings from our Chicago study have enabled us to see the changing culture
of American homosexuality constituted through four distinct generations or
cohorts (see Herdt, 1991, in press). Cohort differences are likely to have consequences for the study of development in general, and in particular with regard
to parent–child relations. Although the oldest living cohort dates from the turn
of the century, many of these surviving persons, now in their 70s and older,
grew into adulthood and discovered their same-sex desires without typically
ever having "come out" to parents or others. Today many of them remain
largely invisible (Berger, 1982; Kehoe, 1986). Whereas the oldest cohorts lived
in secrecy and with fear, suffering the psychosocial costs of this (see e.g., Brown,

1976), in contrast today's youth are developing a future life course by response to these historical issues. The early 1980s seem to have ushered in a new cultural epoch of coming out for teenagers and young adults. They experience a more open society than ever before, as manifested in the institutions and community groups that can be seen as a support to their identity development—such as the gay and lesbian youth group from which we drew the sample for the present study.

The motivations for and timing of coming out to parents are likely to be multidetermined (Myers, 1982) and include political and ideological reasons; needs for honesty and to reduce the strains of passing or deception; increased confidence and self-esteem resulting from self-acceptance; new personal relationships; anger and confrontation. Disclosure of one's gay/lesbian identity to parents can be a stressful and anxiety-provoking situation for any individual (Berzon & Leighton, 1979; Clark 1977; Silverstein, 1977, 1981); such may be more true for a teenager. Concepts of normative socialization during adolescence emphasize heterosexual identity, object choice, and marriage, as the implicit or explicit goals and outcomes of adolescent development. For the youth we have been studying such expectations are experienced as discrepant with their desires and relationships. During early adolescence some of the normative constraints and expectations associated with these heterosexual outcomes, as delineated by Hill and Lynch (1983) in their discussion of gender intensification (see also Hagestad & Neugarten, 1984), may be experienced by gay and lesbian youth in a more vivid and emotionally intense manner. In early adolescence, these developmentalists suggest, sex-role expectations are expressed in more constrained and stereotypic, gender roles.

Many of the youth in our study described feeling the need to conform to the external markers of such normative expectations. One 18-year-old Black male described it this way: "I hide it from no one else besides my family. When I refer to some person I like, I'll say "she" or use different names, like when I am talking on the phone." Indeed, over 70% of the youth in our study have had some type of heterosexual experience—which as a group they rate as less satisfying than the homoerotic ones (Cook, Boxer, & Herdt, 1989). The youth are, in many respects "betwixt and between" different social worlds (Turner, 1967), the primarily heterosexual and heterosocial world of their family and school peers, and that of the gay community of their newly found peer group in Chicago.

In our research interviews many youth have told us that they feel themselves to be the target of a constellation of assumptions about their presumed heterosexuality that do not apply to them, including jokes and jabs about boyfriends or girlfriends, and insinuations about dating or the expression of other heterosexual markers. The experiences typically result in almost all of the youth feeling, at some time, the need to suppress or hide their homosexual desires, particularly from parents.

An adolescent in the process of transition to a gay or lesbian identity has several additional issues to negotiate beyond those of most other adolescents. A double bind may present itself for many youth, because being honest with one's parents (a common value emphasized by most parents) seems contradictory to knowing that news of being gay or lesbian is not likely to be greeted with great joy by parents. One young man described this double bind while discussing his plans for the future. He said: "When I am older I will be able to be more myself. Like I will not have to make up stories about where I am going and who I am with. Like when I am here [at the Gay and Lesbian Youth Group] I tell my mother that I am working."

Thus, coming out in this context means for our population the beginning of the end of secrecy with parents. In previous analyses of our data we have found that most of these youth have first disclosed their sexual orientation to a friend at a mean age of 16, whereas the boys found this significantly more difficult to do than did the girls (Boxer & Cook, 1988).

PARENT–CHILD RELATIONS, HOMOSEXUALITY, AND COMING OUT

Few systematic studies have examined the coming out process and its impact on the quality of the parent–child relationship. Previous investigations, largely based on case reports, portray hiding one's sexual identity from parents as resulting in more distant relationships. Existing data indicate that between approximately 40% to 63% of homosexually or gay- and lesbian-identified respondents have reported being open about their sexual orientation to parents (e.g., Bell & Weinberg, 1978; Cramer & Roach, 1988; Jay & Young, 1979; Kooden et al., 1979; Plummer, 1989). One of the more common but implicit socialization outcomes of the transition to a gay or lesbian identity has been conceptualized as "learning to hide," in which youth have found it necessary to engage in suppression, hiding, and deception regarding their homosexuality in order to not disclose their sexual orientation to parents (Martin, 1982).

A small body of recent literature on gay youth suggests disclosure of sexual orientation to family results in conflict and distress in family relations during an adolescent's transition to a "gay" or "lesbian" identity (Myers, 1982; Plummer, 1989; Robertson, 1981; Troiden, 1989). One recent report, based on a sample of New York City youth attending a center for gay youth, found many individuals whose self-disclosure to parents resulted in a disruption of parent–child ties, at least at the time of the interviews (Martin & Hetrick, 1988). In a small study of multicultural gay and lesbian youth in Toronto, it was found that when minority youth had come out to parents, the youth's relationships to their ethnic communities were altered in the process. Out of concern and care for their families some youth experienced alienation from their communities by excluding themselves from cultural activities to avoid shaming their families (Tremble, Schneider, & Appathurai, 1989).

In a recent survey study of 317 gay and lesbian youth (ages 14 to 23), aspects of these youth's well-being were found to be related to perceptions of parental acceptance of their homosexuality (Savin-Williams, 1989a). Subsequent analyses revealed that positive parental relationships, as reported by the youth, predicted which lesbians felt comfortable with their sexuality and were out to their parents, although positive parental relations did not predict the females' self-esteem. These same relationships did not pertain to the males; although in families where males' rated parents' as an important part of their self-worth, perceived parental acceptance was related to their comfort with being gay (which in turn predicted self-esteem) (Savin-Williams, 1989b). For the males in this sample, being out to mothers but not fathers predicted high self-esteem. (Savin-Williams, 1989b). These data, being correlational, do not establish whether parental self-disclosure leads to higher self-esteem, or whether higher self-esteem may be associated with self-disclosure.

PARENTAL PERSPECTIVES

It is now well recognized that across adjacent and nonadjacent generational positions, family members share expectational sets regarding the advent and timing of individual and shared life events in the family (Greene & Boxer, 1986; Hagestad, 1981; Pruchno, Blow, & Smyer, 1984). An event that occurs in the life of one family member affects others in the family as well. Study of the parent–child relationship reminds us of the intimate interconnections between the lives of parents and adult children, throughout the entire duration of their relationship (Greene & Boxer, 1986). They are consociates, with contingent life careers (Plath, 1980). Children count on a period of strength— almost invulnerability—in their parents up to old age, whereas parents also build strong developmental expectations regarding children. A sense of security and accomplishment in the second half of adulthood depends on the knowledge that offspring have turned out "okay" in their adult life (Cohen & Weissman, 1984; Weissman, Cohen, Boxer, & Cohler, 1989). Indeed, the knowledge that children have been successfully launched into adulthood gives parents the freedom to attend to their own developmental concerns (Cohler & Boxer, 1984). Because of the complex interconnections of lives in the family, critical life events create "countertransitions" (Riley & Waring, 1976). So, for example, a parent's retirement also has meanings and implications for a child. Thus, the coming out process in a child may potentially initiate a parallel process for the parent.

Therefore, a critical dimension to the identity transition process for gay and lesbian youth is the alteration in family relationships produced by the transition. Almost no work on this issue has been conducted to date, and little work, in general, has been conducted that examines the impact of adolescents on parents development and relationships (Boxer, Solomon, Offer, Petersen, & Halprin, 1984; Greene & Boxer, 1986; Silverberg & Steinberg, 1987). Existing literature on coming out to parents includes some practical handbooks for parents (e.g., Borhek, 1983; Fairchild & Hayward, 1979; Jones, 1978; Silverstein, 1977) and for individuals coming out to family members (e.g., Sauerman, 1984; Weinberg, 1972), but little research consideration has been given to understanding these processes in the family (see Muller, 1987; Myers, 1982; Griffin, Wirth, & Wirth, 1986); nor has most of this research examined the impact of a gay or lesbian child on parental well-being or adult development.

One recent report has documented that characteristics predicting parents' levels of acceptance were related to the same qualities associated with homophobia (Cramer & Roach, 1988).[1] A larger cross-national survey of 402 parents of gay and lesbian children (drawn from parent support groups around the country) examined parents' initial reactions to learning of their children's homosexuality (Robinson, Walters, & Skeen, 1989). Sixty-four percent of the parents in this study (75% of whom were mothers) reported experiencing grief-type reactions; these reactions are suggested to result from the loss of former representations of their children and associated life goals related to their presumed heterosexuality. Slightly less than half of the sample (44%) also reported experiencing feelings of guilt. Some parents, at least initially, may feel they have somehow caused their children to become homosexual (see also accounts written by parents with gay and lesbian children in Fairchild & Hayward, 1979). Responses from parents of males were also compounded by their fear of AIDS (Robinson, Walters, & Skeen, 1989).

Most parents are not likely to be pleased to hear the news regarding their child's gay or lesbian identity. Societal conceptions of homosexuality are bound to influence parents' initial responses to their children's self-disclosure. In a recent review of the literature on family members' reactions to the disclosure of homosexuality, Strommen (1989) concluded that disclosure by a child may create a sense of alienation from the child within the parent, a feeling that the parent does not know his or her child (see also Jones, 1978). Within the context of the family, investigators have identified aspects of family process that may influence family members' responses to a gay/lesbian child (Collins & Zim-

---

[1]As with most of these studies this information was not collected from the parents themselves, but from their gay/lesbian children.

merman, 1983; DeVine, 1984).[2] Family themes, family cohesion, values, concerns with conformity, and religiosity, among others, have been found to influence family members' responses to homosexual children (Collins & Zimmerman, 1983; DeVine, 1984; Strommen, 1989). Conflicting and competing issues regarding parental feelings of love for their child coupled with ascribed responsibilities and expectations for childrearing have been thought to conflict with societal conceptions of homosexuality. This may create for parents a kind of cognitive and emotional dissonance that is difficult to resolve (see Strommen, 1989; Weinberg, 1972).

DeVine (1984) and others (Robinson, Walters, & Skeen, 1989; Switzer & Switzer, 1980) have suggested that parents move through a series of stages of awareness and acceptance of their children's homosexuality. However, these processes have not been examined longitudinally. Based on cross-sectional data, it has been suggested (Griffin, Wirth, & Wirth, 1986; Muller, 1987) that some parents become psychologically impeded by this parental "coming out" process and never fully resolve it. Thus, it is particularly important to be able to understand the ways in which the parent may be affected by the child's self-disclosure, and in turn how parent and child may subsequently alter their relationships. Additionally, although changes in the parent–child relationship may be initiated by an adolescent or by parents' reactions to their adolescents, they may also be initiated by parents' own developmental concerns and psychological preoccupations (Boxer, Solomon, Offer, Petersen, & Halprin, 1984).

METHODS AND FINDINGS

The Group

The study (Herdt, Boxer, & Irvin, 1986) on which this chapter is based was an interdisciplinary psychosocial and anthropological investigation of a group of self-identified gay and lesbian youth who belong to the current generation

---

[2]In line with the distinction made in this chapter between homosexual behavior and gay/lesbian identities, it should be noted that the majority of these studies do not make such distinctions. Often the terms may be used interchangeably and thereby confounded. However, it is important to keep in mind that family members in general, and parents in particular, may respond differentially to the cultural label *gay* or *lesbian* versus knowledge of homosexual behavior. A child who has not labeled him or herself as *gay* or *lesbian* and who has no ties to cultural institutions in the gay/lesbian community may present his or her identity very differently than an individual who has become openly integrated into the gay community. These distinctions are confounded with historical time, because earlier studies are less likely to have made such distinctions; newer studies are more likely to draw samples of gay or lesbian identified respondents. The point here is that parents' responses to their child's identity may be differentially mediated by the cultural context. Additionally, as suggested by Strommen (1989), whether a parent is voluntarily told or whether their child's gay/lesbian identity is accidentally "discovered," is highly likely to influence parental response.

of individuals entering adolescence during the AIDS epidemic (preliminary ethnographic findings from the study have been published in Gerstel, Feraios, & Herdt, 1989; see also Boxer & Cohler, 1989).[3] This group of youth living in metropolitan Chicago experience a more open society than ever before, as evidenced by institutions and community groups in the gay/lesbian community of Chicago that support their identity development and social relations. Such a support group for youth was the context for our study, sponsored by a major community-based social service agency that serves the gay and lesbian community in Chicago. The group is situated in-between the youth's mainstream heterosexual parents, on the one hand, and the gay community and lesbian adult advisors, role models, and friends on the other. A cultural system of normative gay/lesbian beliefs, concepts and goals are expressed in the shared discourse of local gay newspapers, churches, shopping areas, and of the youth group itself. This cultural community, in other words, provides an alternative socialization structure to that of the youth's mainstream heterosexual homes. The youth group was begun in 1978 and is recognized as a distinctive sign of the community itself. Because youth who attend the group are in the process of self-identification as gay or lesbian, they may be more resourceful and resilient than other adolescents with homosexual desires. Through the secondary socialization that occurs in the group, they have the opportunity to normalize their experience via introduction to and entry into many domains of cultural life in the gay community. The context of this cultural community, in other words, provides an alternative socialization structure of shared beliefs and cultural practices—to that of the youth's mainstream heterosexual homes (see Murray, 1984).

An obvious caveat about our findings is, therefore, that many adolescents who feel themselves attracted to the same sex do not come to Horizons or participate in the gay community; our sample is an opportunistic one, and generalizations regarding homosexuality among youth in America at large cannot be made. In the analyses presented in this chapter, we confine ourselves to an examination of data collected from individual interviews with the youth. The parental perspective is briefly examined with qualitative data from individual interviews of a sample of parents with young adult gay/lesbian children.

The Sample

Our nonclinical sample was drawn from the Horizons Youth Group over a 2-year period, between 1986–1988. Membership in the group is limited by age, from 14 to 21. Those who achieve their 21st birthday must leave the group,

---

[3]The methods of investigation included data collected through both individual interviews with each teen, and ethnographic study employing standard anthropological field methods. In this report we focus only on the interview study.

which is a source of considerable turmoil to the "graduates." The criteria for being interviewed in our project was that each potential respondent had to have been in attendance at the group for a minimum of three sessions.[4] Most of the youth live at home, go to school, and are within a normal range of psychological functioning.

Two hundred and two youth completed individual, face-to-face, semi-structured interviews with a trained interviewer, as well as a battery of paper-and-pencil assessments. The in-depth protocols took approximately 3 hours, on average, to complete, and all interviews were conducted at the social service agency. The refusal rate among the youth was quite low at 5%. The adolescents in this study are a heterogeneous group who come from all parts of the greater Chicago area. Our sample includes 147 males and 55 females. This unbalanced gender ratio reflects the actual composition of the group. The mean age of the sample is 18.3 (SD = 1.45, r = 14–21; females = 17.96; males = 18.41). Thirty percent of the sample are Black, 40% are White, 12% are Hispanic, 3% Asian American, and the remaining 15% are of mixed ethnic backgrounds. Of the youth, 38% live with both parents, 25% live in single parent households, and the remainder live either on their own or in various types of blended families (7 of the youth were living in shelters at the time of their interviews). The religious backgrounds of the youth are 82% Protestant and Catholic (45% Protestant, 37% Catholic; 9% from mixed religious backgrounds; 4% Atheist/agnostic, 2% Jewish, and 4% had no religious affiliation). Their family backgrounds are fairly evenly divided between working- and middle-class backgrounds. Almost three quarters of these youth (72%) are in school, and close to two-thirds (63%) are employed, either part or full time.

Parents

A pilot sample of 50 parents (approximately equally divided between fathers and mothers) was recruited from a local social support group for parents with gay and lesbian children.[5] These parents are primarily White, middle and

---

[4]This was a requirement necessitated by the Agency's concern regarding the youth's transition into the group.

[5]Although it would have been ideal to have obtained reciprocal data from the same set of parents and youth, we were unable to do so because of the study design. Many of the youth in this study were either in the process of or had not yet disclosed their sexual identity to parents, and we did not wish to threaten the research alliance with respondents by asking them to gain access to their parents. However, in order to gain a parental perspective on this issue, we obtained interviews with parents who were members of a local chapter of a support group for parents with gay or lesbian identified children. Because these adult children were, on average, 10 years older than our youth sample, we must bear in mind that certain cohort differences may be influencing parents' reactions to their gay and lesbian adult children's self-disclosure.

upper middle class, in their 50s, and have young adult sons and daughters who have come out to them, mostly during the children's young adulthood. They have sought social support through membership in the parent group in order to assist them with various aspects of this coming out process. The length of time since their children had disclosed their homosexuality to them ranged from less than 1 year to more than 10 years. Each father/mother was individually administered a semi-structured interview and a battery of paper-and-pencil assessments. In this report we focus on parents' responses to the disclosure of their children's gay/lesbian identity.

MEASURES AND ANALYSES

Parent–Child Relationships

The youth were asked to describe and rate the quality of their relationships with mothers and fathers, recent changes in those relationships, and whether and how their parents were aware of their sexual orientation. Resulting associations between the quality of their relationships with mothers and fathers and disclosure of sexual orientation to parents were evaluated in multivariate regression analyses following the introduction of a series of control variables, including age of respondent (at interview), gender of respondent, living situation, minority status, and degree of self-identification as gay/lesbian. To examine whether disclosure to parents was related to recent change in the relationships, associations between these variables were examined with probit analyses; multiple regression analyses were then employed to determine the quality of changes in parental relationships predicted by self-disclosure to mothers and fathers. The same control variables were employed in all of these analyses.

Sexual Orientation

We have found from both interview and observational data that most of these youth do not manifest confusion about their sexual orientation, but rather come to the youth group with confusion about how to express and manage it. Although these youth self-identify as gay/lesbian, in order to take account of and control for variations in the degree of self-identification as gay/lesbian, we have measured sexual orientation with a revised measure based on an expanded multidimensional Kinsey-type scale (Klein, Sepekoff, & Wolf, 1985). Whereas Kinsey emphasized sexual acts, the measure we are using includes several other variables that influence the individual's functioning and adaptation outside of and beyond simple sexual behavioral acts. Individuals, for example, may define themselves as heterosexual and still engage in homosexual behavior. The revised measure we employed (modeled after the Klein scale, Klein, Sepekoff, & Wolf, 1985) contains seven items on which respondents are asked to rate themselves using a 7-point linear scale (from 1 = opposite-sex only, to 7 = same-sex only). Respondents were asked to rate themselves for past, present (in the last year) and ideal sexual orientation on seven items: a) attraction, b) fantasy, c) behavior, d) emotional preference, e) social preference, f) self-identification, and g) lifestyle. The alpha coefficients for this scale are all above .80 for both males and females (males: $\bar{x}$ = 5.14, SD = .80, α = .82; females $\bar{x}$ = 5.20, SD = .87, α = .89; total $\bar{x}$ = 5.15, α .83). Given the nature of our sample, it is not surprising that the distribution is skewed in the direction of homosexual.

FINDINGS

Disclosure to Parents and Other Family Members

Figure 4.1 displays the percentage of youth who reported that different family members were aware of their sexual orientation. In this report we are concerned only with the parents. Out of all family members, parents are those whom the youth most frequently named as being aware of their sexual orientation. Not surprisingly, a larger number of girls report that their mothers and fathers are aware of their sexual orientation (mothers, 63%; fathers, 37%) than do boys (mothers, 54%; fathers, 28%). Mothers are the more frequent target of this information than are fathers, regardless of the gender of the youth.

Two major types of parental awareness patterns are included in this figure and are disaggregated in Table 4.1. Some youths reported that their parents knew about and were aware of their sexual orientation, although they had not discussed it with their parents. For example, a 15-year-old female told us of how her mother had read her diary, which revealed her being in love with a female classmate and the feelings she had about being a lesbian. When asked if she had ever talked with her mother about this, or if her mother had ever brought it up, she said: "No, it's never been mentioned. It would be too scary to tell your mom. I think I can tell her when I move out to go to college." She continued: "I overheard my Mom tell my Dad that she thought I was a lesbian because of what she read in the diary." Other youth in our study directly discussed and disclosed their sexual orientation to their mothers/fathers. This was the more common mode of parents learning about their children's sexual orientation. For example, an 18-year-old female said: "Yes, I told her. I was so frustrated from hiding that I just told her, so it wasn't that hard. But at that point I didn't care anymore. She thinks it's totally wrong and that I'm making a big mistake."

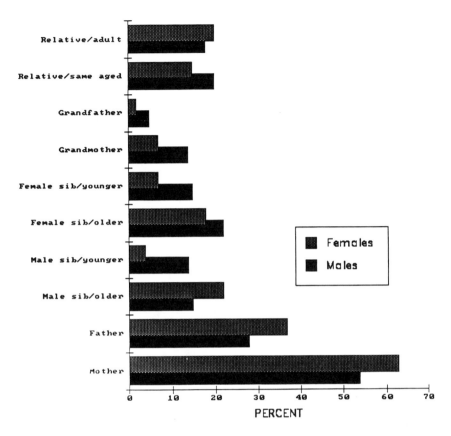

FIG 4.1.   Reports by gay and lesbian youth of family members' awareness of their homosexuality.

From the information in Table 4.1 we created a dichotomous variable that was one of those used to predict parental relationships. We call this the *parental awareness variable*, that is, whether or not the child reported that the parent was aware or not aware of his or her sexual orientation, regardless of how the parent learned of it (i.e., directly or indirectly). To assess direct disclosure to parents, we created another dummy variable used in our regressions, which we have called the *disclosure variable*, where we divided all youth who discussed their homosexuality with parent(s) in one category from those who had not. Both genders disclosed more to mothers than fathers, whereas a larger proportion of girls directly disclosed to both mothers and fathers. Of the total sample of girls, 47% directly disclosed to their mothers, and 24% did so with their fathers; 38% of the males did so with mothers, and 14% with fathers. This *disclosure* variable turns out to be a slightly more powerful predictor than the awareness variable in our multivariate analyses.

TABLE 4.1
Awareness and Disclosure to Parents

	Boys		Girls		Total	
Awareness of Homosexuality	%	N	%	N	%	N
Mother aware	54	79	63	35	56	114
Mother not aware	46	68	37	20	44	88
Total	100	147	100	55	100	202
Father aware	28	42	37	20	30	61
Father not aware	72	105	63	35	70	141
Total	100	147	100	55	100	202
Type of Disclosure						
Mother knows, told by R	38	55	47	26	40	81
Mother knows, not told by R	16	24	16	9	16	33
Mother not aware	46	68	37	20	44	88
Total	100	147	100	55	100	202
Father knows, told by R	14	21	24	13	16	33
Father knows, not told by R	14	21	13	7	14	28
Father not aware	72	105	63	35	70	141
Total	100	147	100	55	100	202

QUALITY OF RELATIONSHIPS

Turning to the nature of the parental relationship as characterized at the time of the interview (Table 4.2), both males and females reported better relations with mothers than with fathers, a difference that was statistically significant. Rated on a 5-point scale from 1 being very negative to 5 being very positive (with 3 being an average or mixed relationship), the mean score for the youth rating mothers was 3.64 and for fathers 2.61 (t = 7.49, p < .0001); there were no significant gender differences between the boys' and the girls' ratings of their parents. Thus, relationships with mothers, not surprisingly, were rated higher than those with fathers. However, relations with fathers were not necessarily more conflictual, but were sometimes less emotionally salient. For example, one male described his relationship with his father: "It is a good relationship. He is not one to make a lot of conversation with you. He and I don't have those heart to heart talks alone, we never have. That's the way we have always been. It works for us."

MULTIVARIATE ANALYSES

A series of multiple regression analyses were separately conducted to predict the quality of relationships with mothers and with fathers. Table 4.3 presents the zero order correlations of the variables included in the following multi-

TABLE 4.2
Quality of Parental Relationships Reported by Youth

Quality of Relationship	Boys		Girls		Total	
	%	N	%	N	%	N
With Mothers						
Very negative	6	9	15	8	9	17
Negative	7	10	7	4	7	14
Average/mixed	29	40	26	14	28	54
Positive	29	40	28	15	29	55
Very positive	29	40	23	12	27	52
Total	100	139	100	53	100	192
With Fathers						
Very negative	28	32	24	11	27	43
Negative	12	14	13	6	12	20
Average/mixed	30	35	39	18	33	53
Positive	22	25	15	7	20	32
Very positive	8	9	9	4	8	13
Total	100	115	100	46	100	161

Quality of Relationship by Parent Gender:
Mothers, $\bar{X}$ = 3.61; Fathers, $\bar{X}$ = 2.64; t = 7.49; $p <$ .0001; df = 164

Quality of Relationship by Child Gender:
Males: Mothers, $\bar{X}$ = 3.66; Females: Mothers, $\bar{X}$ = 3.35, ns
Males: Fathers, X = 2.69, Females: Mothers, X = 2.71, ns

variate regression analyses. With regard to mothers (Table 4.4), neither the mother's awareness of the child's sexual orientation, nor the reported disclosure by the youth to the parent had significant effects on the quality of the relationship. Age was a significant predictor of the relationship, similar to what has been reported in other studies of parent–child relations (Greene & Boxer, 1986; Troll & Bengtson, 1982). Older youth reported better relations with mothers than younger youth. It is interesting to note that there was no effect of either awareness or disclosure.

If mothers are upset to hear that their children are gay or lesbian, they may be masking their reactions and, therefore, their feelings do not directly influence their children's perception of the quality of the relationship. Some mothers do react negatively to the disclosure by their children. However, in the eyes of their children, they do not let it disrupt their relationships. One 19-year-old male told us:

I think she may have realized that when I came out I would need her most . . . she has met my boyfriend and likes him. I don't really know what she thinks about gays. I assume she respects them and their rights. You see, my mother

TABLE 4.3a
Correlation Matrix for Mothers

	(1)	(2)	(3)	(4)	(5)	(6)	(7)	(8)
1. Relationship with mother	1.00	.01	−.01	.01	−.12	−.08	−.03	.21**
2. Mother told (disclosure)		1.00	.71***	.20*	.09	−.02	−.10	−.03
3. Mother aware (Awareness)			1.00	.21*	.11	.07	−.15 +	−.01
4. Sexual identity				1.00	.07	−.09	−.08	.13
5. Gender					1.00	.07	.11	−.06
6. Minority status						1.00	.02	−.08
7. Living status							1.00	−.20**
8. Age								1.00

TABLE 4.3b
Correlation Matrix for Fathers

	(1)	(2)	(3)	(4)	(5)	(6)	(7)	(8)
1. Relationship with father	1.00	.27***	.20*	.03	.04	−.15 +	.12	.14
2. Father told (disclosure)		1.00	.64***	.16 +	.15 +	−.08	−.01	.11
3. Father aware (Awareness)			1.00	.25**	.10	−.07	−.12	−.01
4. Sexual identity				1.00	.08	−.11	−.01	.11
5. Gender					1.00	.09	.01	−.08
6. Minority status						1.00	−.08	−.16 +
7. Living status							1.00	−.06
8. Age								1.00

$+p < .05$; $*p < .01$; $**p < .005$; $***p < .001$.

doesn't treat me as an issue. She regards me as her son who is gay and not her gay son.

Another high school age male told us that his mother found out (indirectly) that he was gay:

She told me she was aware that I was leading an alternative lifestyle and she was concerned about me getting AIDS. I just about died. I felt like I was a big disappointment to my parents. But the joke's on me. Nothing changed between us. I thought there would be a lot of those long dragged out conversations about being gay, but everything remained the same.

With fathers, however, a different and slightly paradoxical set of findings emerged (Table 4.5). In separate multiple regression analyses, both fathers' reported *awareness* of the child's sexual orientation as well as the youths' *direct*

TABLE 4.4
Regression Analyses Predicting Quality of Relationships
with Mothers Among Gay and Lesbian Youth

Quality of Relationship with Mothers	b	Beta	Significance
Mother awareness	.05	.02	
Age at interview	.17	.20	.006
Minority status	− .14	− .05	
Residential status	.05	.02	
Sexual identity	− 1.50	− .01	
Gender	− .30	− .10	
Constant	.81		

R^2 = .061, df = 6/180, ns

Quality of Relationship with Mothers	b	Beta	Significance
Direct disclosure	.07	.03	
Age at interview	.18	.20	.005
Minority status	− .14	− .05	
Residential status	.06	.02	
Sexual identity	− 1.64	− .01	
Gender	− .30	− .11	
Constant	.80		

R^2 = .062, df = 6/180, ns

TABLE 4.5
Regression Analyses Predicting Quality of Relationships
with Fathers Among Gay and Lesbian Youth

Quality of Relationship with Fathers	b	Beta	Significance
Father awareness	.59	.22	.004
Age at interview	.14	.15	.05
Minority status	− .28	− .11	
Residential status	.38	.14	.05
Sexual identity	− 4.82	− .05	
Gender	.14	.04	
Constant	.09		

R^2 = .103, df = 6/158, $p <$ .007

Quality of Relationship with Fathers	b	Beta	Significance
Direct disclosure	.89	.27	.001
Age at interview	.13	.14	.05
Minority status	− .26	− .10	
Residential status	.33	.13	
Sexual identity	− 3.55	− .03	
Gender	.07	.02	
Constant	.20		

R^2 = .129, df = 6/158, $p <$ .001

disclosure to fathers, were significant predictors of the quality of the relationship. Direct disclosure to fathers was the more powerful predictor in this and all subsequent analyses we conducted. Interestingly, those who had discussed their sexual orientation with fathers reported more positive relationships than those who had not. Admittedly, the effects are not large, and the overall models, although significant, account for only between 10%–13% of the variance (which also included measures of age and gender of respondent, as well as their living situation, minority status, and extent of self-identification as gay/lesbian). Those who lived with their fathers reported better relationships than those who did not.

Not unexpectedly, age remained significant in the presence of these variables, with older youth again reporting better relationships than younger youth. To determine whether age was directly related to either parental awareness or to offspring disclosure, we examined these zero-order correlations (see Table 4.3). We found that age was not related to either the parental awareness or disclosure variables. None of the other variables were significant in the model. Overall, then, disclosure and age were simultaneously affecting the quality of the relationship with fathers.

It is certainly possible that those who discussed their sexual orientation with their fathers had begun the disclosure with better father–child relationships. That would not be surprising because coming out to parents may be associated with increased self-esteem, as a part of the personal coming out process of self-acceptance (Myers, 1982; Savin-Williams, 1989a, 1989b). It is important to note that only 14% of the males and 24% of the females had *directly* disclosed to fathers. On the other hand, in the youths' reports of the disclosure experience, many of them report either no response or negative responses after telling their fathers. One male whose father had been told by his mother about his sexual orientation told us: "He is not one to want to talk about it or anything. That's the way my father is. As long as we are okay, he doesn't say anything." Nonetheless, for those who did directly disclose to fathers, this discussion seems to have had a confirming and anxiety-relieving effect on the teens. Many of those who had not yet come out to their fathers and who were sure that their fathers were unaware of their gay or lesbian identity described expecting the very worst of responses. One young man reported: "My father would tear me apart if he found out I was gay." Another said, "He doesn't know . . . he views me as straight. It would be a total shock to him . . ." And when the worst does not occur, many youth feel quite pleased and relieved. An 18-year-old female said: "I told him and it's semi-denial. He says, you know, you just haven't found the right guy yet. But he can deal with it. And at least he didn't weird out on me."

It should be noted, however, that seven youth reported being kicked out of their homes after their parents' discovery of their homosexuality. These estranged youth were living in shelters at the time of their interviews. Obviously, this is not the modal response of the parents, but it poses a difficult and wrenching break for this small number of adolescents. Further research is needed to examine the characteristics and processes in families of gay/lesbian teens who are forced to leave home.

CHANGES IN RELATIONSHIPS

In another set of questions, we asked our sample of youth to describe whether and how they had experienced any type of recent change (during the past year) in their relationships with mothers and fathers. Overall, 64% reported changes in relationships with mothers, whereas 50% reported changes with fathers (Table 4.6). Girls were more likely to report changes in relationships than boys, and boys were much less likely to report change with fathers than with mothers, similar to that reported in other studies of parent–child relations (e.g., Wilen, 1979).

In order to examine whether these relationship changes were associated with disclosure of sexual orientation, we conducted a set of probit analyses (Aldrich & Nelson, 1984) to test the power of disclosure to parents in predicting those who report changes in the relationships and those who did not. A similar pattern of divergence for mothers and fathers again emerged to that revealed in the earlier analyses (Table 4.7 and Table 4.8). Neither parental awareness nor youth disclosure were significant predictors of change in the relationship with mothers. However, direct disclosure to fathers was the most important and significant predictor of change in that relationship, even when controlling for the effects of gender, age, living status, minority status, and degree of sexual orientation. Gender effects were also significant, with girls being more likely to report change than boys, and older youth being more likely to report change

TABLE 4.6
Perceptions of Recent Change in Relationships With Mothers
and Fathers Reported by Gay and Lesbian Youth

	Boys	Girls	Total
	%	%	%
With Mother			
Change	61	73	64
No change	39	27	36
	100	100	100
With Father			
Change	43	67	50
No change	57	33	50
	100	100	100

TABLE 4.7
Probit Analyses Predicting Presence or Absence of Change in Relationships with Mothers

Change with Mothers	Probit Coefficient	Standard Error
Mother awareness	.16	.16
Age at interview	.07	.05
Minority status	.21	.16
Residential status	− .05	.17
Sexual identity	− .00	.01
Gender	.23	.19
Pseudo − R^2 = .50		

Change with Mothers	Probit Coefficient	Standard Error
Direct disclosure	.05	.16
Age at interview	.06	.05
Minority status	.22	.15
Residential status	− .07	.17
Sexual identity	.00	.01
Gender	.24	.18
Pseudo − R^2 = .50		

TABLE 4.8
Probit Analyses Predicting Presence or Absence of Change in Relationships with Fathers

Change with Fathers	Probit Coefficient	Standard Error
Father awareness	.31	.17
Age at interview	.14*	.06
Minority status	− .05	.16
Residential status	.09	.16
Sexual identity	− .01	.006
Gender	.42*	.19
Pseudo— R^2 = .50, *p < .05		

Change with Fathers	Probit Coefficient	Standard Error
Direct disclosure	.50*	.21
Age at interview	.13*	.06
Minority status	− .04	.17
Residential status	.06	.16
Sexual identity	− .01	.005
Gender	.39*	.19
Pseudo— R^2 = .50, *p < .05		

than younger youth. Overall, then, three variables were significant in predicting whether or not change had occurred in relations with fathers: disclosure to father, gender, and age.

We were also interested in knowing whether parental awareness or disclosure of sexual orientation were associated with the direction of change in relationships with parents. We asked those youth who had reported a recent change in their relationships with fathers and mothers to characterize the nature of that change, from much worse to much better, rated on a 5-point scale from 1 being very negative to 5 being very positive change (the mean score for males rating change with mothers was 3.24 and for fathers 3.21; females rating mothers = 3.21, fathers = 2.40)

Multiple regression analyses again revealed a similar pattern of divergence for mothers and fathers. For mothers (Table 4.9), age of the youth was the most important and the only significant predictor of the direction of change in the relationship. Older youth reported more positive changes in relationships than did younger youth. A college-age male in our sample talked about changes in his relationship with his mother: "I can talk to her more because I am mature and I don't see her so much as a mother figure as much as a friend. I can be more comfortable with her now. I feel that I don't need to look up to someone so much." Neither the mother's awareness nor the youth's direct disclosure to her had any significant effects on the quality of change in

TABLE 4.9

Regression Analyses Predicting Quality of Change in Relationships with Mothers Among Gay and Lesbian Youth

Quality of Change with Mothers	b	Beta	Significance
Mother awareness	− .20	− .06	
Age at interview	.30	.28	.002
Minority status	− .10	− .03	
Residential status	− .41	− .13	
Sexual identity	− 7.76	− 7.78	
Gender	− .18	− .05	
Constant	− 2.03		

$R^2 = .123$, $df = 6/114$, p < .01

Quality of Relationship with Mothers	b	Beta	Significance
Direct disclosure	− .07	− .02	
Age at interview	.29	.28	.003
Minority status	− .12	− .04	
Residential status	− .40	− .13	
Sexual identity	− 2.06	− .02	
Gender	− .17	− .05	
Constant	− 1.94		

$R^2 = .119$, $df = 6/114$, $p < .02$

that relationship. Nor were there any gender differences between males and females. A 16-year-old, Black male described the lack of change in his relationship with his mother after she found out he was gay. He said:

> Our relationship hasn't changed. We've talked about it a little. She doesn't accept it as being the truth. She sees me as her asexual child. She said, 'you're too young to think anything one way or the other.' I left it alone. I didn't feel like dealing with it. We never talk about it now.

Turning to the fathers (Table 4.10), neither parental awareness nor direct disclosure predicted the direction (quality) of change in the relationship; however, gender did. Girls were more likely than boys to report negative changes in relationships with fathers. In the interview narratives many of the girls described less warm relationships with fathers, regardless of whether their fathers were aware of or had been told about their sexual orientation. Girls were also more likely to report changes in relationships with fathers than the boys. We can speculate that they may also be more sensitive to the nuances in these relationships with fathers, where the overall relationship is rated less favorably. In other analyses of our data (Cook, Boxer, & Herdt, 1989) we have found that a majority of these young women have experimented with some

TABLE 4.10

Regression Analyses Predicting Quality of Change in Relationships
with Fathers Among Gay and Lesbian Youth

Quality of Change with Fathers	b	Beta	Significance
Father awareness	−.23	−.08	
Age at interview	.21	.20	.05
Minority status	−.52	−.18	
Residential status	−.15	−.05	
Sexual identity	−4.38	−.04	
Gender	−.72	−.24	.02
Constant	.48		

$R^2 = .172$, $df = 6/76$, $p < .02$

Quality of Relationship with Fathers	b	Beta	Significance
Direct disclosure	−.50	−.16	
Age at interview	.20	.19	
Minority status	−.47	−.17	
Residential status	−.18	−.06	
Sexual identity	−3.84	−.04	
Gender	−.72	−.24	.01
Constant	.57		

$R^2 = .192$, $df = 6/114$, $p < .01$

type of intimate heterosexual experience before their first homosexual experience. The transition to a lesbian identity may result, at least temporarily, in a heightened sensitivity and distantiation in their relationships with fathers, because they are rejecting a prescribed heterosexual female role in asserting their independence from men (see Zitter, 1987).

SUMMARY

To sum up, the youth were most likely to disclose their sexual orientation to mothers, although neither mothers' awareness, nor disclosure to mothers were associated with the quality of or changes in these relationships. Older youth reported better relations with mothers than younger youth. Both fathers' awareness, and disclosure to fathers, were associated with more positive parental relationships. Change in father–child relationships was also predicted by direct disclosure. The direction of the change was not, however, accounted for by disclosure. Girls were more likely to report changes in relations with fathers than were boys, and these changes were more likely to be negative.

FINDINGS FROM INTERVIEWS WITH PARENTS

In this sample of parents, most of the children came out to mothers and fathers as young adults rather than during their adolescence. Nonetheless, their perspective further illuminates understanding of the impact of coming out among relationships between parents and their children.

One of the emergent themes from the parent interviews were concerns for the happiness and well-being of their children. After the initial shock, it was not homosexuality, per se, that worried them, but the implications of what that would mean regarding discrimination, homophobia, and attendant concerns about old age. A mother described this when she talked about her response to learning that her son was gay:

> Like most parents I was concerned for his happiness. Was he going to have a satisfying life. It was the social aspects. We knew about the criticisms, discrimination and harassment of gay men. We didn't want that for our child.

Another talked about her response in relation to her daughter:

> When she told me I had already begun to wonder whether she was a lesbian. I felt a little sad when she did tell me. Basically I felt concerned for her. I felt it could cause her pain and grief as time went on.

A father remarked about his daughter:

When she told me I remember thinking to myself—if this was true that she was a lesbian, then life might be more difficult for her than if she were a heterosexual. One still has to live in a society and society does not always look favorably on this way of life. I had seen the movie about Harvey Milk and I didn't want Susan to have to go through that kind of aggravation and discrimination.

Most of these middle-aged parents learned of their children's homosexuality when their children were young adults, typically in their mid-20s. As reported by both mothers and fathers, a majority of the gay/lesbian children of these parents spent some significant amount of time in their life during which they engaged in hiding this aspect of themselves from parents. Many of the parents in our study described shared family realities, prior to the disclosure, that included a demilitarized zone (DMZ) (Hagestad, 1981), that is, areas implicitly agreed on to not be discussed, regarding certain features of the child's adult status transition (e.g., marriage, parenthood, and social relations). Most of these parents reported improved relations with children following the disclosure of their homosexuality. Parents described the hiding from their point of view as a secretiveness on their children's part that they could not understand. Some reported relief that this was *all* that was being hidden and not something they had imagined as much worse (e.g., drug abuse, or drug dealing, and other such illicit activities). A subgroup of these parents reported a protracted period of denial on their parts, and described their resistance to acceptance of their children as gay/lesbian, thereby making the coming out process for their families a much longer and painful one.

We have found that in their initial coming out experiences today, parents of males, in particular, must now deal with the reality of AIDS in a way they may have felt distanced from prior to learning of their sons' gay identity. Many parents with male children expressed strong desires to talk about AIDS with their sons, and here it was the children who often did not wish to discuss it. It then became, for some, a DMZ in the family that parents were asked not to transgress. One mother described her son's attempts to allay her fears by telling her, "It's okay Mom, really, I'm safe and you needn't worry." But mom wanted to discuss how he was safe, when, and under what circumstances. These questions were left unanswered and so were some of her worries. However, in other families where there was more open discussion, parents did not necessarily worry less even though they could discuss their concerns with their gay children.

Robinson, Skeen, and Walters (1987), in their national survey of PFLAG parents (Parents and Friends of Lesbian and Gays, Inc.), found that the AIDS epidemic reopened old psychological wounds for many parents regarding their gay sons. Among some parents fears about AIDS activated previous concerns about their children's homosexuality. On the other hand, some parents have first learned of their sons' homosexuality after being diagnosed with AIDS

(Macklin, 1988). In these families, typically, gay/lesbian identity had never been discussed. In contrast, among the parents we have interviewed, a small number have sons with AIDS; however, because their children were open with them about being gay, their response to their children's illness has been supportive and not conflicted because of homosexuality.

With regard to differences between mothers and fathers, not surprisingly, and not unlike most American families, mothers are typically what we call the kinkeepers of the family (Cohler & Boxer, 1984). They are usually the primary emotion managers (Hochschild, 1983) and relationship negotiators for the generations above and below them. They are, in essence, the linchpins of the family. Mothers are thus typically the first parent to whom the child discloses his or her sexual orientation. Mothers were then often the ones who began to further verbalize aspects of the process to their husbands (when present). Fathers were not less emotional about the process, but they were less likely to verbally articulate their feelings.

A proliferation of adult developmental studies have been emerging over the last 20 years. We know from that body of research of a major psychological change, found in many different populations and different cultural settings, which occurs in adults as they move toward old age (Neugarten, 1977; for a review see also Cohler & Boxer, 1984). This psychological change relates to a heightened sense of introspection, termed "increased interiority" (Neugarten, 1977), which is related to the adult's subjective perception of time left to live (Neugarten, 1967) or a sense of the finitude of life (Munnichs, 1966). For most of the parents, the coming out process further stimulated this inner process of self-examination and introspection. This often began with pragmatic self-questioning, that is, "what did I do to make this happen?" One middle-aged father described this: "I did some self-examining when I first found out. I thought about what really did happen, what was it I did that might have had an effect on this." A late middle-aged mother said:

> It's made me grow. I think I know a lot more now than before. I'm a lot more sensitive to people's needs than before. I'm much more aware of all kinds of people. More sensitive to what people say because a lot of what my daughter was saying meant she was a lesbian, but I just didn't pick up on it. Occasionally I have even been able to help other parents with gay or lesbian children. I think that's a bonus.

For many, this led to a self-examination about what some call the "basics" that is, "Who is my child?" "What do I really want for him/her?" Many of the parents took the opportunity and made the most of it. This was an opportunity for growth and personal development, coincident with transitions in middle age. Some talked about feelings of guilt, not related to the question of causality, but rather because of their initially negative responses to the news of a gay or lesbian child. This introspective process frequently resulted in a more realistic assessment of parental expectations as well as delineated boundaries between parent and child.

Part of this parental self-examination process involved reshaping some of their parental fantasies (Cohen & Weissman, 1984). Every parent has a set of expectations about their children, including an image of future life events, what those should be and when they should occur. One mother put it this way:

> My expectations have changed dramatically. I wanted to see my daughter with a family, the children, you know . . . how parents feel. Then I began to realize that she is so capable of a person—she will be whatever she wants to be in life. Being gay doesn't phase her one way or the other—she's comfortable with it. That makes me feel good.

For some of the parents one disappointment related to the thought of not being able to have grandchildren from their gay/lesbian children. A father talked about this in relation to his young adult son: "One of the things we talked about was whether or not we would have grandchildren. While some gay people are parents, it is not a typical path for most gay people. We aren't counting on it."

Another father talked about his daughter: "I did think to myself, did this mean that she would give me no grandchildren? My egocentric feelings seemed to come out first. I have always liked having kids around and I was wondering whether I would have to give up some of the fantasies that I had about my old age."

In her study, Muller (1987) has found that parents of lesbian daughters have more difficulty in acceptance than parents of sons. She has suggested this may have to do with the greater degree of disruption mothers experience in altering their expectations for their daughters, particularly that they will bear children. In our data we have found that both families with gay sons or lesbian daughters experience this disappointment. However, even the notion of no grandchildren has been turned upside down by some of our parents' gay and lesbian children, who have either adopted or had their own children.

After parents had reoriented themselves to their children's new identity status, they restructured and altered some of their parental expectations regarding the future life course of their children. As one mother put it about her son: "At first when I found out I was disappointed because you do have dreams. Dreams that Jerry would marry some intelligent person and live in the suburbs. And those kind of things you learn to change."

Through the reciprocal socialization from child to parent, many parents talked about being confronted with the reality of their children's sexual identity in a way they never experienced with their heterosexual children. But more than sexuality, parents talked about the many ways that they became socially and culturally enlightened through the coming out process. Others talked about becoming political activists. The mother of a gay son told us: "Being involved with gay people has made me more aware of civil rights and women's rights— suppression is suppression." One parent, in recounting his initial responses to the news of his gay child, said he felt like his liberalism had been challenged for the first time. For all of these parents, cultural stereotypes of homosexuality were altered through learning more about the gay community through their children's lives. One mother described it this way:

My ideas of homosexuality were based on old movies and TV shows. Those images were of feminine males, really impressions that I got because I had no one around to change that. My son is very masculine, so it was hard to believe he was gay. Since then I've gotten quite an education.

Muller's (1987) data indicate that many parents became stuck in the coming out process at an initial phase and were unable to move beyond that. They were able, in essence, to retreat to what Griffin, Wirth, and Wirth (1986) called the "ostrich effect," that is, ignoring or pretending that their children's homosexuality did not exist. In our sample we have encountered some parents who went through a protracted phase of denial after self-disclosure. Preliminary findings suggest this may be related to the age of the child at the self-disclosure. The older the child the more difficult it may be to accept and alter presumed assumptions and expectations; for a younger child the difficulties may be different and more easily attributed to adolescent "identity confusion." One mother discussed her prior denial: "I would tell myself it was just a phase he was going through. At the beginning there was no way I would accept it. I was not willing to admit it to myself or others."

However, the accounts given by those parents who engaged in a high level of denial highlight changes in their acceptance that occurred over time, as well as the differing perceptions of mothers and fathers, in addition to those of sons and daughters. We have also found among our sample of parents that when, historically, the parents (not the children) began the coming out process, affected how they were able to negotiate the process. Just as there are now gay and lesbian adult role models for the youth in our study, so too do parents today find role models to support and facilitate their own coming out process.

We wish to emphasize that coming out is a process, not just an outcome. The coming out process within a family context interfaces with the psychosocial interior of the family as a whole, and with the life course trajectories of individual family members. To more adequately understand this process we must study the family's experiences over time.

DISCUSSION

Coming out to one's parents is a difficult step for an adolescent to take. Even those with the most positive parental relationships reported difficulty in disclosing to them. We know, from other analyses of our data (Boxer & Cook,

1988), that the party to whom youth were more likely to *first* disclose their sexual orientation was a same-age peer and not the parents. Yet disclosure to a peer seems to facilitate subsequent disclosure to parents and other family members.

Based on data from our pilot study of parents, we have been able to glimpse some of the common themes and issues salient to both these parents and to those of the youth we interviewed. The processes of reciprocal socialization (Cook & Cohler, 1986) emerged as a critical component of parents' acceptance of their children's homosexuality. Through ongoing reciprocal socialization with their children, many gained cultural knowledge and personal experience with features of gay and lesbian life that helped facilitate their positive relations with children. The disclosure of being gay or lesbian to one's parents appears to initiate this process of reciprocal socialization, as youth begin to teach their parents about their own desires and feelings, and about the gay and lesbian community. Nonetheless, the initial disclosure appears to be part of a longer developmental process.

From the data on the youth in our sample, many reported that their parents—both those who had some awareness and those who had been told directly—preferred to "sit on" the information or deny it, at least initially. In the descriptions of their disclosures, many adolescents told us that parents responded with such comments as, "you'll outgrow this," or other types of what a large number of the youth themselves referred to as "denial." Among these families, shared family realities included a demilitarized zone surrounding certain features of the child's adult status (e.g., marriage, parenthood, social relations). Some of the youth continue to bring up the issue in their parental relations, whereas others do not.

Although this identity transition begins with the youth, the self-disclosure to parents is likely to initiate a type of family "coming out" process in the parents themselves, whereby parents are given the opportunity to restructure expectations and goals for the future life course of their children. Our work with the teens suggests that coming out has different meanings and impact for mothers and fathers. We are not sanguine about the ease with which this process may occur between the youth and their families. Nevertheless, our data suggest that for mothers, whatever their initial responses to the direct or indirect news of their children's gay and lesbian identity—the overall quality of their relationships are not affected.

For fathers, meanings and responses are different and partially determined by the gender of the child (Boxer, Cook, & Cohler, 1986; Boxer, Solomon, Offer, Petersen, & Halprin, 1984). In our data, fathers' awareness of their children's sexual orientation (either through direct or indirect disclosure) was associated with more positive relationships. Direct disclosure to fathers was associated with changes in relationships, although the direction of these changes was not predictable. For some fathers it may be relieving to be able to understand their children in a new way, and to be aware of an aspect of their lives that was previously hidden or even confusing to them. For others it may result in anger, rage, or some type of rejection.

Our data suggest that fathers and daughters may experience some difficulties unique from those of the other parent-child dyads in the family. Changes in father-child relations were found to be predicted by the gender of the child; the girls reported more negative changes in relationships than did boys, regardless of whether their fathers were aware or unaware of their lesbian identities. Schneider (1989) has discussed some of the differences in the experiences of lesbian youth from those of gay males. The teeen-age women in her study were less influenced by prevailing stereotypes than the males, and they had the advantage of access to a generic women's culture and to the feminist movement that included feminist music, art, humor, and political thought, in addition to the resources of the lesbian community. A process of relationship "cooling" may begin between the fathers and their daughters *prior* to any actual disclosure to fathers.

Although we have been emphasizing the relationships between self-disclosure and parent-child relations, our data also suggest many similarities between the parental relationships of these youth and those found in other studies drawn from presumed heterosexual samples. Males and females in our study reported more positive relationships with mothers than with fathers; and older youth reported better relationships than did younger youth. In addition, girls reported more changes in parental relationships than did boys.

DIRECTIONS FOR FUTURE RESEARCH

Because the data presented in this chapter are correlational in nature we cannot, of course, assume causal relationships between self-disclosure and parental relationships. Antecedent relationships of these youth with their parents may shape many aspects of the self-disclosure process for which we do not have data. For example, Caspi and Moffitt (1990; see also Caspi, Bem, & Elder, 1989) suggest that disruptive life transitions highlight dimensions of personality continuity. It is possible that those youth in our sample whose parents reacted particularly badly to their disclosure also had difficult parental relationships earlier in their lives. Additionally, many youth had not yet directly disclosed their identity status to parents. Further analyses of causal relationships can only be adequately assessed through longitudinal follow-up. As delineated in this chapter, little is known regarding the particular sequence of events that may characterize the coming out process among parents and their children. Understanding the full impact of the self-disclosure process within the family will require prospective studies. Such research must also take account of ethnic and social class differences in cultural norms and responses to homosexuality (see e.g., Jue, 1987). Based on data presented in this chapter, it is difficult to determine now the full effects of coming out on parent–child relations. Follow-up of this sample's transition to adulthood provides the opportunity for further examining this process during a subsequent phase of the life course.

ACKNOWLEDGMENTS

The research reported in this chapter was supported by a grant from the Spencer Foundation ("Sexual Orientation and Cultural Competence in Chicago"). Preparation of this manuscript was facilitated by the Clinical Research Training Program in Adolescence, jointly sponsored by Michael Reese Hospital & Medical Center and the University of Chicago, funded by an institutional training grant from the National Institute of Mental Health (5T32 MH14668-14).

Portions of the data in this chapter were presented at the conference, "Parent Child Relations Across the Lifespan," University of New Hampshire, May 1989; and at the annual meetings of the American Sociological Association, San Francisco, August 13, 1989.

We are indebted to members of the Horizons Youth Group who were willing to share their life stories with us, and to parents from the Chicago Chapter of Parents and Friends of Lesbians and Gays (PFLAG). The authors would also like to express special thanks to Mr. Bruce Koff, Executive Director, Horizons Community Services; Liz Huesemann and the staff of the Youth Group; and to Mike and Vivian Chanon, Gerda Muri, and Nancy Johnson, for all of their help and support in making this study possible. We are particularly grateful to Rachelle Ballmer, for her untiring dedication and assistance in all phases of the conduct of this study.

REFERENCES

Adam, B. (1987). *The rise of a gay and lesbian movement*. Boston: Twayne.

Aldrich, J. H., & Nelson, L. (1984). *Linear probability, logit, and probit models*. Beverly Hills: Sage.

Bell, A., & Weinberg, M. (1978). *Homosexualities*. New York: Simon & Shuster.

Berger, R. M. (1982). *Gay and grey: The older homosexual man*. Urbana, Il: University of Illinois Press.

Berzon, B., & Leighton, R. (Eds.). (1979). *Positively gay*. Milbrae, CA: Celestial Arts.

Borhek, M. V. (1983). *Coming out to parents: A two-way survival guide for lesbians and gay men and their parents*. New York: Pilgrim Press.

Boxer, A., & Cohler, B. J. (1989). The life course of gay and lesbian youth: An immodest proposal for the study of lives. *Journal of Homosexuality, 17*, 315-355.

Boxer, A., & Cook, J. (1988). *Developmental discontinuities in the transition to gay and lesbian adult roles: A study of homosexual youth*. Paper presented at the Midcontinent Meeting of the Society for the Scientific Study of Sex, Chicago, IL.

Boxer, A. M., Cook, J. A., & Cohler, B. J. (1986). Grandfathers, fathers, and sons: Intergenerational relations among men. In K. Pillemer & R. Wolf (Eds.), *Elder abuse: Conflict in the family* (pp. 93–121). Dover, MA: Auburn House.

Boxer, A. M., Solomon, B., Offer, D., Petersen, A. C., & Halprin, F. (1984). Parents' perceptions of young adolescents. In R. S. Cohen, B. J. Cohler, & S. Weissman (Eds.), *Parenthood: A psychodynamic perspective* (pp. 64–85). New York: Guilford.

Brown, H. (1976). *Familiar faces hidden lives*. New York: Harcourt, Brace Jovanovich.

Caspi, A., Bem, D. J. H., & Elder, G. H. Jr. (1989). Continuities and consequences of interactional styles across the life course. *Journal of Personality, 57,* 375–406.

Caspi, A., & Moffit, T. (1990). *Individual differences and personal transitions: The sample case of girls at puberty.* Unpublished manuscript.

Clark, D. (1977). *Loving someone gay.* Milbrae, CA: Celestial Arts.

Cohler, B. J., & Boxer, A. M. (1984). Settling into the world—person, time and context. In D. Offer & M. Sabshin (Eds.), *Normality and the life cycle* (pp. 145–203). New York: Basic Books.

Cohen, R. S., & Weissman, S. (1984). The parenting alliance. In R. S. Cohen, B. J. Cohler, & S. Weissman (Eds.), *Parenthood: A psychodynamic perspective* (pp. 33–49). New York: Guilford.

Coleman, E. (1982). Developmental stages of the coming out process. *Journal of Homosexuality, 7,* 31–43.

Collins, L., & Zimmerman, N. (1983). Homosexual and bisexual issues. In J. C. Hansen, J. D. Woody, & R. H. Woody (Eds.), *Sexual issues in family therapy* (pp. 82–100). Rockville, MD: Aspen Publications.

Cook, J., & Cohler, B. J. (1986). Reciprocal socialization and the care of offspring with cancer and with schizophrenia. In N. Datan, A. L. Greene, & H. W. Reese (Eds.), *Life-span developmental psychology: Intergenerational relations* (pp. 223–243). Hillsdale, NJ: Lawrence Erlbaum Associates.

Cook, J., Boxer, A., & Herdt, G. (1989). *First homosexual and heterosexual experiences reported by gay and lesbian youth in an urban community.* Paper presented at the annual meeting of the American Sociological Association, San Francisco, CA.

Cramer, D. W., & Roach, A. J. (1988). Coming out to mom and dad: A study of gay males and their relationships with parents. *Journal of Homosexuality, 15,* 79–91.

Dank, B. (1971). Coming out in the gay world. *Psychiatry, 34,* 180–197.

D'Emilio, J. (1983). *Sexual politics, sexual communities.* Chicago: The University of Chicago Press.

DeVine, J. L. (1984). A systemic inspection of affectional preference orientation and the family of origin. *Journal of Social Work and Human Sexuality, 2,* 9–17.

Fairchild, B., & Hayward, N. (1979). *Now that you know: What every parent should know about homosexuality.* New York: Harcourt Brace Jovanovich.

Gerstel, C., Feraios, A. J., & Herdt, G. (1989). Widening circles: An ethnographic profile of a youth group. *Journal of Homosexuality, 17,* 75–92.

Greene, A. L., & Boxer, A. M. (1986). Daughters and sons as young adults: Restructuring the ties that bind. In N. Datan, A. L. Greene, & H. W. Reese (Eds.), *Life-span developmental psychology: Intergenerational relations* (pp. 125–149). Hillsdale, NJ: Lawrence Erlbaum Associates.

Griffin, C. W., Wirth, M. J., & Wirth, A. G. (1986). *Beyond acceptance: Parents of lesbians and gays talk about their experiences.* Englewood Cliffs, NJ: Prentice-Hall.

Hagestad, G. O. (1981). Problems and promises in the social psychology of intergenerational relations. In R. W. Fogel, E. Hatfield, S. Kiesler, & E. Shanas (Eds.), *Aging: Stability and change in the family* (pp. 11–46). New York: Academic Press.

Hagestad, G. O., & Neugarten, B. L. (1984). Age and the life course. In E. Shanas & R. Binstock (Eds.), *Handbook of aging and the social sciences* (2nd ed., pp. 35–61). New York: Van Nostrand, Reinhold.

Herdt, G. (1989). Introduction: Gay and lesbian youth, emergent identities, and cultural scenes at home and abroad. *Journal of Homosexuality, 17*, 1–42.

Herdt, G. (1991). Coming out in Chicago: An ethnographic study. In G. Herdt (Ed.), *The ethnography of gay men's lives: Interpreting American culture.* Boston: The Beacon Press.

Herdt, G., Boxer, A. M., & Irvin, F. (1986). *Sexual orientation and cultural competence in Chicago.* Application for funding submitted to the Spencer Foundation, Chicago.

Hill, J. P., & Lynch, M. E. (1983). The intensification of gender-related role expectancies during early adolescence. In J. Brooks-Gunn & A. C. Petersen (Eds.), *Girls at puberty: Biological and psychosocial perspectives* (pp. 201–228). New York: Plenum.

Hochschild, A. (1983). *The managed heart: Commercialization of human feeling.* Berkeley: University of California Press.

Jay, K., & Young, A. (Eds.). (1979). *The gay report: Lesbians and gay men speak out about sexual experiences and lifestyles.* New York: Simon & Shuster.

Jones, C. (1978). *Understanding gay relatives and friends.* New York: Seabury Press.

Jue, S. (1987). Identifying and meeting the needs of minority clients with AIDS. In C. G. Leukefeld & M. Fimbres (Eds.), *Responding to AIDS: Psychosocial initiatives* (pp. 66–71). Silver Spring, MD: National Association of Social Workers, Inc.

Kehoe, M. (1986). Lesbians over 65: A triply invisible minority. *Journal of Homosexuality, 12*, 139–152.

Klein, F., Sepekoff, J., & Wolf, T. (1985). Sexual orientation: A multi-variable dynamic process. *Journal of Homosexuality, 5*, 151–160.

Kooden, H., Morin, S., Riddle, D., Rogers, M., Sang, B., & Strassburger, F. (1979). *Removing the stigma. Final Report. Task force on the status of lesbian and gay male psychologists.* Washington, DC: American Psychological Association.

Macklin, E. (1988). AIDS: Implications for families. *Family Relations, 37*, 141–149.

Martin, A. D. (1982). Learning to hide: The socialization of the gay adolescent. *Adolescent Psychiatry, 10*, 52–65.

Martin, A. D., & Hetrick, E. S. (1988). The stigmatization of the gay and lesbian adolescent. *Journal of Homosexuality, 16*, 163–183.

Muller, A. (1987). *Parents matter.* New York: The Naiad Press.

Munnichs, J. (1966). *Old age and finitude: A contribution to psychogerontology.* Basel: Karger.

Murray, S. O. (1984). *Social theory, homosexual realities.* New York: Gay Academic Union.

Myers, M. F. (1982). Counseling the parents of young homosexual male patients. *Journal of Homosexuality, 7*(2/3), 131–143.

Neugarten, B. L. (1967). The awareness of middle age. In R. Owen (Ed.), *Middle age* (pp. 22–26). London: British Broadcasting Co.

Neugarten, B. L. (1977). Personality and aging. In J. E. Birren & K. W. Schaie (Eds.), *Handbook of the psychology of aging* (pp. 626–649). New York: Van Nostrand-Reinhold.

Plath, D. V. (1980). Contours of consociation: Lessons from a Japanese narrative. In P. B. Baltes & O. G. Brim, Jr. (Eds.), *Life-span development and behavior* (Vol. 3, pp. 287–305). New York: Academic Press.

Plummer, K. (1989). Lesbian and gay youth in England. *Journal of Homosexuality, 17*, 195–223.

Pruchno, R. A., Blow, F. C., & Smyer, M. A. (1984). Life-events and interdependent lives. *Human Development, 27*, 31–41.

Remafedi, G. (1987). Male homosexuality: The adolescent's perspective. *Pediatrics, 79*, 326–330.

Riley, M. W., & Waring, J. (1976). Age and aging. In R. K. Merton & R. Nisbet (Eds.), *Contemporary social problems* (4th ed., pp. 117–129). New York: Harcourt, Brace & Jovanovich.

Robertson, R. J. (1981). Young gays. In J. Hart & D. Richardson (Eds.), *The theory and practice of homosexuality* (pp. 170–176). London: Routledge & Kegan Paul.

Robinson, B., Skeen, P., & Walters L. (1987, April). The AIDS epidemic hits home. *Psychology Today*, pp. 48–52.

Robinson, B. E., Walters, L. H., & Skeen, P. (1989). Response of parents to learning that their child is homosexual and concern over AIDS: A national study. *Journal of Homosexuality, 18*(1/2), 59–80.

Sauerman, T. H. (1984). *Coming out to your parents*. Los Angeles: Federation of Parents and Friends of Lesbians and Gays.

Savin-Williams, R. C. (1989a). Parental influences on the self-esteem of gay and lesbian youths: A reflected appraisals model. *Journal of Homosexuality, 17*, 93–109.

Savin-Williams, R. C. (1989b). Coming out to parents and self-esteem among gay and lesbian youths. *Journal of Homosexuality, 18*(1/2), 1–35.

Schneider, M. (1989). Sappho was a right-on adolescent: Growing up lesbian. *Journal of Homosexuality, 17*(1/2), 111–130.

Silverberg, S. B., & Steinberg, L. (1987). Adolescent autonomy, parent-adolescent conflict, and parental well-being. *Journal of Youth and Adolescence, 16*, 293–312.

Silverstein, C. (1977). *A family matter: A parents' guide to homosexuality*. New York: McGraw-Hill.

Silverstein, C. (1981). *Man to man: Gay couples in America*. New York: William Morrow.

Sladkin, K. (1983, December). Section on American Health, American Academy of Pediatrics. *Pediatric News*, p. 34.

Strommen, E. F. (1989). "You're a what?": Family members reactions to the disclosure of homosexuality. *Journal of Homosexuality, 18*(1/2), 37–58.

Switzer, D. K., & Switzer, S. (1980). *Parents of the homosexual*. Philadesphia: Westminister Press.

Tremble, B., Schneider, M., & Appathurai, C. (1989). Growing up gay or lesbian in a multicultural context. *Journal of Homosexuality, 17*(1/2), 253–267.

Troiden, R. (1989). The formation of homosexual identities. *Journal of Homosexuality, 17*, 43–73.

Troll, L. E., & Bengtson, V. (1982). Intergenerational relations throughout the life span. In B. Wolman (Ed.), *Handbook of developmental psychology* (pp. 890–911). Englewood Cliffs, NJ: Prentice-Hall.

Turner, V. (1967). *The forest of symbols*. Ithaca: Cornell University Press.

Weeks, J. (1985). *Sexuality and its discontents*. London: Routledge & Kegan Paul.

Weissman, S. J., Cohen, R. S., Boxer, A. M., & Cohler, B. J. (1989). Parenthood experience and the adolescent's transition to young adulthood: self-psychological perspectives. *Adolescent Psychiatry, 16*, 155–174.

Weinberg, G. (1972). *Society and the healthy homosexual.* New York: Anchor Press/ Doubleday.

Whitney, C. (1989). Living amid the ruins of the sexual revolution. *Christopher Street, 12*(9), 23–32.

Wilen, J. (1979). *Changing relationships among grandparents, parents, and their young adult children.* Paper presented at the annual meetings of the Gerontological Society, Washington, DC

Zitter, S. (1987). Coming out to mom: Theoretical aspects of the mother–daughter process. In Boston Lesbian Psychologies Collective (Eds.), *Lesbian psychologies: Explorations and challenges* (pp. 177–194). Urbana and Chicago: University of Illinois Press.

The Development of Paternal
and Filial Maturity

Corinne N. Nydegger
University of California, San Francisco

I have not really volunteered to take on the topic of maturity. Rather, the issue has pursued me through years of research. Again and again—in relation to timing of fatherhood, in regard to older fathers' relations with their adult children—maturity was clearly involved. But because the subject seemed the province of ego psychology, I did what most of us do—simply dodged it.

With my most recent work on development in the reciprocal roles of fathers and children, it finally has caught up with me. I can no longer ignore the information from my own respondents, for whom maturity is not merely a psychological construct, but a reality, and indeed a linchpin in their view of role development. So, perhaps belatedly, and with none of the expectable psychological credentials, I address one aspect of maturity, that which is involved in parent–child relations.

FILIAL MATURITY

Over 20 years ago when Blenkner (1965) introduced the concept of filial maturity, it struck a responsive chord among gerontologists. Since that time, few discussions of older parents and their children do not refer to the notion. But referring is all that we have done. No one has tried to critique or clarify the concept, trace children's routes to this state, or identify factors that help or hinder its achievement. Thus, a fruitful concept has been neither examined nor used—merely reified.

It is not difficult to find reasons for giving only obeisance to filial maturity. The notion of maturity is beset with confusions, and our knowledge of the substantive aspects of relations between parents and their children in adulthood is meager. The idea of merging them is daunting. Certainly at this time, such an attempt can only be speculative. But the Parent–Child Relations across the Lifespan conference provided an opportunity to initiate much-needed discussion of filial maturity. Even if my notions prove wide of the mark, I hope they at least serve to place the topic on the family research agenda. It is simply too important to ignore.

What I hope to accomplish here is to indicate some of the difficulties presented by the concept of maturity, distinguish among various developmental models in the literature, and contrast these with what Blenkner and laypersons mean when they speak of maturity in the child's role. Relying on common sense theory, I show that filial maturity is only half the picture, one of a matched pair of concepts, the other being parental maturity. Using data from my own research on fathers and their adult children, I sketch the developmental course of the father's and adult child's roles, and identify two dimensions I regard as central to maturing in these roles. Finally, I critique Blenkner's conceptualization and briefly discuss a few issues that appear to warrant focused research.

THE MANY MEANINGS OF MATURITY

First, then, I must make clear what it was that Blenkner had in mind when she spoke of maturity. Her statement, couched in terms of Eriksonian developmental tasks, is as follows:

> the *filial crisis* may be conceived to occur in most individuals in their forties or fifties, when the individual's parents can no longer be looked to as a rock of support in times of emotional trouble or economic stress but may themselves need their offspring's comfort and support. Successful accomplishment of the *filial task*, or performance of the filial role, promotes *filial maturity*. (1965, p. 57)

Forcefully rejecting the notion of role reversal, she added:

> while it is true that the filial crisis marks childhood's end, the son or daughter does not thereby take on a parental role to his parent. He takes on the *filial* role, which involves being *depended on* and therefore being *dependable* insofar as his parent is concerned.
>
> Healthy resolution of the filial crisis means leaving behind the rebellion and emancipation of adolescence and early adulthood and turning again to the parent, no longer as a child, but as a mature adult with a new role and a different love, seeing him for the first time as an individual with his own rights, needs, limitations, and a life history that, to a large extent, made him the person he is long before his child existed. This is what the parent wants of his children; this is what society expects; this is what many Americans accomplish, with varying degrees of success, in their late forties and fifties. (pp. 57–58).

This short statement is all Blenkner left us, along with a footnote about one impediment to which I refer later. Nothing of significance has been added in the past quarter of a century. Relevant data are accumulating, but have not been integrated with the concept. Keeping in mind the hints Blenkner gave, I looked to the literature in order to evaluate and flesh out these notions.

The Superior State

Literature on the topic of maturity has two main thrusts. One, predominantly psychoanalytic, postulates maturity as an *ideal* and *superior* state, to be attained in mid to late adulthood but only with considerable difficulty, even with professional assistance. Coan (1977) analyzed the various psychologies that, explicitly or implicitly, have taught that this state is the objective of the individual quest for fulfillment. His title (*Hero, Artist, Sage, or Saint?*) indicates that most of the authors he cited clearly view maturity as an *atypical* development. Many regard this state as beyond the reach of most men and women at any age; Maslow is the most obvious example of this point of view. This tradition also influenced the debate among Kohlberg (1973), Gilligan (1977), Perry (1968), and others who are involved in expanding Piaget's ideas about moral development.

Recently, Kiefer (1988) traced the history of this tradition's concept of development and its goal, the state of maturity. His scholarly critique highlighted parallels among the exponents of paths to maturity, from the philosophers of classical Greece through medieval monastics, Renaissance classicists and early secularists, to the modern humanistic psychologies. Kiefer described a persistent four-stage conception of development, a legacy from at least the time of Plato, which has influenced each historic period's handling of these ideas. In Kiefer's words, the Platonic stages "appear so early and so often in our civilization, our thinking about maturity is already to some degree structured by them, whether we know this or not" (p. 196). A parallel in eastern developmental stages also has been noted by Erikson (1959, 1963), Jung (1969), and others.

Kiefer also showed how these stages have, in their turn, been influenced by intellectual changes through time. The most significant change has been in the final stage of maturity, the peak of the developmental trajectory. Maturity is still defined in terms of the self rather than the collectivity (thus remaining firmly in the tradition of western civilization). But the goal is no longer the attainment of any absolute, be it wisdom or divine grace; it is now the fulfillment of the self in the context of a relativistic worldview.

In regard to my concerns here, it could be argued that this secularization of the mature stage should encourage a focus on the meaning of maturity in interpersonal relations. Certainly love is seen as a central issue, but it seems to be defined either as romantic love or a love for mankind in general. This tradition generally ignores intergenerational relations beyond adolescence. Only Erikson explicitly recognized the love between parents and adult children.

Two points in these critiques seem most relevant. First, as Kiefer indicated, the notion of stage-like development underlies all discussions of maturity, lay or professional. Second, Coan raised an important question about the unitary view of maturity. The psychologists he discussed have regarded maturity as a *personal attribute*; once attained, it characterizes the individual and influences all his or her behavior. Coan pointed out that they only presume maturity is not lopsided, uneven in its development. But this presumption is a consequence of the nature of the theories, and has never been seriously questioned, much less subjected to investigation.

Competence

The alternative approach to the issue of maturity is that favored by researchers in child development: It is empirical, focuses on the processes of maturation (especially cognitive), and defines developmental stages primarily in terms of displays of competence. Criteria of maturational progress are therefore reasonably clear in childhood, especially for intellectual growth and self-control; progress in these spheres can be anticipated within fairly well-defined limits. (However, recent studies by Gubrium & Buckholdt, 1977, show that even here, maturity is negotiated.) But the literature suggests that, by adolescence, maturation has become more variable: Not only do children differ greatly one from another, but adolescents are likely to alternate between adult and child-like behavior with bewildering speed. Uneven maturing appears to characterize this life stage.

To my knowledge, within this tradition, only Heath (1965) has attempted to operationalize continued maturation in young adults (aside from Kohlberg's and Perry's narrowly focused work on moral development). Basing his research on the college undergraduate years, Heath targeted issues appropriate to this population; the measures are of intellectual and philosophical developments. He identified five dimensions of maturity, all showing progressive change over the 4-year period. Two may well be limited to college performance (increasingly abstract attitude and progressive integration of new information). The other three dimensions, however, are major elements in the common sense meaning of maturity: increased stability, autonomy, and allocentrism (or put another way, reduced egocentrism).

Work in this research tradition has been based on select and homogeneous samples of undergraduates. Nevertheless, they all show a great deal of variability among individuals in level of maturity expressed, and most students exhibited variability across time or situation. Unevenness of maturity continues to be a feature of development, even in these restricted contexts.

Conceptual Problems

As this brief overview of the two major conceptions of maturing in adulthood indicates, they offer little help in examining the idea of filial maturity. The ideal state models focus on the growth of the self with scant attention to the contexts of lives. Moreover, neither Blenkner nor laypersons refer to maturity as a state of developmental grace. They use the term with a less lofty referent, attainable by the majority of ordinary men and women.

The empirical approach seems to provide a meaning of maturity more consonant with everyday views of what constitutes growing up, becoming adult. But even in the least narrowly focused research, that of Heath, dimensions were derived from strictly intellectual choices; autonomy here means autonomous opinion about political issues, philosophical dilemmas, and the like. Can they be generalized to *interpersonal* maturity? And to later stages of life? For example, dare we assume that a 20-year-old's allocentrism is the same dimension as a 40-year-old child's empathy?

Thus, the literature adds no substance to the concept of filial maturity and only two clues are given as to the nature of its development. First, attaining maturity appears to be a drawn-out process, perhaps characterized by stages, and likely to be marked by developmental unevenness. Second, if Heath's intellectual dimensions can be generalized to interpersonal relations, a central feature of maturity should be a balance between personal autonomy and concern for others. For more pertinent and much richer material, I turned to the interviews with participants in the Fatherhood Project (described later). In contrast to the literature, they provide a detailed, substantive theory of parent and child development to maturity.

Implicit Theory

In everyday usage, the term *maturity* is polysemous. An elementary school child may be called mature; it is also a traditional synonym for legal adulthood; and "mature" is now the preferred euphemism for overweight women and for middle, even old, age. But alongside marketing misuse and traditional reference to adult status, there is also a usage relevant here: people consistently use the term *maturity* to refer to a long-term process of *development in adulthood*, the later stages of the lengthy process of "growing up." This meaning of maturity is embedded in a system of what anthropologists variously call *implicit theory, folk models*, or *emic paradigms*, and what others have called "everyday philosophy" (e.g., Gubrium, 1988) and "naive psychology" (Heider, 1958). I prefer the term *implicit theory* because it emphasizes the fact that all the elements in these theories are seldom fully in persons' consciousness, but must be derived from wide-ranging discussions.

An implicit theory is a set of integrated values, assumptions, and causal relations. They are shared (hence cultural, not merely idiosyncratic) and represent the cognitive bases by means of which behavior is anticipated and explained. And they are an unparalleled source of assistance to the researcher. For example, a few years ago I investigated normative timetables; although focusing on the period of young adulthood, I noted at the time that: "well-developed theory about the course of human development from womb to grave can be derived from the interviews" (Nydegger, 1986a, p. 723). And it was only by using the relevant implicit theory that I was able to show a coherent structure underlying the typically ambiguous data about age norms that had been obtained by traditional methods.

In this theory, maturity is not so much a state as a *process*: maturity is

> a slow process, beginning in adolescence and extending into mid-life. Nor is it uniform across contexts; although the elements of maturity may be general (e.g., responsibility, impulse-control), some roles demand "more maturity" than others. Thus, a 25-year-old emotional adolescent may be sufficiently mature for a responsible job, but not for marriage. Role entries can be ordered by their progressive demands for higher levels of maturity: college, work, marriage, parenthood. (Nydegger, 1986a, p. 724)

Timetables and their norms are based on these predictably different role maturities. Thus, as the literature indicated for younger ages, adult maturing also is seen as uneven. Most important, it is seen as role specific.

The process of maturing is expected to continue well into, even beyond, middle age. But now the terminology changes: mellowing, consolidating, knowing oneself—although the list of characteristics is long, all refer to the same process. However, mid-life maturing does not have as clear markers as in young adulthood (i.e., displays of competence), nor are there well-established age expectations. Maturing in later adulthood also seems to be less role specific; for example, one hears fewer comments about improvement in particular skills (as in dealing with co-workers, or comprehending wives' perspectives). The impression is one of a general, *personal* maturing process. But this is only an impression: This line of inquiry was not pursued as thoroughly as for younger ages. More intensive examination might yield evidence of uneven maturing across roles in late adulthood too.

However, in regard to parents and children, implicit theory fully supports Blenkner's idea of a particular filial maturity. Here, incontrovertibly, is a well-defined maturing that is specific to the role of adult child. Furthermore, we find a parallel maturing specific to the role of parent. Again and again in the interviews, these processes emerge as critical determinants in the complex development of parent–child relations.

Implicit theory differs from both of the research perspectives previously discussed: It conceptualizes maturity neither as a general, personal characteristic, nor as a cluster of intellectual dimensions. Rather, "maturity" is many specific maturities, each developing within a particular set of contextual demands, in interaction with other persons (the role alters), and its progress judged largely in terms of interpersonal behavior. Implicit theory, then, strongly supports Dannefer's contention that development "needs to be understood, conceptualized, and studied as socially organized" (1984, p. 197). This perspective emphasizes the changing demands of various roles and points to a neglected aspect of roles themselves—their own distinctive trajectories over the life course. A brief discussion of this point shows that expectations about the life courses of roles are basic to the implicit theory of maturity.

THE ROLE COURSE

Long-term roles are likely to involve many changes over time. Those changes or transitions that are formalized and ritualized (often grouped as *rites de passage*) have been of particular interest to social scientists and an extensive literature has been built by comparative research. But, strangely, we know very little about the most common changes, those that we all constantly observe: the slowly altering roles of friend, co-worker, family member (Matthews', 1986, study of long-term friendship is the exception). These changes are often recognized only after the fact, as we look back over the years to when the role was young.

    In thinking about roles entered into and sustained during the adult years, I have found it useful to think of the *role course* (Nydegger, 1980, 1986b), essentially the life course of a role. From this point of view, roles can be classified according to the nature of their characteristic changes. One type, for example, is the limiting case of the *stable* role, in which change is neither expected nor desirable: the ward boss, the lawyer in private practice, the lay religious functionary are examples of this kind of role stability. At the other extreme is the *sequencing* role, characterized by predictable transitions in an orderly pattern, as in the typical career ladder. Other types include *transforming* roles, in which major qualitative changes may be more or less anticipated, but have no inherent necessity or order; for example, changes in friendship that result from geographic movements or from alterations in the status of persons involved, such as being married or widowed.

    Finally, there are roles that typically *develop* over time; that is, they exhibit gradual, qualitative modifications that are predictable and directed toward a particular state as the desired goal. "Good" marriages are reputed to have this characteristic, but the most common roles of this type are probably those of parent and child. (If this strikes some as too loose a use of *development*, such roles can be regarded as a special kind of transforming role. I do not think the terminology is important, nor do I want to enter into a debate about the nature of development. I use the term here in its common sense meaning of qualitative change over time toward a goal.)

This is the perspective used by my informants in discussing intergenerational relations over the life course. Their implicit theory specifies unidirectional changes both in the role of parent and that of child and broadly defines the goal of role maturity for each. The impetus for development is to be found in a mix of social, interpersonal, and personal elements. The most important are socially defined role expectations, responses to changes in relevant others, and personal maturing.

THE FATHERHOOD PROJECT

Before describing the development of filial and paternal maturity, I should specify the source of my data. The Fatherhood Project focused on the father–adult child relationship and used an approach anthropologists call *emic*. This approach does more than document the subjective perception of individuals: It shows "how they have given meaning to those perceptions by culturally appropriate ways of organizing, thinking, and feeling about them; literally, the phenomenology of culture" (Nydegger, 1983, p. 452).

In contrast to structural role analysis on the one hand and clinical case study on the other, the intent was to conduct a middle-level analysis of the roles that would describe their distinctive features and their meaning to the actors involved. To this end, we posed deliberately naive questions and used an eclectic mix of methods; but we relied most heavily on lengthy, semistructured taped interviews. Much of this material was coded by an iterative process of response grouping, a method that retains distinctions that are meaningful to informants as well as making it possible to derive implicit theories. (This technique is well described, despite lack of a consistent terminology, e.g., Bernard, 1988; Clark & Anderson, 1967; Nydegger et al., 1983.)

The first phase of the Fatherhood Project involved 267 well-educated middle-class men, aged 45 to 80 years, randomly selected within the greater San Francisco Bay area. Occupations ranged from minor civil service jobs to high-level professional and managerial positions, the majority being businessmen. All had been functioning fathers in their first families until their children were in their late teens; thus, in terms of family, the sample represents the most stable portion of middle-class fathers. For the subsequent study of children, a random sample was drawn from the pool of informants' adult children living within 60 miles of San Francisco. We interviewed 62 sons and 62 daughters, ranging in age from the 20s to the 50s (sample details provided in Nydegger, 1986a).

A major focus of these studies was within-family diversity. Therefore, the traditional indexing of all parent–child relations by one relationship was rejected; we obtained data about all children. The data fully justify the decision:

Dyadic father–child relations are so varied within families that one cannot predict from one dyad to another except in the extreme cases. The way filial and paternal roles are played out, and the pace of their development, proved also to be highly varied.

PARENTAL AND FILIAL ROLE DEVELOPMENT

Despite the frequent invocations of filial maturity, little attention has been paid to developments in the parental role after children are adult. My informants, however, provided a widely shared view of a parental maturing that parallels filial maturing. Their developmental interrelations are complex and deserve focused research. They are summed up in one informants' words: ''You grow into being a parent as your child grows.''

When children are very young, growth in the parental role necessarily is primarily responsive to the child's development. But as the child grows older, developments in filial and parental roles are no longer so closely linked. Thus, their pace may be different and, indeed, one may achieve maturity even if the other never does. However, they do exert a strong influence on one another. For example, it is much easier for each to develop if the other is also developing at roughly the same pace. This paced, parallel development is specified by my informants as the smoothest pathway to the goal of filial/parental maturity.

Let me emphasize that these developments are not norms, nor scenarios of the ideal, but of the expectable. They can be regarded as the cognitive equivalent of modal data. And let me also emphasize that informants are not speaking of interpersonal relations, but rather trying to depict the roles, the context of interpersonal relations (although admittedly, these are not always easily distinguished).

DIMENSIONS OF MATURING

Two dimensions appear to be essential to the development of both filial and parental maturity (perhaps to all intimate roles). One is distancing, the other comprehending. As the first pulls parent and child apart, the second tends to draw them together; development in these roles is the result of balancing these forces at each stage of life. (It is tempting to assume that these dimensions are the adult versions of Heath's autonomy and allocentrism, here exhibited in parent–child interactions, but it must be left to others to establish this correspondence.)

Filial Distancing

Let us look at the child's role first. As psychologists and laymen alike tell us, a critical task for personal development in young adulthood is to separate from the parents and establish one's own identity as an adult (Greene & Boxer, 1986).

And it also is the necessary first step toward development in the filial role. The task in this regard is (in Blenkner's terms) to attain emotional emancipation from the parents, while remaining engaged as a son or daughter. This establishes the psychological distance that is a precondition, not only for the child's objectivity about the self, but also to see the parent more objectively—as a person, not just as "parent."

This process of emotional weaning is slow and likely to be painful for all (Colarusso & Nemiroff, 1981; Erikson, 1963). Beginning with the rebellions and questionings of adolescence, emotional distancing is given impetus by the physical separation from parents customary in our young adulthood. This phase is likely to be accompanied by heightened criticism and reduced contact (the withdrawal widely reported for this period of life, as in Lowenthal et al., 1975). It is generally followed by renewed contact, but now growing emancipation tempers egocentrism, enabling the child to see the parents more realistically.

However, movements toward the child's independence exacerbate the problem of privacy; it continues to be critical in the renegotiated relations between parents and young adult children. Therefore, a prerequisite to further development of the parent and child roles is devising a family etiquette to handle the delicate balance between the parents' right to know and a child's right to privacy (Nydegger & Mitteness, 1988).

A consequence of children's distancing and new, altered perspectives toward themselves and their parents is children's improving ability to see themselves objectively in the child role. One marker of this is beginning to recognize what the parent wants from *them*. When young, we expect our parents to be engrossed by all our enterprises. Distancing and a more realistic appraisal of the relationship force us to realize that we may sometimes bore them or upset them needlessly. For example, despite a mother's professed interest, does she really regard her son's detailed account of his car repairs as another of motherhood's burdens? If she cannot help, will she be pleased by her daughter's recital of marital complaints? Or are both egocentric impositions?

Help and Hindrance: Filial Distancing.   What factors hinder distancing? Strong negative emotions such as resentment or disdain for parental opinions and beliefs often persist well into a child's adulthood; some conflicts are never resolved. If old antagonisms persist or conflicts cannot be dealt with, filial development is likely to be brought to a standstill. Then, faced with the parent's late life need, the child's unresolved anger is readily expressed in bossiness or other forms of retaliation (Hess & Waring, 1978).

On the other hand, positive emotions can be just as problematic, as Blenkner noted. A daughter, for example, may be so emotionally enmeshed with a parent that she cannot distance: She may feel—or be made to feel—guilt at any attempt. Similarly, over-dependence on a parent may rule out any move toward objectivity, which threatens the needed image of a powerful parent. Such children are unlikely to cope well with their aged parent's need: It is too frightening and leads to panic, not mature responsibility. Thus, impediments to filial development can arise from the extremes of either positive or negative relations.

Aids to distancing are less clear, but the interviews suggest that demonstrating maturity in another role provides self-confidence and encourages distancing (the newlyweds in Lowenthal's study are examples). Certainly one factor that helps distancing is maturity of the parents themselves, to which I will return.

Filial Comprehending

The second dimension essential to filial maturity is comprehending the parent. Blenkner stated this clearly: The child must see the parent "as an individual with his own rights, needs, limitations, and a life history that, to a large extent, made him the person he is long before his child existed" (1965, p. 58). I would argue that considerable objectivity—made possible by distancing—is a precondition to this level of understanding.

The growth of comprehension not only lags behind distancing, it is a slower process. Most of my informants could pinpoint a time in their lives when they began to "really" understand their fathers (typically in their early 20s). But they emphasized the gradualness of deepening understanding as they themselves matured, entered the world of work, married, and in their turn, became parents. "I never appreciated my father until I had children myself" is a frequent comment. (Summarizing the literature on intergenerational status similarity, Suitor & Pillemer, 1988, noted that it encourages empathy which increases closeness.)

The final phase of this development is signaled by the child's comprehension of the parent's world and how it shaped the parent's opinions and constrained options. This is much more difficult to achieve than one would expect. In our present-oriented society, it is hard to obtain an accurate picture of our recent past. For example, as a child I knew more about Imperial Rome than World War I; my children could re-fight many Civil War battles, but had minimal knowledge about World War II. Laboring under these disadvantages, comprehending a parent's social context is necessarily a slow process.

Once gained, however, this knowledge serves significantly to reduce conflict in relations with parents, especially fathers (Hagestad, 1984). In a study of "social generations" (Nydegger et al., 1983), my colleagues and I showed that past social trends tend to be perceived as historical processes beyond personal control. History, then, can be used for more than just "understanding" attitudes or behaviors of family members: Knowledge of a parent's social context gives a child the option to excuse or rationalize (as a relic of a past social world) the parent's prejudice or any attitude of which the child disapproves.

This level of comprehension of fathers is not expected to be achieved earlier than the 40s, although for mothers it seems to be somewhat earlier. A number of informants, stymied in this process, reported that they were unable to fully understand the father until he was very old or even until after his death.

Help and Hindrance: Filial Comprehending.   The major hindrance to comprehending is, of course, the child's inability to see the parent objectively. This is commonly the result of insufficient distancing, but another cause is the child's insufficient knowledge of the parents, often due to lack of access to the mother or father in roles other than that of parent. For example, fathers' work relations, pressures, triumphs and setbacks are surprisingly unknown to many children, even of college age, which delays their understanding. In traditional families, this lack of across-role access is most salient for fathers, but will become increasingly salient for mothers as they spend more time in the work world.

Two factors assist the development of comprehension. First, as noted, children's maturing means they have more adult experiences in common with their parents, which deepens their understanding. Second is the parent's willingness to be open with children, to be a person, rather than a plaster embodiment of virtue. This is one aspect of parental maturity, to which I now turn.

PATERNAL MATURING

When we examine the parental role, we find that parents' response to children's independence received no attention until a misreading of their roles led to the "discovery" of an empty-nest syndrome. Some years of argument later, there is general agreement that emptying of the nest is typically greeted with relief. Because children's independence is the final goal of parenting, we should not be surprised by this response. The issue might never have arisen had interpersonal relations not been confused with role expectations. Maintenance of loving ties is one thing; having a dependent adult child is quite another. This point is amply documented in studies such as Greenberg and Becker (1988), Greene and Boxer (1986), and Nydegger (1986c).

Due to the nature of my research, I can only provide specifics of the development of maturity in fathers. Although mothers are involved in the same process, they are quite likely to differ in pace and substance (Hagestad, 1984). The paternal role is first and foremost one of assisting children (especially sons in the past) to become progressively more independent. The way this is done necessarily changes as children grow up and clearly shows a developmental parallel to filial maturing.

Paternal Distancing

The process of paternal maturing involves accepting and encouraging children's efforts to distance from the family. And the father must also distance himself from his children, for his life is not defined solely by the parental role; he must look forward to an altered relationship and reduced involvement. Paternal distancing is expected to begin prior to the child's efforts to distance and to continue to anticipate the child's development. Thus, the father will have the objectivity required to understand the distinctive character of each child at each stage of life, and he can then best assist each child to maximize his or her unique potential. Paternal maturing parallels that described for the maturing child: Ultimately, when all goes well, both father and child relate to each other as mature adults "with a new role and a different love" (Blenkner, 1965, p. 58).

Paternal Comprehending

The other dimension, comprehending, is basic to good parenting at all ages, as well as to the development of a mature relationship. Among other things, being a good parent means socializing children to their future world—at least, doing the best one can at such tricky forecasting. Although the generation gap has turned out to be only a ravine, it is nevertheless true that times change. A father cannot simply assume his children are playing out his own childhood. This means the parent must hear what the child is saying and recognize meaningful changes. Just as one aspect of filial maturity is comprehending parents within their social history, so paternal maturity demands comprehending the child's distinctive social world.

Help and Hindrance: Paternal Maturing. The same factors that hinder filial maturity also impede the maturing of fathers. Strong negative feelings or frustration about a child's faults or failures can lead a father to maintain a kind of involvement no longer appropriate, often locking the pair into persistent conflict. Some fathers still respond to 30- and 40-year-old children in terms of their early behavior, unable to pull back and recognize the children's adulthood.

On the other hand, a father who is too closely identified with a child may fear the child's efforts at independence and seek to delay the child's maturing, and thus his own as well. Although reputedly more typical of mothers, among my informants were a few classic cases of fathers maintaining children's dependence in this way. One father of a son in his mid-20s virtually relived his own life by controlling all his son's decisions, from choice of clothing to choice of career. This was managed through judicious use of emotional and financial rewards along with persistent, "gentle" disparagement of the son's opinions.

A common impediment to comprehension is the father's desire to impose his own views and values on the child or the child's world. That is, a father trying to re-create a young version of himself will misperceive the particular qualities of the child. And if he persists in seeing the modern world in terms only of his own values, he cannot comprehend his child's problems; it is common for fathers to misperceive social changes as children's "wrong-headedness" (Nydegger et al., 1983).

The factors that encourage fathers' distancing and comprehending are those that were noted as assisting filial development: maturity in other roles, shared experience, and openness. For example, our data suggest that fathers who have proven their maturity in other roles find it easier to accept children's strivings for independence and the changes in their relationship. They also are better able to look back at their own youth realistically. (This probably is the main advantage of "late" fathers, for they are notably more reflective about their parenting and more objective about their children. It also suggests that men who have achieved filial maturity may find it easier to develop parental maturity.)

Children's steady maturing also helps fathers to pace their own withdrawal smoothly, as well as adding to the store of shared experiences. And, again, an aspect of interpersonal relations that significantly affects maturing is the willingness of children and fathers to be open with each other. Privacy is to be respected; secrecy can only inhibit understanding.

CENTRAL ISSUES IN FILIAL MATURITY

Numerous conceptual problems arise in thinking about filial maturity. However, I address only four issues, highlighted by this presentation, that are central to Blenkner's conceptualization. I briefly discuss them in the hope that it will stimulate others to look anew at their data, initiate debate, and focus attention on these topics.

Age and Crisis

My informants and Blenkner are in full agreement in their portrayal of the end state of filial maturity. But they disagree on the nature of the developmental process. Blenkner postulated a distinct mid-life stage, marked by a filial crisis; that is, the child experiences a crisis when his "parents can no longer be looked to as a rock of support in times of emotional trouble or economic stress but may themselves need their offspring's comfort and support" (1965, p. 57).

In contrast to this view, my informants reported that children become increasingly aware of their parents' potential dependence as they grow old or show signs of illness. Blenkner is probably correct in having suggested that this awareness, in itself, is a maturing influence. But her term *crisis* is misleading: Typically, this awareness gradually develops during adulthood as parents change, as part of the general process of filial maturing.

Further, informants reported that the age when filial maturity is attained is highly variable: It may be as early as the 30s or delayed until the 60s. It is not necessarily a mid-life phenomenon. Thus, in their view, maturing is seldom precipitated (or even accompanied by) a psychological crisis, it is not dependent on a child's stage of life, or on parental age or need. Rather, it develops gradually, with maturity normally achieved prior to parental old age (and need). Thereafter, if such need occurs, the child is already prepared to cope dependably.

This is not to deny the possibility of a filial crisis such as Blenkner described, or the utility of the concept for clinical practice. But it does contradict her assumption of its generality, much less its necessity. Therefore, I suggest the concept of filial maturity be used without age implications and without an extraneous task-and-crisis framework.

Within-Family Diversity

I have emphasized that filial maturing is a lengthy, complex process, involving children's personal development and their interaction with parents who are also maturing. Therefore, one would expect diversity in maturing within families, and that is what informants reported. The most serious threats to maturing arise from qualities of the parent–child relationship; therefore, the most important source of diversity among siblings probably is the nature of their relations with parents in early adulthood.

Other factors are less obvious, but also contribute to this diversity. Gender of children, for example, is a major patterned source of variability (materials relevant to this discussion are more fully presented in Nydegger & Mitteness, in press). Although sons are expected to distance from parents earlier than daughters, nevertheless they are expected to experience more difficulty achieving filial maturity because of their more complex, tense relations with fathers. For example, sons are less forgiving than daughters, and sons' temporary withdrawal during the early years of marriage and career can more easily grow into estrangement.

Sons do have one advantage: They share a male world with their fathers, thus each finds it easier to understand the other. This distinctive sense of shared maleness grows stronger with age and, regardless of the quality of their relations, provides a commonality. Although traditional daughters have more affectionate relations with fathers, they not only recognize, but emphasize their different worlds; they cannot reach the kind of mutual comprehension attainable by fathers and sons. (Nontraditional, career-oriented daughters have very different relations with their fathers, more like those of sons.)

Any difference in commonality can lead to diversity in filial maturing. Siblings usually differ in the degree to which they share interests with their father, ranging from avocational interests (watching professional football, collecting stamps) to shared work worlds (having a similar or related occupation). A common interest provides a child with a view of the father in a nonfamilial role, promotes understanding, and speeds the pace of filial maturing. Diversity can even result from adventitious circumstance; in one example, an undergraduate daughter shared a long commute with her father for over a year. More time was available for conversation than the other children enjoyed and this daughter developed an early comprehension of her father.

Personal versus Role Maturity

It could be argued that an individual matures in some general way as a person and then "carries over" this maturity into his or her specific roles. As Coan (1977) noted, this is the presumption of the psychoanalytically oriented theorists and it is echoed by my informants in discussions of maturing in mid-life and beyond. Certainly in common parlance, what we mean by maturity seems to be this kind of personal quality or attribute.

However, on more careful second thought, difficulties arise. How is maturity expressed? How do we assess level of maturity? We can only determine "personal maturity" by eliciting motives and noting behavior in a variety of contexts (primarily roles). If maturity is a general characteristic, we would expect it to be expressed more or less equally across these contexts.

Such research has not been done with adults. However, as I noted earlier, the research of this kind that is available shows lopsided, uneven development in children, adolescents, and college students. And my informants' implicit timetable for early adults is actually based on predictably uneven maturing across roles. Moreover, it is not difficult to find anecdotal evidence confirming continued role-specific development. It reaches the status of sitcom cliché for intergenerational family roles: A man is "mature" (as a worker, friend, husband) until his "problem" son drops in, whereupon he loses all objectivity, along with his self-control. Equally popular is the sophisticated "adult" who responds to parental chiding with an infantile tantrum. Often such examples of immaturity are merely temporary lapses, the results of specific tensions. But for some persons, maturity in one particular role is long delayed and may never be attained.

Thus, we have contradictory commonsense notions of adult maturing. A general, personal maturity seems to be the ideal, but uneven development is expected to be frequent. Only research focused on this issue can determine which is the more accurate portrayal of maturing in mid- and later-life.

Affection and Filial Maturity

Blenkner's description of filial maturity explicitly included the child's love for the parent. But is love, or affection, a *necessary* part of filial role development? Empirically, family research has shown that intergenerational affection is generally strong (Bengtson et al., 1985; Troll & Bengtson, 1979). But does this mean it must be conceptually integrated—by definition—into filial maturity? The consequences of so defining maturity are likely to obscure rather than clarify our thinking about family roles. Two examples make this point.

First, research (Finley et al., 1988; Troll & Bengtson, 1979) shows that the relationship between affection and filial obligation (one aspect of filial maturity) is highly variable. That is, a child may exhibit comprehension of the parent and his or her needs and responsibly meet these needs, but be motivated by a sense of obligation rather than affection. Are we to conclude that this lack of affection means the child is filially immature? This seems to me (and to my informants) a misreading of filial development and a flagrant mislabeling of the child.

Maturity presumably means comprehending the parent realistically. But, realistically, not all parents are lovable. If we view affection as intrinsic to maturity, we would be forced to the untenable conclusion that comprehension should stop short of accuracy in such cases. To comprehend may be to forgive, but it does not necessarily mean to love.

Second, our thinking about family roles shows a persistent confusion between interpersonal relations and role performance. Some of this is due to the real problems posed by expressive roles. But much of it is due to our emphasis on affection as virtually the only tie among family members. As a result, our family roles are seen as so different from other family systems that the extensive literature on kinship worldwide appears to be irrelevant. Thereby we distort and constrain our thinking.

This emphasis on emotion at the expense of obligation has come under attack from various perspectives and is well summarized by Jarrett (1985). We should consider its effects on our assumptions about affection as a *sine qua non* of filial development. As I have noted, strong positive ties can both help and hinder filial maturity, and there is no reason to assume maturity cannot develop in their absence. Therefore, I suggest it would be wise analytically to disentangle these separate factors.

SUMMARY

In this discussion, I have tried to clarify the common sense meaning of the term *filial maturity*. Data from my research on fathers demonstrates that filial maturity and parental maturity are matched concepts, exhibiting parallel development. Two dimensions are central to the transformation of these roles: distancing and comprehending. Development is helped and hindered by a mix of social, interpersonal, and personal influences.

Four issues were highlighted by the discussion of filial maturity: (a) Blenkner's assumptions that maturity is age specific and precipitated by a filial crisis seem unwarranted: (b) There are numerous sources of within-family diversity in routes to filial maturity, both idiosyncratic (such as quality of relations) and patterned (such as gender); (c) The question of a general "personal maturing" in adulthood versus role specific maturing cannot be addressed with currently available data; and (d) To enhance clarity of thought about family roles, it is wiser to disentangle affection from filial maturity.

SUGGESTIONS FOR FUTURE RESEARCH

Given the unexamined status of the concepts of filial maturity and parental maturity, research into any aspect of their development would be valuable. Here, I restrict my suggestions to a few arising from the previous discussion.

The two main research thrusts described earlier have defined maturity in different ways. Nevertheless, each suggests potentially fruitful approaches that need not compete, but could complement one another. For example, the "ideal state" perspective emphasizes maturity as a personal goal, a notion that has exerted a remarkably strong influence on our thinking about development. If attention were turned to how this state would be evidenced in interpersonal, and especially intergenerational, relations, it would enrich our understanding of the personal aspects of family roles development. This approach is also well suited to place changing views of filial and parental maturity in their appropriate sociohistorical matrices.

The empirical tradition has identified specific developmental dimensions in young adulthood. Answering the questions I raised earlier in regard to this work is an essential first step in tracing the development of maturity: Can "intellectual" dimensions such as Heath's be generalized to interpersonal maturity? And to later stages of life? Are the dimensions I have called *distancing* and *comprehension* special instances of Heath's autonomy and allocentrism? What other dimensions are needed?

I have identified various influences on the routes to filial and parental maturity and hypothesized that achieving filial maturity eases one's path to parental maturity. I hope these comments provoke focused research. Tracing these influences will help to clarify the nature of diversity in parents' relations to their children as well as variations in their maturing.

Another area that would amply repay attention is that of the consequences of maturity for intergenerational relations. If a child's maturing involves a reappraisal of both self and parent, accompanied by increased objectivity, how is this evidenced? One likely outcome is significantly altered communication: Does information control shift from defending privacy to curbing one's tongue to avoid giving offense?

Finally, once the concept of filial maturity has been clarified and at least some of its markers identified, its connections to related concepts can be evaluated: Does filial anxiety (Cicirelli, 1988) precede maturity, as a spur to development, or can it curb progress? What is the relationship between filial maturity and affection? And is there a late life *general* attribute of "personal maturity" or is maturity a congeries of role-specific maturities, each developing at its own tempo?

ACKNOWLEDGMENTS

The author acknowledges the support of NIMH (MH29657) and NIA (AG00097 and AG03871).

REFERENCES

Bengtson, V., Cutler, N., Mangen, D., & Marshall, V. (1985). Generations, cohorts, and relations between age groups. In R. Binstock & E. Shanas (Eds.), *Handbook of aging and the social sciences* (pp. 304–338). New York: Van Nostrand Reinhold.

Bernard, H. (1988). *Research methods in cultural anthropology*. Newbury Park, CA: Sage.

Blenkner, M. (1965). Social work and family relationships in later life with some thoughts on filial maturity. In E. Shanas & G. Streib (Eds.), *Social structure and the family: Generational relations* (pp. 46–59). Englewood Cliffs, NJ: Prentice-Hall.

Cicirelli, V. (1988). A measure of filial anxiety regarding anticipated care of elderly parents. *The Gerontologist, 28,* 478–482.

Clark, M., & Anderson, B. (1967). *Culture and aging*. Springfield, IL: Charles Thomas.

Coan, R. (1977). *Hero, artist, sage, or saint?* New York: Columbia University Press.

Colarusso, C., & Nemiroff, R. (1981). *Adult development*. New York: Plenum Press.

Dannefer, D. (1984). Adult development and social theory: a paradigmatic reappraisal. *American Sociological Review, 49,* 100–116.

Erikson, E. (1959). *Identity and the life cycle*. New York: International Universities Press.

Erikson, E. (1963). *Childhood and society*. New York: Norton.

Finley, N., Roberts, M., & Banahan, B. (1988). Motivators and inhibitors of attitudes of filial obligation toward aging parents. *The Gerontologist, 28,* 73–78.

Gilligan, C. (1977). In a different voice: Women's conceptions of self and morality. *Harvard Educational Review, 47,* 481–517.

Greenberg, J., & Becker, M. (1988). Aging parents as family resources. *The Gerontologist, 28,* 786–791.

Greene, A., & Boxer, A. (1986). Daughters and sons as young adults: Restructuring the ties that bind. In N. Datan, A. Greene, & H. Reese (Eds.), *Life-span developmental psychology: Intergenerational relations* (pp. 125–149). Hillsdale, NJ: Lawrence Erlbaum Associates.

Gubrium, J. (1988). *Analyzing field reality*. Newbury Park, CA: Sage.

Gubrium, J., & Buckholdt, D. (1977). *Toward maturity*. San Francisco: Jossey-Bass.

Hagestad, G. (1984). The continuous bond: A dynamic, multigenerational perspective on parent–child relations between adults. *Minnesota Symposia on Child Psychology* (Vol. 17, pp. 129–158). Hillsdale, NJ: Lawrence Erlbaum Associates.

Heath, D. (1965). *Explorations of maturity*. New York: Appleton-Century-Crofts.

Heider, F. (1958). *The psychology of interpersonal relations*. New York: Wiley.

Hess, B., & Waring, J. (1978). Parent and child in later life: Rethinking the relationship. In R. Lerner & G. Spanier (Eds.), *Child influences in marital and family interaction* (pp. 241–273). New York: Academic Press.

Jarrett, W. (1985). Caregiving within kinship systems: Is affection really necessary? *The Gerontologist, 25*, 5–10.

Jung, C. (1969). *Psychology and religion: West and east. Vol. 11. Collected works*. Princeton: Princeton University Press.

Kiefer, C. (1988). *The mantle of maturity*. Albany, NY: State University of New York Press.

Kohlberg, L. (1973). Continuities in childhood and adult moral development revisited. In P. Baltes & W. Schaie (Eds.), *Life-span developmental psychology: Personality and socialization* (pp. 180–204). New York: Academic Press.

Lowenthal, M., Thurnher, M., & Chiriboga, D. (1975). *Four stages of life*. San Francisco: Jossey-Bass.

Matthews, S. (1986). *Friendships through the life course*. Beverly Hills, CA: Sage.

Nydegger, C. (1980). Role and age transitions: A potpourri of issues. In C. Fry & J. Keith (Eds.), *New methods for old age research: Anthropological alternatives* (pp. 127–145). Chicago: Loyola University of Chicago.

Nydegger, C. (1983). Introduction. In C. Nydegger (Ed.), Anthropological approaches to aging research [Special issue]. *Research On Aging, 5*, 451–453.

Nydegger, C., Mitteness, L., & O'Neil, J. (1983). Experiencing social generations: Phenomenal dimensions. *Research On Aging, 5*, 527–546.

Nydegger, C. (1986a). Timetables and implicit theory. *American Behavioral Scientist, 29*, 710–729.

Nydegger, C. (1986b). Age and life-course transitions. In C. Fry & J. Keith (Eds.), *New methods for old age research: Strategies for studying diversity* (pp. 131–161). South Hadley, MA: Bergin & Garvey.

Nydegger, C. (1986c). Asymmetrical kin and the problematic son-in-law. In N. Datan, A. Greene, & H. Reese (Eds.), *Life-span developmental psychology: Intergenerational relations* (pp. 99–123). Hillsdale, NJ: Lawrence Erlbaum Associates.

Nydegger, C., & Mitteness, L. (1988). Etiquette and ritual in family conversation. *American Behavioral Scientist, 31*, 702–716.

Nydegger, C., & Mitteness, L. (in press). Fathers and their adult sons and daughters. In S. Pfeifer & M. Sussman (Eds.), Families: Intergenerational and generational connections [Special issue]. *Marriage and Family Review*.

Perry, W., Jr., (1968). *Forms of intellectual and ethical development in the college years*. New York: Holt, Rinehart & Winston.

Suitor, J., & Pillemer, K. (1988). Explaining intergenerational conflict when adult children and elderly parents live together. *Journal of Marriage and the Family, 50*, 1037–1047.

Troll, L., & Bengtson, V. (1979). Generations in the family. In W. Burr, R. Hill, F. Nye, & I. Reiss (Eds.), *Contemporary theories about the family* (Vol. 1, pp. 127–161). New York: The Free Press.

III

BETWEEN-FAMILY AND WITHIN-FAMILY APPROACHES

The Developmental Importance of Differences in Siblings' Experiences Within the Family

Judy Dunn
Pennsylvania State University

A CHALLENGE TO THOSE STUDYING THE FAMILY

A major challenge to current ideas on the nature of familial influences on individual development has been posed by evidence from developmental behavior genetics. Children who grow up within the same family—siblings who share 50% of their segregating genes, the same parents, and the same family environment—develop to be strikingly different in personality, in adjustment, in confidence and self-esteem, and in psychopathology. Such differences between siblings have been documented in an extensive range of studies by behavior geneticists, and they present the challenge to those interested in the impact of parent–child relationships on individual development (Dunn & Plomin, 1990; Plomin & Daniels, 1987; Rowe & Plomin, 1981; Scarr & Grajek, 1982). What the data from studies of siblings, adoptive siblings, and twins show us is that the sources of environmental influence that make individuals different from one another work *within* rather than *between* families. To understand the salient environmental influences we have to be able to explain what makes two children different from one another within the family. The factors that are shared cannot per se be the environmental influences that exert significant effects on children.

At first sight this seems a counter-intuitive finding. After all, most of the family factors that have been studied appear to be shared by siblings (e.g., social class, the quality of the marital relationship, the mother's mental health, parents' child-rearing attitudes). But the message from the behavioral genetics data is not that family factors such as these are unimportant; it is rather that their impact, if it is associated with developmental outcome, must be specific to each child. What this means is that there must be an important change in perspective in how we view family influence. We need to document those experiences that are specific to each child—and necessarily, therefore, we need to study more than one child per family. Studies that focus on individual outcome of one child per family cannot use such data to discover the processes that link apparently shared family factors to outcome differences. The question "Why do siblings growing up in the same family turn out to be so different?" is key to documenting the significant environmental influences on individual differences in general, and to answer that question a new perspective on the salient influences within the family is needed.

To introduce this new perspective, consider an incident from an observation made on a 30-month-old child with his mother and his 14-month-old sister. Andy, a sensitive and rather anxious 30-month-old boy, overhears his mother make a very warm, proud comment on his assertive and exuberant younger sister Susie. She (Susie) has just succeeded in achieving a forbidden goal—in the face of repeated prohibitions by her mother:

Mother to Susie (affectionately): Susie you *are* a determined little devil!
Andy (sadly): *I'm* not a determined little devil!
Mother to Andy (laughing): No! What are you? A poor old boy!

This little incident serves to illustrate a pattern of the relationships between the three family members that was often repeated during the observations: the mother praising Susie affectionately, Andy sadly drawing attention to himself with a negative comment about himself, and his mother then confirming his comment. But beyond illustrating a *particular* family triad of relationships, the example does more: It highlights some of the key aspects of the new perspective on salient experiences within the family.

First, note the difference between the siblings. Andy and Susie differed markedly in temperament, and self-confidence: It is just one example of the differences documented in the wide range of studies to which we have already referred. The evidence for such differences in personality will probably come as no surprise to those who have more than one child, as such differences between their children are frequently noted by parents. Second, note that Andy, in the emotional circumstances of the family, is making a self-evaluative comment. Yet he is only 2 1/2-years-old. At this age, according to the received view of the development of self-reflective powers, he should not be able to evaluate himself in this way. Is this then an aberrant example? Or could we be misrepresenting children's abilities by studying their social cognitive development only outside the family? The evidence of recent systematic studies of children at home shows that the power and subtlety of their social understanding has been considerably underestimated (Dunn, 1988a). This research also indicates that social comparison between siblings is frequent from a very early stage.

The third relevant aspect of the incident between Andy and his mother and sister is this: Andy intervenes in his mother's "conversation" with his sister, with his self-comparison. He is monitoring their interaction, and interpolates his comment on himself. This kind of intervention into the talk of others in the family turns out to be relatively frequent even with such very young children. Andy's intervention is far from unusual. A recent study of families with preschool children found that on average 20% of the conversational turns of secondborn children in their third year followed speech addressed to others (Dunn & Shatz, 1989). One implication of the findings is that the salient verbal environment for young children is not solely the speech addressed to them. They are interested in, and attentive to the speech between others, and by 36 months are effective conversationalists who can join such talk between others and turn it to their own interests. This is important: Most of the talk in families is not addressed to the 2-year-old. Yet the great majority of studies of communicative development focus on the child–mother dyad, and attempt to document the child's direct experience within the dyad. Such a focus may fail to capture much of what is significant in the children's verbal environment.

The fourth point concerns the mother's behavior to her two children. She talks and behaves differently to her two children—with a warm pride in her daughter, and a dismissive laugh at her son. The relationship between Andy and his mother is notably different from that of his sister. And again, this is not an unusual or aberrant example. Differences in parents' relationships with their different children are not the exception—but extremely common (Brody, Stoneman, & Burke, 1987; Bryant & Crockenberg, 1981; McHale & Gamble, 1987; Stocker, Dunn, & Plomin, 1989).

In this brief incident we see then, that as young as 36 months, children are attentive to the relationships between their siblings and their parents, that they are prompt to compare themselves with their siblings, that the relationships between parent and each sibling differ, and that by studying just Andy's relationship with his mother we would be missing out on what appear to be potentially important experiences for him. Children grow up as family members, not solely as members of a parent–child dyad. But it would also be deeply misleading to attempt to characterize the family atmosphere in global terms applicable to all the children within the family. The experience of growing up in that family was very different for Andy and for his sister. The challenge of the behavior geneticists' evidence is that it makes clear that it is precisely those differences in experience that we must begin to document if we are to understand the development of individual differences. What could the significant processes be, the experiences specific to each child that affected their individual development?

In what follows I put forward some tentative answers to this question, drawing on data from studies conducted in the United States and in England. It should be recognized at the outset that facing these challenging questions is important not only for answering questions about the particular developmental domains on which I focus, but more generally for understanding the origins of individual differences and the ways in which parental influence works. The chapter focuses on aspects of the development of social understanding as an illustrative case, specifically the development of the ability to understand others' feelings, and of self-esteem. However, it must be emphasized that the general argument has far broader implications that concern a very wide range of developmental domains. A full discussion of the argument and evidence is given in a recent book (Dunn & Plomin, 1990).

DIFFERENTIAL PARENT–CHILD RELATIONSHIPS

A range of possible sources of nonshared experiences within the family have been proposed (Rowe & Plomin, 1981). Included in this number are differences in the relationships that parents have with each child, differences in the experiences of siblings within their relationship with one another, differences in their experiences outside the family (e.g., with peers or with teachers) and chance events such as illnesses that affect one child but not the other. This chapter considers briefly two of these: differential parent–child relationships and differences in experiences within the sibling relationship.

To what extent do mothers behave differently with their different children? And are such differences related to individual outcome of the children? These questions can be asked in two different ways. First, the question can be posed in terms of whether parents behave differently to their children when they are the same age: To what extent is their behavior consistent to each sibling when he or she was an infant, a child, and an adolescent? Second, we can also ask whether at any one chronological time point parents behave differently to their two children, who are, of course, different ages. Either of these forms of differential behavior might influence the development of differences between the children.

Studies of the siblings participating in the Colorado Adoption Project (Plomin, DeFries, & Fulker, 1988) give us information on how the same mother behaved toward her two children when each was 12, 24, and 36 months (the consistency of her behavior), and also information on the stability of her behavior with each child as an individual over time (Dunn & Plomin, 1986; Dunn, Plomin, & Daniels, 1986; Dunn, Plomin, & Nettles, 1985). The results showed that although the mothers were relatively consistent in their behavior with and affection toward their different children *when they are the same age*, their affectionate, verbal, and controlling behavior to each individual child changed over time, as the children grew up. It was not stable to the same child over time. Some mothers were particularly affectionate toward their children when they were babies, others were especially affectionate when they were with their communicative 2-year-olds or 3-year-olds. The developmental stage of the child was importantly related to the mother's behavior with that child.

Thus, at any one time point, the same mother is likely to be behaving differently toward her two children. And studies of families with two children that document a mother's interaction with both her children amply confirm the point. For example, in the Cambridge Sibling Study, families with two children were observed at home with long naturalistic observations—a methodology rather different from that of the Colorado study. The results showed that there were no significant correlations between the mothers' affectionate, or restraining, punitive behavior with their two children, and no significant correlations in amount of conflict or of joint play between the mother–child and mother–sibling dyads. Such results are in some ways unsurprising, as Scarr (1987) commented:

> It is not surprising that 12-month-olds are treated more similarly to each other than they are to 24-month-olds, regardless of family ties. Can you imagine speaking to a one-year-old as you would to a 2-year-old, even if you are the most insensitive parent in the world? (p. 38)

These differences take on added significance when we take account of the evidence that children attend to and respond to the interaction between other family members, and that they are sensitive to perceived differences in their parents' behavior toward them, vis-à-vis their sibling. The example of Andy and his sister illustrates the salience of affectionate interaction between his mother and his sister for one 3-year-old boy. Two lines of relevant evidence stand out from recent developmental work. First, a wealth of studies have now documented that children from the end of their first year are interested in the behavior of their parents, and especially to emotional exchanges between others. In a classic study, Zahn-Waxler, Cummings, Radke-Yarrow, and their colleagues documented the development of children's responses to emotional displays by other family members (Radke-Yarrow, Zahn-Waxler, & Chapman, 1983), and in a series of experimental studies they have shown that children who witness angry exchanges between adults react immediately, their play and aggressive behavior toward a peer also being affected (Cummings, Ianotti, & Zahn-Waxler, 1985; Cummings, Zahn-Waxler, & Radke-Yarrow, 1981). Using naturalistic observations of siblings at home, we found that children witnessing disputes between their mothers and siblings rarely ignored such disputes but usually acted promptly to support or to punish one of the antagonists (Dunn & Munn, 1985). And in a study of first-born children's relationships before and following the birth of a sibling, we found that the first-born's behavior was profoundly affected by their mothers' interaction with the younger sibling (Dunn & Kendrick, 1982; Kendrick & Dunn, 1980, 1982).

A second source of evidence for the impact of parent–sibling relationships on young children comes from the children's own perceptions of their parents' behavior. Children as young as 5–6 years old when interviewed about their parents' relationships with their siblings and themselves usually report that there are differences (Koch, 1960); so too do children of 10–11 years, and adolescents (Furman & Buhrmester, 1985; Daniels, Dunn, Furstenberg, & Plomin, 1985).

So parents behave differently toward their different children, and their children respond to such differences, and comment on them in no uncertain terms. Are these differences significantly related to the children's developmental outcome? First, it should be noted that there is now an accumulation of evidence that differential parental behavior is linked to the quality of the relationship between the siblings, with more conflict and hostility between siblings found in families in which there is more differential parental treatment. This association has been reported for preschool children (Dunn, 1988b), for siblings in middle childhood (Brody, Stoneman, & Burke, 1987; Bryant & Crockenberg, 1981; Furman & Buhrmester, 1985; Stocker, Dunn, & Plomin, 1989), for children with disabled siblings (McHale & Gamble, 1987), and for children following divorce (Hetherington 1988). As Hetherington commented, "It was the disparity in treatment rather than the absolute levels of parental behavior that had the most profound effects on sibling relations." Her results indicated that when one child was treated with less warmth and affection and more coercion and restrictiveness than the other, then both siblings directed more aggressive and avoidant behavior toward the other than the children in families in which the siblings were treated more equally. It is important to note that the direction of effects in these associations is not clear.

Parental differential treatment is, then, associated with differences in the quality of the sibling relationship. But the challenge posed initially was that of describing the experiences specific to each child that were linked to individual developmental outcome. The next question addressed here is therefore whether differences in maternal behavior are associated with the children's adjustment, and their social understanding.

A number of lines of evidence are beginning to indicate that differences in parental behavior may be associated with outcome measures of children's adjustment. In a study of a nationally representative sample of adolescents, Daniels and her colleagues found that siblings who perceived more maternal closeness, more say in family decision making, and more parental expectation of responsibility than their siblings were better adjusted psychologically than their siblings (Daniels et al., 1985). The measures of adjustment here included parents', adolescents', and teachers' ratings of emotional distress, delinquency, and disobedience, and the adolescents' own self-reports of dissatisfaction. Note that again we cannot come to any conclusions about the direction of effects, because these are correlational data. A second study by Daniels, this time focusing on very young siblings participating in the Colorado Adoption Project, found that differences in the siblings' experience of the family environment, measured on the FES and the HOME, although small in scale, were significantly related to differences in the behavior of the young siblings (Daniels, 1985).

In both these studies, the outcome measures employed were the *differences* between the siblings. But the general argument for the significance of non-shared environmental influence proposes that individual developmental outcome—rather than sibling differences in outcome—should be related to the experiences within the family that are specific to each individual child. As yet few studies have examined possible connections with individual outcome. However, some interesting results are emerging from the longitudinal follow-up of the Cambridge Sibling Study that are relevant. The siblings were first studied early in the preschool period, with naturalistic observations of family interaction, and interviews with the mothers (Dunn & Munn, 1985, 1986, 1987). When the siblings reached middle childhood (aged on average 9 and 7 years) they were assessed on a variety of aspects of their social understanding and self-esteem, including an assessment of their ability to judge other people's feelings and motives, the Rothenberg Social Sensitivity assessment (Rothenberg, 1970).

It seems very likely that a number of different processes influence the development of this centrally important aspect of human understanding. But it is notable that one such source of influence was the experience of differential maternal affection and discipline during the earlier preschool period. There were considerable differences in the affection mothers showed toward their different children; what emerged as important in relation to the older siblings' affective-perspective-taking abilities was the *relative* difference in the affectionate behavior the mother showed to her two children during the observations. The greater the difference in maternal affection in favor of the younger sibling in the preschool period, the better the older sibling was at affective-perspective-taking in middle childhood [$r\,(40) = .46, p < .05$].

These data were from observations of the families. The pattern of results from the maternal interview on the mothers' perceptions of differences in their own affection, attention and discipline toward their two children was very similar.

The processes of influence here may be operating within the family at a number of different levels—from the broad emotional dynamics of differences in warmth expressed, to more cognitive attributional differences. Recall the example of Andy and his sister that we began with. There were differences in the mother's emotional tone as she spoke to her two children, as well as differences in the specific content of her comments. Her voice was warm and affectionate in her comments to her daughter—and much less so in her dismissive comments to her son. For Andy, either—or both—of these aspects of differential treatment might be salient. It could be that the most important difference, for Andy, was the content of his mother's comments to his sister and to himself. But it could also be the discrepancy in the warmth and affection of her tone to Susie and to himself that he noticed. An exciting direction for future research is to explore the relative significance of the different dimensions of differential behavior toward siblings, and to trace developmental changes in their significance. Parents (both mothers and fathers) show differing affection and responsiveness, differing attention, differing control, and discipline toward their various children (Dunn, Stocker, & Plomin, 1990). Any or all of these dimensions of difference might be important for the children's development. Parents also differ in their expectations and their attributions concerning their children. It seems likely that differences in what is being attributed to children, and the explicit comparisons between siblings will assume more importance as children reach middle childhood.

A second aspect of the children's development that was assessed in the follow-up stage of the Cambridge Sibling Study was the children's perceived self-competence, as measured on the Harter scales (Harter & Pike, 1984). How children feel about themselves in middle childhood is an interesting and important matter: Children who have low self-esteem are at some risk for later depressive mood and emotional problems. Yet we know little about the early family correlates of differences in children's sense of self-worth, or their perceptions of their own competence in different domains. First, it should be noted that there were no significant correlations between the scores of the two siblings in a family on the self-competence measures. That is, although they were growing up within the same family, there were marked differences in how the two siblings felt about themselves. We should not assume then that there are simple links between parental child-rearing attitudes, or maternal personality, or the quality of the marital relationship (all factors that have been suggested to influence the development of self-esteem) and children's perceived self-competence. Rather, the results of the Cambridge study showed that for the older siblings, differential maternal behavior was systematically related to the outcome measure. A significant proportion of the variance in the older siblings' self-esteem was accounted for by maternal differential behavior, this time assessed contemporaneously in an interview with the mother. In families in which mothers reported being more affectionate and attentive to the younger than the older sibling, the older siblings had lower self-esteem. Again we should be cautious about inferring causal influence, or assuming the direction of effects in these correlational data.

DIFFERENCES IN EXPERIENCES WITHIN
THE SIBLING RELATIONSHIP

The second arena of differential experiences within the family to be considered is that of the sibling relationship itself. Whereas it is generally acknowledged by those studying the marital relationship that there can be marked differences between spouses in their experiences within the relationship—"his and her marriage" as Bernard (1982) phrased it—the question of how far siblings experience their relationship differently has not until now been raised. Studies of the sibling relationship have generally focused on the dyad, characterizing the relationship along dimensions of dyadic conflict, rivalry, cooperation, and so on (e.g., Furman & Buhrmester, 1985), or on the behavior of each individual child. If instead of focusing on the siblings as a dyadic unit, we ask how similarly or differently the two siblings behave toward each other, we find that there can be marked differences between the children in the affection, or control shown to the other. Whatever the source of information—maternal interview, observations of children, or children's own accounts—the picture from both the Colorado and the Cambridge projects is that on average, only one third of siblings behave similarly toward each other in affectionate or controlling behavior. For conflict and aggression there is more reciprocity, but the relative differences in negative behavior are, it turns out, important for the developing self-esteem of the second-born. In the Cambridge study we find that the perceived self-competence of the second-born in middle childhood is correlated with observational and interview assessments of differences in the siblings' behavior to one another from the preschool period. The important feature is the *relative* difference in negative behavior shown by older and younger child. The direction of the association is that the more negative the younger sibling was toward the older, relative to the older's negative behavior to the younger, the higher the self-esteem of the younger 3 years later, at the middle childhood assessment. The correlations were positive for each of the domains of self-competence assessed in the Harter test: social, physical appearance, athletic ability, school achievement, and conduct. It is interesting that this pattern was clear for the second-born siblings, but not for their older siblings. A number of studies have found that the quality of sibling interaction shows clearer patterns of association with outcome for later-born than for firstborn children (Dunn, 1983). It is also worth noting that it was relative differences in negative rather than in positive friendly behavior that appear to be linked with self-esteem.

It must be emphasized that these results come from relatively small samples of families; much more work needs to be done to clarify the nature and extent of differential experiences within the family, and their developmental pattern. The challenge posed by the behavior genetics data on siblings is that the salient influences that affect individual development work within families, and are specific to each child within the family and cannot be studied or understood by conventional "between-family" comparisons. The findings serve as initial evidence that examining within-family differential experiences of siblings will enlarge our understanding of the salient processes of family influence, and show us a way to begin to understand how experiences within the family influence development.

DIRECTIONS FOR FUTURE RESEARCH

In summary, the following points sccm most useful to begin to clarify the complex processes involved in the nonshared experiences of siblings within the family:

1. Differential experiences within the mother–child and the sibling relationships of siblings are likely to occur at a number of different levels, from a broad emotional level to more specifically cognitive-attributional level. Differential experiences at any or all of these levels may be developmentally significant. Research designs should be sensitive to this range of possible levels of influence.

2. The developmental impact of differential experiences is likely to differ for different aspects of children's outcome. The experiences that influence self esteem for instance are likely to differ from those that affect skills of conflict resolution, or understanding others' feelings and intentions.

3. The extent of the developmental impact of the various differential experiences is likely to change with the developmental stage of the children, and with the family position and gender composition of the individual. However no research to date has focused on this issue.

4. Mothers differ in the extent to which they treat their children differentially. Evidence suggests that these differences are related to maternal personality, age, education, and to siblings' temperament (Dunn & Plomin, 1986), during the preschool period; further research is needed on older children to explore these influences on differential behavior.

5. Similarly, the extent of differential experiences within the sibling relationship varies greatly between sibling pairs. Factors associated with such variation are the temperamental match of the siblings, and age differences (Dunn & Plomin, 1990).

6. The issue of the direction of effects is of major importance. Future studies must attempt to clarify how differences between siblings contribute to or elicit differential experiences within the family.

It should be noted that the argument and evidence for this new perspective on the nature of family influence is set out in much more detail in a recent book (Dunn & Plomin, 1990) to which the interested reader is referred.

ACKNOWLEDGMENTS

The study of the siblings participating in the Colorado Adoption Project (CAP) is supported by the National Science Foundation (BNS-8806589). The CAP is supported by HD-10333, HD-18426, and MH-43899. The Cambridge Sibling Study was supported by the Medical Research Council; the author was supported while preparing this chapter in part by a grant from NICHD, HD-23158-03).

REFERENCES

Bernard, J. S. (1982). *The future of marriage.* New Haven, CT: Yale University Press.

Brody, G. H., Stoneman, Z., & Burke, M. (1987). Child temperaments maternal differential behavior, and sibling relationships. *Developmental Psychology, 23*, 354–362.

Bryant, B., & Crockenberg, S. (1981). Correlates and dimensions of prosocial behavior. *Child Development, 51*, 529–544.

Cummings, E. M., Ianotti, R. J., & Zahn-Waxler, C. (1985). The influence of conflict between adults on the emotions and aggression of young children. *Developmental Psychology, 21*, 495–507.

Cummings, E. M., Zahn-Waxler, C., & Radke-Yarrow, M. (1981). Young children's responses to expression of anger and affection by others in the family. *Child Development, 52*, 1274–1282.

Daniels, D. (1985). *Understand the family environment: A study of adoptive and nonadoptive infant siblings.* Unpublished doctoral dissertation, University of Colorado, Boulder.

Daniels, D., Dunn, J., Furstenberg, F., & Plomin, R. (1985). Environmental differences within the family and adjustment differences within pairs of adolescent siblings. *Child Development, 56*, 764–774.

Dunn, J. (1983). Sibling relationships in early childhood. *Child Development, 54*, 787–811.

Dunn, J. (1988a). *The beginnings of social understanding.* Cambridge, MA: Harvard University Press.

Dunn, J. (1988b). Connections between relationships: Implications of research on mothers and siblings. In R. A. Hinde & J. Stevenson-Hinde (Eds.), *Relationships within families: Mutual influences* (pp. 168–180). Oxford: Oxford University Press.

Dunn, J., & Kendrick, C. (1982). *Siblings: Love, envy and understanding.* Cambridge, MA: Harvard University Press.

Dunn, J., & Munn, P. (1985). Becoming a family member: Family conflict and the development of social understanding in the second year. *Child Development, 56*, 480–492.

Dunn, J., & Munn, P. (1986). Sibling quarrels and maternal intervention: Individual differences in understanding and aggression. *Journal of Child Psychology and Psychiatry, 27*, 583–595.

Dunn, J., & Munn, P. (1987). The development of justification in disputes with mother and sibling. *Developmental Psychology, 23*, 791–798.

Dunn, J., & Plomin, R. (1986). Determinants of maternal behaviour towards young siblings. *British Journal of Developmental Psychology, 4*, 127–137.

Dunn, J., & Plomin, R. (1990). *Separate lives: Why siblings are so different.* New York: Basic Books.

Dunn, J., Plomin, R., & Daniels, D. (1986). Consistency and change in mothers' behavior towards two-year-old siblings. *Child Development, 57*, 348–356.

Dunn, J., Plomin, R., & Nettles, M. (1985). Consistency of mothers' behavior towards infant siblings. *Developmental psychology, 21*, 1188–1195.

Dunn, J., & Shatz, M. (1989). Becoming a conversationalist despite (or because of) having an older sibling. *Child Development, 60*, 399–410.

Dunn, J., Stocker, C., & Plomin, R. (1990). Nonshared experiences within the family: Correlates of behavioral problems in middle childhood. *Development and Psychopathology, 2*, 113–126.

Furman, W., & Buhrmester, D. (1985). Children's perceptions of the qualities of sibling relationships. *Child Development, 56*, 448–461.

Harter, S., & Pike, R. (1984). The Pictorial Scale of Perceived Competence and Social Acceptance for children. *Child Development, 55*, 1969–1982.

Hetherington, E. M. (1988). Parents, children and siblings: six years after divorce. In R. A. Hinde & J. Stevenson-Hinde (Eds.), *Relationships within families* (pp. 311–331). Oxford: Oxford University Press.

Kendrick, C., & Dunn, J. (1980). Caring for a second baby: Effects on interaction between mother and first-born. *Developmental Psychology, 16*, 303–311.

Kendrick, C., & Dunn, J. (1982). Protest or pleasure? The response of first-born children to interactions between their mothers and infant siblings. *Journal of Child Psychology and Psychiatry, 23*, 117–129.

Koch, H. L. (1960). The relation of certain formal attributes of siblings to their attitudes held towards each other and towards their parents. *Monographs of the Society for Research in Child Development, 25*(4).

McHale, S. M., & Gamble, W. C. (1987). Sibling relationships and adjustment of children with disabled brothers and sisters. *Journal of Children in Contemporary Society, 19*(3/4), 131–158.

Plomin, R. & Daniels, D. (1987). Why are children brought up within the same family so different from one another? *Behavioral and Brain Sciences, 10*, 1–16.

Plomin, R., DeFries, J., & Fulker, D. W. (1988). *Nature and nurture during infancy and childhood.* Cambridge: Cambridge University Press.

Radke-Yarrow, M., Zahn-Waxler, C., & Chapman, M. (1983). Children's prosocial dispositions and behavior. In P. H. Mussen (Series Ed.), *Handbook of child psychology, Vol. IV: socialization, personality, and social development* (pp. 469–545). New York: Wiley.

Rothenberg, B. B. (1970). Children's social sensitivity and the relationship to interpersonal competence, intrapersonal comfort, and intellectual level. *Developmental Psychology, 2*, 335–350.

Rowe, D. C., & Plomin, R. (1981). The importance of nonshared (E1) environmental influences in behavioral development. *Developmental Psychology, 17*, 517–531.

Scarr, S. (1987). Distinctive environments depend on genotypes. *Behavioral and Brain Sciences, 10*, 38–39.

Scarr, S., & Grajek, S. (1982). Similarities and differences among siblings. In M. E. Lamb & B. Sutton-Smith (Eds.), *Sibling relationships: Their nature and significance across the lifespan* (pp. 357–381). Hillsdale, NJ: Lawrence Erlbaum Associates.

Stocker, C., Dunn, J., & Plomin, R. (1989). Sibling relationships: Links with child temperament, maternal behavior and family structure. *Child Development, 60*, 715–727.

Mothers' Language with First- and Second-Born Children: A Within-Family Study

Kathleen McCartney
University of New Hampshire
Wendy Wagner Robeson
Wellesley College
Elizabeth Jordan
University of New Hampshire
Vera Mouradian
University of North Carolina at Greensboro

The question of whether children evoke social experiences from parents and others has been posed both by critics of socialization research (Bell, 1968; Bell & Harper, 1977) and by developmental behavior geneticists (Plomin, DeFries, & Loehlin, 1977; Scarr & McCartney, 1983). Critics of socialization research argue that there are reciprocal influences within parent–child relationships. Developmental behavior geneticists argue that child effects on adults reflect a process of genotype $\rightarrow$ environment effects. More specifically, genetic predispositions of children are hypothesized to be systematically associated with the environments children evoke and actively seek out. Recent theory along these two lines has led to an increased interest in child effects on adults.

A REVIEW OF RESEARCH ON DIFFERENTIAL PARENTAL TREATMENT OF SIBLINGS

The study of differential parental treatment of siblings has been used to document child effects on parents. Researchers are currently studying in what domains and in which contexts siblings receive different behaviors from parents. In the existing scant literature there is as much evidence for consistency of parental treatment as there is for differential parental treatment.

Studies that have directly investigated differential parental treatment have focused on its sequelae rather than its antecedents. Several researchers have been interested in the effect of differential treatment on the quality of sibling relationships (see Dunn, 1988, for a brief review) and its effect on adolescent adjustment (Daniels, Dunn, Furstenburg, & Plomin, 1985). In one study that

125

assessed differential treatment directly, Brody, Stoneman, and Burke (1987) operationalized it as the proportion of time spent with one child over another. This definition reflects level, or amount, of interaction. Interestingly, they found that increased differential behavior affected the sibling relationship. For example, when mothers spoke more with a younger sibling, there was, not surprisingly, less verbal interaction with siblings, and there was less prosocial behavior between siblings. Apparently, one or more of the siblings perceives the imbalance.

Other within-family studies of differential parental behavior typically consider only consistency of parental behavior. Dunn and her colleagues have conducted a within-family, longitudinal study of mother–child interaction of first-born and second-born children, when the children were 12 months (Dunn, Plomin, & Nettles, 1985), 24 months (Dunn, Plomin, & Daniels, 1986), and 36 months old (Dunn & Plomin, 1986). At 12 months, mothers were consistent in their affectionate, verbal, and controlling behaviors, based on zero-order correlations between mothers' behavior toward her two children. Dunn then compared these correlations to reliability indexes and concluded that consistency approaches reliability. In this light, differential maternal treatment appears to be an unlikely source of individual differences. At 24 and 36 months, consistency was replicated for affection and verbal responsiveness; at 36 months it was also replicated for control. These consistency indexes are particularly impressive given the low stability in maternal behavior from 12 to 24 months and from 24 to 36 months. Thus, mothers' behavior appears to be sensitive to children's developmental status.

Dunn's subjects included both biological siblings, who are 50% similar genetically on average, and adopted siblings, who share no genes on average. If parents' treatment of biological siblings is more similar, then this would suggest that differential treatment might be guided by predispositions. At 12 months, Dunn found no difference in consistency for verbal and control behaviors, but the pattern of correlations for affection was different for the two groups, such that it was lower for adoptive siblings. At 24 months, supportive presence, which is related to affection, was significantly lower for adoptive siblings. At 36 months, mothers were more consistent toward biological siblings on intrusiveness, shares joy and attention, and on the factor scale of affection.

Dunn's comparison of biological and adoptive siblings offers a powerful means of examining differential treatment as it is related to genetic predispositions. These results suggest that genetic similarity is related to consistency of maternal treatment. Thus, differential treatment may be related to differences in genetic predispositions.

However, these and additional studies document maternal consistency rather than adaptability or differential treatment. For example, Corter, Abramovitch, and Pepler (1983) found consistency for both negative behaviors, such as commanding, threatening, and punishing, and for positive behaviors, such as caretaking, helping, giving praise, and comfort. Brody, Stoneman, and Burke

(1987) reported consistency for verbalizations, prosocial behavior, and antagonistic behavior. Bryant and Crockenberg (1980) documented consistency on a number of maternal behaviors, especially unsolicited disapproval, unsolicited help, and ignoring the child. In these three studies, too, consistency analyses are made up of zero-order correlations.

Does the presence of consistency reflect on absence of adaptability? The answer to this question appears to be no, unless the consistency correlations are perfect, which they are not. Dunn's comparison of consistency correlations to reliability correlations is helpful; however, comparisons reveal that there is nevertheless variance unaccounted for. What is needed is a direct assessment of differential treatment.

PURPOSE OF THE PRESENT STUDY

The purpose of the present study was to assess both consistency and adaptability of mothers' language to first- and second-born children. Differential behavior was assessed as a function of mothers' adaptability to existing differences between their two children. We hypothesized that there would be evidence for consistency, based on the existing literature, and that there would be evidence for adaptability, based on the literature on child-directed language to children (for a review see Hoff-Ginsberg & Shatz, 1982).

The importance of the theory guiding this research must be emphasized. There are behavior genetics studies that use twins and adopted children to demonstrate a heritable component in language ability. There are language socialization studies that demonstrate a relationship between mothers' verbal input and children's language. There are few studies that attempt to model the process through which genetic predispositions and environments combine in development. This study attempted to do exactly this through the study of mothers' adaptability.

The focus on language production serves two methodological purposes. First, heritability estimates are higher in the intellectual-language domain than in the social-affective domain (Scarr & Kidd, 1983). Second, language production can be measured validly and reliably via naturalistic observation. In addition, the role of experience in language learning has been hotly debated by developmental psycholinguists (Hoff-Ginsberg & Shatz, 1982). This study is not about whether there is a relation between language input and acquisition, but rather about language adaptability, which is sometimes referred to as tailoring by developmental psycholinguists. Tailoring has typically been assessed by correlating an index of mothers' language at Time 1 with an index of children's language at Time 2, while controlling statistically for children's language at Time 1.

We argue that this method assesses individual differences among mothers.

It is likely that all mothers tailor to some extent, because it is in some sense adaptive to do so in that it facilitates communication. However, a more effective means to assess mothers' tailoring directly is to assess her language with more than one partner.

A WITHIN-FAMILY STUDY
OF MOTHERS' LANGUAGE USE

Method

Forty mothers and their first-born children participated in a longitudinal observational study of mother–child interaction, which began when the children were 21 months old. The children were evenly divided between girls and boys. Twenty-one months was chosen because it is the earliest age that one would predict that all children would have at least minimum productive language (i.e., mean length of utterance in morphemes—MLU—of 1.0). This prediction was born out; MLU ranged from 1.0 to 3.3. Mother–child dyads were recruited in Cambridge/Arlington, Massachusetts from local town birth records, from a community health maintenance organization, and from canvassing local shopping centers in an effort to obtain as random a sample as possible. In spite of this effort, the sample consists primarily of middle- and upper middle-class families, which is typical in studies of mother–child interaction. The average number of years of education for mothers was 16 years.

Two researchers conducted the home observations; one served as the interviewer and session coordinator and the other served as the video camera operator. While the video camera operator set up the equipment, the interviewer explained to mothers that the purpose of the research was to do a developmental study of how mothers and children play together. First, mothers completed a demographic questionnaire. Then, mothers were encouraged to play with their children the way they normally do, despite the fact that there were two researchers in their living rooms with a video camera. We realize that this is easier said than done, particularly for mothers, if not for toddlers. Mothers and their children were videotaped while interacting alone for 25 minutes. They were provided with novel toys that were chosen to promote social rather than parallel play. The toys were a play house with furniture, people, and a car; two puppets; and a toy telephone. Following the play session, mothers rated their children on the toddler temperament scale (Fullard, McDevitt, & Carey, 1978). Following the home visit, mothers completed the California psychological inventory (CPI: Gough, 1975) to assess their own personality. Mothers mailed their responses to the CPI to the project address.

Of these 40 mothers, 21 gave birth to a second child by the time their firstborns were 5 years old; the average spacing between births was 32 months (range from 18 to 46 months). When the second-borns were 21 months old, they were observed interacting with their mothers, following the same procedures as with the first-borns. First-borns were not present during the observations.

First-borns and their mothers were later observed when the children were 28 and 35 months; second-borns were later observed at 35 months. Data collected from these sessions is not discussed here. The subjects for this report were 21 triads, consisting of mothers, their first-borns at 21 months and their second-borns at 21 months. Mothers, of course, were observed twice.

Data Coding

The videotapes were transcribed to provide natural language samples of mothers and toddlers. Rules for transcription were adapted from Ochs (1979). Children's verbal production, mothers' verbal production, and notes about nonverbal context were recorded in sequential order. Punctuation was used to mark utterance boundary, interruption, unclear reading, repetition, and intonation. Each transcript was checked twice, by two different coders, to ensure accuracy. Data transcription is extremely time consuming. Each mother-child session took approximately 15 hours to transcribe, and the transcripts provide only the raw data for coding.

Measures

Mothers' and Children's Syntax.   The standard index of syntactic production is the mean length of utterance in morphemes. A morpheme is the smallest meaningful unit of language. For example, car consists of one morpheme, but cars consists of two, because the ''s'' inflection represents knowledge of the plural (see Newport, Gleitman, & Gleitman, 1977). Although MLU is a sensitive indicator of children's syntactic level at this age range (see Dale, 1976), it has its limitations, most notably that it may be biased by the discourse behavior of the conversational partner (Wells, 1981).

Brown (1973) suggested using an upper bound index, the number of morphemes in the single most syntactically complex utterance, for a closer approximation of competence. We coded the median upper bound of the five most syntactically complex utterances. In addition, six specific syntactic structures were coded: nouns per utterance, inflections per noun phrase, verbs per utterance, auxiliaries per verb phrase, wh-questions per utterance, and negatives per utterance. There is evidence that auxiliaries may be particularly related to environmental input (e.g., Moerk, 1980). Verbal fluency of mothers and children was assessed by total number of utterances.

Mothers' Discourse.   Discourse can be defined as the function of an utterance; function may, of course, be related to form. We coded six discourse functions that we thought, based on prior research, might serve a teaching function.

Extensions are responses that are generally intended to add to and further the conversation. They incorporate some part of the child's utterance, but the mother is clearly speaking for herself. For example, a child might say, "That the suitcases," and a mother might reply "And this is the thing that carries the suitcase."

Expansions repeat the meaning of the child's previous utterance and are generally intended to verify, clarify, interpret, or summarize. They are often characterized by grammatical corrections. For example, a child might say, "This too big," and a mother might reply, "This is too big." Repetitions refer to the mother's repetitions of the child's utterances. The remaining three functions were types of interrogatives: general Wh-questions (e.g., "What is that?"), yes–no questions with subject–verb inversion (e.g., "Is he hungry?") and yes–no questions with rising intonation (e.g., "You like this↑?").

Children's Temperament. The Toddler Temperament Scale (TTS: Fullard, McDevitt, & Carey, 1978) is a 97-item questionnaire designed as a parent-report measure for 1- to 3-year-olds. The items comprise nine scales: activity, rhythmicity, approach/withdrawal, adaptability, intensity, mood, attention, distractibility, and threshold response. We suggest that the construct, approach-withdrawal, is a precursor to sociability. Some of the approach/withdrawal items are: child is shy on meeting another child for the first time, child approaches new visitors at home, and child accepts new surroundings within 10 minutes. Buss and Plomin (1984) reported that the trait sociability or its opposite, shyness, may be more stable than other temperamental traits. In terms of reliability and validity, the TTS is comparable to other paper-and-pencil measures of temperament (Hubert et al., 1982). Nevertheless, the psychometric properties of all paper-and-pencil measures of temperament are only moderate.

Mothers' Personality. The California psychological inventory (CPI: Gough, 1975) was used to assess mothers' personality. The CPI consists of 480 true–false items that yield 18 standard scores, including sociability. The reliabilities of the scales are moderate; the validity of the scales has been documented in many studies (see Megargee, 1972).

Results

Consistency of Mothers' Language with Their Two Children

The consistency of mothers' language was assessed by correlating measures of a mother's language with her first-born child with identical measures of her language with her second-born child. The syntactic level of mothers' language was quite consistent with first-borns and second-borns (see Table 7.1). The diagonal of the correlation matrix in Table 7.1 is most important and shows consistency of the same variable over time, across children. Six of the eight syntax variables were significant; more important, the effect sizes of these correlations were for the most part large. In addition, mothers' verbal fluency, as indexed by total number of utterances, was highly consistent.

With respect to mothers' discourse, mothers' interrogatives were consistent, although mothers' extensions, repetitions, and expansions were not as consistent (see Table 7.2). Interestingly, developmental psycholinguists have sug-

TABLE 7.1

Significant Correlations Between Mothers' Language With First-Borns and Mothers' Language With Second-Borns

Mothers' Language With First-Borns	Mothers' Language With Second-Borns								
	1.	2.	3.	4.	5.	6.	7.	8.	9
1. MLU	.76***	58**		.60**	.51*		.56**	.52*	
2. Median upper bound	.64**	.44*						.61**	
3. Total utterances			.70***						
4. Non phrases/ utterance	.52*	.43†	.45*	.52*				.59**	
5. Verb phrases/ utterance	.48*			.45*	.77***			.50*	
6. Inflections/ noun phrase						.34			
7. Auxiliaries/ verb phrase	.46*						54*		
8. Wh-questions/ utterance								.06	
9. Negatives/ utterance									.08

†p < .10; *p < .05; **p < .01; ***p < .001.

TABLE 7.2

Significant Correlations Between Mothers' Discourse With First-Borns and Mothers' Discourse With Second-Borns

Mothers' Discourse With First-Borns	Mothers' Discourse With Second-Borns					
	1.	2.	3.	4.	5.	6.
1. Extensions	.41†					
2. Repetitions		.13		−.39†		.57**
3. Expansions		.49*	.34			.40†
4. Wh-questions		.58**	−.41†	.43†		−.51*
5. Yes–no inversion questions					.67***	
6. Yes–no rising intonations					−.49*	.57**

†p < .10; *p < .05; **p < .01; ***p < .001.

gested that these three functions might be particularly important for teaching language (Snow, Perlmann, & Nathan, 1987). The question that remains is whether less consistent features of language are more likely to be tailored to individual differences between offspring.

Adaptability of Mothers' Language to Children's Language

Each mother's language was assessed twice: at Time 1 with her first-born and at Time 2 with her second-born. Each child's language was assessed once at 21 months. To assess adaptability of mothers' language, we correlated the difference between the two sibling's language with the difference between a given mother's language with her two children. For example, for any given variable, say MLU, we subtracted the second-born's score from the first-born's score. We then subtracted the mother's score with her second-born from mother's score with her first-born. By correlating these two difference scores, adaptability can be assessed and is indicated by a positive correlation. Although difference scores are typically criticized for their unreliability, Richards (1976) has shown in simulation studies that difference scores are equivalent to other means of assessing growth or change (e.g., regression).

The complete matrix of adaptability correlations with respect to mothers' syntax and children's syntax is presented in Table 7.3. Again, the diagonal

TABLE 7.3

Significant Correlations Between Differences in Mothers' Syntax With Her Two Children and Differences in Children's Syntax With Their Mother

Children's Syntax	Mothers' Syntax Variables								
	1.	2.	3.	4.	5.	6.	7.	8.	9
1. MLU	.32			.44*					
2. Median upper bound		.05							
3. Total utterances		.20						−.38†	
4. Noun phrases/ utterance	.56**		−.45*	.67**				.51*	
5. Verb phrases/ utterance					.17				
6. Inflections/noun phrase		−.58**				.02		−.46*	
7. Auxiliaries/ verb phrase		−.50*					.05	.57**	
8. Wh-questions/ utterance				.48*				.14	
9. Negatives/ utterance			.37†						.39†

†p < .10; *p < .05; **p < .01.

is most informative, in that it represents specific syntactic tailoring, or adaptation, by mothers. Note that there is significant specific tailoring only for noun phrases. There is one trend worthy of consideration: Mothers adapt their wh-questions to three measures of children's syntax. Note that some of these correlations are negative. These negative correlations may be spurious; they tend to occur with low frequency syntax categories. Certainly, there is little reason to believe that smaller differences in mothers' language would be associated with larger differences between siblings' language.

The complete matrix of adaptability correlations with respect to mothers' discourse and children's syntax is presented in Table 7.4. Perhaps not surprisingly, mothers' interrogatives, which were consistent across children, were not adapted. However, mother's extensions, repetitions, and expansions, which were far less consistent, were adapted to individual differences in children's syntactic abilities. Thus, adaptability and consistency in mothers' language varies across functions.

Adaptability of Mothers' Language to Children's Temperament

Mothers' language may also be adapted to other individual differences between her two children. For example, we expected that a mother would have more language exchanges with her more sociable child. More specifically,

TABLE 7.4

Significant Correlations Between Differences in Mothers' Discourse
With Her Two Children and Differences in Children's Syntax With Their Mother

Children's Syntax Variables	Mothers' Discourse Variables					
	Extensions	Repetitions	Expansions	Wh-questions	Yes–no inversions	Yes–no rising intonation
MLU	.44*	.68***	.44*			
Median upper bound	.49*	.73***	.46*			
Total utterances				−.38†		.42†
Noun phrases/ utterance		.49*				
Verb phrases/ utterance	.59**	.56**	.44*			
Inflections/noun phrase		−.43†				
Auxiliaries/ verb phrase	.42†	.72***	.38†	.47*		
Wh-questions/ utterance		.42†				
Negatives/ utterance	.42†		.41†			

†$p < .10$; *$p < .05$; **$p < .01$; ***$p < .001$.

mothers' utterances should be adapted to sociability. The factor, approach–withdrawal, on the TTS corresponds to sociability. There was no evidence that mothers adapted the number of utterances spoken to children's sociability. Mothers' utterances were negatively adapted to children's mood, but this appears to be a spurious finding. There was little evidence that mothers adapted any aspect of their syntax to their children's temperament. Similarly, there was little evidence that mothers adapted any aspect of their discourse to their children's temperament. There were several scattered findings that can be attributed by chance based on the alpha level of .05.

The Relation Between Mothers' Personality and Language

It seems likely that any consistency in language might in part be the result of some aspect of mothers' personality. To test this, we correlated the 18 CPI variables with the eight measures of mothers' syntax and with total number of utterances, separately for first-borns and second-borns. Of the 162 correlations, 10 were significant for first-borns and 14 were significant for second-borns. Two correlations replicated across children. Mothers who rated themselves high on well-being made fewer utterances to first-borns ($r = -.73$) and second-borns ($r = -.64$); similarly, mothers who rated themselves high on self control made fewer utterances to first-borns ($r = -.59$) and second-borns ($r = -.54$). Thus, mothers' adjustment may be related to the amount they talk.

Birth Order Differences

There were no differences between first-borns and second-borns on the eight syntax variables and on total number of utterances. Nevertheless, mothers' language was affected by the birth order of their conversational partners. Mothers spoke in a syntactically more complex way to first-borns, as indexed by four of the eight syntax variables: for MLU [$t(19) = 4.93, p < .05$], for noun phrases per utterance [$t(20) = 3.45, p < .01$], and for verb phrases per utterance [$t(20) = 2.80, p < .05$]. The difference on median upper bound approached significance [$t(20) = 1.93, p < .10$]. However, mothers talked more to second-borns: for total number of utterances [$t(20) = 2.93, p < .05$]. This difference may reflect mothers' increasing comfort concerning the videotaping procedures. There was also one birth order difference on mothers' use of discourse: Mothers asked more yes–no questions with rising intonation of second borns [$t(20) = 3.06, p < .05$].

It is not clear whether these difference will eventually promote language differences between the children. In fact, in some studies first-borns have scored better on various language measures (see Bates, 1975), perhaps because they receive more language stimulation from parents or because they are less likely to be exposed to the imperfect language of a language-learning sibling; however, the vast majority of birth-order studies are flawed in that they are between-family studies in which variables like age, birth order, and birth interval are confounded. It is also not clear whether differences in language tailoring will eventually promote language differences between siblings, but there appear to be differences here as well. For first-borns, mothers' MLU was positively associated with upper bound (r = .49, p < .05) and verb phrases per utterance (r = .45, p < .05). In addition, the relation between mothers' MLU and first-borns' MLU approached significance (r = .36, p < .10). For second-borns, there were no significant correlations between mothers' MLU and any index of children's syntactic production. The correlation between mothers' MLU and second-borns' MLU was .06. We are currently coding second-borns' syntactic production at 35 months to investigate whether birth order differences in level and tailoring have any impact on child language abilities.

Age Spacing of Siblings

Age spacing of siblings is a potential source of differential treatment of siblings. To assess this, the age difference between siblings was correlated with differences in mothers' syntax and discourse use. There were no significant correlations for 15 mother language variables.

Gender Differences

There were no differences in mothers' syntax or discourse as a function of children's gender for first-borns for second-borns. Neither were there any gender differences in children's syntax.

In an effort to determine whether differential treatment by mothers might be affected by children's gender, we compared the difference in mothers' language to same-gender pairs, of which there were 7, to the difference in mothers' language to mixed-gender pairs, of which there were 13. One might expect greater differential treatment for mixed-gender pairs. In fact, there was no evidence for this. There were no significant findings for the nine syntax variables and there were none for the six discourse variables.

Discussion

It is important to note that this is not a study about language acquisition. In fact, we doubt whether correlational data like these can be used to establish the acquisition of language structures. Rather, this is a within-family study of mother–child interaction in a language-learning context.

These data show clearly that there is evidence for both consistency in a mother's language with her two children and adaptability in a mother's language with her two children. Thus, this study demonstrates differential maternal treatment of children, at least with respect to mothers' use of discourse functions that seem to serve a teaching function. The question that remains is: What is the source of this differential treatment? It is tempting to conclude that the differential parental treatment is child-driven, such that mothers responded to differences between their two children. Yet, child-driven sources are but one class of potential sources of differential parental treatment.

Potential Sources of Differential Parental Treatment of Siblings

We present here a taxonomy of potential sources of differential parental treatment of siblings (see Table 7.5). Each of these sources needs to be considered when studying differential parental treatment.

Child-driven sources of differential parental treatment are the focus of research on child effects. There are at least three types of child-driven sources. One type can be labeled *predispositions* that are genetic in origin. This is what Scarr and McCartney (1983) referred to when they discussed genotype → environment effects. For example, a child who is genetically predisposed to be sociable may receive more social interactions with parents than a sibling who is not so predisposed. A second type of child-driven sources can be labeled *abilities,* which are the product of genetic predispositions and experiences; thus, abilities reflect phenotypes.

The small body of research on child effects indicates that various child abilities and predispositions influence adult behavior. Cantor and her colleagues (Cantor & Gelfand, 1977; Cantor, Wood, & Gelfand, 1977) found that adult males and females attended more to child confederates who had been trained

TABLE 7.5
Potential Sources of Differential Parental Treatment of Siblings

Child-driven sources
  Predispositions
  Abilities
  Social construction/attitudes

Parent-driven sources
  Social construction/attitudes
  Sensitivity to actual differences between siblings

Relationship-driven sources
  Match between parent and child
  Interactional synchrony

Family context
  Birth orders of children
  Ages of children
  Sex of children
  Spacing between children

to be responsive than to those trained to be unresponsive. In addition to responsiveness, children's person orientation also affects adult behavior. Keller and Bell (1979) found that the person orientation of child confederates determined the strategies used by adults to elicit helping behavior from the children. Although none of these studies include parent–child dyads, it may be that similar child effects are found in the context of the family.

Social constructions and attitudes of children of varying sorts may also be sources of child-driven differential treatment. An example of this is sibling de-identification, which Schacter (1982) has defined as a process through which family members define siblings as different or contrasting. In addition, the siblings themselves may choose to define themselves as different (or similar for that matter). If siblings deliberately choose dissimilar paths as a way of establishing an identity, then their behaviors could lead to differential behavior by others. Birth order researchers have suggested that this is in fact the case with respect to family roles and career choices (Wagner, Schubert, & Schubert, 1979).

Differential parental treatment may also be parent-driven. Parent-driven sources rely on the parents' detection or construction of differences among children. It is reasonable to expect that parental sensitivity and attention to real sibling differences affect the probability of responding differentially. Various *social constructions* and attitudes of parents may affect treatment. For example, Schachter and Stone (1985) found that mothers' ratings of their children's temperament were less similar for first-borns and second-borns than for second-borns and third-borns. Of course, it is possible that mother's perceptions are grounded in reality, that is that they reflect *sensitivity to actual differences between siblings*. Mothers' ratings might in fact reflect greater sibling de-identification among first sibling pairs, perhaps because they are most likely to be compared with one another among possible sibling pairs. Alternatively, it may be that mothers' ratings reflect their own social constructions.

There is some evidence to support the view that parents' ratings contain both an objective and a subjective component (see Bates, 1980). Individual differences among mothers on age, parity, and personality are associated with their ratings of infant difficultness (Bates, Freeland, & Lounsbury, 1979). Mebert (1989) has documented that prenatal predictions of temperament are in fact associated with postnatal ratings. It is unlikely that prenatal predictions reflect anything other than maternal constructions. In spite of the mounting evidence for the existence of maternal constructions, their influence on maternal behavior and the mother–child relationship remain to be examined.

Differential parental treatment might also result from relationship-driven sources. In any relationship, each partner in the interaction has an effect on the other, and the relationship itself is said to have an effect on the behavior of each person in the relationship (Kenny & La Voie, 1984). One recent study of parent and child play found that relationship effects outweigh the effects of the individual participants (Stevenson, Leavitt, Thompson, & Roach, 1988).

The unique relationship between the parent and each child may contribute to differences in the treatment of siblings. The parent–child relationship may be characterized in terms of the match between parent and child and interactional synchrony. *Match* refers to the similarity between parent and child on characteristics such as attitudes, affect, and activity level. Lerner and Lerner (1986) discussed the idea of match more broadly with respect to the physical and social components of a setting. When there is a "good fit" between a child and a setting, this leads to positive behaviors and emotions; the fit is therefore thought to be adaptive. Although there are no existing data to adequately test this, it is consistent with the finding that one child within a family is often the target of child abuse by parents (Parke & Collmer, 1975) and that favorite adult children are those with shared interests and values (Aldous, Klaus, & Klein, 1985).

The other characteristic of the relationship, *interactional synchrony,* is the cyclical, rhythmic property of the interaction. Tronick, Als, and Brazelton (1980) and Lester, Hoffman, and Brazelton (1985) have studied the rhythmic nature of mother–infant play. Both research teams observed that synchrony involves coordination of individual behavior cycles to produce a smooth, unified whole that defines the dyadic interaction. Lester and his colleagues (1985) found that there is less synchrony between mothers and preterm infants than between mothers and term infants. They believe that such differences in synchrony may be correlated with differences in socioemotional development.

Finally, family context variables may also lead to differential parental treatment of siblings. Sibling constellation variables such as *birth order, age, gender, and spacing* have been studied to varying degrees, but mostly using a between-family methodology. Birth order differences may reflect parental perceptions, the environment provided by the sibling(s), or indeed differences in the intrauterine environment (Maccoby, Doering, Jacklin, & Kraemer, 1979). Jones and Adamson (1987) studied 21-month-olds, half of whom were first-borns and half of whom were second-borns. There were birth order differences in the language of the children, such that second-borns used more social regulatory speech, and in the language of the mothers, such that mothers of second-borns used less metalingual speech (e.g., they asked their children fewer questions). In general, however, within-family studies have failed to find effects for family constellation variables (Dunn, Plomin, & Nettles, 1985). Unfortunately, there are few within-family studies of siblings. Even birth order studies have typically used a between-family methodology. Studies typically consider only consistency of parental behavior, and not differential parental behavior.

Sources of Differential Treatment in the Present Study

To some extent, differential maternal language use in the present study is child-driven in that differences in mothers' language was associated with differences in children's language. To some extent, differential maternal language use is mother-driven in that at least one social construction, namely birth order, seems to affect mothers' language use; we can label this a social construction because there are no corresponding birth order differences in the children's language. The question of whether differential maternal language use is relationship-driven was not assessed in this study. The study of relationship-driven sources may very well replace the study of child-driven and parent-driven sources. Family context variables were assessed in this study and did not seem to account for differential maternal language use at all; however, power was low in these analyses.

Future Directions for Research on Parent–Child Relations

We have argued that the parent–child relationship must be studied as a relationship; that is, parent effects cannot be studied without studying child effects. Furthermore, we have demonstrated the value in studying child effects through the study of differential parental treatment of siblings. Finally, we have offered a taxonomy of potential sources of differential parental treatment of siblings that we hope will guide future research. We offer several specific suggestions as well.

A fruitful way to study adaptability is to study an individual with different partners (see Bell & Harper, 1977). We have used this strategy by studying mothers and children in semi-natural contexts; however, this strategy can be used experimentally, too. Both experimental and nonexperimental manipulations of partners should be conducted to determine whether findings replicate.

Child effects and parent effects should be assessed in the same study. One way to conduct such a study would be to use a round-robin methodology (Kenney & LaVoie, 1984), where each individual in a relationship is observed with multiple partners. We have conducted such a study and our preliminary analyses reveal that child effects, mother effects, and relationship effects operate simultaneously (McCartney & Jordan, in prep.).

It seems like a truism that relationship effects are transactional. Thus, the answers to many of our questions about reciprocal influence in parent–child relations probably lies in longitudinal research that takes into account the dynamics of the evolving relationship. Individual patterns in growth (Ragosa, Brandt, & Zimowski, 1982) may very well be associated with the relationship between a parent and child on various indicators of personality and intelligence.

Finally, it seems critical to remember that any effects may vary across and/or within domains. Here, the existing literature should help identify domains in which we can expect parent effects, child effects, and relationship effects.

ACKNOWLEDGMENTS

This research was supported by a grant to the first author (McCartney), by NIMH (R01 MH41807). Many research assistants helped to collect and code the data that are presented here. The authors are especially grateful to three of them: Kate Dobroth, Maura Kerrigan, and Annie Senghas. The authors also thank Sandra Scarr for her helpful comments on an earlier version of this chapter.

REFERENCES

Aldous, J., Klaus, E., & Klein, D. M. (1985). The understanding heart: Aging parents and their favorite children. *Child Development, 56,* 303–316.

Bates, J. E. (1975). Peer relations and the acquisition of language. In M. Lewis & L. A. Rosenblum (Eds.), *Friendship and peer relations* (pp. 259–292). New York: Wiley.

Bates, J. E. (1980). The concept of difficult temperament. *Merrill-Palmer Quarterly, 26,* 299–319.

Bates, J. E., Freeland, C. B., & Lounsbury, M. L. (1979). Measurement of infant difficultness. *Annual Progress in Child Psychiatry and Child Development,* 248–264.

Bell, R. Q. (1968). A reinterpretation of the direction of effects in studies of socialization. *Psychological Review, 75,* 81–95.

Bell, R. Q., & Harper, L. V. (1977). *Child effects on adults.* Lincoln, NE: University of Nebraska Press.

Brody, G. H., Stoneman, Z., & Burke, M. (1987). Child temperaments, maternal differential behavior, and sibling relationships. *Developmental Psychology, 23,* 354–362.

Bryant, B. K., & Crockenberg, S. B. (1980). Correlates and dimensions of prosocial behavior: A study of female siblings with their mothers. *Child Development, 51,* 529–544.

Brown, R. (1973). *A first language: The early stages.* Cambridge, MA: Harvard University Press.

Buss, A. H., & Plomin, R. (1984). *Temperament: Early developing personality traits.* Hillsdale, NJ: Lawrence Erlbaum Associates.

Cantor, N. L., & Gelfand, D. M. (1977). Effects of responsiveness and sex of children on adults' behavior. *Child Development, 48,* 232–238.

Cantor, N. L., Wood, D. D., & Gelfand, D. M. (1977). Effects of responsiveness and sex of children on adult males' behavior. *Child Development, 48,* 1426–1430.

Corter, C., Abramovitch, R., & Pepler, D. J. (1983). The role of the mother in sibling interaction. *Child Development, 54,* 1599–1605.

Dale, P. S. (1976). *Language development: Structure and function.* New York: Holt Rinehart & Winston.

Daniels, D., Dunn, J., Furstenburg, F. F., & Plomin, R. (1985). Environmental differences within the family and adjustment differences within pairs of adolescent siblings. *Child Development, 56,* 764–774.

Dunn, J. (1988). Connections between relationships: Implications of research on mothers and siblings. In R. A. Hinde & J. Stevenson-Hinde (Eds.), *Relationships within families: Mutual influences* (pp. 168–180). New York: Oxford University Press.

Dunn, J., & Plomin, R. (1986). Determinants of maternal behavior towards 3-year-old siblings. *British Journal of Developmental Psychology, 4,* 127–137.

Dunn, J., Plomin, R., & Daniels, D. (1986). Consistency and change in mothers' behavior toward young siblings. *Child Development, 57,* 348–358.

Dunn, J., Plomin, R., & Nettles, M. (1985). Consistency of mothers' behavior toward infant siblings. *Developmental Psychology, 21,* 1188–1195.

Fullard, W., McDevitt, S. C., & Carey, W. B. (1978). *The toddler temperament scale.* Unpublished manuscript, Temple University, Department of Educational Psychology, Philadelphia, PA.

Gough, H. (1975). *California Psychological Inventory.* Palo Alto, CA: Consulting Psycholinguists Press.

Hoff-Ginsberg, E., & Shatz, M. (1982). Linguistic input and the child's acquisition of language. *Psychological Bulletin, 92,* 3–26.

Hubert, N. C., Wachs, T. D., Peters-Martin, P., & Gandour, M. J. (1982). The study of early temperament: Measurement and conceptual issues. *Child Development, 53,* 571–600.

Jones, C. P., & Adamson, L. B. (1987). Language use in mother–child and mother–child–sibling interactions. *Child Development, 58,* 356–366.

Keller, B. B., & Bell, R. Q. (1979). Child effects on adults' method of eliciting altruistic behavior. *Child Development, 50,* 1004–1009.

Kenny, D. A., & La Voie, L. (1984). The social relations model. In L. Berkowitz (Ed.), *Advances in experimental social psychology* (Vol. 18, pp. 141–182). New York: Academic Press.

Lerner, R. M., & Lerner, J. V. (1986). Contextualism and the study of child effects in development. In R. L. Rosnow & M. Georgoudi (Eds.), *Contextualism and understanding in behavioral science: Implications for research and theory* (pp. 89–104). New York: Praeger.

Lester, B. M., Hoffman, J., & Brazelton, T. B. (1985). The rhythmic structure of mother–infant interaction in term and preterm infants. *Child Development, 56,* 15–27.

Maccoby, E. E., Doering, L. H., Jacklin, C. N., & Kraemer, H. (1979). Concentrations of sex hormones in umbilical cord blood: Their relation to sex and birth order of infants. *Child Development, 50,* 632–642.

McCartney, K., & Jordan, E. (in prep). *A social relations approach to the study of mother–child relations.*

Mebert, C. J. (1989). Stability and change in parents' perceptions of infant temperament: Early pregnancy to 13.5 months postpartum. *Infant Behavior and Development, 12,* 237–244.

Megargee, E. I. (1972). *The California Psychological Inventory Handbook.* San Francisco: Jossey-Bass.

Moerk, E. L. (1980). Relationships between parental input frequencies and children's language acquisition. *Journal of Child Language, 7,* 105–118.

Newport, E. L., Gleitman, H., & Gleitman, L. R. (1977). Mother, I'd rather do it myself: Some effects and noneffects of maternal speech styles. In C. E. Snow & C. A. Ferguson (Eds.), *Talking to children: Language input and acquisition* (pp. 109–148). Cambridge, England: Cambridge University Press.

Ochs, E. (1979). Transcription as theory. In E. Ochs & B. S. Schieffelin (Eds.), *Developmental pragmatics* (pp. 43–72). New York: Academic Press.

Parke, R., & Collmer, C. W. (1975). Child abuse: An interdisciplinary analysis. In E. M. Hetherington (Ed.), *Review of child development research* (Vol. 5, pp. 509–590). Chicago, IL: University of Chicago Press.

Plomin, R., DeFries, J. C., & Loehlin, J. C. (1977). Genotype-environment interaction and correlation in the analysis of human behavior. *Psychological Bulletin, 84,* 309–322.

Ragosa, D., Brandt, D., & Zimowski, M. (1982). A growth curve approach to the measurement of change. *Psychological Bulletin, 92,* 726–748.

Richards, J. M. (1976). A simulation study comparing procedures for assessing individual educational growth. *Journal of Educational Psychology, 68,* 603–612.

Scarr, S., & Kidd, K. K. (1983). Behavior genetics. In M. Haith & J. Campos (Eds.), *Manual of child psychology: Infancy and the biology of development* (Vol. 2, pp. 345–434). New York: Wiley.

Scarr, S., & McCartney, K. (1983). How people make their own environments: A theory of genotype → environment effects. Child Development, *54,* 309–322.

Schachter, F. F. (1982). Sibling deidentification and split-parent identification: A family tetrad. In M. E. Lamb & B. Sutton-Smith (Eds.), *Sibling relationships: Their nature and significance across the lifespan* (pp. 123–197). Hillsdale, NJ: Lawrence Erlbaum Associates.

Schachter, F. F., & Stone, R. K. (1985). Difficult sibling, easy sibling: Temperament and the within-family environment. *Child Development, 56,* 1335–1344.

Snow, C. E., Perlmann, R., & Nathan, D. (1987). Why routines are different: Toward a multiple-factors model of the relation between input and language acquisition. In K. E. Nelson & A. van Kleek (Eds.), *Children's language* (Vol. 6, pp. 65–97). Hillsdale, NJ: Lawrence Erlbaum Associates.

Stevenson, M. B., Leavitt, L. A., Thompson, R. H., & Roach, M. A. (1988). A social relations model analysis of parent and child play. *Developmental Psychology, 24,* 101–108.

Tronick, E., Als, H., & Brazelton, T. B. (1980). Monadic phases: A structural descriptive analysis of infant-mother face to face interaction. *Merrill-Palmer Quarterly, 26,* 3–24.

Wagner, M. E., Schubert, H. J. P., & Schubert, D. S. P. (1979). Sibship-constellation effects on psychological development, creativity, and health. In H. W. Reese & L. P. Lipsett (Eds.), *Advances in child development and behavior* (Vol. 14, pp. 58–148). New York: Academic Press.

Wells, C. G. (1981). *Learning through interaction: The study of language development.* Cambridge: Cambridge University Press.

Adolescent Happiness
and Family Interaction

Kevin Rathunde
Mihaly Csikszentmihalyi
The University of Chicago

Few family studies have investigated the subjective rewards that adolescents experience at home, which may build toward positive developmental outcomes. This despite the fact that extensive research into "optimal experiences" (interest, flow, intrinsic motivation, peak experiences) suggest they are among the most important influences on growth, such as the full utilization of potential, and the achievement of a sense of self-determination and creativity (Amabile, 1983; Csikszentmihalyi & Csikszentmihalyi, 1988; deCharms, 1976; Deci & Ryan, 1985; Dewey, 1913; Groos, 1898; Harter, 1978; Maslow, 1968; White, 1959). Identifying which factors enhance momentary experience may stimulate new ideas on how to improve adolescent life, and therefore aid the structuring of enjoyable and effective developmental contexts. Toward this end, this chapter focuses on one dimension essential for healthy families—the experience of happiness.

Our assumption is that adolescents who report being happy in everyday activities of life—in schoolwork, housework, and other usually unpleasant routines—have benefited from family environments that facilitate such experience. To investigate happiness and family life the first questions addressed by this study are descriptive: What kinds of activities do adolescents engage in at home with their parents? Which activities are engaged without them? Which one makes adolescents happier?

These questions are answered using the Experience Sampling Method (Csikszentmihalyi & Larson, 1987; Csikszentmihalyi, Larson, & Prescott, 1977)—a method designed to provide systematic access to subjective experience through daily self-reports of momentary thoughts and feelings in natural settings. The data were obtained from a sample of 165 talented high school students who wore electronic pagers for one week and filled out approximately 2,400 short questionnaires in response to signals received at home.

After describing the group as a whole, the study investigates the differing family types and parental behaviors that correlate with happiness. Previous research (Rathunde, 1988, 1989b) found that teens who perceived their families as integrated and differentiated reported improved subjective experience and performance in a variety of productive settings, including work at school. This chapter focuses on teens' subjective feelings of happiness in a variety of activities at home, in an attempt to illuminate these positive family dynamics in more detail.

COMPLEX FAMILIES AND THE QUALITY OF EXPERIENCE AT HOME

A growing theme in the study of families and adolescent development concerns the importance of finding a balance, between family integration, and individual differentiation (see Grotevant & Cooper, 1983; Olson, Sprenkle, & Russell, 1979). Integration allows family members to maintain relations with others through a shared investment of attention in common goals (traditions, beliefs, values, etc.); differentiation allows an individual to construct a separate self through having the control to invest in personal goals (Csikszentmihalyi & Rochberg-Halton, 1981; Damon, 1983). When a system, whether biological, cognitive, familial, or societal, is both integrated and differentiated, it is commonly referred to as *complex*. When a system has low integration and differentiation its organization can be thought of as *simple*.[1]

Just as an infant's secure attachment allows the emergence of exploration and independence (Ainsworth, Bell, & Stayton, 1971; Matas, Arend, & Sroufe, 1978), a teen-ager's sense of community in a complex family allows autonomous challenges to be embraced with a sense of confidence (the same dynamic, it could be argued, is true for all persons despite their age, see e.g., Maslow, 1968). The paradoxical idea that is implicit in the notion of family complexity—a sense of ''dependence'' for a feeling of ''independence''—also corresponds to the observations of some biologists concerning human development. For instance, they point out that due to the lengthy period in which par-

---

[1]The terms *complex* and *simple* describe a family's internal organization. Complex should be distinguished from ''complicated,'' which commonly implies a deleterious lack of organization; simple should not be taken to imply ''simple-minded.'' In fact, the parents and children of families described as simple in this chapter do not differ in terms of education or intelligence from other family groups. The complexity of a family is directly related to the amount of attention, or psychic energy, that its members invest in each other as individuals (differentiation), and in common family goals (integration). Thus, a simple family organization is one that reduces opportunities for members to invest attention in shared activities or personal projects.

ents must invest time and energy into taking care of their children (a condition of "neoteny" in biological parlance), human infants gain more opportunities to play in and explore their environments, resulting in greater behavioral flexibility and cognitive development (Fagan, 1981). If one extends this reasoning to adolescent development, teens who maintain some reliance on parents can reap the benefits of extended periods of challenge seeking and exploration, which presumably are important for development and growth.[2]

Although the advantages of belonging to a family where attachment and autonomy are both valued is being described with increasing frequency (see also Irwin, 1987), understanding why such a pattern seems to work so well is open to interpretation. The perspective of this chapter is that such a combination of family qualities is associated with children's investment of attentional energy in growth-enhancing activities, and thereby with the quality of their subjective experience.

The emphasis on experience adds a perspective that is missing from other family studies that rely on direct observations of family interaction. The approach here is informed by research on flow experiences, which are characterized by unselfconsciousness, clarity of goals and feedback, high concentration on a specific activity, and a heightened sense of control and intrinsic motivation (Csikszentmihalyi, 1975, 1990). The family model used in this chapter initially arose from asking: "What type of family environment might be associated with optimal experience?" (Rathunde, 1988, 1989a, 1989b). This question can only be answered by collecting experiential reports from children, and interpreting them within a theoretical framework suited for thinking about such experience. Furthermore, because the "functional significance" or subjective meaning of an interpersonal context is the most important dimension to consider when assessing contextual influences on intrinsic motivation (Deci & Ryan, 1987), a priority was also placed on childrens' perceptions of their families.

Thus, a questionnaire was constructed to measure relevant contextual dimensions, that is, those that corresponded to the characteristics of flow described earlier. Four factors resulted—support, harmony, involvement, and freedom (see methods)—that were related to the dynamics of optimal experience in the following way. Flow is generated by the interrelation of high perceived skills and challenges, or the coexistence of potent capacities and opportunities for attentional investment. It was hypothesized that support and harmony (integration) in a family would help children to "save" energy by reducing feelings of defensiveness and confusion, thus making it easier for them to enjoy and get interested in various tasks at hand. Families who, in addition, encouraged their childrens' personal involvement and freedom (differentiation), were expected to facilitate habits of pursuing important and challenging goals. In sum-

---

[2]The assumption here, of course, is that such time for "exploration" is used wisely, and that teens do not take advantage of their parents support by wasting their time.

mary, the context of optimal experience in a family was thought to be similar to Dewey's (1938) conception of the context of interest in a classroom: adults provided conditions that enabled children to get momentarily involved with activities that had a long-term aim.

This chapter focuses on just one dimension of positive subjective experience—happiness—in order to provide a more detailed breakdown of the day-to-day activities of adolescents while at home. In addition, it compares complex and simple families on the Parent-Practices Questionnaire (Devereux, Bronfenbrenner, & Rogers, 1969) which asks specifically about parental behaviors. The Complex Family Questionnaire (CFQ) used in this study relies on adolescents' observations of family routines and expectations, not on adolescent perceptions of specific parental behaviors. Thus, the comparison of these two instruments may provide useful descriptive information on the interactional patterns of these parents and teen-agers.

In addition to the comparison of family measures, two hypotheses are proposed. First, because complex homes are theoretically more conducive to investments of attention in challenging tasks, we expect teens from such families to be happier doing productive activities such as everyday maintenance routines and homework. However, teens' reports of happiness while engaged in widely enjoyed leisure activities (e.g., watching TV) are not expected to differ as the result of family differences.[3] A second hypothesis states that if a complex family provides a more supportive and interesting environment for adolescents, one might expect teens from such families to be happier around other family members, such as their parents, and to have more contact with them over the course of a week.

These hypotheses are stated based on a comparison of complex versus simple families, presumably the two types showing the clearest difference in adolescent quality of experience and productive use of attention. However, data is presented for four family types distinguished by the CFQ—complex (only) integrated (only) differentiated, and simple.

METHOD

Subjects

Subjects are 165 boys and girls from two middle-class suburban high schools in the Chicago area. These students were nominated by their teachers as having superior talent in the fields of math, science, art, music, or athletics, guid-

---

[3]The fact that these teen-agers are recognized as talented adds significance to this first hypothesis. In other words, the choice of whether to spend more time doing productive or leisure activities is a salient one in these students' young lives. Such choices are likely to play an important role in determining which ones in the group will develop their talents.

ed by the criterion that the students were involved with school organizations (math teams, orchestra, athletic teams) or advanced placement classes. Students and parents were contacted by mail with explanations of the study and were told its purpose was to identify factors that help or hinder development. No compensation for participation was offered and half of those contacted consented to participate.

Procedure

In the first year of the study, each student met with a member of the research staff three to four times at a school office. He or she participated in an in-depth interview, and filled out several questionnaires, including the Parent-Practices Questionnaire (Devereux, Bronfenbrenner, & Rogers, 1969). Students were given materials for the Experience Sampling Method (ESM) which uses electronic pagers and a corresponding booklet of self-report forms with both open-ended and scaled items (Csikszentmihalyi & Larson, 1987; Csikszentmihalyi, Larson, & Prescott, 1977). Students carried their pagers for 1 week while being sent 7–9 random signals daily between the hours of 7:00 a.m. and 10:00 p.m. during the week, and 7:00 a.m. and midnight on the weekends.

At the end of the third year of the study additional family information was collected using the Complex Family Questionnaire (CFQ), and other information relevant to teens' development of talent was gathered (e.g., teacher ratings, grades, students' future plans, etc.). Approximately 83%, or 165 out of the original 200 students in the study completed the CFQ; this group constitutes the present sample.

Measures

Complex Family Questionnaire (CFQ). This measure was designed so that teen-agers could assess their day-to-day family routines and shared expectations. The assumption is that such routines and expectations reveal a family's "paradigm," which has a profound effect on members' phenomenology, and can "guide the family to sample certain segments of its world and ignore others" (Reiss, Oliveri, & Curd, 1983, p. 80).

The 24 items used were organized around the factors of support, harmony, involvement, and freedom, aspects of family interaction important for teen's quality of subjective experience (see Rathunde, 1988, 1989a, 1989b). They were presented as questions to be answered on 4-point scales: 1 = definitely no, 2 = usually no, 3 = usually yes, 4 = definitely yes. Items were worded in both positive and negative directions. They were phrased in an "observational" style, addressing the family system as a whole (e.g., "If you are feeling depressed, or are having a problem, do others notice even though you may not say anything about it?'' [support], ''Would you say there was much bickering or arguing in your family? [harmony], ''Are family members serious and intense when engaged with things that are important to them?'' [involvement], ''Is it hard to find privacy, and escape into your ''own world'' at home when you need to?'' [freedom]).

Exploratory factor analysis using varimax rotation and an analysis of internal consistency (Cronbach's alpha) were used to assess the reliability of the measure. These analyses supported the theoretically generated components of complex families. Four factors emerged with eigenvalues greater than 1.0, accounting for 43% of the variance. Four subscales were constructed: support (eight items, α = .78); harmony (five items, α = .72); involvement (seven items, α = .50); and freedom (four items, α = .62). Measures of internal consistency do not yield appropriate indicators of reliability when assessing a small number of items, however, the alphas for support, harmony, and freedom were moderately high and satisfactory, and the alpha for involvement was only slightly lower. The lower ''involvement'' alpha suggests that some of the responses concerning opportunities for intense personal involvement (e.g., questions about political, spiritual, or competitive involvement) were not highly intercorrelated. Nevertheless, these responses still provided pertinent information about basic channels for attentional investment.

Subscales were not constructed for use in a linear analysis, whereby the relative contribution of each scale would be assessed in the sample as a whole; rather, they were used to create a fourfold family typology for comparison (see also Baumrind, 1987; Hinde & Dennis, 1986; Reiss, Oliveri, & Curd, 1983). The assumption here is that keeping the ''family'' as the primary unit of analysis has several advantages in terms of conceptualizing family interaction and stating hypotheses, and presenting and communicating results. The subscales were utilized to construct a family typology in the following way. (a) an integration score (α = .84) was computed for each family by adding the subfactors ''support'' and ''harmony''; (b) a family differentiation score (α = .60) was computed by summing ''involvement'' and ''freedom''; (c) median splits were made on the distributions of the integration and differentiation scores, allowing four groups to be distinguished: complex families (high/high, N = 48); integrated families (high/low, N = 34); differentiated families (low/high, N = 26); and simple families (low/low, N = 56).

The Parent-Practices Questionnaire (PPQ). The PPQ (Devereux, Bronfenbrenner, & Rogers, 1969) contains 30-items (scaled 1–5 ''never'' to ''very often'') which measure 14 dimensions of parental behavior as seen by the child (see Appendix). Several of these dimensions (e.g., nurturance, consistency, instrumental companionship, and encouragement of autonomy) are relevant for the four factors on the CFQ (support, harmony, involvement, and freedom, respectively). For this reason, they are well suited for comparative purposes. The PPQ was completed 2 years prior to filling out the CFQ, thus in addition to providing information on their perceptions of specific parental behaviors, the comparison permits one to assess teens' perceptions of their families over time. The 30-items were answered separately regarding perceptions of mother and father behaviors. For comparison to the CFQ—which assesses perceptions of the entire family system—scores for mother and father were combined, creating one index of, for instance, parental nurturance.

Experience Sampling Method. The ESM gives systematic access to subjective experience in naturalistic settings. Measures of adolescent happiness at home will be obtained using one variable—happy—from the ESM self-report form. "Happy" is a variable based on a 7-point semantic differential, the opposite being "sad." The adolescents indicated how happy they were at 2,400 random moments when the pager signaled them at home, approximately 15 beeps per student (students averaged 35 beeper responses for the entire week). Raw scores for happiness were first converted to z scores based on the groups' average for its 2,400 responses (e.g., a happiness score of 0.0 when, for instance, watching TV, indicates that this activity produces average happiness at home.) Mean z scores for happiness were computed for each family group, in several different activities, and used for comparison.

Percent of Time Doing (Various Activities). Adolescents also responded to the open-ended ESM question: "What were you doing as you were beeped." Answers were originally coded into approximately 230 subcategories of activities (interrater agreement $> 90\%$). This chapter breaks down these activities into 10 categories for describing the overall adolescent pattern. Percentage scores were computed as a ratio of the total number of ESM signals responded to while doing a particular activity, to the total number of signals responded to at home (e.g., If 600 of 2,400 ESM responses were coded as "eating," "percent eating" would equal 25%). Because all ESM signals were sent randomly, and subjects had an equal opportunity to answer them, these percentages are used as estimates of adolescent time usage at home.

RESULTS

Happiness at Home

Table 8.1 summarizes teens' time budgets and mean happiness scores in various activities, both for the overall week at home and for times when they were with their parents. By far the largest percentage of home time use (28%) was spent involved with various media (TV, radio, or print); although these ac-

TABLE 8.1
Percent of Time Spent and Average Happiness in Various Activities at Home
for the Overall Week and Just With Parents

	Overall		With Parents	
Activity	% time	happiness	% time	happiness
Media	27.9	−.03	32.2	.04
Homework	16.7	−.19	9.8	.08
Maintenance	13.0	−.12	7.2	.10
Miscellaneous	11.3	.04	9.9	.27
Housework	6.7	.07	6.6	.01
Eating	6.4	.11	13.1	.05
Games/Hobbies	6.2	.30	4.3	.31
Talking	6.0	.27	13.2	.01
Telephone	4.9	.20	1.5	.45
Socializing	.9	.35	2.1	.31

Note: The number of ESM signals for the overall week = 2,410, with parents = 515.
Happiness scores are z scores (0.0 = average happiness at home).

tivities produced only average happiness (−.03). Next came homework (17%), and despite being talented in at least one subject at school, homework produced significantly less than average happiness at home ($p < .001$). The next largest category—maintenance (13%)—also produced less than average happiness ($p < .05$). When grouped together, what might be termed *home routines:* maintenance (e.g., dressing, washing, etc.), miscellaneous (e.g, puttering around the house, looking for something), housework (cleaning, cooking, washing dishes), and eating accounted for 37% of time spent at home, and produced average to low happiness. Finally, the least often engaged activities produced greater happiness: games/hobbies ($p < .001$), talking ($p < .01$), and chatting on the telephone ($p < .05$). A Spearman rank-order correlation coefficient (rank by time vs. rank by happiness) was computed to assess this reverse trend. Results showed that the activities engaged most often at home produce the least happiness, that is, frequency and happiness were negatively correlated ($r = .93$).

When teens were at home with their parents, they spent approximately half as much time doing homework and maintenance activities, and about twice as much time talking, eating, and socializing. When teens' happiness doing these activities with parents present was compared to the times parents were not around (not represented in Table 8.1), only two significant differences appeared: happiness while talking was significantly higher when parents were not around ($p < .001$), and homework seemed to be more enjoyable with parents present ($p < .05$).

In conclusion, we see that teen-agers report being happier at home in the relatively rare instances when they are engaged in games, hobbies, and active social interaction. They are quite unhappy when involved with activities that should prepare them for productive adult roles (i.e., when they are studying, working, or doing necessary maintenance chores). Eating, housework, and television viewing provide average levels of happiness at home.

FAMILY COMPLEXITY AND PARENTAL PRACTICES[4]

Table 8.2 summarizes the highest and lowest means for complex, integrated, differentiated, and simple families on the 14 dimensions of the PPQ. The descriptive pattern that emerged from this arrangement of high and low means suggested family differences that were consistent with the family typology based on the CFQ. In other words, adolescents who perceived their families as "integrated" (based on the CFQ), 2 years earlier had rated their parents highest on nurturance and indulgence, and the lowest on their use of punishment, rejection, and power. Those in the differentiated group had rated their parents highest on achievement demands, rejection, prescription responsibilities, and the lowest on indulgence. Teens who perceived family complexity had rated their parents highest on instrumental companionship, principled discipline, and consistency, whereas simple families had the lowest means on these dimensions, and the highest means on parental use of physical punishment, deprivation of privileges, and use of power.

Six significant differences ($p < .05$, see Table 8.3) emerged between complex and simple families, five of which (nurturance, consistency & principled discipline, instrumental companionship, and encouragement of autonomy) resembled the main dimensions the CFQ was designed to measure: "support," "harmony," "involvement," and "freedom." Adolescents from simple families also rated their parents higher on the dimension "parental protectiveness," although the title of this factor is somewhat misleading. Protectiveness in this context actually implies a lack of parental trust (e.g., "She worries that I can not take care of myself").

---

[4]We prefer in this chapter to use an analysis of variance across type of family context to summarize the data. It is expected that integration or differentiation may be of greater or lesser consequence in relation to particular dependent variables (i.e., one or the other may produce stronger main effects), but the overall comparison of "families" across the entire set of data is felt to provide a more appropriate level of abstraction for presenting, communicating, and interpreting the findings. However, it is important to demonstrate that both integration and differentiation are important, or that there is sometimes an interaction between them, in order to justify the use of a multidimensional construct (see Carver, 1989). This issue was addressed in prior research (Rathunde, 1989b) which demonstrated positive main effects for family integration, differentiation, and their interaction in various analyses. Thus, it was clear that both components had an impact on teens' experience, and that they sometimes "synergistically" interacted to produce a positive effect. Some of these previous findings are discussed later.

TABLE 8.2

Family Group Comparison on the Parental-Practices Questionnaire
Grouped by High and Low Means

Highest mean on PPQ	Lowest mean on PPQ
1. Complex	
Instrumental companionship	Achievement demands
Principled discipline	Deprivation of privileges
Parental consistency	Protectiveness
	Affective punishment
2. Integrated	
Nurturance	Physical punishment
Indulgence	Expressive rejection
Encouragement of autonomy	Prescription responsibility
	Parental use of power
3. Differentiated	
Achievement demands	Principled discipline
Expressive rejection	Indulgence
Prescription responsibility	
Protectiveness	
Affective punishment	
4. Simple	
Physical punishment	Nurturance
Deprivation of privileges	Instrumental companionship
Parental use of power	Encouragement of autonomy
	Consistency

TABLE 8.3

Family Group Comparison on the Parental Practices Questionnaire

Variable (n)	Complex (46)	Integ. (34)	Differ. (22)	Simple (54)	F	T
Nurturance	22.8	23.0	20.2	18.8	9.4****	4.4****
Instrumental companionship	13.6	13.0	13.0	12.1	1.9	2.3**
Physical punishment	6.9	6.7	7.1	7.3	.8	− 1.1
Acievement demands	5.6	5.7	6.6	6.5	1.7	− 1.8*
Expressive rejection	11.0	10.8	14.2	12.2	6.0****	1.8*
Principled discipline	15.4	15.0	12.8	13.4	4.8***	3.0***
Deprivation privileges	6.7	6.9	7.6	7.9	1.4	− 1.9*
Prescription responsibility	16.7	16.6	16.9	16.7	.1	0
Indulgence	6.0	6.5	5.4	5.7	2.2*	.8
Protectiveness	8.4	9.7	11.7	10.7	5.3***	− 3.3***
Affective punishment	8.8	9.3	11.2	10.1	2.9**	− 2.0*
Use of power	12.3	11.1	12.4	12.5	1.5	− .3
Encourage autonomy	15.8	16.0	14.8	13.6	6.4****	3.4***
Consistency	17.1	16.5	16.3	15.6	2.9**	2.9***

Note: Contrasts (*t*-values) compare the complex and simple groups. For these analyses, reported p-levels are one-talied.

*p < .10; **p < .05; ***p < .01; ****p < .001.

Happiness and Family Context

To facilitate family group comparisons, the 10 major activities in the home were further compressed into four categories: home routines (maintenance + miscellaneous + housework + eating), leisure (media + games/hobbies), productive (98% of which is homework), and interaction (talking, telephone, and socializing). Data are summarize for all four family types, with a priori comparisons of complex and simple families.

A 4 X 4 analysis of variance was performed on happiness scores, category of activity X family type. Main effects on overall happiness for category of activity [$F(3,2380)$ = 11.44, p < .001] and family type, $F(3,2380)$ = 11.55, p < .001] were found as expected; there was no interaction (see Fig. 8.1).

One-way ANOVAs were also performed on each activity separately, two of which—home routines (p < .001) and productive work (p < .001)—reached significance. Complex families showed the highest overall happiness at home, especially in family routines and productive work. In both of these contexts, a priori contrasts between complex and simple families reached significance (p < .01). However, the four groups reported similar amounts of happiness in leisure activities (mainly television viewing), which we expected adolescents to enjoy regardless of family context. Neither did the groups differ on happiness in interaction, presumably for the same reason. Teen-agers from differentiated families reported the lowest happiness in all four contexts, especially in productive activities like doing homework.[5]

Finally, it was expected that the presence of parents would be more damaging to teens' happiness in simple, rather than complex families, and those in the latter group would thus have more parental contact. To carry out the first part of this analysis, we compared the average happiness scores of teenagers from these two groups, both with and without parents, while doing the same 10 activities. Results showed that for teens from complex homes, the presence of parents improved happiness in 7 out of 10 activities compared (the exceptions being socializing, playing games, and doing miscellaneous activities). Children in this group, for instance, were happier eating with their parents than eating alone or with siblings. In contrast, when parents were around their children in simple families, happiness was lower in 7 of 10 activities (the exceptions were homework, maintenance, and media). A Chi-square test on these

---

[5]To assess separate effects for integration, differentiation, and their interaction, a 2 X 2 ANOVA (high/low integration by high/low differentiation) was also performed on the ESM reports of happiness in routine and productive activities. Family integration produced a significant main effect in both contexts and differentiation did not, however, there were significant interactions for each. The interaction is evident in two areas: (a) the presence of differentiation without integration is particularly deleterious to adolescent happiness doing homework, and (b) the copresence of these two dimensions is particularly beneficial to teens' happiness while doing home routines (see Fig. 8.1).

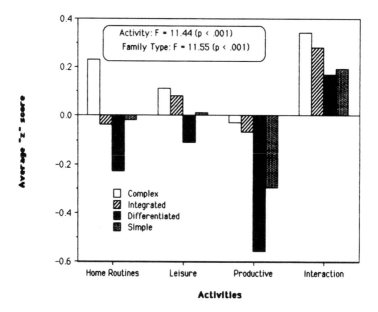

FIG. 8.1.   Mean happiness by family type in various activities.

proportions (i.e., complex/simple X percent higher happiness/lower happiness with parents) was significant (X^2 = 3.2, $df = 1$, p < .05, one-tailed).

Teens from complex homes also had the most contact with parents (i.e., at least one parent was present approximately 24% of the time when these teenagers responded to the beeper at home, or 165 out of 675 beeper responses); the corresponding figure in simple families was the lowest of the four groups— 19%. A Chi-square test on these proportions (complex/simple X percentage with/percentage without parents) also showed a significant difference (X^2 = 5.29, $df = 1$, $p = .01$, one-tailed). Although this time difference appears small, if one estimates that teens spend about 7 waking hours a day at home (approximately 50 hours per week), and if the random sampling of the beeper accurately reflects parental contact, this means that teens from complex homes would have 2 to 3 hours more contact with their parents per week.

DISCUSSION

The overall findings of the study supports initial expectations: (a) some convergent evidence supporting the family typology was provided by the PPQ; (b) happiness in home routines and homework was highest for children in complex families, but not in leisure; and (c) teens from such families had more contact with their parents over the course of the week, and their presence generally enhanced their childrens' happiness.

Adolescent responses on the PPQ were consistent with their membership in complex, integrated, differentiated, and simple family types. In addition to the pattern that emerged for the 14 overall parental behaviors, the particular dimensions that reached significance when comparing complex and simple families were precisely the ones that most resembled the four subfactors on the CFQ. For instance, teen-agers from complex homes reported more familial support on the CFQ, or being at ease and finding a sense of togetherness at home. Two years earlier on the PPQ, these same adolescents reported their parents were more "nurturant": comforting when there was a problem, and available to talk. Their higher ratings of harmony on the CFQ suggested an expectation for family life to have little conflict and to be calm, orderly, consistent, and clear. The complex group earlier affirmed parental "consistency" on the PPQ (e.g., "When I do something s/he doesn't like, I know exactly what to expect from him/her"), and "principled discipline" (e.g., "When she wants me to do something, she explains why"). Involvement on the CFQ meant that teen-agers in the complex group perceived family members as intense and active in various ways. Their earlier PPQ endorsement of "instrumental companionship" suggested that parents had acted as important resources of information and instruction for them. Finally, higher responses on the CFQ dimension of freedom indicated teens' expectations for a complex home to provide quiet and privacy to work, and the opportunity to chose intrinsically motivating activities without constant interruption. Two years earlier these same teenagers reported their parents' "encouragement of autonomy": "S/he lets me make my own plans. . ." and ". . . try new things on my own."

Other findings suggest the importance of the copresence of integration and differentiation at home, and how the existence of one or the other can change the way teenagers interpret the actions of parents. For instance, teens in differentiated families more often view parental discipline as based on the use of guilt (affective punishment) and nagging (expressive rejection), whereas discipline is perceived as firmness and fairness (consistency and principled discipline) in a complex family. The missing component that brings about this change of interpretation is the presence of family integration in complex homes (i.e., both the differentiated and the complex groups are high on the CFQ dimension of "differentiation," but the latter group is also high on the dimension of "integration"). The synchronous presence of integration allows a similar message—"be responsible, independent, and mature"—to be filtered through a context that is also supportive and reliable. Perhaps this is why the young members of differentiated and simple family groups found the least happiness in home routines, whereas those in complex families clearly found the most happiness. It seems reasonable that the consistency, clear rules and standards, as well as the warmth and cooperation in complex families have made the everyday routines both more efficient and enjoyable (i.e., one knows what one has to do, has done it many times before, and others pitch in).

Attitudes toward school performance also take on different connotations in a context that includes family integration. For instance, parents in differentiated families are seen by their children as putting extrinsic pressure on them to achieve (i.e., achievement demands). Parents in complex families are, in contrast, seen as helpful teachers (instrumental companionship). Ironically, the differentiated groups' happiness while doing homework was the lowest mood score across all activities and groups, whereas teen-agers in complex families— with the lowest achievement demands—reported the highest happiness when doing homework. In general, a differentiated organization, not a simple one, produced the lowest happiness in all four major activity contexts. It seems that this type of family system, which sets high standards and expectations for the individual child, but does not provide appropriate emotional supports, has the most aversive effect on a adolescents' moods at home.

Integrated families, on the other hand, seem to have parents who make few demands, and who do not stress individual assertion. The integrated group had the highest "parental indulgence," and the lowest "prescription of responsibilities." This finding corresponds to previous research, which found that of the four family types, teens from complex homes spent the most time doing productive activities, whereas those from integrated families spent the most time involved in leisure pursuits (e.g., they invested 8% more time in leisure than the other groups, when just looking at the proportion of time they spent with their parents; Rathunde, 1989b).

This pattern of results suggests that one of the main advantages of complex families, from the perspective of the child's development, is that they offer a context where productive activities like homework and routine home maintenance can be experienced as relatively happy. These important activities typically produce sadness in teen-agers, but in complex families even these challenging tasks are experienced with moderate happiness. If productive activities are experienced as subjectively rewarding, one would expect that they will be repeated in the future. Thus children from complex families are more likely to engage in demanding tasks, and therefore grow more readily into productive roles than children from differentiated and simple families.

Some confirmation of these positive developmental expectations has been found (see Rathunde, 1989b). For instance, consistent with the findings reported here for productive work at home, teens from complex families reported a superior quality of experience in a variety of productive contexts at school. They reported being more happy, alert, and concentrated in their talent areas (math, science, music, athletics, and art), and in their regular classes and studies. In addition, while doing these activities they were more often in a state of flow. They performed better at school—as indicated by their teachers' grades and ratings—although not possessing superior ability or intelligence (PSAT scores). Teachers in the students' particular talent areas rated them as more open to new and difficult challenges which utilized their full potential, able to concentrate and pay attention with persistence, and more likely to find the intensity of this process enjoyable. The single item that most distinguished the complex group on the teachers' ratings was their "quality of attention." Teens from complex families had higher teacher ratings in four of the five talent areas, the exception being "athletics" where they scored just below the differentiated group.

The Question of Response Bias

The data suggests that differences between family groups cannot be explained simply as biases in the adolescents' perceptions. Teen-agers reported being equally happy when involved in leisure or interaction, regardless of differences between their families. If higher reports of happiness were simply the result of a positive style of responding to the ESM, differences would be evident across all contexts. Rather, it is plausible that leisure is enjoyed by most teen-agers, whereas home routines and homework generate more variance in their happiness. Different mood reactions in the presence or absence of parents also argues against the response bias explanation. In other words, teens' moods in complex families improved in 7 of 10 activities with parents present, whereas the opposite pattern occurred in simple families. This suggests that whatever their response styles, the former group had a more positive reaction to parents, with whom they also had more contact with over the week of experience sampling.

Finally, questionnaires filled out by the parents of these two family types paralleled their childrens' perceptions of differences concerning family support and harmony, and personal involvement and freedom (Rathunde, 1989b). For instance, parents in complex versus simple families reported higher rewards from helping their child mature, less disagreement with their spouse, more life satisfaction, and they placed a greater emphasis on the importance of intrinsic versus extrinsic rewards for their child's future career. When teacher responses are also taken into account, two independent sources of information are seen as corroborating important aspects of the teen-ager's reports, thus making improbable the validity of a bias explanation of the results.

GENERAL ISSUES AND CONCLUSIONS

Ideas about the benefits of a balanced family system are, of course, not new. Similar suggestions for a combination of family supports and demands, connection and separation, have convincingly been argued by several others (Baumrind, 1987; Grotevant & Cooper, 1983; Maccoby & Martin, 1983). What the present approach emphasizes, however, is recognizing the important roles that

attention and positive subjective experience play in making these contexts effective. When adopting this more phenomenological or moment-to-moment
perspective, a greater emphasis is placed on the many small experiential "building blocks" that over time accumulate toward positive outcomes. The perspective in the present chapter is that a complex family creates a prolonged supportive environment where children are more likely to invest time and energy
in growth-producing activities, and thereby experience positive subjective rewards in the process.

Children do not need parental support and stimulation to enjoy peer interaction, watching television, or playing a game. They will be happy in these
activities regardless of family context. But they do need such home qualities
in order to find enjoyment in activities that require additional effort, such as
studying or helping out around the house. Because it is precisely these activities one must learn to enjoy if one is to lead a productive and happy adult life,
an important aspect of a complex family is its ability to promote happiness
in children when engaged in challenging tasks. Because the day to day routine
in such families does not drain childrens' energy in insecurity, confusion, re-
bellion against lack of autonomous opportunities, and so on, and because it
encourages children to make choices and get involved, a pattern of engaging
challenging and growth-oriented tasks develops more easily.

To create more complex homes, parents can be less vigilant about pressing
their children to achieve, and pay more attention to helping them discover the
ongoing rewards of pursuing goals. In other words, pressuring children may
be successful in communicating the need for making plans and working dili-
gently, but it may destroy the relaxed and supportive context that best suits
such work. Parents (and teachers) can facilitate the day to day process by noticing how a child is feeling, especially when involved with tasks that test the limits
of their attentional control. Thus, an initial step in creating complex homes
is recognizing when optimal experience is or is not occurring, and when a child
is feeling bored, anxious, or apathetic. Only then can a parent take further
steps or exercise other skills that can help the child to stay on task.

This seems a simple enough prerequisite, but upon reflection it is a rare
and difficult practice. Seldom does the busy teacher or parent have the time
to invest in becoming such a skilled observer. Nevertheless, one can simply
ask a child how they are feeling, and much can be learned by noticing physical
cues such as facial expressions, posture, fidgetiness, and so on. Homes that
are integrated make family members' thoughts and feelings more transparent
to one another, thus improving communication of this kind. Offering the right
suggestion, providing some needed distraction or information, or simply giving a timely hug that benefits the child's momentary state of mind, ultimately
depends on such closeness and family integration.

Just as important is knowing what not to say, and when not to interfere
with a child's actions and decisions. Family differentiation provides each fam-

ily member some opportunities to select and involve themselves with interesting challenges, to set goals, and to plan and pace actions designed to achieve them. When such opportunities are denied, a child is less likely to develop selective habits, even if the home is warm and loving. Perhaps the best way parents can express the values of differentiation is to model self-determined involvement by pursuing goals they deem important. Another way is to invite dialogue that challenges each family member to defend and support their point of view. Such talks may help a child to discover ways they are unique from other family members, and thereby increase their awareness of further opportunities to distinguish themselves.

An environment where a child feels comfortable and secure, and where he or she can exercise some selective control, provides flexible conditions for education and development. To create such an environment can also be an enjoyable challenge in its own right, one that can make parenting more rewarding.

DIRECTIONS FOR FUTURE RESEARCH

This chapter focused on young people who had demonstrated superior intellectual, physical, or artistic talents, and a special emphasis was placed on the relationship between family context and the productive use of attention. The results of the study, however, need not be confined to talented adolescents. In other words, there is no necessary assumption of talent in order for a complex family system to enhance childrens' experience and development. Thus, the results here should be applicable to the general population of teen-agers (and presumably younger children as well). It is even possible that complex families may show a stronger association with positive adolescent experience and performance in a normal population of teen-agers and parents, due to the greater variability of the sample (i.e., the talented sample may have a restricted range of "good" students and "good" parenting). These are questions for future research.

Follow-up studies that are more specific in their focus, and which utilize additional "experience-near" methodologies besides the ESM (e.g., more interviews and direct observations of family interactions), would also be helpful in fleshing out a more detailed picture of everyday life in complex families. In particular, more specific information is needed on how the perceptions of integration and differentiation develop in a family.

Two broad assumptions that inform this approach could prove fruitful for subsequent research on the family. One is that by examining the flow of attention in optimal experiences, much can be learned about structuring social contexts so as to facilitate productive and enjoyable uses of attention. In other words, that something important can be learned about family life by exploring, for instance, the subjective rewards of an expert musician playing a challenging piece. Although at first glance this seems unlikely, further scrutiny suggests that despite vast differences in the size and content of "domains" or activities (e.g., music, family life, or cultural life) they are all processed through a consciousness that has certain parameters for optimal functioning. When the domains are structured such that the capacity of an individual's attention is conserved—through actions that are highly practiced and automatic, and where the domain continually affords new opportunities that demand the fruits of such practice and more, the full utilization of attention allows optimal subjective rewards to emerge.

A second, and perhaps more central assumption, is that much can be learned by seeking out the best examples of human functioning. This was the inspiration behind Maslow's (1968) work on peak experiences that he drew from Aristotle: "It is the things which are valuable and pleasant to a good man that are really valuable and pleasant." The same logic can be applied to family systems, and other social or cultural systems—even though it is seldom so applied in contemporary thought. One reason, perhaps, is because researchers' attempts to guard against their implicit prejudices have made them forego any conceptions of optimal functioning. This often prudent fear, however, can work against the desired ideal of learning to appreciate the complexity of various systems in their own light; it is precisely the study of optimally functioning individuals and systems that can provide the most instructive lessons on the appreciation of individual variation, and of group unity.

ACKNOWLEDGMENT

This research was supported by a grant from the Spencer Foundation.

REFERENCES

Ainsworth, M. D. S., Bell, S. M., & Stayton, D. J. (1971). Individual differences in strange-situation behavior of 1-year-olds. In H. R. Schaffer (Ed.), *The origins of human social relations*. London: Academic Press.

Amabile, T. M. (1983). *The social psychology of creativity*. New York: Springer-Verlag.

Baumrind, D. (1987). A developmental perspective on adolescent risk taking behavior in contemporary America. In C. E. Irwin (Ed.), *Adolescent social behavior and health* (pp. 93–125). San Francisco: Jossey-Bass.

Carver, C. (1989). How should multifaceted personality constructs be tested? *Journal of Personality and Social Psychology, 56*, 577–85.

Csikszentmihalyi, M. (1975). *Beyond boredom and anxiety*. San Francisco: Jossey-Bass.

Csikszentmihalyi, M. (1990). *Flow: The psychology of optimal experience*. New York: Harper and Row.

Csikszentmihalyi, M., & Larson, R. (1987). Validity and reliability of the experience-sampling method. *Journal of Nervous and Mental Disease, 175*, 526–536.

Csikszentmihalyi, M., Larson, R., & Prescott, S. (1977). The ecology of adolescent activity and experience. *Journal of Youth and Adolescence, 6,* 281–294.

Csikszentmihalyi, M., & Rochberg-Halton, E. (1981). *The meaning of things: Domestic symbols and the self.* New York: Cambridge University Press.

Csikszentmihalyi, M., & Selega Csikszentmihalyi, I. (Eds.). (1988). *Optimal experience: Psychological studies of flow in consciousness.* New York: Cambridge University Press.

Damon, W. (1983). *Social and personality development.* New York: W. W. Norton.

deCharms, R. (1976). *Enhancing motivation: Change in the classroom.* New York: Irvington.

Deci, E. L., & Ryan, R. M. (1985). *Intrinsic motivation and self-determination in human behavior.* New York: Plenum.

Deci, E. L., & Ryan, R. M. (1987). The support of autonomy and the control of behavior. *Journal of Personality and Social Psychology, 53,* 1024–1037.

Devereux, E., Bronfenbrenner, U., & Rogers, R. (1969, May). Child-rearing in England and the United States: A cross-national comparison. *Journal of Marriage and Family,* 257–270.

Dewey, J. (1913). *Interest and effort in education.* Cambridge: The Riverside Press.

Dewey, J. (1938). *Education and Experience.* New York: Macmillan.

Fagen, R. (1981). *Animal play behavior.* New York: Oxford University Press.

Groos, K. (1898). *The play of animals.* (E. L. Baldwin, Trans.). New York: Appleton.

Grotevant, H. D., & Cooper, C. R. (Eds.). (1983). *Adolescent development in the family.* San Francisco: Jossey-Bass.

Harter, S. (1978). Pleasure derived from optimal challenge and the effects of extrinsic rewards on children's difficulty level choices. *Child Development, 49,* 788–799.

Hinde, R. A., & Dennis, A. (1986). Categorizing individuals: An alternative to linear analysis. *International Journal of Behavioral Development, 9,* 105–119.

Irwin, C. E. (Ed.). (1987). *Adolescent social behavior and health.* San Francisco: Jossey-Bass.

Maccoby, E. E., & Martin, J. A. (1983). Socialization in the context of the family: Parent–child interaction. In E. M. Heatherington (Ed.), *Handbook of child psychology: Vol. 4. Socialization, personality, and social development* (pp. 1–101). New York: Wiley.

Maslow, A. H. (1968). *Toward a psychology of being.* New York: D. Van Nostrand.

Matas, L., Arend, R. A., & Sroufe, L. A. (1978). Continuity of adaption in the second year: The relationship between quality of attachment and later competence *Child Development, 49,* 547–556.

Olson, D., Sprenkle, D., & Russell, C. (1979). Circumplex model of marital and family systems: I. Cohesion and adaptability dimensions, family types, and clinical applications. *Family Process, 18,* 3–28.

Rathunde, K. (1988). Family context and optimal experience. In M. Csikszentmihalyi & I. Selega Csikszentmihalyi (Eds.), *Optimal experience: Psychological studies of flow in consciousness* (pp. 342–363). Cambridge: Cambridge University Press.

Rathunde, K. (1989a). The context of optimal experience: An exploratory model of the family. *New Ideas in Psychology, 7,* 91–97.

Rathunde, K. (1989b). *Family context and optimal experience in the development of talent.* Unpublished doctoral dissertation, University of Chicago, Chicago, IL.

Reiss, D., Oliveri, M. E., & Curd, K. (1983). Family Paradigm and adolescent social behavior. In H. D. Grotevant & C. R. Cooper (Eds.), *Adolescent development in the family* (pp. 77–92). San Francisco: Jossey-Bass.

White, R. W. (1959). Motivation reconsidered: The concept of competence. *Psychological Review, 66,* 297–333.

Appendix: Parent-Practices Questionnaire
(from Devereux, Bronfenbrenner, & Rogers, 1969)

A. Nurturance
   1. She comforts and helps me when I have trouble.
   2. She makes me feel I can talk with her about everything.
   3. She makes me feel she is there when I need her.

B. Physical punishment
   4. She slaps me.
   5. She physically punishes me.
   6. She says she will physically punish me if I don't behave better.

C. Achievement demands
   7. She keeps after me to do better than other children.

D. Instrumental companionship
   8. She helps me with homework or lessons, if there is something I don't
       understand.
   9. She teaches me things I want to learn.

E. Expressive rejection
   10. She nags at me.
   11. She scolds me.

F. Principled discipline
   12. When she punishes me, she explains why.
   13. When she wants me to do something, she explains why.

G. Deprivation of privileges
   14. She punishes me by not allowing me to be with my friends.
   15. She punishes me by not letting me use my favorite things.

H. Prescription of responsibilities
   16. She expects me to keep my things in good order.
   17. She expects me to help around the house or yard.

I. Indulgence
   18. She lets me off lightly when I do something wrong.
   19. She cannot bring herself to punish me.

J. Protectiveness
   20. She worries that I cannot take care of myself.
   21. She won't let me go places because something might happen to me.

K. Affective punishment
   22. When I do something she doesn't like, she acts hurt and disappointed.
   23. She punishes me by trying to make me feel guilty or ashamed.

L. Power
   24. She wants to know exactly where I am going when I go out.
   25. She expects me to tell her exactly how I spend my pocket money.

M. Encouragement of autonomy
   26. She encourages to try new things on my own.
   27. She lets me make my own plans about things I want to do even though I
       might make a few mistakes.

N. Consistency
   28. I know what she expects of me and how she wants me to behave.
   29. When I do something she doesn't like, I know exactly what to expect
       from her.

Relationships With Children and Distress in the Elderly

Karl Pillemer
Cornell University
J. Jill Suitor
Louisiana State University

For at least three decades, the importance of kin in the lives of the elderly has been of central interest to gerontologists. After a period in which it was widely believed that families abandoned elderly relatives, social scientists convincingly demonstrated that children and parents continue to interact and depend on one another for both emotional and instrumental support throughout the life course (cf. Bengtson & Robertson, 1985; Brody, Johnsen, Fulcomer, & Lang, 1984; Cicirelli, 1983; Johnson Bursk, 1977; Nydegger, 1983; Shanas, 1979; Troll, Miller, & Atchley, 1979).

Of the numerous themes in the growing literature on relationships between elderly parents and adult children, one seems particularly predominant. This is the role of elderly parents as sources of stress and burden for their adult offspring. Numerous theoretical, empirical, and popular works have identified parental needs for physical and emotional support and resulting dependency as major causes of psychological distress for adult children. As we discuss later, this view has become such a dominant paradigm in the field that it has tended to obscure other important research questions (cf. Barnett, Kibria, Baruch, & Pleck, in press). In particular, it has led researchers to neglect the study of the effects of adult children's problems on elderly parents' well-being.

In the present chapter, we hold that such a unidirectional approach is overly limited. We argue instead that the negative influence of adult children on elderly parents' psychological well-being must be considered. We provide evidence from several bodies of research that suggests that problems in the lives of children are a potentially important cause of psychological distress for elderly parents. Next, we present data from a random sample survey of elderly persons in Boston that support this claim. We conclude with a proposed agenda for future research on this topic.

PITY THE POOR CHILD: DOMINANCE
OF THE CAREGIVING PERSPECTIVE

Steinberg (1988) has noted that in the study of adolescence, early research presumed the unidirectional influence of parents on children. Such a perspective long dominated research on infancy and childhood, as well (Bell, 1979). In the past decade, however, researchers have moved in the direction of a more bi-directional view of family influence (Steinberg, 1988) in studying the early stages of the family life cycle.

It is therefore curious to note that the unidirectional influence of parents on children is still widely presumed in family gerontology. The predominant view holds that parents become old, frail, and demanding. These characteristics in turn lead to inequities in the relationship that stress and depress the child.

The literature on family caregiving to older people can be taken as evidence of this bias (for a review, see Silliman & Sternberg, 1988). In the past decade, several hundred articles have been published on the difficulties experienced by family caregivers. Many of these works focus on adult children's feelings of helplessness, apprehension, social alienation, and financial stress (cf. Pett et al., 1988). During the same period, our extensive literature review uncovered only one article specifically devoted to exploring the impact of problems or difficulties in *children's* lives on elderly parents (Greenberg & Becker, 1988). It has, quite simply, been assumed that in later life, parents create more trouble for their children than the reverse.

This bias is evident in many books and articles that purport to cover parent–child relationships in later life more generally. For example, Blenkner's (1965) article "Social Work and Family Relationships in Later Life" dealt only with the child's experience. The child, through a process Blenkner terms *filial maturity,* must come to accept being depended on by parents. Similarly, Brody's (1982) "They Can't Do It All: Aging Daughters with Aged Mothers" cites only the strains experienced by middle-aged daughters when mothers become dependent, including practical problems of managing competing demands on their time and energy, as well as emotional stress, guilt, and feelings of inadequacy. Many other articles identify parental demands on adult children as the key dynamic of families in later life (cf. Cicirelli, 1983; Robinson & Thurner, 1979; Shanas, 1979).

Introductory textbooks are particularly likely to focus only on parents' effects on children's well-being. For example, Cox (1984), in his chapter on "Family Patterns in Later Life" examined "the adjustments and family patterns that emerge following such events as the last child leaving home, the growing dependence of aging parents, the retirement of the husband, and the withdrawal of the family from previous levels of social involvement'' (p. 157). In Schaie and Willis' (1986) widely used *Adult Development and Aging,* intergenerational relations are discussed primarily in terms of parents' impact on adult children. Thus, the chapter on ''Adult Children and Their Elderly Parents'' is framed around parental dependency, role reversal, parents moving in with children because of illness, and so forth.

Sussman's (1985) formulation of parent–child relations across the life-span states the predominant view succinctly. He proposes the existence of a cyclical shift in interaction with parents. First, parents provide a substantial amount of assistance to their offspring, even into the children's early married life. Then, as children become more independent—and possibly move away—a break occurs in the intergenerational relationship. Finally, as elderly parents begin to decline in health, they come to depend on their children, leading to problems of stress and diminished well-being of their offspring.

Our point here is not that these writers are in some way incorrect or misguided. However, just as others have argued regarding relationships between parents and younger children, we assert that this view is too narrow. It does not take into account, nor is it able to explain, relationships in which parents are in good health—a state that characterizes a substantial proportion of the aged population. It also does fails to recognize that adult children are likely to affect their *parents*. As we discuss later, considerable evidence exists that suggests that this effect may be decidedly negative. In particular, adult children may suffer from a variety of mental and physical problems that result in psychological distress for their parents.

WHY SHOULD WE STUDY THE EFFECTS
OF CHILDREN'S PROBLEMS ON ELDERY PARENTS?

Direct investigations of the effects of children's problems on elderly parents are scarce indeed. In fact, researchers on the psychological well-being of the elderly have not included variables related to parent–child interaction. However, there is substantial evidence from research on related areas that a relationship between the two areas exists; so much so that the neglect of this issue in the gerontological literature is somewhat remarkable. In this section, we briefly discuss the related research on the effects of children's problems on parents at other stages of the family life cycle. Our goal is to demonstrate that parents' experience of later life can better be understood by studying problems in their children's lives, and examining the impact of these problems on the parent–child relationship.

Adolescents and their Parents

Numerous researchers have investigated ways in which the transformations brought about by adolescence affect parents (cf. Silverberg & Steinberg, 1987). In particular, increasing demands for autonomy by adolescent children, and the parent–child conflict that frequently results, may act as a stressor for parents. Silverberg and Steinberg's (1987) research, for example, indicated that when children became more emotionally autonomous, fathers reported more midlife identity concerns, as well as lower life satisfaction. Mothers were adversely affected by the degree of conflict they experienced with their adolescent offspring. Steinberg (1987) and others (cf. Hill et al., 1985) have also demonstrated that the onset of puberty can in certain circumstances result in increased conflict among all family members.

To be sure, elderly parents' relationships with adult children cannot be directly equated with parent–adolescent relationships. However, as Hess and Waring (1978) have noted, it is not necessarily the case that the conflicts of adolescence are resolved when children become adults. Although in some cases value congruence and trust come to characterize intergenerational relations, this is not necessarily the case: "Struggles for control, patterns of blaming, and disappointments about achievement . . . may linger to undermine the possibility of a comfortable relationship between parents and children in the later years" (p. 251).

The Effects of Disabled and Emotionally Disturbed Children

Substantial research has also been conducted on parents of children with physical and mental disorders. Mash and Johnson (1983) summed up the existing research on this issue as follows: "Parenting itself can be a generally stressful event . . . and the manifestation of major and persistent child problems may be the most significant dimension of stress across a range of unpleasant parental effects" (p. 86). For example, mothers of children with such diverse conditions as hyperactivity, cerebral palsy, epilepsy, and developmental delay have interactions with children that are more stressful and less rewarding than mothers of healthy children (Mash & Johnson, 1983).

Parental difficulties may begin with the birth of the disabled child. Fortier and Wanlass (1984) provided evidence that the initial diagnosis of the disability has a seriously negative impact on the family. Similarly, Olshansky (1962) and Wikler et al. (1981) identified feelings of chronic grief and mourning in families of retarded children. As the child grows older, it is clear that parents continue to be subject to severe stress (Beckman-Bell, 1981; Byrne & Cunningham, 1985; Holroyd & McArthur, 1976; Kazak & Marvin, 1984; McKinney & Peterson, 1987; Schilling et al., 1985; Slater & Wikler, 1986; Sherman &

Cocozza, 1984; Spink, 1976; Tavormina et al., 1981; Waisbren, 1980). It is very plausible that adult children's mental and physical difficulties would affect older parents' well-being in broadly similar ways.

Mentally Ill Young Adults

The rapid deinstitutionalization of mental patients has led to increased academic attention to the problems of families with mentally ill members. In a recent review article, Gubman and Tessler (1987) noted that a variety of behaviors exhibited by the mentally ill can cause distress for families. These behaviors include argumentativeness, withdrawal, bizarre behavior, verbal abuse, and threatened or actual harm to others or themselves. In coping with such behavior problems, families become burdened by disturbed household routines, financial strain, missed work, and reductions in social activities, leisure pursuits, and interaction with other family members.

The work of Cook (1988; Cook & Cohler, 1986) provided evidence that parents are extremely vulnerable to these types of stress. Parents with adult schizophrenic children experienced feelings of hopelessness and despair, concern for the child's future, and anger at disruptive behavior. Mothers in particular experienced high levels of anxiety, depression, and emotional drain. Again, it is likely that troublesome behavior by the child would continue to negatively affect parents throughout the life cycle.

Launching Young Adult Children

Studies of the effects of the departure of children from the parental home *(launching)* also indirectly support the assertion that children may have negative effects on parents' psychological well-being. Although the research is not entirely unequivocal, in general it seems clear that parents have higher levels of psychological distress than non-parents (McLanahan & Adams, 1987). This is evident in the fact that individuals whose children have reached adulthood and left the parental home have been found to have higher levels of psychological well-being than do those whose children remain in the home (cf. Atchley, 1987; George, 1980; Glenn & McLanahan, 1981; Lowenthal et al., 1975; Radloff, 1980).

We believe that the effects of launching would appear to be even greater if children's physical and psychological problems had been taken into account. The relatively small differences in well-being between persons whose children do or do not remain in the home may be due to the pooling of children with and without problems. Although the departure of children with no major problems may have little or mildly negative effect on parents' well-being, the departure of children with severe problems is likely to have major positive effects.

Domestic Violence Against the Elderly

The literature on domestic violence provides direct evidence that adult children's problems affect elderly parents' lives detrimentally. Early speculation about family abuse of the elderly centered around the notion that such maltreatment resulted from the strains of caregiving. It was held that as parents become elderly, frail, and dependent, they cause stress for their otherwise well-meaning caregivers, who then react with violence (cf. Steinmetz, 1988). This view, however, has been largely discredited by recent research demonstrating that physical violence and chronic verbal aggression against the elderly result instead from the deviance and dependency of the abuser. A number of studies have shown that adult children who abuse their elderly parents are likely to suffer from a range of mental and physical problems, and to be heavily dependent on the victim (Anetzberger, 1987; Bristowe & Collins, 1989; Pillemer, 1985; Wolf & Pillemer, 1989). They are also more likely to be substance abusers, and to have a history of psychiatric hospitalization and arrest. Thus, the recent elder abuse literature provides a graphic demonstration of the impact problems in children's lives can have on elderly parents.

In summary, these bodies of research demonstrate that problems experienced by children are strongly related to parental distress. With the exception of the elder abuse literature, the studies reviewed all dealt with younger populations. It is important to discuss in more detail why we anticipate that children's problems will have a similarly strong impact on parental well-being in later life. In particular, some observers have noted that ties between the generations are now more voluntaristic than in the past. That is, elderly parents' relationships with grown children are characterized by choice, rather than by an obligation to remain together, as is the case with minor children (cf. Hess & Waring, 1978; Suitor & Pillemer, 1988). It might therefore seem that children's problems would have only a relatively slight effect on parents. There are several grounds, however, on which to assert that troubled adult children will affect aged parents negatively.

First, and most obvious, troubled children's concrete behaviors may bring about adverse reactions on the part of parents. In studies of younger children, such aversive behaviors include uncontrollability, defiance, anger, and negativity. Such threatening behaviors by children with emotional difficulties or substance abuse problems would be likely to cause as much, if not more distress to elderly parents.

Second, morale may suffer if adult children's problems require parents to continue to provide them with care and support. Such continued assistance is associated with increased psychological distress among the elderly (cf. Cohler & Grunebaum, 1981; Hess & Waring, 1978; Kerchoff, 1966; Mutran & Reitzes, 1984; Rosow, 1967). Thus, to the extent that problems experienced by children lead to their increased dependency, the psychological well-being of their parents would be expected to suffer.

Third, the problems experienced by children may prevent them from providing expected assistance to elderly parents. For example, Cicirelli (1983) found that children who had been divorced provided less help to elderly parents. It may be that parents who have high filial responsibility expectations (Seelbach & Sauer, 1977) are resentful or disappointed when these cannot be fulfilled.

Finally, parents frequently identify strongly with their children, and view their accomplishments and difficulties as signs of their own success or failure. There is ample evidence from the clinical literature (particularly that inspired by a psychoanalytic perspective) that parents remain heavily invested in their children's lives. Benedek (1959) argued that parents participate vicariously in their children's lives, using the latter as ways of working out solutions to important issues throughout the life course (see also Farrell & Rosenberg, 1981; Grunes, 1977).

Social scientists have also noted that children remain important to parents over the life cycle (cf. Aldous, 1978; Johnson & Bursk, 1977; Litwak, 1960; Moss, Moss, & Moles, 1985; Rosow, 1970). Bengtson's concept of the "developmental stake" (Bengtson & Kuypers, 1971) is relevant here. Bengtson and other researchers have found that elderly parents tend to report greater attachment and communication with their offspring than do the adult children themselves. The elderly also focus on similarities between them and their adult children, and to emphasize intergenerational continuities. This stake in their offspring might lead to discomfort about problems in children's lives.

Evidence for this point comes from recent studies of "off-time" transitions on the part of children. Hagestad (1986) found that mothers of adult children tend to have strong developmental expectations for children (see also Greene & Boxer, 1982). They form plans for their children, and assume that these will be fulfilled in the long run. They hope that their children will "grow up, establish themselves as functioning adults, and become important supports" (p. 685). Her interviews revealed that mothers derived a personal sense of accomplishment from knowing that their children had mastered life tasks, and done so in the normal sequence. Mothers of children who were not "on schedule" in becoming independent adults experienced strain and a sense of personal failure. To some extent, they felt that they could not carry on with their own lives until their children progressed successfully.

Similarly, Aldous (1978) noted that children who have not successfully negotiated leaving the parental home and becoming independent serve as a reminder that parents have not successfully achieved their task of socialization. Cook and Cohler (1986) provided empirical evidence of the distress that results from the failure of schizophrenic children to develop and separate in a normal fashion.

In summary, there is ample theoretical formulation and empirical data to hypothesize that problems in the lives of adult children will negatively affect elderly parents' psychological well-being. Further, the distress caused may be as serious and extensive as that caused by impaired elderly persons on their caregiving children. In the following section, we examine the question of the degree to which adult children's problems affect elderly parents, using data from a large random-sample survey of the elderly.

AN EMPIRICAL TEST OF THE IMPACT
OF CHILDREN'S PROBLEMS

The data used to test the hypothesis that children's problems have a negative impact on the psychological well-being of their parents were collected between September 1985 and February 1986 in the Boston, Massachusetts metropolitan area, as part of a larger study of the family relations of the elderly.

Under Massachusetts law, each municipality in the state is required to compile and publish an annual listing of the residents of every dwelling. These lists contain the name, birthdate, and occupation of all residents. A random sample was drawn of persons 65 years of age and older listed in the 1985 published town lists. Once elders were identified, they were classified on the basis of their living arrangements (living alone, living with spouse, living with adult child, living with both spouse and adult child). Samples were drawn from each of these categories, oversampling for persons living with spouses and/or adult children. This procedure resulted in a final eligible sample of 2,813, 72% (N = 2,020) of whom participated in the study.

Telephone or in-person interviews were conducted, which lasted approximately 30 minutes, and covered such areas as social relationships, health and functional status, and family conflict and abuse. In-person interviews were conducted with persons who had hearing difficulties, who did not have telephones, or who preferred an in-person interview for any reason. Approximately one third of the sample were interviewed in person. The findings presented in this chapter were unaffected by the mode of interview.

A subsample was randomly selected from the larger sample for follow-up interviews, in which issues regarding family relations and psychological well-being could be examined in more detail. These follow-up interviews were conducted by telephone or in person according to the mode of the initial interview and depending on the respondent's wishes. Of the 251 persons designated for follow-up interviews, 215 (86%) agreed to be interviewed.

In this chapter, we analyze data from the follow-up subsample. The analysis is restricted to this group, as measures of psychological well-being were included only in the follow-up interview. In order to test this hypothesis, it was necessary to further restrict the subsample. Specifically, the study design was such that each follow-up respondent was asked detailed questions about only one relative, which included items about mental and physical health problems.

The selection procedure was as follows. All respondents who were living with a child were asked questions about that child. In the remainder of the subsample, if the respondent had non-coresident children and was not currently married, questions were asked about a randomly selected child. When the respondent was both married *and* living with a child, a random selection was made as to whether the respondent answered questions about the spouse or child. Respondents who were married and living with no children answered questions about their spouse. For the present analysis, data were analyzed on only the 100 respondents who answered questions regarding children.

Measurement of the Variables

Psychological distress was measured with the Center for Epidemiologic Studies Depression (CES-D) Scale. The CES-D scale has been demonstrated to be a reliable and valid index of depressive symptomatology (Radloff, 1977), and has been used extensively in surveys of the elderly (Radloff & Teri, 1986). The items composing the scale ask how many days in the preceding week the respondent felt a certain way (e.g., "You felt depressed," "You felt hopeful about the future"). Response categories are: less than 1 day, 1–2 days, 3–4 days, 5–7 days. The items were combined in a scale in which a higher score indicates more severe depression. This scale has a reliability coefficient (Cronbach's alpha) of .86.

To measure children's problems, an index of mental and physical health difficulties was created from three items. Elderly respondents were asked whether their child had "any serious mental or emotional problems," "any serious problems with his or her physical health," and whether the child's "activities are limited by ill health or any disabilities." A dummy variable was created based on whether the respondent had answered affirmatively to any of these questions (0 = no; 1 = yes).

Three other variables that have been found to be related to depression in previous studies were included in the analysis as controls. These included: (a) age, measured in years; (b) subjective rating of own health (1 = poor, 2 = fair, 3 = good, 4 = excellent); and (c) gender (1 = male, 2 = female). We also included a measure of whether the parent and child were living together, as some writers have suggested that parental distress may be greater when the generations co-reside (cf. Suitor & Pillemer, 1987).

Of the subsample, 76% were female and 24% male. Of the sample, 60% were between 65 and 74 years of age, 33% were between 75–84 years old, and 7% were 85 years old or above. Seventy-eight percent had incomes of less than $15,000, and 22% over $15,000. Only 13% were currently married, and 87% were not. All of the respondents were White. Although the sample thus appears to be predominantly poor, widowed women, self-reported health was relatively high: 17% said their health was excellent, 46% good, 33% fair, and only 4% poor. In 37% of the cases, the child who was asked about lived with the respondent. Twenty-four percent of the respondents reported that their children had serious physical or mental problems.

Table 9.1 presents the regression results when children's mental and physical health problems are entered into the equation. The hypothesis regarding the effects of child's mental and physical health was supported: Parents whose children were mentally or physically ill reported higher levels of depression ($p < .001$) even when controlling for parents' health, age, or gender, or residence sharing. Of course, these findings are subject to the limitations of secondary analysis of a data set that was not originally intended to address the topic at hand. We do not have, for example, descriptions of the actual problems of the children, nor are we able to determine the precise nature of the impact of the children's problems; that is, was the negative impact due to greater demands on parents' resources, children's inability to help, and so forth. As an exploratory study, however, the results are sufficiently striking to merit extensive further exploration.

DIRECTIONS FOR FUTURE RESEARCH

Three general areas appear to us to be particularly promising for future research: (a) studies to confirm or refute the relationship between children's problems and parents well-being found in the exploratory analysis just presented; (b) research on the mechanisms by which children's problems have an impact on parents; and (c) studies of factors that may mediate the impact of children's problems on parents.

TABLE 9.1
Regression of Child Problems and Control Variables on Parents' Depression

Variable	Unstandardized Coefficients		Standardized Coefficients
Living arrangement	.580		.037
Child problems	3.569**		.339
Parents' age	.020		.022
Parents' health	3.212**		.406
Gender	2.714*		.156
R^2		.309**	
N		100	

*$p < .05$; **$p < .001$.

Studies of the Effects of Children's Problems

Clearly, the greatest need is for research that will more firmly establish that elderly parents are adversely affected by their children's problems. One of the most promising ways in which to accomplish this is to include items relating to children in future studies of depression in the elderly. Studies of depression in the aged have not included items on problematic relationships with children; the data presented suggest that such items may have major potential to account for variance in depression.

In addition, studies that have examined the impact of children on the elderly have tended to focus only on whether the elderly person *ever* had children, or on the frequency of interaction. It is important to begin to examine the *quality* of interactions with children, and the characteristics of the children themselves. It may be that elderly persons who have frequent contact with children are in fact doing so because they must help their troubled offspring.

Examine the Ways in Which Children's Problems Affect Parents

We noted earlier that it is not yet known precisely why children's problems negatively affect parents. Specifically, we posited three possible causes: (a) that parents must provide help to children, which interferes with the parents' lives; (b) that problem children are unable to provide their parents with help that the latter expect; and (c) that parents have strong identification with and normative expectations for children that are violated by problem children. Other mechanisms might also be included: For example, children's problems may lead to parent–child conflict, which in turn could lead to distress. Studies should be designed to specify the mechanisms by which children's problems affect elderly parents.

Explore Mediating Factors

It would be worthwhile to examine factors that may mediate the impact of children's problems. Several potential mediating factors are discussed here.

Gender of Parent.   It is clear from the literature that mothers relationships with children in later life are more intense than those of fathers, and that they remain more invested in the parental role (Hagestad, 1986; Rossi & Rossi, this volume). Further, researchers have found that of parents with physically or emotionally disabled young children, mothers experience more stress and greater reductions in psychological well-being. Cook's (1988) study of mentally ill young adults also found a more serious impact on mothers than fathers. This pattern may hold as well for elderly parents.

Marital Status of Parent. It is clear that the stresses of parenthood are greater for single parents. However, it has also been demonstrated that adult children can cause difficulties in parents' marital relationships, which might in turn have detrimental affects on the latter's well being (Suitor & Pillemer, 1988).

Living Arrangement. Some investigators have speculated that sharing a residence with an adult child can lead to psychological distress in elderly parents (Schnaiberg & Goldenberg, 1986). Although some more recent evidence contradicts this notion (Pillemer & Suitor, in press), it is possible that living with a troubled child would increase the stress of the child's problems.

Type of Problem Experienced by Child. With young children, parental distress seems to vary with type of disability. Such a pattern might hold for elderly parents as well.

CONCLUSION

The major implication of this chapter is that we must cease to focus solely on how hard it is for children to have elderly parents, and begin looking at reciprocal influences between children and parents in later life. Our discussion here strongly suggests that certain aspects of the parenting experience affect older persons' psychological well-being. Thus, although the literature on family caregiving has focused on the impact of *parents'* failing health and increased dependence on their children, this study suggests that attention should also be paid to the children's problems as possible correlates of negative affect in the elderly. Such research is critically needed if we are to more fully understand the effects of family relations on psychological well-being in later life.

REFERENCES

Aldous, J. (1978). *Family careers: Developmental changes in families.* New York: Wiley.
Atchley, R. C. (1987). *Social forces in later life: An introduction to social gerontology.* Belmont, CA: Wadsworth.
Anetzberger, G. J. (1987). *The etiology of child abuse by adult offspring.* Springfield, IL: Charles C. Thomas.
Barnett, R. C., Kibria, N., Baruch, G., & Pleck, J. (in press). Quality of adult daughters' relationships with their mothers and fathers. *Journal of Marriage and the Family.*
Beckmen-Bell, P. (1981). Child-related stress in families of handicapped children. *Topics in Early Childhood Special Education, 1,* 43–53.

Bell, R. (1979). Parent–child and reciprocal influences. *American Psychologist, 34,* 821–826.

Benedek, T. (1959). Parenthood as a developmental stage: A contribution to the libido theory. *Journal of the American Psychoanalytical Association, 7,* 389–417.

Bengtson, V. L., & Kuypers, J. A. (1971). Generational difference and the developmental stake. *Aging and Human Development, 2,* 249–259.

Bengtson, V. L., & Robertson, J. (1985). *Grandparenthood.* Beverly Hills, CA: Sage.

Blenkner, M. (1965). Social work and family relationships in later life with some thoughts on filial maturity. In E. Shanas & G. Streib (Eds.), *Social structure and the family: Generational issues* (pp. 46–59). Englewood Cliffs, NJ: Prentice-Hall.

Bristowe, E., & Collins, J. B. (1989). Family mediated abuse of non-institutionalized frail elderly men and women living in British Columbia. *Journal of Elder Abuse and Neglect, 1,* 45–64.

Brody, E. M. (1982, Winter). They can't do it all: Aging daughters with aging mothers. *Generations,* 18–37.

Brody, E. M., Johnson, P. T., Fulcomer, M. C., & Lang, A. M. (1984). Women's changing roles and help to elderly parents: Attitudes of three generations. *Journal of Gerontology, 38,* 597–607.

Byrne, E. A., & Cunningham, C. C. (1985). The effects of mentally handicapped children on families—A conceptual review. *Journal of Child Psychology and Psychiatry, 26,* 847–864.

Cicirelli, V. (1983). A comparison of helping behavior to elderly parents of adult children with intact and disrupted marriages. *The Gerontologist, 23,* 619–625.

Cohler, B. J., & Grunebaum, H. U. (1981). *Mothers, grandmothers and daughters: Personality and childcare in three generation families.* New York: Wiley.

Cook, J., (1988). Who 'mothers' the chronically mentally ill? *Family Relations, 37,* 42–49.

Cook, J., & Cohler, B. J. (1986). Reciprocal socialization and the care of offspring with cancer and with schizophrenia. In N. Datan, A. Greene, & H. Reese (Eds.), *Life-span developmental psychology: Intergenerational relations* (pp. 223–243). Hillsdale, NJ: Lawrence Erlbaum Associates.

Cox, H. (1984). *Later life: The realities of aging.* Englewood Cliffs, NJ: Prentice-Hall.

Farell, M., & Rosenberg, S. (1981). Parent–child relations at middle age. In C. Getty & W. Humphreys (Eds.), *Understanding the family: Stress and change in american family life* (pp.). New York: Appleton-Century-Crofts.

Fortier, L. M., & Wanlass, R. L. (1984). Family crisis following the diagnosis of a handicapped child. *Family Relations, 33,* 13–24.

George, L. K. (1980). *Role transitions in later life.* Belmont, CA: Wadsworth.

Glenn, N. D., & McLanahan, S. (1981). The effects of offspring on the psychological well-being of older adults. *Journal of Marriage and the Family, 43,* 409–421.

Greenberg, J. S., & Becker, M. (1988). Aging parents as family resources. *The Gerontologist, 28,* 786–791.

Greene, A. L. & Boxer, A. M. (1982). Daughters and sons as young adults: Restructuring the ties that bind. In N. Datan, A. Greene, & H. Reese (Eds.). *Life-span developmental psychology: Intergenerational relations* (pp. 125–149). Hillsdale, NJ: Lawrence Erlbaum Associates.

Grunes, J. (1977). Parenthood issues in the aging process. In R. S. Cohen, B. J. Cohler, & S. H. Weissman (Eds.), Parenthood: A psychodynamic perspective (pp. 103–111). New York: Guilford.

Gubman, G., & Tessler, R. (1987). The impact of mental illness on families. *Journal of Family Issues, 8,* 226–245.

Hagestad, G. O. (1986). Dimensions of time and the family. *American Behavior Scientist, 29,* 679–694.

Hess, B., & Waring, J. (1978, October). Changing patterns of aging and family bonds in later life. *The Family Coordinator,* 303–314.

Hill, J. P., Holmbeck, G. N., Marrow, L., Greene, T., & Lynch, M. E. (1985). Menarcheal status and parent–child relations in families of seventh grade girls. *Journal of Youth and Adolescence, 14,* 301–316.

Holroyd, J., & McArthur, D. (1976). Mental retardation and stress on the parents: A contrast between down's syndrome and childhood autism. *American Journal of Mental Deficiency, 80,* 431–436.

Johnson, E. S., & Bursk, B. J. (1977). Relationships between the elderly and their adult children. *The Gerontologist, 17,* 90–96.

Kazak, A. E., & Marvin, R. S. (1984). Differences, difficulties and adaption: Stress and social networks in families with a handicapped child. *Family Relations, 84,* 67–77.

Kerchoff, A. C. (1966). Family patterns and morale in retirement. In I. H. Thompson & J. C. McKinney (Eds.), *Social aspects of aging* (pp.). Durham, NC: Duke University Press.

Litwak, E. (1960). Geographical mobility and extended family cohesion. *American Sociological Review, 25,* 9–21.

Lowenthal, M. F., Thurner, M., & Chiriboga, D. (1975). *Four stages of life.* San Francisco, CA: Jossey-Bass.

Mash, E. J., & Johnston, C. (1983). Parental perception of child behavior problems, parenting self-esteem and mothers' reported stress in younger and older hyperactive and normal children. *Journal of Consulting and Clinical Psychology, 51,* 86–99.

McKinney, B., & Peterson, R. A. (1987). Predictors of stress in parents of developmentally disabled children. *Journal of Pediatric Psychology, 12,* 133–150.

McLanahan, S., & Adams, J. (1987). Parenthood and psychological well-being. *Annual Review of Sociology, 13,* 237–257.

Moss, M., Moss, S., & Moles, E. (1985). The quality of relationships between elderly parents and their out of town children. *The Gerontologist, 25,* 134–140.

Mutran, E., & Reitzes, D. G. (1984). Intergenerational support activities and well-being among the elderly: A convergence of exchange and symbolic interaction perspectives. *American Sociological Review, 49,* 117–130.

Nydegger, C. (1983). Family ties of the elderly in a cross-cultural perspective. In B. Hess & E. W. Markson (Eds.), *Growing old in America* (pp. 387–400). New Brunswick, NJ: Transaction.

Olshansky, S. (1962). Chronic sorrow: A response to having a mentally defective child. *Social Casework, 43,* 190–194.

Pett, M., Caserta, M. S., Hutton, A. P., & Lund, D. (1988). Intergenerational conflict: Middle-aged women caring for demented older relatives. *American Journal of Orthopsychiatry, 58,* 405–417.

Pillemer, K. (1985). The dangers of dependency: New findings on domestic violence against the elderly. *Social Problems, 33,* 147–158.

Pillemer, K., & Suitor, J. (1988). Elder abuse. In V. Van Hasselt, R. L. Morrison, A. S. Bellack, & M. Hersen (Eds.), *Handbook of family violence* (pp. 247–270). New York: Plenum.

Pillemer, K., & Suitor, J. J. (in press). Sharing a residence with an adult child: A cause of psychological distress in the elderly? *American Journal of Orthopsychiatry.*

Radloff, L. S. (1977). The CES-D scale: A self-report depression scale for research in the general population. *Applied Psychological Measurement, 1,* 385–401.

Radloff, L. S. (1980). Risk factors for depression: What do we learn from them? In D. Belle & S. Salinson (Eds.), *Mental health of women: Fact and fiction* (pp. 93–109. New York: Academic Press.

Radloff, L. S. & Teri, L. (1986). Use of the center for epidemiological studies-depression scale with older adults. *Clinical Gerontologist, 5,* 119–135.

Robinson, B., & Thurner, M. (1979). Taking care of aged parents: A family cycle transition. *The Gerontologist, 19,* 586–593.

Rosow, I. (1970). Old people: Their friends and neighbors. *American Behavioral Scientist, 14,* 59–69.

Rosow, I. (1967). *Social integration and the aged.* New York: The Free Press.

Schilling, R. F., Shinke, S. P., & Kirkham, M. A. (1985). Coping with a handicapped child: differences between mothers and fathers. *Social Science Medicine, 21,* 857–863.

Shanas, E. (1979). The family as a support system in old age. *The Gerontologist, 18,* 3–9.

Schaie, K. W., & Willis, S. L. (1986). *Adult development and aging* (2nd ed.). Boston: Little Brown.

Schnaiberg, A., & Goldenberg, S. (1986, August). *From empty nest to crowded nest: Some contradictions in the returning-young-adult syndrome.* Paper presented at the annual meeting of the American Sociological Association, New York City.

Sherman, B., & Cocozza, J. (1984). Stress in families of the developmentally disabled: A literature review of factors affecting the decision to seek out-of-home placements. *Family Relations, 33,* 95–103.

Seelbach, W. C., & Sauer, W. J. (1977). Filial responsibility expectations and morale among aged parents. *The Gerontologist, 17,* 492–499.

Silliman, R., & Sternberg, J. (1988). Family caregiving: Impact of patient functioning and underlying causes of dependency. *The Gerontologist, 28,* 377–382.

Silverberg, S., & Steinberg, L. (1987). Adolescent autonomy, parent-adolescent conflict, and parental well-being. *Journal of Youth and Adolescence, 16,* 293–312.

Slater, M., & Wikler, L. (1986, September/October). Normalized family resources for families with a developmentally disabled child. *Social Work,* 385–390.

Spink, D. (1976). Crisis intervention for parents of the deaf child. *Health and Social Work, 1,* 140–160.

Steinberg, L. (1987). Impact of puberty on family relations: Effects of pubertal status and timing. *Developmental Psychology, 23,* 451–460.

Steinberg, L. (1988). Reciprocal relations between parent-child distance and pubertal maturation. *Developmental Psychology, 24,* 122:128.

Steinmetz, S. (1988). *Duty bound: Elder abuse and family care.* Beverly Hills, CA: Sage.

Suitor, J., & Pillemer, K. (1987). The presence of adult children: A source of stress for elderly couples' marriages? *Journal of Marriage and the Family, 49,* 717–725.

Sussman, M. (1985). The family of life of older people. In R. Binstock & E. Shanas (Eds.), *Handbook of aging and the social sciences* (pp. 414–447). New York: Van Nostrand Reinhold.

Tavormina, J. B., Boll, T. J., Dunn, N. J., Luscomb, R. L., & Taylor, J. R. (1981). Psychosocial effects on parents of raising a physically handicapped child. *Journal of Abnormal Child Psychology, 9,* 121–131.

Troll, L., Miller, S., & Atchley, R. (1979). *Families in later life.* Belmont, CA: Wadsworth.

Wasibren, S. (1980). Parents reactions after the birth of a developmentally disabled child. *American Journal of Mental Deficiency, 4,* 345–351.

Wikler, L., Wasow, M., & Hatfield, E. (1981). Chronic sorrow revisited: Parent v. professional depiction of the adjustment of parents of mentally retarded children. *American Journal of Orthopsychiatry, 51,* 63–70.

Wolf, R., & Pillemer, K. (1989). *Helping elderly victims: The reality of elder abuse.* New York: Columbia University Press.

Family Conflict When Adult Children and Elderly Parents Share a Home

J. Jill Suitor
Lousiana State University
Karl Pillemer
Cornell University

During the past two decades, there has been considerable effort devoted to examining parent–child relations in the later years. One of the issues in which there has been increasing interest is the quality of family relations when adult children continue to live, or return to live in their parents' homes. In this chapter, we summarize the findings of our study of family relations when the generations coreside, and discuss directions for future research on this topic.

When we began searching the literature on the effects of intergenerational residence sharing, we found a small number of conceptual papers (cf. Mancini & Blieszner, 1985; Schnaiberg & Goldenberg, 1986; Shehan, Berardo, & Berardo, 1984) and numerous popular press articles (Brooks, 1981; Disario, 1982; Fischer, 1986; Toufexis, 1987; Walters, 1986) that discussed the ways in which family relations *might* be affected by adult children's presence in their parents' homes. With few exceptions, these authors argued that this living arrangement would have a detrimental effect on both the parents' marital relationships and on their relationships with their adult children.

The authors believed that this would happen for a variety of reasons. They argued that parents and children would be likely to experience conflict over such issues as renegotiating roles, adult children's attempts to maintain independence while living in their parents' homes, either party becoming too dependent on the other for economic support or services, and parents' disappointment that their children had failed to achieve economic success and independence, or had allowed a marriage to fail. They suggested that the high levels of parent–child conflict in the household would "spill over" to affect the parents' marital relationship. In addition, they argued, parents' marital relationships would suffer because the presence of an adult child would reduce the parents' sense of freedom and privacy, as well as increase their financial burdens.

Both the scholars and journalists based their arguments primarily on a combination of anecdotal evidence from their own lives and those of their friends, and the experiences of clients in family therapy settings. The only empirical paper on the subject supported their assertions. Clemens and Axelson (1985) reported that in many cases, adult children's return placed a strain on the parents' marriage, and in almost half of the cases, parents reported serious conflicts with at least one of their resident adult children. However, Clemens and Axelson's methodology was seriously flawed, calling into question the generalizability of their findings. This is because their data were collected from a very small number of parents (n = 39), most of whom were participating in a workshop on parenting the young adult—obviously parents who were already concerned about the effects of the presence of their adult children. Still, the arguments made by both academics and journalists regarding the effects of coresidence on family relations seemed plausible; thus, we went into the investigation expecting that we would find high levels of conflict in coresidential families. The first analysis we conducted involved examining whether the presence of adult children had detrimental effects on elderly couples' marriages.

PARENTS' MARITAL QUALITY AND CORESIDENCE

The literature on life-cycle variations in marital quality could certainly be used to suggest that the presence of adult children would affect elderly couples' marital relationships negatively. This literature has long argued that the departure of children has a salutary effect on couples' relationships (cf. Anderson, Russell, & Schumm, 1983; Atchley, 1987; Lowenthal, Thurnher, & Chiriboga, 1975; Rollins & Cannon, 1974). In particular, it appears that certain patterns that are associated with declines in marital quality across the transition to parenthood (cf. Cowan et al., 1985; White, Booth, & Edwards, 1986) are reversed at the time that children leave the parental home as adults. For example, launching is associated with a move toward a less traditional division of household labor (Atchley, 1987; Troll, Miller, & Atchley, 1979), greater satisfaction with the division of labor (Schafer & Keith, 1981; Suitor, 1991), more joint leisure time (Atchley, 1987; Starr & Weiner, 1981; Troll et al., 1979), and more privacy (Starr & Weiner, 1981). In addition, if the children are truly "launched," as opposed to attending college, financial pressures are likely to be reduced when children leave the parental home.

Taken together, this set of findings led us to expect that adult children's failure to leave the parental home upon reaching adulthood, or return to the home, would have detrimental effects on older couples' marriages, because coresidence would reverse the processes usually begun at the time of launching.

THE STUDY

To investigate this issue, we used data that were collected between September 1985 and February 1986 in the Boston metropolitan area as part of a larger study of the family relations of the elderly.

Under Massachusetts law, each municipality in the state is required to compile and publish an annual listing of the residents of every dwelling. These lists contain the name, birth date, and occupation of all residents. A random sample was drawn of persons 65 years of age or older listed in the 1985 published town lists. Once elders were identified, they were classified on the basis of their living arrangements (e.g., living only with spouse, living with spouse and adult child). Samples were drawn from each of these categories, with oversampling for persons living with spouses and/or adult children. This procedure resulted in a final eligible sample of 2,813, 72% (n = 2,020) of whom participated in the study.

Most of the data were gathered in telephone interviews that lasted between 30 and 45 minutes and covered such areas as the respondents' physical health, ability to perform activities of daily living, family interaction, family conflict and abuse, and satisfaction with relationships with both family and friends.[1]

Subsample Characteristics

To examine the effects of residence sharing on parents' marital quality, we used the subsample of 677 parents who were married, living with their spouses, and had at least one child 18 years of age or older. The mean age of the respondents in this subsample was 71.7 (SD = 6.1). Fifty-four percent of the respondents were men; 46% were women. Thirty-two percent had completed less than 12 years of education, 38% had completed high school, 12% had completed some college, and 19% were college graduates. One-hundred forty-six of the respondents were sharing a residence with an adult child.[2]

The respondents who were residence sharing were not asked why their adult children were living at home with them. However, a comparison between parents whose children were and were not living with them showed that the presence of adult children was not significantly related to the parents' age, income, current health status, or change in health status during the previous 5 years. Thus, we can assume that parents' increased dependency was not the major precipitant to sharing a home in the majority of cases.

---

[1]In approximately one quarter of the cases, a telephone interview was not possible, and the respondent was interviewed in person. Regression analyses including mode of interview as a dummy variable indicated that the mode of interview did not affect any of the findings reported in this chapter.

[2]Additional information about the characteristics of the subsample is presented in Suitor and Pillemer (1987).

RESIDENCE SHARING AND MARITAL CONFLICT

The first hypothesis examined was whether individuals sharing their home with an adult child experienced greater marital conflict than did individuals whose adult children lived elsewhere. To measure marital conflict each respondent was asked a series of nine items regarding the frequency with which he or she had disagreements with his or her spouse during the previous year. The specific topics for disagreement included: (a) how money was spent, (b) who should do household chores, (c) relationships with children, (d) relationships with other relatives, (e) television, (f) food, (g) one of them drinking too much, and (h) relationships with friends. The respondents were also asked whether there were any other topics over which they had serious disagreements with their spouse during the previous year. For the present analysis, the response categories for each item were "never," "once," and "two or more times." The nine items were then combined to form the marital conflict scale.[3]

Consistent with other studies of marital conflict and satisfaction in the later years (cf. Gilford & Bengtson, 1979; Johnson, 1985), the respondents in the present study reported low levels of conflict. Slightly more than half of the respondents reported having had no disagreements during the previous year, and the mean conflict score was only 2.2 (SD = 3.3; range = 0-16).

Effects of Residence Sharing on Parents' Marital Conflict

Much to our surprise, there was no support for the hypothesis that individuals sharing a residence with their adult children experience greater marital conflict. Parents who shared their home with an adult child experienced no greater marital conflict than did those whose children lived elsewhere (see Table 10.1).

As shown in Table 10.1, we chose to include parent's subjective health, age, and educational attainment as controls in the analysis.[4] It is worth noting that the findings regarding both age and educational attainment were consistent with those of other studies. Age has been found to be strongly inversely related to a variety of types of family violence (cf. Pillemer & Suitor, 1988; Straus et al.,

---

[3]The reliability coefficient (Cronbach's alpha) for the marital conflict scale was .744.

[4]Health was measured by the question "How would you rate your overall health at the present time—excellent, good, fair or poor?" Educational attainment was an ordinal measure with seven categories ranging from eighth grade or less to graduate training. We included age of the youngest partner, rather than the age of the respondent him or herself. Initial analyses had shown that it was important to consider the age of the respondent's spouse, as well as the age of the respondent, because the age of each partner was strongly related to marital conflict. Further analysis revealed that the age of the youngest partner was even more important in explaining conflict than was the average age of the couple.

TABLE 10.1
Regression Analysis of Marital Conflict by Husbands and Wives

Variables	Husbands		Wives	
	Unstand. Reg. Coef.	Stand. Reg. Coef.	Unstand. Reg. Coef.	Stand. Reg. Coef.
Living arrangement	.105	.013	.015	.002
(1 = coresiding)	(.425)[a]		(.399)	
Health	.196	.044	.097	.029
(1 = poor; 4 = excellent)	(.232)		(.196)	
Educational attainment	.241***	.129	.231**	.126
(1 = less than eighth grade; 7 = graduate school)	(.097)		(.098)	
Age of youngest partner	−.077***	−.146	−.059	−.121
	(.027)		(.027)	
R^2	.041***		.030*	
N	367		310	

*$p < .01$; **$p < .05$; ***$p < .01$.
[a]Standard errors are reported in parentheses.

1980; Suitor, Pillemer, & Straus, 1990). Whereas educational attainment has been found to be positively related to verbal aggression between spouses.[5] Thus, it appears that the measure of marital conflict we employed was related to other factors as expected.

Several factors may contribute to the negative finding regarding residence sharing and marital conflict. First, many of the changes in marital structure and interaction that accompany the completion of the launching stage may occur even when children remain in or return to the parental home as adults. For example, the day-to-day responsibilities involved in parenting a minor child impose constraints that are likely to be substantially lower when a residence is shared with an adult child. The presence of minor children (even when adolescents) may reduce parents' time for direct interaction with one another, as well as hinder their ability to spend time together away from home, particularly for long periods, such as vacations. In contrast, adult children are likely to demand less time on a day-to-day basis and pose fewer obstacles to parents spending time away together. Similarly, the presence of adult children may not precipitate a more traditional division of household labor; mothers who felt compelled to perform household labor for their children in the earlier years are probably less likely to feel constrained to provide those services once their children have reached adulthood.

[5]The relationship between age and marital conflict has been reported in recent unpublished analyses of national survey data by Glenda Kaufman Kantor and by the first author of the present chapter.

A second factor that may contribute importantly to these negative findings is the degree of choice involved in sharing a residence with an adult child. Except in extreme cases, it is normatively prescribed that parents share their dwelling with their minor children. Whereas it is expected that parents share their residence with their adult child if there are no other options available, in most cases there is a degree of choice on both parents' and children's parts. Parents who believe that their adult child's presence will have a disruptive effect on their lives may be less willing to share their residence with the child.

Although this analysis answered our initial question—does the presence of adult children affect elderly parents' marital relationships—it led us to several other questions regarding residence sharing and family conflict. The next question we addressed was "What are the conditions under which residence sharing affects parents' marital relationships?"

Explaining Marital Conflict When Parents and Children Live Together

When we began to consider the factors that might affect marital conflict during coresidence, one variable of particular interest was the frequency of conflict between the elderly parents and their adult children. Mancini and Blieszner (1985) and Shehan et al. (1984) suggested that the quality of the parent–child relationship might be a factor in understanding the effects of residence sharing on family relations. Therefore, our next analysis involved examining whether the level of parent–child conflict affected parents' marital relations when adult children were present in the home. In addition, we investigated whether any characteristics of the parent or child affected parents' conflict. To conduct this part of the analysis, we analyzed data on only the 146 parents who were sharing their home with an adult child.

These coresidential families were somewhat more likely to include an adult daughter than an adult son (55% daughters; 45% sons). The mean age of the adult children was 32.9 (*SD* = 8.3). Seventy-six percent of the children had never been married, 18% were formerly married, and only 7% were currently married. Sixty-three percent of the adult children had always resided with their parents, even though most of these individuals had reached adulthood many years earlier (mean age 31.8; *SD* = 8.1). Of those who had returned to the parental home, the length of time since they returned varied substantially, ranging from less than 1 year to 44 years (*M* = 11; *SD* = 13.8).

We measured parent–child conflict by using a scale similar to that used to assess marital conflict. The scale was composed of the same items included in the marital conflict scale, with the following exceptions: items regarding conflicts over the child's job and over his or her use of drugs were added, whereas the item regarding conflict over relationships with children was deleted.[6]

---

[6]The parent–child conflict scale has a reliability coefficient (Cronbach's alpha) of .683.

Consistent with what the earlier authors had argued, we found that parents' marital conflict was strongly related to parent–child conflict, as shown in Table 10.2. In fact, none of the other variables even approached significance.

It is possible that the relationship between parent–child conflict and marital conflict could be accounted for, in part, by two other factors. First, persons who are willing to report experiencing conflict with one family member may be more willing to report conflict with another. Second, some individuals probably experience greater conflict in all of their relationships than do others. Thus, some may be more likely both to report and to experience higher levels of conflict with all family members. Although we cannot completely dismiss these possibilities, data collected on the respondents' conflict with other co-residents suggests that individual differences in reporting or experiencing conflict cannot account for the relationship between marital and adult child–parent conflict. Thirty-two of the respondents shared their home with another relative, as well as the adult child (e.g., sister, sibling-in-law, etc.). Among these respondents, correlations between conflict with spouses or children and conflict with other coresidents were very weak (−.02 between conflict with spouse and other coresidents; and

TABLE 10.2
Regression Analysis of Marital Conflict
(Only Parents Sharing Residence With Adult Child)

Variables	Unstandardized Regression Coefficients	Standardized Regression Coefficients
Parent's gender[a]	− .711	− .105
(1 = female)	(5.28)[b]	
Parent's health	.177	.040
(1 – poor; 4 – excellent)	(.329)	
Parent's education	.223	.110
(1 = less than eighth grade; 7 = graduate school)	(.152)	
Age of youngest partner	.037	.071
	(.049)	
Length of coresidence	− .021	− .086
	(.019)	
Child's gender	.131	.020
(1 = female)	(.490)	
Child's age	− .002	− .004
	(.037)	
Conflict with child	.684*	.498
	(.102)	
R^2		.296*
N		146

*p < .001

[a]Given the relatively small number of married respondents living with an adult child, the subsample was not separated by gender for this analysis.

[b]Standard errors are reported in parentheses.

-.04 between conflict with children and other coresidents). Thus, there did not appear to be a general tendency for persons who reported conflict with spouses or children to be more likely to report conflict with other family members.

The importance of parent–child conflict in explaining marital conflict led us to feel that the next steps in our analyses should be examinations of the extent of parent–child conflict in coresidential families, and the correlates of that conflict.

PARENT–CHILD CONFLICT
IN CORESIDENTIAL FAMILIES

To investigate the extent and correlates of parent–child conflict in coresidential families, we used a slightly different subsample from that used to examine parents' marital conflict. For this analysis, we used the subsample of 372 respondents who had an adult child sharing their home. This subsample included parents who were divorced and widowed, as well as those who were married. As a result, a higher proportion of elderly parents in the analysis of parent–child conflict were women (63%) than was the case in the analysis of marital conflict (46%); and a greater proportion had total family incomes of less than $15,000 (60% in the subsample including all coresiding parents; 40% of married coresiding parents). In other respects, the subsample used for the present analysis was similar to that used for the analysis of marital conflict.[7]

Frequency of Parent–Child Conflict
in Coresidential Families

An examination of the frequency of disagreements between adult children and their elderly parents showed very low levels of conflict. Almost two thirds (64%) of the respondents reported that they had no disagreements with their resident children during the previous year, and only 28% reported having had two or more disagreements.

These findings are surprising in the face of the high levels of intergenerational conflict that others have suggested might occur when the generations coreside (e.g., Clemens & Axelson, 1985; Schnaiberg & Goldenberg, 1986; Shehan et al., 1984). In part, the difference between the amount of conflict reported here and that suggested by others may lie in the fact that the parents who participated in the present study were elderly, whereas most authors have focused on coresidential families in which middle-aged parents share their home with young adult children. Age has been found consistently to be negatively related to family conflict and violence (cf. Pillemer & Suitor, 1988; Straus, Gelles, & Steinmetz, 1980; Suitor et al., 1990); therefore, relationships involving

---

[7]Additional information about the characteristics of this subsample is presented in Suitor and Pillemer (1988).

younger parties would be expected to yield higher reports of conflict. In addition, the literature on adult development and intergenerational relations (cf. Bengtson, 1979; Blenkner, 1965; Hagestad, 1987) suggests that middle-aged parents and their children would experience more conflict than would older parent–child dyads. Thus, it is likely that parent–child conflict would have been greater if the sample had included middle-aged parents and their children.

It is still important to consider whether the low level of parent–child conflict might have resulted from some other aspect of the methodology we employed. In particular, we need to question whether the low level of conflict resulted from the measure we used, or from the fact that the data were collected from the parents rather than the adult children.

It seems unlikely that the low levels of conflict reported can be accounted for by the measure. First, as noted earlier, one of the items in the conflict scale asked whether there were any other topics over which the respondent had disagreements with his or her child. Thus, the parents were provided an opportunity to include conflict they had experienced over issues not already addressed by the scale, such as their living arrangements, or the child's financial dependence. Second, noticeably higher levels of conflict were reported when using the almost identical scale to measure conflict between married respondents and their spouses, suggesting that the respondents were willing to report disagreements with other family members over these issues. Thus, it does not appear that the low levels of conflict can be accounted for by the measure.

It is likely, however, that greater conflict would have been reported if the data had been collected from the adult children rather than their elderly parents. The tendency for individuals to present overly harmonious pictures of their family relationships has long been recognized (cf. Edmunds, 1967; Schumm & Bugaighis, 1986; Schumm, Jurich, Bollman, & Bugaighis, 1985). This concern is particularly salient when collecting data from older family members, because the elderly generally receive higher scores on social desirability scales than do their younger counterparts (Campbell, Converse, & Rodgers, 1976; Gove & Geerken, 1977). In addition, research on intergenerational relations has shown that parents tend to report greater closeness and consensus than do their adult children (cf. Bengtson & Kuypers, 1971; Bengtson, Mangen, & Landry, 1984; Troll & Bengtson, 1979). Thus, the fact that our data were collected from the parents, rather than the adult children, is likely to have somewhat attenuated the level of conflict reported.

But even if we assume that adult children would have reported somewhat higher levels of conflict, the findings suggest that adult children and elderly parents who share a residence experience relatively little conflict. Although we cannot test this possibility with the present data, we believe that the low levels of conflict we found may be a reflection of the selectivity involved in decisions regarding coresidence. As noted earlier, it is *not* normatively prescribed that parents share their dwelling with their adult children. In fact, the establishment of an independent residence is widely considered to be one of the major tasks of normal adult development (cf. Schaie & Willis, 1986). Thus, parents and children who choose to coreside are likely to be those whose relationships are characterized by levels of conflict that would not be disruptive in their lives.

One of the obvious questions our initial analysis of parent–child conflict left unanswered was, "What factors contribute to conflict—what factors distinguish between those parent–child dyads who do and those who do not experience conflict when coresiding?" This was the next question we addressed.

Explaining Parent–Child Conflict in Coresidential Families

In the absence of almost any work on residence-sharing families, we turned to the broader literature on affective relations between the generations to develop a theoretical framework for explaining intergenerational conflict in coresidential families.

A review of the literature suggested that the factors affecting adult child-parent relations could be framed within two theoretical perspectives: (a) exchange relations, and (b) social structural positions.

Exchange Relations. Exchange theory (Blau, 1964; Homans, 1961) has been widely used to explain family relations throughout the life cycle. This perspective has gained particular attention within the gerontological literature since the mid-1970s (e.g., Cicirelli, 1981; Dowd, 1975, 1980; Pillemer, 1985; Sussman, 1976). A brief review of exchange theory as it has been applied to the family will demonstrate its relevance to intergenerational relations.

Exchange theory suggests that individuals attempt to minimize their costs and maximize their rewards in interactions. This approach also holds that individuals expect their provision of rewards to another to be reciprocated— although not necessarily immediately or in kind. In non-family relationships, when reciprocity is no longer achieved, the relationship is very likely to end. However, as Gelles (1983) has noted, families provide special instances of exchange in which it may not be feasible to end relationships, even when reciprocity is absent. In such situations, conflict would be expected to occur (cf. Gelles, 1983; Goode, 1971).

Such a conceptualization of family relations seems quite applicable to adult children and elderly parents. Studies of the family relations of the elderly have often highlighted imbalanced exchanges and perceptions of inequity between the generations as causes of family disharmony. For example, several investigations have suggested that an increase in parents' dependence on their adult children may reduce positive feelings between the generations. Thompson and Walker's (1984) study revealed that middle-aged daughters and their mothers who reported the lowest levels of reciprocal aid scored lowest on attachment, whereas Adams (1968) found that affectional ties were weaker when adult children's provision of help to their widowed parents was not reciprocated. Similarly, Cicirelli (1983a, 1983b) reported that high levels of both parental dependency and children's helping behaviors could lead to negative feelings on the part of adult children.

The family violence literature also provides support for the expectation that imbalanced exchanges would lead to intergenerational conflict: both Quinn and Tomita (1986) and Steinmetz and her colleagues (Steinmetz, 1983; Steinmetz & Amsden, 1983) have reported that unusually high levels of dependency on adult children are related to physical and psychological abuse of elderly parents.

The exchange perspective may also help to explain the reduction in adult children's feelings of closeness and attachment when parents' health declines (cf. Baruch & Barnett, 1983; Johnson & Bursk, 1977). As parents' health deteriorates, adult children are likely to need to increase their level of support to previously independent parents substantially, as well as accept a lessening or termination of the parents' provision of support—thus disrupting the previously established flow of support between the generations.

In summary, the preponderance of evidence from this series of studies suggested that both the disruption of the previously established flow of support, and perceived inequity of support play an important part in the quality of adult child–parent relations. As parents become increasingly dependent and reciprocity diminishes in the relationship, the exchange comes to be perceived as unfair by the child, which may in turn result in conflict. On this basis, we anticipated finding lower levels of conflict in dyads in which elderly parents were in better health and were less dependent on their adult children.[8]

Social Structural Factors. Whereas the gerontological literature has focused primarily on the dependency of parents as a major determinant of the quality of parent–adult child relationships, other potentially important variables emerge from the broader sociological literature on interpersonal relations. In particular, social structural positions have been shown to be important in

---

[8]Parent's dependency on his or her adult child was measured by using an adaptation of the OARS scale of functional dependency (cf. George, Landesman, & Fillenbaum, 1982). The respondent was asked whether he or she was able to perform each of several activities of daily living without any assistance, with only some assistance, or was completely unable to perform this activity. The specific activities included such things as shopping for food or clothes, housecleaning, cooking, dressing, bathing, eating, and walking. If the respondent required assistance, he or she was asked who usually provided that assistance for each activity. Respondents received a dependency score of one for each activity for which they usually received assistance from the adult child, and a score of zero for each activity for which they did not receive assistance from the child. The scores were summed across the 10 items. Because few respondents reported that they received assistance from the child for more than three activities, the dependency scores were collapsed into categories of 0, 1, 2, and 3.

understanding the development and maintenance of relationships throughout the life cycle (cf. Bell, 1981; Feld, 1982; Hetherington, Cox, & Cox, 1976; Lazarsfeld & Merton, 1954; Suitor, 1987a, 1987c).

In the analysis of parent–child conflict, we focused on three social structural variables that have been found to be important in explaining relations between adult children and elderly parents, as well as interpersonal relations more generally: (a) marital status similarity, (b) age, and (c) gender.

Marital Status Similarity.   One of the most consistent patterns found in the study of intergenerational relations is an increase in closeness in parent–child relations when children begin to share a larger number of adult statuses with their parents (Adams, 1968; Baruch & Barnett, 1983; Fischer, 1981; Komarovsky, 1962; Wilen, 1979; Young & Willmott, 1957). One of these patterns is that children's transition from singlehood to marriage is associated with an increase in positive affect from both the parents' and adult children's perspectives (Adams, 1968; Baruch & Barnett, 1983; Komarovsky, 1963; Wilen, 1979; Young & Willmott, 1957). Research on the effects of marital status similarity has been conducted almost exclusively with parents and children who did not share a residence. Status similarity should have at least as great an effect on parent–child relations in families in which the generations coreside as in families in which the generations live apart. If anything, the value similarity and role congruence associated with status similarity would seem to be even more important when individuals are forced into contact through coresidence. Thus, we anticipated that conflict would be lower in dyads where the adult children and their elderly parents occupied the same or similar marital status.[9]

Child's Age.   The literature suggested that child's age would also be important in understanding parent–child conflict. Theories of adult development and intergenerational relations argue that maturational changes are likely to decrease differences between parents and adult children, thus reducing the bases for conflict between them. For example, Bengtson (1979) suggested that as children mature, their orientations become more similar to those of their parents; whereas Blenkner (1965) proposed that adult children's identification with their elderly parents increases as a part of developing "filial maturity." Similarly, Hagestad (1987) posited both that differences between parents and children become muted across time, and that there is greater tolerance for differences that remain.

---

[9]Marital status similarity was based on the combination of the parent's and child's marital status. For the present analysis, similarity was dichotomized. A respondent received a similarity score of one if: (a) he or she and the resident child occupied the same marital status (e.g., both currently married, both currently divorced, etc.); or (b) he or she was widowed and the resident child was married. Respondents who did not meet one of these criteria were assigned a score of 0.

Data collected from both adult children and elderly parents also suggest more harmonious relations when children are older. Cicirelli (1981) reported a negative relationship between adult children's ages and their reports of conflict with their mothers and fathers. Likewise, Aldous and her colleagues (Aldous, Klaus, & Klein, 1985) found that both fathers and mothers were more likely to report that they used their older, rather than their youngest children as confidants. Last, Hagestad's (1986) interviews with middle-generation mothers indicated that they expected their children's maturation to result in the same increases in understanding they had experienced with their own mothers after reaching adulthood.

In addition, as noted earlier, research on family conflict and aggression has consistently reported a decline in aggression across age groups (e.g., Pillemer & Suitor, 1988; Straus et al., 1980; Suitor et al., 1990), providing a third basis for anticipating that child's age would be negatively related to parent–child conflict. On these bases, we anticipated that conflict would be lowest among families in which the coresident children were older.

Gender. The last structural factor of interest was gender. A review of the literature suggested that gender of both parent and child affect intergenerational relations. Studies of the effects of gender consistently demonstrate stronger affectional ties between mothers and daughters than any other combination. For example, mothers report more positive affect with adult daughters than adult sons (Angres, 1975), are more likely to rely on daughters than sons as confidants (Aldous et al., 1985; Lopata, 1979), and are less likely to become angry (Lopata, 1979) or disappointed (Aldous et al., 1985) with daughters. In addition, adult daughters report greater feelings of closeness to mothers than fathers (Adams, 1968; Cicirelli, 1981), and are more likely to rely on mothers as confidants (Suitor, 1984). Based on these findings, we anticipated that conflict would be lowest in mother–daughter dyads.

The literature on other gender combinations suggested that conflict would be lower in both mother–son and father–daughter pairs than in father–son pairs. Adult sons report greater closeness to mothers than fathers (Adams, 1968; Lowenthal, Thurnher, & Chiriboga, 1975), whereas fathers report somewhat weaker affectional ties with adult sons than daughters (Miller, Bengtson, & Richards, 1987), and are more likely to report being disappointed with sons (Aldous et al., 1985).

Taken together, these findings led us to anticipate that the least conflict would be found in mother–daughter pairs, and the most in father–son pairs. In the mixed pairs, we expected that there would be less conflict in mother–son than father–daughter pairs.[10]

---

[10]For the present analysis, parents' and children's genders were combined into four dummy variables: (a) mother–daughter pairs, (b) mother–son pairs, (c) father–daughter pairs, and (d) father–son pairs. The variables "mother–daughter," "mother–son," and "father–daughter" were entered into the regression equation; "father–son" was used as the reference category.

In summary, the literature we reviewed led us to anticipate that conflict between parents and their resident adult children would be lowest when: (a) the parent was in good health, (b) the parent was less dependent on the adult child, (c) the child and parent occupied the same or similar marital status, and (d) the child was older. In addition, we anticipated that the least conflict would be found in mother–daughter dyads, followed by mother–son dyads, father–daughter, and father–son dyads.

There was one additional factor that we thought was important to consider in the analysis that could not be subsumed under exchange relations or social structural positions. We anticipated that conflict would be inversely related to the length of time since the parents and children had begun sharing a residence. We expected that parents and children who experienced high levels of conflict would not continue to live together; thus, pairs who had coresided for a longer period would be those who had been able to resolve any new or reactivated conflicts (Steinman, 1979) in their relationships. In addition, life events experienced by one or both members of a dyad often precipitate tension in their relationship, because the previously established role expectations have been altered (cf. Benjamin, 1981; Suitor, 1987b; White, Booth, & Edwards, 1986). On these bases, we expected that adult child–parents conflict would be greater in families in which the generations had recently begun to share a home.

Correlates of Parent–Resident Adult Child Conflict

The multiple regression analysis provided support for two of the three hypotheses regarding the effects of social structural positions, but for neither of the hypotheses regarding the effects of exchange and dependency.[11] As shown in Table 10.3, parent–adult child conflict was significantly lower in dyads in which the resident child was older, and in which the parent and child occupied the same or similar marital status. Contrary to expectations, there was no support for the hypotheses regarding gender, parent's health, parent's dependency, or length of coresidence.

These findings contribute to a growing literature showing the importance of social structural factors in understanding intergenerational relations. Initially, it would appear that the findings contradict other studies on the importance of exchange in explaining intergenerational relations. We believe, however, that our nonfindings *are* the result of issues involving exchange and equity. The fact that the respondents were sharing their own residence with the child may have affected the relationship between parent's dependency and conflict. It is possible that both parents and children in these living situations

---

[11]For the present analysis, parent–child conflict scores were logged to meet the distributional requirements of OLS. One unit was added to each respondent's summed conflict score to permit computation of the logged variable.

TABLE 10.3
Regression Analysis of Parent-Child Conflict

Variables	Unstandardized Regression Coefficients	Standardized Regression Coefficients
Parent's dependency	−.020	.024
(0 = no dependency;	(.048)[a]	
3 = high dependency)		
Parent's health	−.013	−.015
(1 = poor; 4 = excellent)	(.050)	
Parent's education	−.002	−.005
(1 = less than eighth grade;	(.028)	
7 = graduate school)		
Marital status similarity	−.238*	
(1 = status similar)	(.129)	−.104
Child's age	−.016**	−.242
	(.004)	
Length of coresidence	−.001*	−.014
	(.003)	
Gender combinations		
Mother–daughter	−.112	−.071
	(.108)	
Mother–son	−.107	−.071
	(.104)	
Father–daughter	−.118	−.061
	(.122)	
R^2		.088**
N		372

*$p < .10$; **$p < .001$.
[a]Standard errors are reported in parentheses.

view the exchange of housing for assistance with activities of daily living as equitable—thus reducing the likelihood of conflict over issues of dependency, as well as reducing the overall likelihood of conflict.

Coresidence in the Parent's Home Versus the Child's Home

The apparent importance of equity in explaining the low levels of parent–child conflict when adult children return to live or continue to live in their parents' homes raises yet another question—"Is conflict higher if the adult child and elderly parent live together in the *child's* rather than the parent's home?" Are exchange relations be seen as less equitable in those situations, resulting in greater conflict?

To address this question, we used data on conflict experienced by the 51 respondents in the original sample who coresided in the child's home, and compared those data to the data on the conflict experienced by the 372 respondents who shared their own homes with their adult children.

An initial bivariate analysis indicated that the frequency of parent–child conflict was *lower* when the generations coresided in the adult child's home than when they coresided in the parent's home. However, a multivariate analysis revealed that the relationship between conflict and place of coresidence could be accounted for by differences in the ages of adult children in these two living arrangements. Adult children tended to be older in households in which the generations shared the adult child's home than households in which they shared the parent's home. When age was included in the analysis, the original relationship between conflict and place of coresidence disappeared completely, as shown in Table 10.4.

Unfortunately, the data we had collected did now allow us to determine whether the generations perceived this coresidential living arrangement as equitable. However, it is possible to speculate that elderly parents who share their adult children's homes may contribute to the household such that the arrangement is seen as equitable by both generations. For example, less frail

TABLE 10.4
Regression Analysis of Parent–Child Conflict
(Coresidence in the Child's Home Versus the Parent's Home)

Variables	Unstandardized Regression Coefficients	Standardized Regression Coefficients
Place of coresidence	– .026	– .012
(1 = child's home)	(.105)[a]	
Parent's dependency	.001	.001
(0 = no dependency;	(.038)	
3 = high dependency)		
Parent's health	– .033	– .040
(1 = poor; 4 = excellent)	(.040)	
Parent's education	– .002	– .001
(1 = less than eighth grade;	(.023)	
7 = graduate school)		
Marital status similarity	– .153	– .086
(1 = status similar)	(.098)	
Child's age	– .015*	– .255
	(.003)	
Gender combinations		
Mother–daughter	– .099	– .069
	(.090)	
Mother–son	– .062	– .044
	(.088)	
Father–daughter	– .097	– .052
	(.104)	
R^2	.096*	
N	423	

*$p < .001$.
[a]Standard errors are reported in parentheses.

elderly parents may provide assistance in the form of light housekeeping or yard work, or care for grandchildren. More frail elderly parents may be seen as contributing to the household by providing companionship, or general supervision of grandchildren, even if they do not engage in more active child care or household tasks.

DIRECTIONS FOR FUTURE RESEARCH

In summary, the findings discussed in this chapter suggest that it is only under particular circumstances that residence sharing creates family conflict. In most cases, coresidence is associated with low levels of both marital conflict and parent–child conflict. Adult children's presence is the most likely to have a detrimental effect on parents' marital quality when there is conflict between the parents and children—a situation that is the most common when adult children are younger, and do not occupy the same or similar marital status as their parents.

We believe that there are a number of important questions that we could not answer with the present data, particularly regarding the degree of choice involved in forming coresidential families, and the effects of perceptions of equity and exchange. In our view, further research on these issues should include the following components.

First, data should be collected from both the elderly parents and their adult children, to avoid any biases that may occur from interviewing only one member of the dyad. Second, measures of conflict should be administered to a comparison group of parent–child dyads who are not living together. Third, information should be collected regarding the degree of choice that both the parents and children felt was involved in the decision to live together. Fourth, parents and resident children should be asked about their perceptions of equity regarding both their living arrangement and the level of the parent's dependency. Last, qualitative, as well as quantitative data should be collected to examine changes in family relations as parents and children coreside, as well as the circumstances that lead the generations to begin to or discontinue sharing a home.

For more than a decade, gerontologists have attempted to combat the myth that families no longer maintain a belief in filial responsibility (cf. Brody, Johnsen, & Fulcomer, 1984; Brody, Johnsen, Fulcomer, & Lang, 1983), and abandon their elderly relatives or fail to meet their needs (cf. Shanas, 1979). Perhaps another myth is one that holds that there will be high levels of conflict when the generations live together. On the contrary, it appears from the present study that most elderly parents and adult children live together quite harmoniously.

These findings may have important implications for practice and policy. In American society, parents and children are often discouraged from forming coresidential families. Our findings question the appropriateness of this counsel. At the present time, housing is a major issue for the elderly—particularly as they begin to need assistance with activities of daily living. At the same time that elderly parents are having difficulty remaining in homes that they own and do not want to give up, many adult children are having difficulty finding affordable housing. Perhaps elderly parents and their adult children can reduce both of their housing difficulties by considering coresidence as an option. We expect that future research will help to determine whether policies should be developed to facilitate this living arrangement.

REFERENCES

Adams, B. (1968). *Kinship in an urban setting.* Chicago: Markham.

Aldous, J., Klaus, E., & Klein, D. M. (1985). The understanding heart: Aging parents and their favorite child. *Child Development, 56,* 303–316.

Anderson, S. A., Russell, C. S., & Schumm, W. R. (1983). Perceived marital quality and family life-cycle categories: A further analysis. *Journal of Marriage and the Family, 45,* 127–139.

Angres, S. (1975). *Intergenerational relations and value between young adults and their mothers.* Unpublished doctoral dissertation, University of Chicago, Chicago, IL.

Atchley, R. C. (1987). *Aging: Continuity and change.* Belmont, CA: Wadsworth.

Baruch, G., & Barrett, R. (1983). Adult daughters' relationships with their mothers. *Journal of Marriage and the Family, 45,* 601–606.

Bell, R. R. (1981). *World of friendship.* Beverly Hills: Sage.

Benjamin, E. (1981, August). *It's not easy being single after years of marriage: The social world of separated and divorced parents.* Paper presented at the annual meetings of the Society for the Study of Social Problems, Toronto, Canada.

Bengtson, V. L. (1979). Research perspectives on intergenerational interaction. In P. K. Ragan (Ed.), *Aging parents* (pp. 37–57). Los Angeles: University of Southern California.

Bengtson, V. L., & Kuypers, J. A. (1971). Generational difference and the developmental stake. *Aging and Human Development, 2,* 249–259.

Bengtson, V. L., Mangen, D. J., & Landry, P. H. Jr. (1984). The multi-generation family: Concepts and findings. In V. Garms-Homolova, E. M. Hoerning, & D. Schaeffer (Eds.), *Intergenerational relationships* (pp. 63–80). Lewiston, NY: C. J. Hogrefe.

Blau, P. M. (1964). *Exchange and power in social life.* New York: Wiley.

Blenkner, M. (1965). Social work and family in later life, with some thoughts on filial maturity. In E. Shanas, & G. Streib (Eds.), *Social structure and the family: Generational relations* (pp. 46–59). Englewood Cliffs, NJ: Prentice-Hall.

Brody, E. M., Johnsen, P. T., & Fulcomer, M. C. (1984). What should adult children do for elderly parents? Opinions and preferences of three generations of women. *Journal of Gerontology, 39,* 736–746.

Brody, E. M., Johnsen, P. M., Fulcomer, M. C., & Lang, A. M. (1983). Women's changing roles and help to elderly parents: Attitudes of three generations of women. *Journal of Gerontology, 38,* 597–607.

Brooks, A. (1981, January 19). When married children come home to live. *The New York Times,* p. 10.

Campbell, A., Converse, P. E., & Rodgers, W. L. (1976). *The quality of American life.* New York: Russell Sage.

Cicirelli, V. (1981). *Helping elderly parents: Role of adult children.* Boston: Auburn House.

Cicirelli, V. (1983a). Adult children and their elderly parents. In T. H. Brubaker (Ed.), *Family relationships in later life* (pp. 31–46). Beverly Hills, CA: Sage.

Cicirelli, V. (1983b). Adult children's attachment and helping behavior to elderly parents: A path model. *Journal of Marriage and the Family, 45,* 815–826.

Clemens, A. W., & Axelson, L. J. (1985). The not-so-empty nest: The return of the fledgling adult. *Family Relations, 34,* 259–264.

Cowan, C. P., Cowan, P. A., Hemming, G., Garrett, E., Coysh, W. S., Curtis-Boles, H., & Boles, A. J., III. (1985). Transition to parenthood: his, hers and theirs. *Journal of Family Issues, 6,* 451–482.

Disario, A. (1982, July). Back to the nest: When it works out and when to get out. *Glamour,* pp. 51–52.

Dowd, J. J. (1975). Aging as exchange: A preface to theory. *Journal of Gerontology, 30,* 584–594.

Dowd, J. J. (1980). Exchange rates of old people. *Journal of Gerontology, 35,* 596–602.

Edmunds, V. H. (1967). Marital conventionalization: Definitions and measurement. *Journal of Marriage and the Family, 29,* 681–688.

Feld, S. L. (1982). Social structural determinants of similarity among associates. *American Sociological Review, 47,* 797–801.

Fischer, A. (1986, July). Hi, Mom, I'm home . . . again. *Redbook,* pp. 96–97, 136.

Fischer, L. R. (1981). Transitions in the Mother–Daughter Relationship. *Journal of Marriage and the Family, 43,* 613–622.

Gelles, R. (1983). An exchange/social control theory. In D. Finkelhor, R. J. Gelles, G. T. Hotaling, & M. Straus (Eds.), *The dark side of families: Current family violence research* (pp. 151–165). Beverly Hills: Sage.

George, L. K., Landesman, R., & Fillenbaum, G. (1982). *Developing measures of functional status and service utilization refining and extending the OARS methodology.* Final Report to the NRTA-AARP Andrus Foundation.

Gilford, R., & Bengtson, V. (1979). Measuring marital satisfaction in three generations: positive and negative dimensions. *Journal of Marriage and the Family, 41,* 387–398.

Goode, W. J. (1971). Force in the family. *Journal of Marriage and the Family, 33,* 624–636.

Gove, W. R., & Geerken, M. (1977). Response bias in surveys of mental health: An empirical investigation. *American Journal of Sociology, 82,* 1289–1317.

Hagestad, G. O. (1986). Dimensions of time and the Family. *American Behavioral Scientist, 29,* 679–694.

Hagestad, G. O. (1987). Able elderly in the family contact: Changes, chances and challenges. *Gerontologist, 27,* 417–428.

Hetherington, E. M., Cox, M., & Cox, R. (1976). Divorced fathers. *Family Coordinator, 25,* 417–422.

Homans, G. (1961). *Social behavior: Its elementary forms.* New York: Harcourt, Brace, Jovanovich.

Johnson, C. L. (1985). The impact of illness on late-life marriages. *Journal of Marriage and the Family, 47,* 165–172.

Johnson, E. S., & Bursk, B. (1977). Relationships between the elderly and their children. *Gerontology, 17,* 90–96.

Komarovsky, M. (1962). *Blue-collar marriage.* New York: Random House.

Lazarsfeld, P. F., & Merton, R. K. (1954). Friendship as a social process: A substantive and methodological analysis. In M. Berger, T. Abel, & C. H. Page, (Eds.), *Freedom and control in modern society* (pp. 18–66). New York: Octagon.

Lopata, H. Z. (1979). *Women as widows: Support systems.* New York: Elsevier.

Lowenthal, M. F., Thurnher, M., & Chiriboga, D. (1975). *Four stages of life.* San Francisco: Jossey-Bass.

Mancini, J. A., & Blieszner, R. (1985). Return of middle-aged children to the parental home. *Medical Aspects of Human Sexuality, 19,* 192–194.

Miller, R. B., Bengtson, V. L., & Richards, L. (1987, August). *Patterns and predictors of parent–child relationships in aging families.* Paper presented at the annual meetings of the American Sociological Association, Chicago.

Pillemer, K. (1985). The dangers of dependency: New findings on domestic violence against the elderly. *Social Problems, 33,* 146–158. Pillemer, K., & Suitor, J. J. (1988). Elder abuse. In V. Van Hasselt, H. Bellack, R. Morrison, & M. Hersen (Eds.), *Handbook of family violence* (pp. 247–270). New York: Plenum.

Quinn, M. J., & Tomita, S. K. (1986). *Elder abuse and neglect: Causes, diagnosis, and intervention strategies.* New York: Springer.

Rollins, B. C., & Cannon, K. L. (1974). Marital satisfaction over the life cycle: A reevaluation. *Journal of Marriage and the Family, 36,* 271–283.

Schafer, R. B., & Keith, P. M. (1981). Equity in marital roles across the family life cycle. *Journal of Marriage and the Family, 43,* 359–368.

Schaie, K. W., & Willis, S. L. (1986). *Adult development and aging.* Boston: Little, Brown.

Schnaiberg, A., & Goldenberg, S. (1986, August). *From empty nest to crowded nest: Some contradictions in the returning-young-adult syndrome.* Paper presented at the Annual Meetings of the American Sociological Association, New York.

Schumm, W. R., & Bugaighis, M. A. (1986). Marital quality over the marital career: Alternative explanations. *Journal of Marriage and the Family, 48,* 165–168.

Schumm, W. R., Jurich, A. P., Bollman, S. R., & Bugaighis, M. A. (1985). His and her marriage revisited. *Journal of Family Issues, 6,* 221–227.

Shanas, E. (1979). The family as a social support system in old age. *Gerontologist, 19,* 169–174.

Shehan, C. L., Berardo, D. H., & Berardo, F. M. (1984). The empty nest is filling again: implications for parent–child relations. *Parenting Studies, 1,* 67–73.

Starr, B. D., & Weiner, M. B. (1981). *Sex and sexuality in the mature years.* New York: Stein & Day.

Steinman, L. A. (1979). Reactivated conflicts with aging parents. In P. Ragan (Ed.), *Aging parents* (pp. 126–143). Los Angeles: University of Southern California Press.

Steinmetz, S. (1983). Dependency, stress, and violence between middle-aged caregivers and their elderly parents. In J. I. Kosberg (Ed.), *Abuse and maltreatment of the elderly,* (pp. 134–139). Littleton, MA: John Wright PGS.

Steinmetz, S., & Amsden, D. J. (1983). Dependent elders, family stress, and abuse. In T. H. Brubaker (Ed.), *Family relationships in later life* (pp. 173–192). Beverly Hills, CA: Sage.

Straus, M. A., Gelles, R. J., & Steinmetz, S. K. (1980). *Behind closed doors: Violence in the American family.* New York: Anchor/Doubleday.

Suitor, J. J. (1984, September). *Family members' support for married mothers' return to school.* Paper presented at the annual meetings of the New York State Council on Family Relations, Ithaca, New York.

Suitor, J. J. (1987a). Friendship networks in transition: Married mothers return to school. *Journal of Social and Personal Relationships, 4,* 445-461.

Suitor, J. J. (1987b). Marital happiness of returning women students and their husbands: Effects of part- and full-time enrollment. *Research in Higher Education, 27,* 311-331.

Suitor, J. J. (1987c). Mother-daughter relations when married daughters return to school: Effects of status similarity. *Journal of Marriage and the Family, 49,* 435-444.

Suitor, J. J. (1991). Marital quality and satisfaction with the division of household labor across the family life cycle. *Journal of Marriage and the Family, 53,* 221-230.

Suitor, J. J., & Pillemer, K. (1987). The presence of adult children: A source of stress for elderly couples' marriages? *Journal of Marriage and the Family, 49,* 717-725.

Suitor, J. J. & Pillemer, K. (1988). Explaining conflict when adult children and their elderly parents live together. *Journal of Marriage and the Family, 50,* 1037-1047.

Suitor, J. J., Pillemer, K., & Straus, M. A. (1990). Marital violence in a life course perspective. In M. A. Straus & R. Gelles (Eds.), *Physical violence in American families* (pp. 305-317). New Brunswick, NJ: Transaction.

Sussman, M. (1976). The family life of old people. In R. H. Binstock, & E. Shanas (Eds.), *Handbook of aging and the social sciences* (pp. 218-243). New York: Van Nostrand Reinhold.

Thompson, L., & Walker, A. J. (1984). Mothers and daughters: Aid patterns and attachment. *Journal of Marriage and the Family, 46,* 313-322.

Troll, L., & Bengtson, V. (1979). Generations in the family. In W. R. Burr, R. Hill, F. I. Nye, & I. L. Reiss (Eds.), *Contemporary theories about the family* (Vol. 1, pp. 127-161). New York: The Free Press.

Troll, L. E., Miller, S. J., & Atchley, R. C. (1979). *Families in later life.* Belmont, CA: Wadsworth.

Toufexis, A. (1987, May 4). Show me the way to go home. *Time,* p. 106.

Walters, B. K., Sr. (1986, August 25). Parenting on the downside. *U.S. News and World Report,* p. 63.

White, L. K., Booth, A., & Edwards, J. N. (1986). Children and marital happiness: why the negative correlation? *Journal of Family Issues, 7,* 131-148.

Wilen, J. B. (1979, November). *Changing relationships among grandparents, parents, and their young adult children.* Paper presented at the annual meetings of the Gerontological Society of America, Washington, DC.

Young, M., & Willmott, P. (1957). *Family and kinship in east London.* Baltimore, MD: Penguin.

IV

SOCIAL STRUCTURE
AND THE FAMILY

Normative Obligations
and Parent-Child Help Exchange
Across the Life Course

Alice S. Rossi
Peter H. Rossi
University of Massachusetts

This chapter reports two lines of analysis from a larger study of the parent–adult child relationship: first, the structure of normative obligations toward a range of specified kinpersons, which permits us to specify the respects in which obligations toward parents and children differ from the obligations felt toward less closely related kin; and second, an overview of the help exchanged between parents and adult children from the early adulthood of the children to the very elderly years of the parents (Rossi & Rossi, 1990). We begin, however, with a discussion of the major issues posed in the study, and their translation into the research design we adopted to pursue them, so that these two more specific themes reported in later sections can be located in the framework of the larger study.

CONCEPTUAL ISSUES IN THE LARGER STUDY

Four major concerns were brought together in the study. The first and largest framework within which we explored the relationship between parents and adult children is the life course context. Hagestad (1984) has pointed out that research on the parent-child relationship has been focussed at the very earliest and very latest phases of the life course, with developmental psychologists concerned with the years of infancy through adolescence, and social gerontologists with the very elderly years of the parents when their children are middle-aged. Left relatively uncharted is the long stretch of time when the children are young adults and their parents are still vigorous and healthy middle-aged adults. Our expectation was that childhood dependence on parents is followed by several decades during which the parent–child relationship is re-negotiated and help flows in both directions in a more reciprocal fashion, paving the way to the time when some elderly parents become dependent for personal care and psychological support from their adult children. Assuming our predictions held that interaction and help exchanges are mutually gratifying and reciprocal in the years when children move from young to middle aged adults, late life dependency of parents on children is not an abrupt inversion from child dependency to parental dependency, but a far smoother further development in a relationship that accommodates to the changing needs of the relationship partners.

A second major concern was with gender of parent and child. Indeed, we held the view that we are not justified in speaking of "parents" and "children" unless it has been empirically established that gender does not matter (i.e., that there are few or no differences in this core family relationship among the basic four dyads of mother–daughter, mother–son, father–daughter, and father–son). Our expectation was that gender was an important structural axis around which family relations are organized, such that the greatest intimacy, most frequent interaction, and most extensive help exchange would be found in the mother–daughter relationship, the least intimacy, contact and help between fathers and sons, with the cross-sex dyads falling between the same-sex dyads.

A further concern was to specify gender beyond reliance merely on the sex of respondents. It has been fashionable in sociology to argue that gender is largely a *social construction*, a product of differential sex-role socialization, with biological sex dimorphism contributing minimally to observable differences in social behavior and affect of men and women. If this were true, it should follow that measures of the content of sex-role socialization and the personal attributes left as a residue of that socialization should "explain" an initial empirical observation of a gender difference. To our knowledge, however, this has not been done. Interpretations of gender differences, as a consequence, have tended to be post hoc explanations, rather than empirically grounded demonstrations that gender is socially constructed. Consequently, we wished to measure sex-role socialization and personal attributes, in order to test these assumptions. Toward that end, we explored the extent to which parental training during the formative years followed traditional lines or not (i.e., whether daughters were taught domestic skills to a greater extent than sons, and sons taught masculine and cognitive skills to a greater extent than daughters). Furthermore, we also devised abbreviated measures of femininity and masculinity, although we label these constructs *expressivity* and *dominance* to avoid any assumption of a necessary linkage to a biological substrate. These measures were designed both to help explain differences between men and women in their parental and adult child roles, and to explore intragender variation in the family behavior of men and women.

A third major concern was with the question of how parents and children differ in their perceptions of the relationship between them. Bernard (1972) made the important point that every marriage is two marriages, a "his" marriage and a "her" marriage; in a similar way, we expected the parent–child relationship to be viewed differently by the two generations. All too often reports about family relationships are obtained from a single informant, typically a woman reporting on her marital and maternal roles. The implication of Bernard's point is that data on a social relationship needs to be obtained from both partners to the relationship, which is what we have done by interviewing both parents and their adult children.

The fourth concern was to provide *interpretive depth* to the study by exploring the impact of early family life on contemporary relations between the generations. No other human relationship has as long a history as that between a parent and child, going back as it does not merely to the birth of the child, but to the qualities parents brought to their marriage, and their hopes and dreams about the children yet unborn. And no other adult figures are as important to the qualities children carry into adulthood as parents are, from shared genes to personality characteristics, status attainment, basic values, and perhaps even the parenting styles children bring to the rearing of their own children, a particularly likely prospect in a society that has never defined parenting skills as a legitimate area for formal schooling.

To include data on early family life necessarily involved asking retrospective questions, which goes against the prejudices of American sociologists, unlike our European counterparts who are less hesitant about obtaining life history data from contemporary informants. Although sociologists concede that individual behavior and beliefs are powerfully affected by race, social class, and gender, they have been less willing to concede influences rooted in early family life, we suspect because such formative influences are less amenable to change, and hence may represent barriers to purposive social and political action to which many sociologists are committed. We do not subscribe to this view, and assumed the inclusion of date on early family life was an excellent way to build a bridge between life span psychology and life course sociology. Our goal was to test the extent to which the quality of early family life shows persistent effects on later parent–child relationships, independent of the press of current needs and resources of the two generations.

DESIGN FEATURES OF THE STUDY

The design decision that flowed from these four concerns was to obtain a primary data set from an age representative, random probability sample of adults, which we drew from the greater Boston metropolitan area, resulting in 1,400 personal interviews with respondents ranging in age from 19 to 92.

At the end of these personal interviews, respondents filled out a self-administered vignette booklet on normative obligations, to be described later, as well as a self-rating sheet on personal traits. These self-ratings provided measures of expressivity and dominance, described earlier, and drive, a measure of age-related energy level.

In the main sample interviews, identical questions were asked concerning the relationship of the 1,400 respondents to each of their children, and each of their parents, if they were still alive. We measured four dimensions of the relationship, following Bengtson and Schrader's (1982) specification of intergenerational solidarity: affective closeness, social interaction, value consensus, and help exchange. We also obtained retrospective ratings concerning early family life, including measures of affection and authority of respondents' mothers and fathers, the social and emotional significance of other kin while respondents were growing up, the number and type of "troubles" the family experienced, extent and type of skill transmission by parents to children (to explore gender-role socialization), a global rating of the cohesiveness of the early family, and so forth.

At the end of the interviews, the cooperation of respondents was sought to obtain the names, addresses, and telephone numbers of each of their adult children and their parents. From this pool of information, we drew spinoff samples of parents and adult children, and conducted telephone interviews with them. No restriction was placed on their location except that they reside in the continental United States or Canada.[1] Special attention was given to select cases that assured an equitable distribution of the four gender-specific dyads of parents and children. Telephone interviews are conducted with 323 parents and 278 adult children. Figure 11.1 provides an overview of the three samples involved in the study and the base Ns by sample and gender. Note the convention followed in labelling the three generations represented in the three samples: G2 refers to the main sample middle generation, G1 to the parents of these respondents, and G3 to the adult children of the respondents.

There were clearly measurement implications to this design. For one, constructs had to be measured by clearly posed questions with a narrow range of response categories, so that they would be appropriate to both a personal and telephone interview. Second, constructs had to be measured efficiently, with few items, simply because so many dimensions were to be measured for each parent and each child of the respondent.[2] Interview time was thus largely a function of the number of living parents and adult children: An interview with a respondent with only one child and no living parent took an average

---

[1]This is important because socially mobile children tend to be geographically mobile as well.

[2]With a Boston sample, it was no surprise to find many older adults had had eight or more children. We set an upper limit of seven children for whom detailed information was obtained for each child.

Generation	Respondents	# Reported by G2	# Respondents		# Nonrespondents
G1 (Parents)	323	599 Living Fathers	129 Fathers	< ---- >	470 Fathers
		835 Living Mothers	194 Mothers	< ---- >	641 Mothers
			↑ ↓		
G2 (Main Sample Respondents)	1393		588 Men 805 Women		
			↓ ↑		
G3 (Adult Children)	278	550 Sons	136 Sons	< ---- >	414 Sons
		531 Daughters	142 Daughters	< ---- >	389 Daughters

Note: ↑ Information ABOUT a parent (or child).
     ↓ Information FROM a parent (or child).
< ---- > Comparison to test for selection bias.

FIG. 11.1. Case distribution of respondents in three samples, and nonrespondents in G1 and G3 generations.

of little less than 1 hour, but an interview with a respondent both of whose parents were alive and who had six adult children took over 2 hours.

We turn now to the design and findings on normative obligations.

DESIGN AND MEASUREMENT OF KIN OBLIGATIONS

Sociologists talk and write a great deal about social norms—those prescriptive and proscriptive standards of socially approved behavior—and most social scientists would agree that the family is the primary context for the acquisition and application of social norms. But there is far more theory than empirically grounded findings concerning the social norms that govern social life, even those concerning family and kinship relationships and behavior, where one would most expect to find them. Indeed, in 1964 a *Handbook on Sociology* by Faris contained an excellent lengthy chapter on norms, values, and sanctions, but in 1988, a handbook with the same title, edited by Smelser, contains no chapter and only four entries in the index to "norms."

We believe the measurement practices that have dominated sociology and social psychology have been barriers to the empirical study of social norms. These practices seem designed to *avoid* finding evidence for precisely those norms, about which there is a large degree of social consensus. Our impulse as researchers is to reject items with highly skewed response distributions, because they tell us little about interindividual variation, and it is such variation that is at the heart of most of our research. We prefer items with maximum variance, hence minimum agreement among respondents, a strategy that makes good sense in explaining variation in, say, degree of aggressiveness among male adolescents, but does not make good sense for sociologists trying to understand the overall normative patterning of human behavior, including kin obligations.

Hence, to study social norms, we must depart from customary measurement practices. We also face difficulties in problem formulation. Norms do not exist in a vacuum: They are embedded in highly specific ways in social life, with only a loose fit between actual behavior and the normative order. Much of the work of our legal system lies precisely in making determinations about how legal norms apply to specific instances of behavior. The general principles may be embodied in the statutes, but attorneys, juries, and judges have to fit specific instances of behavior into the meaning of those principles. We might all agree that we feel more obligation to provide help to a sibling than to a cousin, but would probably have trouble explaining why this is so in terms of any general principles, and we would probably also have trouble articulating where, across many domains of potential need, our obligations end to either a sibling or a cousin. In other words, we can expect a much greater degree of consensus in a society when norms are stated in general terms and a lesser degree of consensus over how norms apply in specific behavioral contexts, and in the specific kinpersons involved in those contexts.

The implication we drew from these considerations is this: An understanding of the role of norms in affecting concrete kin relationships requires understanding how such general rules are interpreted in *specific settings* with *specific kinpersons*. Because there are so many potential applications to kin, the issue becomes how properly to "sample" from among the many possible settings and the many different categories of kin to which the general norm may apply, in order to gain an appreciation for how general norms are translated into specific guides to behavior. This also implies that our goal is to *infer* the general structure of obligations through the patterning of reactions to specific instances involving a range of specified kinpersons.

This is the premise underlying the technique we adopted to measure kin obligations, the factorial survey method (Rossi & Nock, 1982). Our purpose was to specify empirically how the level of obligations adults feel toward parents or children differs from the obligation they feel toward other, less closely related kin—grandparents, grandchildren, parents-in-law, aunts, uncles, nephews, cousins—or to such non-kin as friends, neighbors, or an ex-kinperson like an ex-spouse.

The essence of the factorial survey method used is to present respondents with a set of vignettes, each containing a short description of a specific kinperson in common situations that might evoke a sense of obligation to make some appropriate gesture toward that person. One of two types of situations was described in the vignettes:

1. *Crisis events*, in which the situation of need was triggered by a traumatic event in the life of a kinperson. We selected four crisis events: undergoing major surgery, experiencing serious personal problems, having lost almost everything to a household fire, and running out of unemployment benefits. On these crisis events, respondents rated how obligated they would feel, in an 11-point scale, to offer "comfort and emotional support" or "some financial help." On the assumption that obligation level might vary as a function of the *duration* of a crisis, each event was further characterized as one that would last either "for a few weeks" or "a very long time."

2. *Celebratory events*, in which we specified three events: winning an award after years of effort; going to have a birthday; and just moving into a new place. The obligation ratings for the celebratory events were to either "give something appropriate to the occasion," or "to visit" the person.

The seven circumstances therefore represent our "sample" of specific *types of circumstances* that might predispose to varying degrees of obligation on the part of respondents toward the kind of person described in the vignette. The most important dimension of the vignette design was the kinperson or non-relative involved in the obligating circumstances: They included 74 relationships, so structured to distinguish between male and female, and between a married state and an unmarried or widowed state. Gender of each kin type was specified because it is a major variable in the study, and our expectation was that women kin would evoke higher levels of obligation than men kin. Marital status was specified because we expected kin with no marital partner would evoke higher levels of obligations than those with a spouse (e.g., unmarried daughters vs. married daughters). The kin designated ranged from the four grandparents, (each described as a grandmother or grandfather on either the maternal or the paternal side of the family—(e.g., your mother's mother—), through the respondents' generation (siblings and cousins) to children and grandchildren (e.g., son's son, daughter's son). In addition to these consanguineal kin, we included parents-in-law, children-in-law, and in light of high divorce and remarriage rates, stepparents and stepchildren, all specified in terms of gender and marital status. To provide a contrast with the level of felt obligation to kin, we also included friends, neighbors, and former spouses as designated categories.

Each respondent rated 32 vignettes,[3] each set being a separately and independently drawn probability-based sample of all possible vignettes. The vignette booklets were printed by computer and contained that respondent's unbiased sample from the total set of 1,628 unique vignettes. Some 1,200 respondents completed the vignette booklets, thus producing approximately 36,000 vignettes for analysis. Two examples of such vignettes follow:

---

[3]One of the 32 vignettes was a "practice" vignette, so interviewers could gauge whether the respondents understood the task.

Sample Crisis Vignette

Your unmarried sister has undergone major surgery and will be bedridden for
a few weeks. This problem is straining her financial resources. How much of
an obligation would you feel to offer her some financial help?

Sample Celebratory Vignette

Your widowed father is going to have a birthday. How much of an obligation
would you feel to give him something appropriate to the occasion?

KIN NORM FINDINGS

Symmetry

The most important result of the aggregate level of analysis of these vignette
ratings was the beautiful symmetry of the normative pattern they revealed:
Normative obligations to kin are highly structured, and only modestly affected by variation in situational stimuli. The most important dimension in this
structure is the degree of relatedness between ego and the kinperson in question. Figure 11.2 provides a graphic overview of these results. The obligation
ratings were more responsive to the number of connecting links between respondents and the specified kinpersons than they were to the type of relative within
a link category. Most of the variance in mean obligation ratings was accounted for by the number of links between ego and the kinperson. Mean ratings
decline as you move either *up* or *down* the direct generational line from ego,
with roughly the same level of obligation in each position relative to ego, as
they do on the collateral range dimension as well. As seen in Fig. 11.2, for
example, primary kin—parents and children—evoke identical high mean ratings (8.3 on the 11-point scale). They are followed by kin related to ego through
one connecting link (grandparents with a mean of 6.3 and grandchildren with
6.5), followed by kin related through *two* connecting links (e.g., 4.0 for aunts,
4.8 for nephews), to the lowest kin obligation, first cousins related through
three connecting links (parent, grandparent, and parent's sibling), with a mean
rating of 3.2.

KINDRED CORE, PERIPHERY, AND NON-KIN

A second finding from the analysis of normative obligations is that the primary
relations of respondents to parents or to children are relatively impervious to
distinctions that matter in other kin relationships. Gender and marital status
of parent or child make little difference in the obligation levels of respondents,
nor does the gender of respondents show any consistent or significant varia-

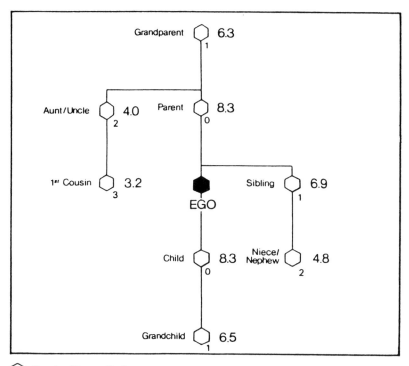

Grandparent 6.3
1

Aunt/Uncle 4.0 Parent 8.3
2 0

1ˢᵗ Cousin 3.2 Sibling 6.9
3 1

EGO

Child 8.3 Niece/Nephew 4.8
0 2

Grandchild 6.5
1

○ Gender Unspecified

FIG. 11.2.   Mean rating on financial aid obligations by number of connecting links between ego and kinperson: selected consanguineal kin only.

tion in the mean ratings of obligations to these primary kin. There is only a minor tendency to feel more obligation toward widowed mothers and unmarried daughters than to parents or children of either gender who are married.

Third, affinal kin, acquired through marriage or remarriage, evoke lower obligations than consanguineal kin in comparable positions, but the nature of the position is important. Thus, obligations to stepparents, who fill the *position* of parents, and to stepchildren, who fill the *position* of children, are higher than to more distant blood kin.

Roughly equivalent ranking of obligation means can be seen in Fig. 11.3, showing an "obligation wheel," with the highest obligations in the core of the wheel, with means over 8, and declining obligation levels as you move toward the periphery of the wheel, with mean ratings under 3. Within any one circled band around the core, then, you can see the kin and nonkin types that share roughly the same levels of obligation. The upper half of the wheel

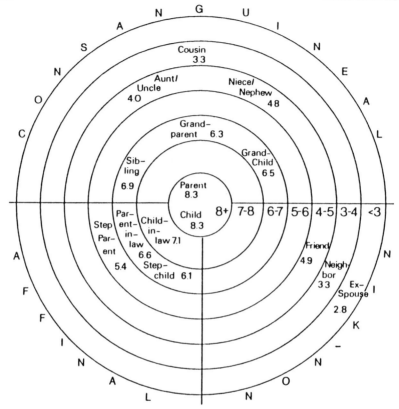

FIG. 11.3.   Layering of normative obligations: mean ratings of financial aid
obligations by degree and type of relationship (G2 Sample).

includes all consanguineal kin; affinal kin are in the lower *left* quadrant and
non-kin in the lower *right* quadrant. Here it can be readily seen that parents-
in-law, stepchildren, siblings, grandparents, and grandchildren (all with one
connecting link to ego) share the same obligation ring; friends are on a par
with aunts and uncles, nieces and nephews; and neighbors with cousins. Out
at the extreme periphery are ex-spouses, shown here with a mean rating of
2.8. When marital status of the ex-spouse is taken into account, the rating drops
even further to a mere 2.0 on the 11-point scale if an ex-spouse has remarried.

GENDER AND KIN OBLIGATIONS

Several interesting findings concern gender of the kinperson in the vignette,
or gender of the respondent. Women kin evoke more obligation than men kin,
especially if they are unmarried or widowed; women secondary or distant kin,
and women non-kin evoke more obligation than men in such categories. Gender

of respondents shows a similar pattern: Men and women agree and do not differ in obligation levels to primary kin, but women show higher obligations to secondary and distant kin than men do.[4] Women are also particularly important as connecting links: There are significant increments to obligation level if the connecting link is a woman, in particular ego's mother (i.e., the link to a maternal grandmother, or the link to a maternal aunt). Higher levels of obligation are felt toward mother's mother than to the other three grandparents, and higher obligations to mother's sister than to any other aunt or uncle.

Thus, the assymetrical tilt to the maternal side of the family that has been found on other dimensions of the intergenerational relationship—social interaction, subjective feelings of closeness, and the specific kin who were salient in youth—is mirrored in normative obligations as well.

This assymetrical maternal tilt is rooted in the specially close bond between mothers and daughters, a closeness that begins in childhood and becomes even more salient in adulthood, in part because the spheres of shared concern and interest is much greater in female–female family ties than in male–male or female–male ties. When gender of respondent and vignette kinperson is considered *jointly*, the female–female bond predominates in being associated with elevated obligation levels. This accords with other findings in our study as well: for example, tension in the parental marriage has no effect on the affective closeness between children and their mothers, especially daughters, whereas there is less intimacy between children of both genders and their fathers when the parental marriage is tense.

Relations between grandparents and grandchildren are also impacted by marital tension in the middle generation: Grandchildren themselves (G3 children of our G2 respondents) report being markedly less intimate with paternal grandparents if their parents' marriage is not a happy one, but parental marital tension has no effect on the closeness of grandchildren and maternal grandparents, especially the maternal grandmother. This takes on particular interest because most research on divorce (e.g., Cherlin & Furstenburg, 1986) suggested a reduction of intimacy and contact between children of divorce and their paternal grandparents as a *result* of the divorce, whereas our data suggest this cooling out takes place *prior* to divorce, as a result of tension in the parental marriage. Indeed, all the evidence in our study supports the notion that men—whether as sons, fathers or grandfathers—hold a more precarious position within the kindred than do women in their roles as daughters, mothers, or grandmothers.

One finding might at first blush seem to violate the principle of higher obligations toward women than men kin. We found that both men and women report higher obligations to sons-in-law than to daughters-in-law. The explanation, in our judgment, is that daughters-in-law are more closely tied to their *own* parents, especially their mothers, whereas sons-in-law are brought closer

---

[4]Black and Irish-Catholic respondents, like women respondents, show higher levels of obligation to secondary and distant kin.

to their parents-in-law as a consequence of their wives' closer ties to their own parents. We concluded that this one reversal from the general pattern represents an exception that proves the rule.

Individual Variation in Kin Norms

Thus far we have reported on the overall structure of kin obligations, relying on mean ratings of obligations. To analyze individual variation in normative obligation levels, we first used the standard deviations around the average ratings as a strategy to identify those parts of the kinship structure over which there is more or less agreement among respondents concerning the obligating strengths of particular types of kin. By this procedure, the types of kin with the largest standard deviations are the relatives about whom kin norms are least well socially defined.

We briefly summarize several findings from the analysis of individual variation in normative obligations:

1. The highest consensus is over obligations to primary kin, and consensus declines the more links there are between ego and the kinperson in question.

2. Consensus is affected by the kind of obligation involved: People are in more agreement on obligations to provide financial aid (crisis events) or gifts (celebratory events) than they are to provide comfort (crisis events) or to pay visits (celebratory events). One infers that people agree that money should move in narrower kin circles than expenditures of emotional energy or time.

3. The strength of adult obligations to kin has its roots in early childhood experiences. For this analysis we used *adjusted obligation indices*, which measure how much respondents expressed a stronger or weaker sense of obligation to kin than is average for the kin type rated.[5] We found higher levels of obligations to kin among those who grew up in intact families than those whose families were broken by death or divorce, a finding that is independent of an array of *current* characteristics. This effect is only shown where primary kin are concerned. It seems likely that the broken home experience lowers obligation to one of the parents, no doubt the noncustodial parent. The fact that one parent, typically the father, left the family, may also project the notion to a child that men have lower commitments to their children, a powerful lesson that may have the long-term effect of lowering the child's sense of obligation to parents and to children.

---

[5]Respondents each rated 32 vignettes, but the sample of vignettes for each respondent was drawn randomly from the total pool of vignettes. Hence, although the vignette sets were "on average" identical, sampling variation meant they were also different one from the other. The "adjusted" obligation indices remove the effects of such sampling variation, by taking into account the particular mix of kintypes in each respondent's vignette sample. They are computed by subtracting from each rating given by a respondent, the average rating given to that kin type in the vignette sample.

Respondents who were reared by parents high on our affection scales acknowledge stronger obligations to kin, not just parents and children but to *all* kin, and interestingly, among primary kin, the reported degree of parental affection elevates the sense of obligation to *children* even more than to the *parents* who were the source of that affection, a rather neat illustration of the point often made that parental love and care provide a fundamental base for later trust in and care shown toward others and the capacity to transmit such caring to the next generation.

Having grown up in families beset by "troubles" of various sorts showed opposite effects on obligation level, as a function of the type of troubles. Those whose families experienced troubles with a likely *emotional* base (alcoholism, psychiatric troubles, physical or sexual abuse, quarreling among adults) showed significantly *lower* obligations to kin and *higher* obligations to non-kin. This suggests that a background experience of poor parental models turns the children away from the family and toward people they could choose to relate to outside their kindred. By contrast, *adversity* in the family of origin (rebellious children, prolonged illness, a death, trouble with external school or police authorities) had the effect of *strengthening* kin obligations. Family ties under these circumstances may have involved pulling together, protecting and caring for family members under adverse or threatening circumstances that left a residue of commitment and a stronger sense of responsibility that extends beyond primary kin to more distant ranges of the kindred.

4. Divorce has the effect for adults that broken homes have for children: both depress the overall strength of obligations to others. Respondents who have ever been divorced are adults who typically have attenuated relations with the kin of former spouses, but in addition, we find that divorced men (compared to married men) show significantly less strong obligations to children, whereas divorced women show just as high an obligation to children as married women do.

5. Having at least one child elevates obligations to *all* primary and secondary kin, reflecting the fact that the birth of a child is a *lineage* event, with repercussions beyond the immediate parents, for the child is a grandchild, niece or nephew as well. Becoming a parent awakens or reinforces the ties and responsibilities of new parents to kin all told; as many adults have experienced, it is sometimes a shock to realize that your parents-in-law are now blood kin of your child.

6. We thought it possible that kin obligations may be a specific instance of the variety of role obligations to which we are all subject. As citizens, for example, we have obligations to perform such duties as filing honest tax returns, serving on juries, voting, contributing to charity, and performing volunteer work. We obtained ratings on how important respondents considered it to be to fulfill such civic duties. The civic duty index showed one of the most significant coefficients on strength of kin obligations. Developmentally, of course, it is likely that we are socialized to family and kin norms long before the ethic

of public and charitable contributions become relevant. Hence we view the early family experiences as predisposing first to kin obligations, and later in the child's development, to obligations to a wider world of community and the society at large.

7. Our last finding on normative obligations provides a link to the topic of parent–child help exchange. The finding may come as a surprise to some: a *negative* relationship between age and the strength of obligations. The older the respondent, the lower the level of felt obligation toward kin and non-kin. There is no particularly sharp inflection point along the life course in this pattern, but a gradual linear decline in the strength of obligations adults report the older they are, a pattern that holds for all types of kin and of non-kin as well.

Age differences in cross-sectional data are notoriously difficult to interpret with confidence, because developmental, or life course patterns may mask cohort effects. On the other hand, a cohort interpretation would be more consistent with a positive age relation to normative obligations than a negative relationship, on the reasoning that older respondents attained less education than young respondents, and the elderly adults are closer to their families' ethnic cultures, which might predispose to higher obligations toward kin. But the age decline in obligation is not restricted to relatives; it applies to friends and neighbors as well. Age of respondent shows a negative coefficient on obligation level even when ethnic origin, educational attainment, religiosity, and numerous personal traits and family background characteristics are present in a multiple regression equation. We return to this issue in the concluding section of the paper.

HELP EXCHANGE BETWEEN PARENTS AND ADULT CHILDREN

We share only a short overview of our findings on the help exchanged between parents and adult children; a more comprehensive treatment appears in Rossi and Rossi (1990).

Measurement of Help Exchange

We obtained measures of the help given to and received from each living parent and adult child of our G2 main sample respondents. The identical questions were asked in the G1 parent spinoff sample and the G3 child spinoff sample. This meant we had to rely on very efficient, simple examples of the variety of help that is exchanged between parents and adult children. We opted to tap a diversity of types of help, rather than detail on a limited array, and with questions calling merely for a ''Yes'' or a ''No'' response (e.g., ''Over the past year or so, have you given your mother any advice on a decision she had to make? Just answer Yes or No''). No attempt was made to gauge the amount of time or the frequency that each type of help was given or received. We also wanted to use the identical measures in all three samples, so they had to apply as readily to parents as to children, to men as to women, and with a reasonable balance between help that requires physical proximity (such as help with chores or care during an illness) and help that is not dependent on physical proximity (such as providing money or a loan, giving a special gift, giving advice or comfort), which could be done by mail or telephone.

The final list consisted of nine types of help, so that the help indices measure the *extent* of help given or received, and the extent to which the *same* types of help were exchanged between parent and child (in a reciprocity index).

Help Exchange Over the Life Course

An overview of our findings is presented in Fig. 11.4 and 11.5. Fig. 11.4 shows the mean ratings on the extent of help given by parent to child (in Panel A) and by the child to the parent (in Panel B). The solid lines refer to help exchange with respondents' mothers, the broken lines to help exchange with fathers. Age of parent in 5-year intervals is shown on the horizontal axis, and the mean help scores in a converted 0–100 scale on the vertical axis.

Several things are dramatically shown in Fig. 11.4: Most striking is the sharp and steady decline in the extent of help given by both mothers and fathers to adult children over the life course. Many of the youngest parents have children between 18 and 22 who are still attending school and largely dependent economically on their parents. Even at that stage of life however, a good deal of help flows from child to parent (on almost all types of help except money). Second, at no point is the help exchange with fathers greater than with mothers. And third, children's help to parents declines rapidly while parents are between 40 and 65 years of age, but after 65, help levels remain stable in the case of help to mothers, but are more erratic in the case of fathers.

Figure 11.5 shows essentially the same data, but this time with the gender of both parent and child specified. Thus, help exchange between mothers and daughters is shown in Panel A in the upper left quadrant, between fathers and sons in Panel D in the lower right quadrant. Help flows from parent to child show significant declines with age of the parent in all four dyads in much the way we have seen in Fig. 11.4 earlier. By contrast children's help to parents shows more of a plateau across the life course, with no upturn of help to fathers, whereas both daughters and sons show an upturn in help level provided to their mothers. Daughters show this inflection point earlier, when mothers are in their 60s, whereas sons show such an upturn only when their mothers are in their late 70s.

Part of the reason why the gender of the child makes a difference in these inflection points is a consequence of the type of help that tends to differentiate

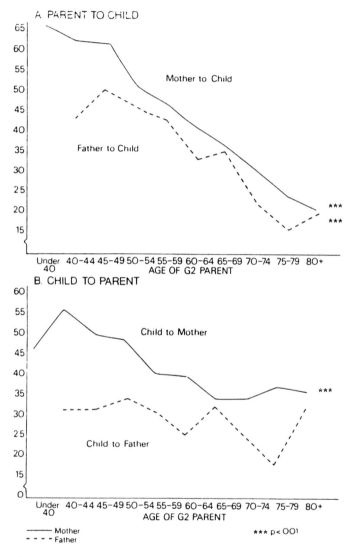

FIG. 11.4. Life course trajectory in help exchange between G2 parents and G3 children by gender of parent (G2 sample, childset file). (Mean ratings on help indices, 0-100 metric.)

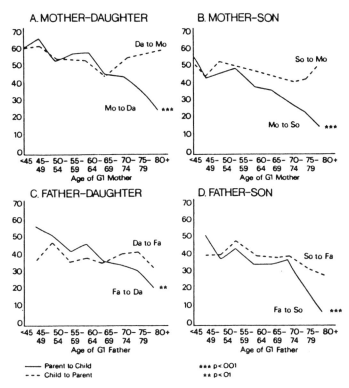

FIG. 11.5.   Life course trajectory in extent of help exchange between G1 parent and G2 child by gender of parent and child and age of parent (G2 sample).
(Mean ratings on help indices, 0-100 metric.)

sons from daughters. Sons give advice and money more than daughters do,
whereas daughters show a greater prevalence of comfort giving, care during
illness, and help with domestic chores. Personal caregiving may occur regardless of marital status of the parents, but advice and financial assistance are
more common when mothers are widowed.

An important point about intergenerational help patterns is the life course
trajectory in economic resources of the two generations. Although educational
attainment remains relatively stable beyond 25 years of age, earnings do not.
Bearing in mind an average age difference between parents and adult children
of 28 years, it is instructive to examine mean annual income of parents and
adult children by the age of parent or the child. Figure 11.6 shows the pattern,
as reported by G1 parents in our spinoff sample, and by G2 respondents as
the adult children. Note that when the children are in their 20s, their income
is low compared to that of their parents who are in their 40s and 50s and at
their peak lifetime earnings level. As children move into their 30s, their own

income rises, while that of their parents has begun its decline. Parents who survive into their 70s are at the lowest income levels of all, especially mothers, many of whom have exhausted private savings as a result of terminal illness expenses of their husbands and whose pension or social security benefits as widows are low. By contrast, their sons and daughters, now middle-aged, are at their peak earnings level.

This economic reality is the important background to the last example from our data set, shown in Fig. 11.7. This figure restricts the help measure to the percent reporting they gave or received "money or a loan" from a parent or child during the past year. The gradual shift in the balance of income level between parents and children across the life course is mirrored in the money flows between the generations, most sharply in the mother–adult child relationship (Panels A and B). Both sons and daughters show a steady increase in giving money to mothers as the mothers age, whereas up to the age of 60, a larger proportion of mothers report giving money to both sons and daughters than the latter report receiving from their mothers. Paternal money giving also shows a decline with the age of the father, but children do not show any significant change over the life course in the frequency of giving money to their fathers. This pattern no doubt reflects the lesser need for financial assistance among elderly fathers, but we suspect it also goes against the grain of gender role expectations on the part of older men. This is suggested by the further finding that it is precisely in reports on money flows that the greatest discrepancies occur between the data obtained from elderly fathers concerning being helped financially by their sons or daughters, and their children's reports of the frequency with which they gave money to their fathers. Men are far more prone to under-report financial help from children than women are. In fact, on many types of help, women report receiving more help than their children report giving to their mothers!

Determinants of Help Exchange

We conducted a very detailed analysis of the determinants of the help exchanged between the generations. Here, we can highlight only a few results. Help levels are responsive to the current circumstances in the lives of both parents and adult children (e.g., children give more help to widowed parents or parents in poor health, and parents give more help to unmarried than to married children, especially their unmarried or divorced daughters). We also find that *net* of these current characteristics, early family life has direct effects on the extent of help exchange between the generations. Children from families they rated as highly cohesive[6] when they were growing up, report higher levels of help given

---

[6]The family of origin cohesion index is based on ratings of the extent to which family members showed love and affection for each other, worked together well as a team, did interesting things together on weekends, and generally found home a fun place to be.

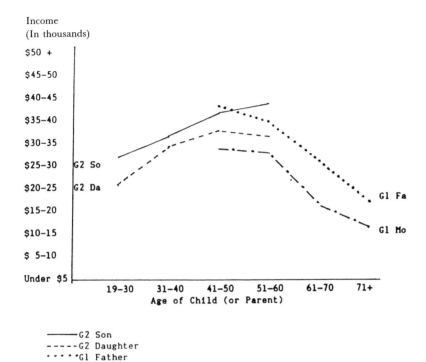

FIG. 11.6. Mean annual total income in 1984 of G1 parents and G2 adult children (G1 & G2 samples).

and received from their parents. So too, the level of affective closeness that characterized the relationship during the child's adolescence shows a continuing effect on the extent of help exchanged between the generations. Furthermore, sons and daughters who are high on expressivity not only give more varied help to parents; they also report receiving more help from their parents. This is particularly the case for high expressive sons in their relationship to their fathers. One infers that if more sons were socialized to become highly expressive men, some of the gap between men and their parents or children, compared to women and their parents and children, would be closed.

One last finding links the two topics we have covered in this chapter: Those who showed high levels of kin obligations in our vignette study also report more varied and reciprocal exchanges of help with their parents and children, and once again, this was a significant coefficient, net of many past and present characteristics of the respondents. In the analysis of individual variance in the level of normative obligations to kin, we found that the measure of expressivity washes out the effect of gender, whereas in the help pattern, gender remains a significant determinant of help exchange, net of expressivity level. This no

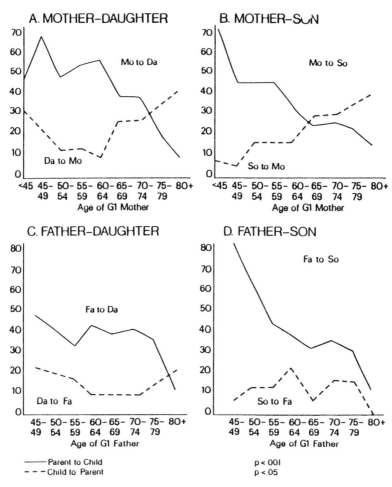

FIG. 11.7. Life course trajectory in the exchange of *money or loans* between G1 parents and G2 adult children by gender of parent and child and age of G1 parents (G2 sample). (Percentage report *giving* or *receiving* money or a loan during the past year.)

doubt reflects the fact that the normative data are hypothetical, whereas the help measures are reports of actual behavior, in which social expectations of appropriate gender-linked types of help may override any personal predisposition toward expressivity.

DIRECTIONS FOR FUTURE RESEARCH

This last finding taps a topic on which we are most anxious to gather new data that would build on the results from the Boston kinship study. Our kin obligation design was unique as an approach to the study of social norms, and it yielded some very interesting results. But there are also critical issues that will remain unresolved until we take some important additional steps in research. At the top of our priority list is further investigation of the relationship between age or phase of the life course and kin obligations. Because obligation level goes down systematically with each older age group does not mean that adults feel others are more obligated to them the older they are. We feel it is imperative to investigate the strength of obligations adults feel *others owe to them*, before drawing any firm interpretations about the normative structure of kin obligations shown in our present data.

Our expectations concerning what we would find in this reverse flow direction are these: When the parent–child relationship is viewed in a life course framework, it is clearly the case that for the early years of child rearing, children are largely the recipients of parental care and support. As children move into early adulthood they have a high degree of felt obligation for all their parents have done for them. During the long stretch of years in early adulthood, when the child is a mature and independent adult, there is a high level of reciprocity in the help exchange between the generations. Nowadays many American parents provide a boost to the status attainment of their children even into their 20s and 30s, including help with educational expenses for children seeking advanced degrees, down payments on a house, or advice and referrals to customers and clients that are relevant to the child's occupation. But children also help their parents in numerous ways during these years. In other words, some balance may be reached in which help in equal amounts flows in both directions between parents and children. Once the parents enter their 70s, some reversal of help flows may occur: the parents have discharged their responsibilities toward their children, the children are at their peak earnings and may continue to provide help of various sorts to their elderly parents. It is rarely the case, however, that elderly parents become the total dependents on their children that the children had been on them during infancy and childhood. Elderly parents in traditional societies may feel less obligated to others and expect others to be more obligated to them, but in western societies, elderly parents derive gratification from having discharged their obligations to others and from the knowledge that their children are doing all they can in rearing the grandchildren.

There is also likely to be an accompanying shift in the subjective dependency between the generations over the life course, a shift illuminated by the "strength of weak ties" theory. In childhood and adolescence, fewer of the parents' needs are gratified by children than children's needs are gratified by their parents. With weaker ties, parents hold the power. At the end of the life course, the scenario has reversed, with the power now in the hands of the children, because children have less need of elderly parents than elderly parents have need for their children. But with the American penchant for independence, the elderly are not likely to reveal the full extent of their own subjective needs and will take what pride they can from maintaining their independence for as long as possible.

One especially important next step in the study of kin obligations is to vary the crisis situations to a greater extent than we did in our study. We relied upon noncontroversial circumstances: a household fire, surgery, emotional problems, or loss of job. We would like next to include triggering events that tap ethical and legal boundaries, such as a parent or a child or a brother-in-law who has a gambling debt or was arrested for driving while drunk. We expect to find much greater variance in the strength of obligations even toward primary kin with the inclusion of such ethically borderline situations.

Finally, we need to take our own argument to heart and include spouses in any next step in the study of kinship obligations. We had rejected that possibility out of hand, because we assumed our respondents would find it foolish in the extreme to be asked how obligated they would feel to provide comfort or financial support to a wife or husband who had major surgery. But to exclude a kin type because we anticipate an extraordinarily skewed response distribution is to violate our own position that the study of social norms requires a departure from customary measurement procedures, and to miss the opportunity to compare the level and kind of obligations that inhere in the marital relationship with the obligations we have found in the parent–child relationship. As an example of one highly specific hypothesis in a future study of this kind, we expect higher obligation levels to parents or adult children who engaged in unethical or illegal behavior than to wives and husbands under similar circumstances. We have the option of terminating a marriage and pushing an ex-spouse to the periphery of the obligation wheel. Some of us may sever ties to parents, perhaps especially fathers, but few of us are likely to sever ties to our children, however heartbreaking and unethical we judge their behavior to be.

Our kinship study has provided a rich data-set that has been fascinating to analyze and to report on. Now the future beckons, and we are eager to replicate our study with national data and some revision in the measurement of the major constructs, and thus to deepen our understanding of the relationship between parents and children.

REFERENCES

Bengtson, V. L., & Schrader, S. (1982). Parent–child relations. In D. J. Morgan & W. A. Peterson (Eds.), *Research instruments in social gerontology* (Vol. 2, pp. 115–128). Minneapolis, MN: University of Minnesota Press.

Bernard, J. (1972). *The future of marriage*. New Haven, CT: Yale University Press.

Cherlin, A. J., & Furstenberg, F. (1986). *The new American grandparent*. New York: Basic Books.

Faris, R. E. L. (Ed.). (1964). *Handbook of sociology*. Chicago, IL: Rand McNally.

Hagestad, G. O. (1984). The continuous bond: a dynamic multigenerational perspective on parent–child relations between adults. In M. Perlmutter (Ed.), *Parent–child relations in child development, The Minnesota symposium on child psychology* (Vol 17, pp. 129-158). Hillsdale, NJ: Lawrence Erlbaum Associates.

Rossi, A. S., & Rossi, P. H. (1990). *Of human bonding: parent–child relations across the life course*. Hawthorne, NY: Aldine de Gruyter.

Rossi, P. H., & Nock, S. L. (Eds.). (1982). *Measuring social judgments: The factorial survey method*. Beverly Hills, CA: Sage.

Smelser, N. (Ed.). (1988). *Handbook of sociology*. Newbury Park, CA: Sage.

Transitions in Work and Family Arrangements: Mothers' Employment Conditions, Children's Experiences, and Child Outcomes

Elizabeth G. Menaghan
Toby L. Parcel
The Ohio State University

The increased prevalence of maternal employment and nonmaternal child care in the United States and other industrialized countries has prompted wide discussion regarding the impact of these conditions on adult lives and on child outcomes. Much of this discussion has viewed mothers' employment as a social problem and has emphasized research contrasting the children of employed and nonemployed mothers. Perhaps the single clearest conclusion after decades of such studies is that there is no strong positive or negative effect of maternal employment (Hoffman, 1983, 1989), and that there are wide variations in effects observed. In this chapter, we focus explicitly on an important source of those variations among employed mothers: We emphasize variations in the occupational and economic experiences that employed mothers encounter, and discuss how those maternal experiences can be expected to affect their children's everyday lives.

Consistent with Bronfenbrenner's (1979) framework for studying human development and Elder's (1974) exemplary analyses, we seek to bridge the disciplinary and subdisciplinary boundaries that too often put pieces of the same puzzle into separate research traditions. Even within studies of the family, marital interaction has tended to be of primary interest to family sociologists, whereas parent–child interaction has been emphasized by developmental psychologists (Furstenberg, 1985). To a still greater extent, analogous divisions of labor have left the economy, socioeconomic status, and occupations to one set of researchers, and family interaction and child development to others. Such divisions leave unexplored the mechanisms by which each affects the other.

In our own model, we have integrated insights from a diverse set of research traditions to provide an understanding of how social structure shapes family interaction and human development. We argue that maternal employment experience is influenced by the larger economy as well as by maternal characteristics, and that women are often restricted to positions lower in status, wages, and stability. We argue that the quality of the child's home environment, as well as the quality and stability of nonmaternal settings, is negatively affected by unsatisfying, unstable maternal employment and insufficient economic resources. We expect high rates of instability in nonmaternal child care arrangements and in maternal household composition to adversely affect child outcomes. The quality of both maternal and nonmaternal child care will have direct positive effects on child outcomes, with family environment potentially having more powerful effects but with the strength of these relationships varying with the amount of the child's exposure to each arrangement. Thus, adult experiences in the labor force shape children's experiences at home and elsewhere, in ways that tend to perpetuate socioeconomic inequalities. In this chapter we emphasize the flow of influence from adults' participation in occupational life to children's everyday experiences; but we acknowledge that children's experiences may also feed back over time to influence adult labor force participation.

Although much of the current debate contrasts maternal care with other arrangements, viewing the former as desirable and the latter as potentially damaging, we emphasize the parallels between ''good'' nonmaternal care arrangements and ''good'' home environments. We argue that ''mother care'' and ''other care'' (Scarr, 1984) have much in common: Similar features of maternal and nonmaternal care settings affect caregiving behaviors, and the same caregiving behaviors are associated with better child cognitive and emotional outcomes in each setting.

Figure 12.1 summarizes the more detailed conceptual model described later. Our discussion begins with the most exogenous influences. Accordingly, we

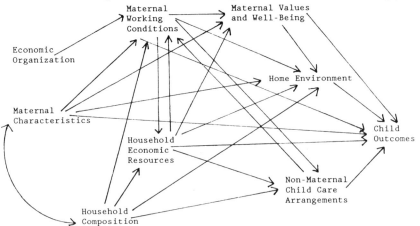

FIG. 12.1   Conceptual model: Child outcomes as a function of maternal working conditions and children's everyday experiences.

first consider determinants of maternal labor market experiences. We discuss both individual characteristics of the mother, including educational attainment and cognitive aptitudes, as well as broader economic and labor market conditions that influence how these characteristics are translated into jobs.

Having outlined individual and social determinants of maternal occupational experiences, we next develop our argument regarding their consequences for children's everyday experiences. We discuss both relationships between working conditions and home environments, as well as those between working conditions and nonmaternal child care arrangements. Regarding the first, we discuss how maternal occupational characteristics (such as autonomy, substantive complexity, time pressure, wage levels, and career ladders) are expected to affect the quality of the home environment and mother–child interaction. Here we view maternal values and maternal psychological well-being as important mediators of these occupational effects.

Regarding the second, we outline relationships between occupational characteristics, particularly wage levels and work schedules, and nonmaternal child care arrangements. These relationships are likely to be nonrecursive or reciprocal: Although the dominant sociological view emphasizes how working conditions and economic pressures will constrain child-care arrangements, child-care availability may also constrain maternal work opportunities.

We then sketch out how children's experiences at home and elsewhere are linked to cognitive, social, and emotional outcomes. We describe the parallels as well as the differences between these two major contexts. We especially note how common features of these two major social contexts affect caregiving behaviors, which are in turn linked to child cognitive and emotional development.

Finally, we note limitations to our conceptual model, including the absence of paternal characteristics and the importance of modeling changes in working conditions and child-care arrangements, and discuss directions for future research, including a brief outline of plans to extend the model to address these limitations.

THE ECONOMY, STATUS ATTAINMENT, AND MATERNAL OCCUPATIONAL OUTCOMES

We argue that maternal employment experiences are influenced by both individual characteristics and dimensions of economic organization (Fig. 12.1). We first focus on these two exogenous sets of characteristics affecting maternal employment experience. We draw on sociological status attainment models and economic human capital theories to identify key maternal characteristics: educational, training, and work experience investments and additional personal characteristics such as mental ability, family background, locus of control and achievement orientation. We discuss research and theory on economic organization from both sociology and economics to identify relevant dimensions of economic organization, such as size, profitability and economic concentration of firms, that have implications for the working conditions mothers face on the job.

Individual Characteristics

Status attainment research within sociology and the human capital tradition within economics both argue that characteristics of individuals determine their earnings. The status attainment perspective emphasizes the role of socialization experience, particularly education, as it affects adult socioeconomic status (Blau & Duncan, 1967; Featherman & Hauser, 1978). Originally conceptualized as a model to explain the association between fathers' and sons' occupational statuses, the perspective has demonstrated that this association is primarily due to the intervening role of schooling, with additional measures of school experiences such as peer influences, mental ability and teachers' expectations frequently included (e.g., Alexander & Eckland, 1975; Alexander, Fennessey, McDill & D'Amico, 1979; Howell & McBroom, 1982). Although such models have been fruitful for investigation of socioeconomic attainment and for studying race and gender differences in occupational outcomes and earnings (see Featherman's, 1976, summary), their emphasis on individual characteristics, particularly education, in influencing economic well being has been heavily criticized (Berg, 1970; Horan, 1978; Parcel & Mueller, 1983).

The human capital tradition within economics offers compatible arguments that also call attention to educational attainment and training. This tradition posits the importance of investment in human capital as rendering payoffs in earnings over the life course (see Becker, 1964; Mincer, 1974; Schultz, 1962, for classic statements). Investments that individuals control are typically education, training and work experience, and economists argue that individuals undertake these investments as a function of anticipated payoffs. Although human capital theory clearly acknowledges investments that institutions make in the human capital of individuals, there remains a significant emphasis on individual initiative as the primary cause of individual economic outcomes, a notion associated with a supply side, conservative world view (Blaug, 1976). Both status attainment and human capital perspectives are useful in suggesting personal characteristics of workers that influence their labor market positions, and have inspired extremely fertile research traditions documenting such effects (Boissiere, Knight, & Sabot, 1985; Brown, 1989; Smith, 1984, provide recent illustrations).

Economic Organization

Interest in "the new structuralism" (Baron & Bielby, 1980) within sociology grew up in opposition to the functionalist, supply side views underlying status attainment and human capital models. These more structural arguments include early theories of a dual economy (Averitt, 1968; Beck, Horan & Tolbert, 1978) and a dual labor market (Doeringer & Piore, 1971), as well as the resource approach to economic segmentation subsequently developed by Hodson and Kaufman (1982), Hodson, (1983) and Schervish (1983). The earlier models are most useful in suggesting dimensions along which economic segments vary, whereas the resource approach encourages us to view these characteristics as resources or vulnerabilities affecting adult and family outcomes.

The initial theories of economic segmentation (Averitt, 1968; O'Connor, 1973) posit that the economy is divided into discrete segments, with the economic organization of firms differing between/among segments. Averitt argued that the economy is divided into a center (or core) and periphery. Firms in the economic core are large, capital intensive, highly profitable, oligopolistic (i.e., they control a large share of the market for their respective products), vertically integrated, operating within the context of national or international markets, and are frequently unionized. Such firms are rich in resources and relatively protected from competition. Partly for this reason, they may be better able to offer relatively high wages and attractive fringe benefits to employees. In contrast, firms on the periphery are small, operate with limited and/or antiquated capital, and are marginally profitable, competitive (i.e., controlling a small market share for their products), not vertically integrated, providing products for local or regional markets, and infrequently unionized. Employees of firms on the periphery are less likely to have the insurance benefits or wage levels obtained by those in the core of the economy. Thinking of firms falling along a continuum, we conceptualize firms varying in size, profitability, market share, vertical integration, scope of markets, and extent of unionization. As we develop later, individuals encounter different occupational conditions and opportunities depending on whether their firm has more core or peripheral characteristics (see also Parcel & Sickmeier, 1988).

Theory similarly dichotomized labor markets in the United States into two separate and strikingly unequal parts (Doeringer & Piore, 1971; Osterman, 1984). For example, Doeringer and Piore (1971) have argued that jobs in the primary labor market have better working conditions and are more stable than those in the secondary labor market. Jobs in the primary labor market pay well, are of moderate to high status, have safe and often pleasant working conditions, are attached to job ladders of some length that assure some degree of upward mobility within the firm or occupation, and are generally cushioned against layoffs during cyclical downturns. The upper tier primary jobs are those with the highest pay and status and the longest job ladders; they require educational credentials, and performance is often regulated via internalized codes of conduct. Professional and managerial jobs fall into this category.

Lower tier primary labor market jobs have lesser status and sometimes lesser pay, with workers being attached to shorter job ladders. Specialized skills are required, and work is regulated via formalized, though not internalized, work

rules. Positions are often unionized. The better blue-collar positions are frequently labeled as lower tier primary jobs, although some characterize craft
jobs as upper tier. In contrast, jobs in the secondary labor market are low in
status and in pay, and are often performed under unpleasant and at times un-
safe working conditions. They require minimal skill, and work rules are infor-
mally defined and enforced. Work is unstable in that the jobs are created and
eliminated as a function of cyclical demand. Again, thinking in terms of con-
tinua, jobs vary in wage levels, degree of job security, the extent to which they
afford chance for upward mobility via job ladders, degree of formalization of
work rules, safety and pleasantness of working conditions, status, and the degree
of skill/nature of credentials needed for entry.

Finally, Edwards (1975) argued that primary labor market jobs are more
prevalent in the core of the economy whereas the periphery contains a preponderance of secondary labor market jobs. Although empirical evidence suggests
that assuming direct correspondence between sectors and markets is unwarranted (Parcel, 1987; Parcel & Sickmeier, 1988), researchers agree that it is
useful to view labor market conditions within the context of underlying market sectors.

Although these perspectives identified characteristics useful in describing
market segments, the resource perspective has offered a useful interpretation
of how these characteristics affect individual workers (Hodson, 1983, 1984;
Schervish, 1983). This approach suggests that jobs vary in status, earnings,
and pleasantness and safety of working conditions. They vary in their stability, in the degree of skill and educational credentials required, and in the degree
which the work is routinized. One can view characteristics such as these as
resources that may translate into worker earnings and other socioeconomic outcomes, and may also benefit employers (see also Grant & Parcel, 1990; Hodson, 1986). For example, being on a job ladder may afford the worker opportunities for upward mobility while the firm gains by having ready replacements
for workers who terminate employment or engage in intra- or interfirm mobility. This illustration also suggests that we examine the sequences of jobs individuals hold. For example, multiple periods of involuntary employment since
leaving school and a high proportion of months unemployed may suggest secondary labor market participation, as would holding a succession of low status,
low wage jobs interspersed with periods of unemployment. Alternatively, a
career progression consisting of jobs with successively higher wages, higher
status, and greater complexity would suggest a primary labor market participation pattern. Again, following Edwards' (1979) notions loosely, we can conceptualize how characteristics of economic sectors influence working conditions,
and this is reflected in the upper left-hand portion of our model.

Structuralists point out that there are not enough positions with primary
labor market characteristics for workers who obtain appropriate training. Berg
(1970) eloquently argued that as aggregate qualifications of job applicants rise,

so do the requirements for obtaining good jobs, independent of whether work in the positions actually requires such training or knowledge. More recently, heated debates regarding whether there is deskilling or upgrading in the U.S. economy (e.g., Cyert & Mowery, 1987; Spenner, 1983) suggest the possibility that many of the new jobs being created in today's burgeoning service and retail industries have secondary labor market characteristics. Growth of secondary market type positions suggests an increase in the number of families whose occupational and economic resources we argue are detrimental to child outcomes.

The structuralist approaches pay particular attention to the role that systematic discrimination plays in allocating workers to sectors, markets, and jobs. Workers allocated to the secondary labor market-type positions are disproportionately young, female, and members of racial minority groups. Positions with primary labor market characteristics are more likely to be reserved for white males. Recent study of occupational sex segregation further documents the tendency for women and men to cluster in different sets of jobs (Jacobs, 1989; Reskin, 1984; Reskin & Roos, 1990), and although such segregation does not necessarily dictate differential allocation of working conditions, such segregation does tend to differentiate working conditions by gender (see Lennon, 1987), thus potentially influencing child outcomes.

Other Influences on Maternal Employment Conditions

The level of other economic resources available from household members can also influence child outcomes. Market resources importantly impact family income through wages and salaries paid to adult family members. In addition, mothers' current marital status and marital history, and mothers' fertility histories and plans influence the economic standing of families and the extent of the "resource stretch." Although we do not develop these arguments conceptually here, these factors must be taken into account in empirical estimation.

In summary, we emphasize that variations in maternal employment experiences do not occur randomly. In addition to the individual characteristics such as intelligence, initiative, and educational attainment that are often emphasized in the sociological and economic literatures, it is important to consider the structural factors that affect the occupational opportunities of individual women. We have emphasized the latter because such structural forces are relatively neglected in many accounts of maternal employment and family life.

EFFECTS OF MATERNAL EMPLOYMENT CONDITIONS
ON MOTHER–CHILD INTERACTION

We now move to the intermediate portion of our model, and ask, How do maternal employment conditions affect children's lives? As Fig. 12.1 depicts, we want to trace two sets of effects in this chapter: those on mother–child interaction and those on nonmaternal child care arrangements. We discuss the first set of effects in this section. We emphasize both the substantive conditions of individual jobs and the wages that are attached to them. We first draw from social structure and personality frameworks, and direct attention to variations in employment conditions that affect parental values for their children, adult emotional well-being, and parent–child interaction.

Employment Experience and Maternal Values

Melvin Kohn and his colleagues have been particularly influential in developing the theoretically expected relationships between social class, and especially occupational conditions, and parental values (e.g., Kohn, 1963, 1976, 1977; Kohn & Schooler, 1982, 1983; Pearlin & Kohn, 1966). Kohn viewed social class as importantly determined by occupation. Parental occupations influence the values that parents hold, and these values are important determinants of parental child-rearing behaviors. According to Kohn, white-collar parents place more emphasis on self direction and internalization of norms, whereas blue-collar parents stress conformity to externally imposed standards. These values are, in turn, a function of the actual working conditions the parents themselves face in their jobs. White-collar work more often involves manipulation of ideas or symbols, or involves interpersonal dealings; it may be complex and be performed under conditions of indirect supervision, permitting greater autonomy and self-direction. Blue-collar work more often requires manipulation of things, is more standardized and is more closely supervised. Kohn and his colleagues argued that job incumbents come to value the characteristics demanded on the job more generally, for themselves and for their children. Kohn's theory regarding the impact of working conditions on adult parental values has been empirically supported (Kohn, 1977), although his data did not permit him to demonstrate a link between parental values and parental behavior.

Bronfenbrenner (1979, Bronfenbrenner & Crouter, 1982) also built on Kohn's work in constructing his ecological theory of human development, and argued that the working conditions that parents face affect the values they use in interactions with their children. For Bronfenbrenner, this relationship cannot be accounted for by the effects of third variables such as family structure, family dynamics, class origins, subjective class identification, job dissatisfaction or bureaucratic versus entrepreneurial job settings.

Employment Experience and Maternal Well-Being

In addition to affecting parental values, occupational conditions also affect important aspects of intellectual and psychological functioning. The conditions of work that are common in less valued, and less well-paid, jobs—routinization, low autonomy, heavy supervision, and little demand or opportunity for substantively complex work—erode intellectual flexibility (Kohn & Schooler, 1973, 1978) and exacerbate psychological symptoms (Kohn & Schooler, 1983; Miller, Schooler, Kohn, & Miller, 1979). Other studies outside the United States (e.g., Kohn et al., 1990; Pearlin & Kohn, 1966; Miller, Slomczynski, & Kohn, 1985; Naoi & Schooler, 1985; Slomczynski, Miller, & Kohn, 1981) have replicated the finding that occupational conditions affect psychological functioning.

This tradition of work initially focused almost exclusively on the occupational experiences of men; in contrast to its emphasis on variations in employment conditions, investigations of women's employment experiences have been dominated by a social problems framework that emphasized the fact of employment (and maternal absence from the home) and gave little attention to variations in the substantive content of her employment. However, Miller, Kohn, and their colleagues (1979) have shown that occupational conditions have psychological and cognitive effects on female as well as male workers: more substantively complex work is associated with greater intellectual flexibility and more flexible and responsive social orientations; job pressures and uncertainties are associated with lower flexibility and lower self-esteem and self-efficacy (see also Gecas & Seff, 1989; Mortimer & Borman, 1988; Spenner & Otto, 1985). Other studies also find that less substantively complex and desirable working conditions have negative impacts on adult well-being. Lennon (1987) reported that women's overall feelings of demoralization or "psychological malaise" were influenced by the substantive complexity of their occupations, with those in more complex occupations less demoralized. The same pattern is found using measures of occupational prestige or status (Repetti & Crosby, 1984; Saenz, Goudy, & Lorenz, 1989). Menaghan and Merves (1984) showed that emotional distress is greater when workers experience time pressures, depersonalization, noxious job conditions, and have few opportunities for advancement.

Implications for Mother–Child Interaction

The adult distress aroused by low occupational and economic standing has expectable intergenerational consequences: mothers with less internal locus of control and higher psychological distress display less attentive, responsive, and stimulating parental behavior (Belsky, 1984a; Menaghan, 1983). Thus, when juxtaposed, these studies suggest that occupational experiences will affect mothers' interaction with their children, and thus influence children's cognitive achievements and emotional well-being: occupational conditions come to influence children's development through adult values and well-being. In support of this line of reasoning, Piotrkowski and Katz (1982) argued that the qualities that are demanded of mothers on the job influence the content of socialization for their children and are reflected in their children's academic behaviors.

We note that both maternal job experiences and children's academic behaviors may be affected by other variables as well. For example, we have argued earlier that maternal intelligence and education influence the jobs that mothers are able to obtain; such variables may also have direct effects on children's educational achievement. Some might even argue that the link between maternal employment experiences and child academic outcomes may be spuriously produced by such common causes, rather than reflecting the causal impact we theorize. To test such arguments, researchers need to keep in mind the endogenous character of maternal employment experience, and bring into their empirical analyses such potential sources of spuriousness. Such research demands a multivariate analytical approach. As we detail in the final section of this chapter, our own empirical work suggests that both individual characteristics and current employment experiences have independent effects on child outcomes, and the effects of maternal occupational experiences cannot be dismissed as spuriously produced by the effects of stable individual maternal characteristics.

Economic Pressures, Parental Well-Being, and Parent–Child Interaction

We have argued that maternal working conditions affect maternal well-being and thus mother–child interaction at home; in turn these factors shape the development of these workers' children (see Fig. 12.1). In addition to maternal working conditions, maternal earnings affects maternal and child well-being. When earnings from jobs are low, workplace vulnerabilities create economic environments where children are vulnerable to unfavorable child outcomes.

We see several pathways for such effects. Low wage jobs constrain parents' ability to provide adequate housing, health care, and material stimulation, leaving children vulnerable to unfavorable child outcomes. Economic pressures also affect parental values and feelings of mastery and self-efficacy. Gecas (1979, 1981) has summarized research showing how the degree of economic deprivation associated with low earnings affects parental values, psychological states such as feelings of control and self-esteem, and family patterns of organization. In turn, parental values, parental psychological states, and family structure all shape parent–child interaction. For both men and women who head households, levels of earned income affect feelings of efficacy, and improvements in earnings are associated with improvements in efficacy net of other demographic characteristics and parental responsibilities (Andrisani, 1978; Duncan & Liker, 1983; Duncan & Morgan, 1980; Downey & Moen, 1987). Economic strain and worry have pervasive effects on marital and family satisfaction, and on mothers' perceived problems with their children (Piotrkowski, Rapoport, & Rapoport, 1987; Voydanoff, 1987; Voydanoff & Donnelly, 1988).

In their observational study of mothers' environmental stressors and family interaction patterns, Conger, McCarty, Yang, Lahey, and Kropp (1984) show that mothers in more adverse socioeconomic conditions have more emotional distress and more negative perceptions of their children; these in turn are related to the general emotional tone of mothers' behavior with their children. Siegal (1984) provided a comprehensive summary of the many empirical studies linking economic conditions to adult psychological distress and disturbed family relationships (see also Menaghan, 1990). He argued that the economic conditions that parents face affect their child-rearing behaviors and capabilities, and cited extensive literature indicating an association between economic deprivation and parental abuse and neglect of their children as consistent with this explanation. In their own review of this body of literature, Mirowsky and Ross (1986) eloquently concluded that people in lower socioeconomic positions have a triple burden: there are more problems to deal with, their personal histories are likely to have left them feeling powerless, and that sense of powerlessness discourages them from taking full advantage of what resources and capacities they do have. The result: "a multiplication of despair" (1986, p. 30).

Other characteristics of the mother's life situation, of course, will also affect the processes we have described. For example, the impact of maternal wages and pay on the family's economic resources will be greater when there are no other wage earners in the household. Conversely, given the greater economic returns to men's employment experiences, the presence or absence of a stably employed man will have a large impact on household economic adequacy.

Thus, we expect poor wages and concomitant economic deprivation to be inversely related to the quality of parental child interactions (and also, as we argue later, to the quality and stability of nonmaternal child care arrangements), and negatively related to child outcomes. In addition, jobs with poor economic returns seriously constrain mothers' ability to secure safe housing or to provide material stimulation to their children when they are with them.

EFFECTS OF MATERNAL EMPLOYMENT
ON CHILD-CARE ARRANGEMENTS

We now move to our arguments linking maternal working conditions with children's experiences in nonmaternal child-care arrangements, the other major set of effects depicted in Fig. 12.1. This is a surprisingly neglected topic. While pointing out positive and negative features of care, few child-care studies explore whose children are apt to experience better or worse arrangements. We argue that characteristics of employment such as wages and hours, as well as family composition, influence the quality and continuity of the supplemental care arrangements mothers make. In this section we review literature from several disciplines to help explicate the relationships between maternal working conditions and child care arrangements.

Formal and Informal Care Arrangements

Economists have argued against the often deterministic cast of sociological models that predict child-care arrangements from maternal occupational demands and resources. They contend that individuals (presumeably women) choose both work situations and child-care arrangements to maximize their overall utility, which in this case is general household well-being. For example, Heckman (1974) assumed that informal mechanisms of child care are available to many mothers at low cost while formal mechanisms are more costly. He provided evidence to suggest that the choice of child care, the decision to work and hours worked are jointly determined, and are dependent on women's expected wages and the prices of child care alternatives. Demographers (e.g., Presser & Baldwin, 1980) also noted that mothers' participation in the labor force and number of hours worked are affected by actual and perceived lack of desirable care for their children; such constraints may be particularly strong for mothers who are young, Black, single, and at lower levels of socioeconomic status (Presser & Baldwin, 1980). Actual patterns of labor force participation among the National Longitudinal Survey of Youth's young mothers support the argument that more advantaged mothers are selected into employment, whereas less advantaged ones are selected out: Among young mothers with a 3- to 6-year-old child, those currently employed were older, better educated, had higher scores on standardized tests of cognitive ability, and were from more advantaged families of origin (Menaghan & Parcel, 1991; Parcel & Menaghan, 1990a). Presser (1987) has argued that the phenomenon of parents' working different shifts in dual earner households is a response to difficulties in finding adequate care for children.

Other work focuses more exclusively on the determinants of choice of mode of child care. Such research is concerned with formal, group care in centers or schools versus informal arrangements in the neighborhood or in the child's own home. Robins and Spiegelman (1978) found that use of formal care varies positively with female head's wage rate, the price of the care, and by family structure, with families that included teenagers or nonhead adults less likely to use formal care unless there are both preschool and school-age children in the family. Duncan and Hill (1975, 1977) found that choice of mode of child care is independent of socioeconomic variables except for wife's wage rate, which is associated with choice of formal mechanisms of child care. Choice of formal mechanisms is also associated with region, because formal child care is more likely to be used in the south and less likely to be used in the north central region, and with city size, because formal modes are more likely to be used in larger cities. Stolzenberg and Waite (1984) provided evidence that the cost of formal child-care arrangements varies geographically, although they do not report how averages vary by census region. Although they provide no evidence to suggest that region directly affects child outcomes, these studies suggest some possible indirect effects operating through mode of child care used. Lehrer (1983) and Lehrer and Kawasaki (1985) argued that among married mothers, husbands' permanent income, wife's wages, age structure of children in the household, and level of the wife's labor supply affect the type of child care chosen. Leibowitz, Waite, and Witsberger (1988) found that maternal education and earnings are positively associated with choice of at home care for younger children and formal center care for children 3 years old and over.

Maternal Values and Child-Care Arrangements

Another way that employment experiences affect child-care arrangements is through their effects on parental values. We have argued with Kohn and others that employment experiences influence maternal values. Other research suggests that parental values in turn influence child-care choices. Phillips, McCartney, and Scarr (1987) reported that among Bermudan families using child-care centers, parental values about child development were related to the quality of the child-care center in which their children were enrolled: Higher valuation of social skills, and lower valuation of conformity, was associated with enrollment in higher quality centers. As Kohn's framework would suggest, parental valuation of conformity was itself related to the mother's occupation (K. McCartney, personal communication, June 1989). Parents in such occupational settings are also more likely to earn adequate incomes, permitting them to purchase higher quality care.

Recent research also suggests other experiences that affect parental values and parental child care choices. Howes and Stewart's (1987) study of parents using family day-care homes found that in families with lower levels of stress and higher levels of social support, mothers were more apt to value nurturant, nonrestrictive childrearing approaches. In turn, these maternal evaluations were associated with locating and selecting higher quality child-care arrangements and making fewer changes in child-care arrangements.

To summarize our account thus far, we suggest that economic organization as well as individual characteristics shape women's employment experiences. Those employment experiences affect economic well-being, psychological well-being, and parental values; these in turn affect the quality of both the care mothers directly provide and the supplemental care that mothers arrange. This argument has an additional important implication: the quality of maternal care and the quality of nonmaternal care have common precursors and they will be positively correlated. The already advantaged (occupationally, economically, socially, and psychologically) are also more able to arrange good supplemental care for their children, whereas less advantaged mothers are more likely to be limited to poorer child-care arrangements as well. Except in the small numbers of cases of care subsidized by third party payments, we suggest that it is unlikely that children from families with limited economic and psychological resources will encounter compensating non-maternal arrangements. Rather than compensating for initial differences and disadvantages, nonmaternal care arrangements are apt to reflect existing inequalities among families.

CHILDREN'S CARE EXPERIENCES
AND CHILD DEVELOPMENT:
MATERNAL AND NONMATERNAL EFFECTS

As noted in the beginning to this argument, we juxtapose maternal and nonmaternal care of children, because theoretically both should contribute to child well-being. For maternal as well as nonmaternal caregivers, we argue that more sensitive, predictable, and responsive care facilitates child development, and that adults are more able to provide such care when physical and personal resources are sufficient. When circumstances are less favorable, "individual attention to children falls victim to the exigencies of coping with an overextended set of resources" (Belsky, 1984b, p. 27; see also Ainsworth, Blehar, Waters, & Wall, 1978).

Both low quality interaction with socializing adults and unstable, unpredictable social contexts compromise children's attachment and security, with attendant negative effects on learning. Stability is important in children's everyday environments for several reasons. Anderson (1980) argued that day-care arrangements that are temporarily stable reduce the demand for repeated adjustments to new settings and new caregivers; both the daily mother–child separations and reunions, and the routines and environmental demands of the child-care arrangement, become predictable to the child. These stable, predictable arrangements are less likely to disturb the child's security or development than a sequence of settings and shifts in caregivers (see also Benn, 1986). Parke and his colleagues (1988) pointed out that more stable arrangements also maintain the stability of the child's peer group; for young children in particular, greater peer familiarity is associated with greater social competence. It is not surprising then that toddlers who had experienced more changes in child care arrangements have been characterized by lower social competence with peers (Howes & Stewart, 1987), and with poorer academic progress several years later (Howes, 1988). The child may experience varying degrees of instability depending on the form of child care: A child could remain at the same child-care center, so that the physical environment and the group of peers is stable, yet experience several turnovers in adult caregivers; in contrast, environment, peers, and caregiver change simultaneously when a child moves from one informal arrangement to another (see also Phillips & Howes, 1989 and Hayes, Palmer, & Zaslow, 1990, on the extensive turnover among child caregivers).

In family settings, of course, the importance of stable, predictable caregiving has been widely recognized (e.g., Bowlby, 1969). Like nonparental childcare arrangements, family environments vary in the temporal stability of adult members. In particular, marital disruptions, dating, remarriages, and disruptions of remarriages expose children to many changes in residence and in caregivers. Even when residence with the mother continues, there are likely to be changes in mothers' psychological well-being and the quality of care they provide; such instability has been linked to a higher risk of academic and behavior problems (Furstenberg & Seltzer, 1986).

In both maternal and nonmaternal care settings, the quality of interaction is affected by social structural features of care (such as caregiver–child ratios, group size, and caregiver training). For example, the National Day Care Study of 67 day-care centers (Ruopp & Travers, 1982) and others (Clarke-Stewart, 1982) established the negative role of large group size and poor caregiver-child ratios: As these increased, scheduling became less flexible; caregivers engaged in less facilitative social stimulation, expressed less positive affect, and were more restrictive and negative; and children spent more time in solitary activities, were more frequently unhappy, and were less frequently involved in any sustained activity. In turn, less frequent and less positive adult–child and peer interaction has been associated with lower cognitive and social competence (McCartney, 1984; Phillips, McCartney, & Scarr, 1987).

Thus, nonmaternal child care can have quite different effects depending on its quality. Effects of infant day care in particular are hotly debated (Belsky, 1986; Clarke-Stewart, 1989; Phillips, McCartney, Scarr, & Howes, 1987). Enrollment in high quality day care may prevent the decline in cognitive functioning from infancy through age six that has been observed among economically disadvantaged home-reared children (Ramey, Dorval, & Baker-Ward, 1981; see also Howes, 1988). In contrast, several recent studies (McCartney, Scarr, Phillips, Grajek, & Schwartz, 1982; Vaughn, Gove, & Egeland 1980), have suggested that enrollment in unstable and/or poor quality day care prior to age one increased emotional and social problems in subsequent years, provoking renewed concern with negative effects of infant day care. Howes and Stewart (1987), however, concluded that age at entry per se is less critical than quality and stability of care.

This picture is consistent with, and predictable from, extensive research on parental caregiving and child development. A large body of literature supports the expectations that low quality interaction with socializing adults and unstable, unpredictable social contexts compromise children's attachment and security, with attendant negative effects on social competence and cognitive advance (Crouter, Belsky, & Spanier, 1984; Estrada, Arsenio, Hess, & Holloway, 1987). For example, Estrada and her colleagues demonstrated that the emotional quality of mother–child interaction in the preschool years (as indicated by greater warmth, flexibility, sensitivity, and responsiveness) predicts higher child cognitive performance and higher school achievement at subsequent ages, net of maternal IQ effects. Observations of children's approaches to problem-solving efforts suggest that children in higher quality mother–child dyads were more comfortable with other adults, more likely to choose challenging tasks and initiate new activities, showed more persistence, and were less likely to resist mothers' efforts to assist them. They suggest that a positive affective relationship in the preschool years may function much like secure attachment in infancy (see Bowlby, 1969) by providing a stable emotional base from which children can explore their world. Thus, higher quality affective relationships may enhance children's social competence and their willingness to approach and persist in cognitive tasks.

Parents are more apt to provide quality care when physical and personal resources are sufficient: Parents who have fewer social supports and more family stressors express less nurturant, more restrictive attitudes regarding their children (Howes & Stewart, 1987). Minturn and Lambert (1964) found that mothers responsible for caring for several children who are isolated from and unsupported by other adults are more restrictive and hostile, contributing to a deteriorating parent–child interaction. As in child-care studies, research on families suggest that smaller numbers of children are associated with more effective home environments, characterized by more affective warmth and greater cognitive stimulation (Bradley & Caldwell, 1984; see also Blake, 1989). For both maternal and nonmaternal settings, the socialization literature suggests additional reasons why high ratios of caregivers to children will be associated with better outcomes. As the ratio of parents/caregivers to children decreases, the effectiveness of socialization efforts generally declines. Two processes are involved here: Caregivers spend less time in direct, sustained interaction with any single child; and a larger group of children is more likely to organize into a context of socialization itself, developing goals and norms different from, and often antithetical to, those of the caregiver (Gecas, 1981, p. 196).

In cultures such as our own that emphasize direct maternal care of young children within nuclear families, the total number of other nurturing adults that are available for children and mothers is often constrained by family composition. The prime variation is in the presence or absence of a biological or social father; only 4% of children living with two working parents, and 22% of children living with an employed single parent, have an additional adult relative living with them (Hernandez & Myers, 1988), and contact with nonresident biological fathers is generally quite low (Furstenberg & Nord, 1985). Male partners (and other adults in the household) potentially provide alternative adults to shoulder child-rearing responsibilities, expose the child to a greater range of adults with whom to interact, and offer more routine and sustained models of adult–adult interaction. In summary, we expect that unsupported, unrelieved child care, by mothers as well as nonmothers, will be of lower quality. Higher total numbers of children will also be associated with negative outcomes.

The Relative Impact of Maternal and Nonmaternal Care

Figure 12.1 depicts both mother–child interaction and nonmaternal care experiences affecting child cognitive, social, and emotional outcomes; and we have argued that the same features of family and nonfamily environments affect the quality of care. Socialization theory suggests, however, that the effects of family experiences may be more powerful than the effects of structurally similar nonmaternal child-care arrangements. In general, socialization is more effective in situations of high affectivity, and in which the socializing agents have considerable power or control over the initiates (Gecas, 1981); in this regard, children's nuclear family settings are more likely than other settings to be characterized by more intense, affectively charged interaction, in addition to large socialization ratios.

Thus, the more affectively charged interaction common in family environments may generate more powerful effects than will supplemental care arrangements. In addition, even children in "full-time" nonmaternal care spend much larger amounts of time in their families than in such arrangements. Because we expect the effects of children's environments to vary with the amount of the child's exposure to each arrangement, because the amount of time spent at home outweighs time with other caregivers, and because family environments are more affectively charged than other socialization settings, we expect the effects of family on child outcomes to outweigh the effects of other caregivers.

BASES FOR STATISTICAL INTERACTION

The Role of Gender

We recognize that several of the relationships we posit may vary by gender of the child. Several studies suggest that nonmaternal care effects are more positive for girls than for boys. Crouter, Belsky, and Spanier (1984); Hoffman and Nye (1974); and Bronfenbrenner, Alvarez, and Henderson (1984) argued that girls of working mothers may be more positively affected than boys by the out-of-home socialization experiences they receive in nonmaternal care settings, when background and relevant child attributes are controlled. Others, however, find no significant gender differences (Howes & Stewart, 1987).

Boys may also be more sensitive to the quality of care in the home environment. Studies suggest that young boys display more negative effects, particularly aggression and behavior problems, following marital disruption and subsequent mother-headed family structures (e.g., Crouter et al., 1984; Hetherington, Cox, & Cox, 1978). It is not yet clear whether the negative effects on girls are less or whether the form of girls' problems simply attracts less initial attention/alarm, or only becomes visible at later ages in the context of dating and sexual activity (see Parcel & Menaghan, 1989, for some suggestive evidence). Although these findings might buttress the argument that young boys are generally more vulnerable to complex or unstable social contexts, they also suggest an alternative explanation. Because unmarried mothers of young children are more apt to be in the labor market and to work more hours when they are employed, any differential effect of maternal employment may be confounded with differential effects of maternal marital status. The separate effects of these related circumstances have not yet been established.

The Role of Ethnicity

Given extensive literature regarding racial differences in the content of socialization and in processes of socioeconomic attainment, we expect that the model we have developed may operate differently for children of White and non-White mothers. Although arguments regarding the differential effectiveness of every resource included in the model would be difficult to sustain, racial differences should be frequent enough to warrant systematic investigation regarding the presence and degree of such findings.

LIMITATIONS OF THE MODEL
AND DIRECTIONS FOR FUTURE RESEARCH

In developing our model of maternal employment, adult–child interaction, and child outcomes, we have sought to move beyond what others have called a "social address" (Bronfenbrenner & Crouter, 1982) or "states and rates" (Furstenberg & Seltzer, 1986) approach to social context. These approaches essentially contrast two social categories (e.g., mother employed/not employed; child in child care/not in child care; family with two parents/one parent) on a number of outcome variables. Such designs are inherently flawed: they generally ignore the wide range of variation that exists within such groups; in addition, they do not take into account the many other, often preexisting, differences between groups.

Not surprisingly, such approaches have yielded few significant or consistent findings: even when one is able to document group differences, the question of how or why such differences are produced remains. Without understanding the process by which positive or negative effects are produced, neither theory nor intervention is advanced. Rather than relying on gross dichotomies, we have sought to elaborate the variations in experience within such categories as maternal employment and both maternal and nonmaternal child care, and articulate the processes by which those variations exert their impacts.

We have argued that variations in characteristics of firms and maternal background influence maternal working conditions, as does household economic well-being. Maternal working conditions influence maternal values, which in turn influence the quality of the home environment. Child outcomes are a function of several of these more exogenous influences, but are most directly influenced by the quality of the home environment and the quality and stability of nonmaternal child-care arrangements. To date, we have demonstrated empirical justification for three critical portions of this model, using the 1986 child–mother data set of the National Longitudinal Survey of Youth (NLSY). In analyses of the young (21-28) employed NLSY mothers of 3- to 6-year-old children, we have estimated multivariate models predicting child home environment and children's outcomes from maternal characteristics, current family situation, and current occupational experiences (Menaghan & Parcel, 1991; Parcel & Menaghan, 1988; Parcel & Menaghan, 1990a; Rogers, Parcel, & Menaghan, 1991). We find that the substantive complexity of maternal occupations has significant positive effects on home environments even after controlling for the significant positive effects of smaller family size and maternal self-esteem, locus of control, age, and educational attainment (Menaghan & Parcel, 1991). Higher maternal wages, smaller family size, and better child home environments affect child verbal facility even after controlling for measured maternal ability and other maternal resources (Parcel & Menaghan, 1990a). Maternal working conditions with greater working control of the labor process reduce maternal reports of child behavior problems, as do higher maternal mastery, stable family composition, and stronger home environments (Rogers, Parcel, & Menaghan, 1991).

Despite the interdisciplinary sweep and relatively broad scope of this model, we have nonetheless neglected several additional topics inherently related to these processes. First, because we study biologically related parents and children, an ideal model would also evaluate and control possible genetic linkages that may influence both parent and child behavior (Plomin & Daniels, 1987; Plomin & DeFries, 1983; Scarr & McCartney, 1983). This remains as an important goal for future research.

Second, we have neglected to fully consider the role of fathers in the processes we have studied. Paternal employment experiences obviously make a difference in the emotional and economic circumstances of mothers and children. When both parents are present and both are in the labor force, fathers contribute a high proportion of the total family income (Sorensen & McLanahan, 1987). And although mothers retain most of the responsibility for care of children even when they work, paternal working conditions will still influence the content of the socialization she provides. Even considering that increases in marital disruption and out-of-wedlock births are reducing the amount of time children in the aggregate spend with fathers in the home, most children still spend considerable portions of their lives with both mothers and either biological fathers or stepfathers. Thus, paternal working conditions must also be considered; our later research is aimed at remedying this gap (Menaghan & Parcel, 1989).

Third, we have neglected the fact that many of our model variables themselves change over time. Both mothers and children may experience multiple transitions during the first few years of a child's life: Young workers are more likely to move among several different jobs and to experience periods of unemployment, and women's work lives are more likely to be interrupted repeatedly to accommodate family needs (U.S. Bureau of the Census, 1987). Their children's lives may be punctuated accordingly by a sequence of care arrangements. In addition, for many, the early adult years are times of marital and nonmarital partner change: Marital disruptions and new partnerships introduce a series of changes in family environments that have repercussions on both mothers and children. Family households may also be changed by the incorporation of children's aunts, uncles, or grandparents, and the birth of additional children. Such changes may permit or require different care arrangements, bring in additional income or increase economic pressures, and lead to changes in employment hours or conditions.

Most broadly, stability and change in child environments and child outcomes is a function of the quality and stability of both parents' work lives as well as the quality and stability of the parents' relationship with one another. Future work must more fully incorporate paternal variables and model change over time to provide a more complete portrayal of how parental work experiences and child environments may threaten or enhance early development, and to document the duration and possible reversibility of early developmental deficits. Although such incorporation is beyond the scope of this chapter, our current work is investigating these possibilities (Parcel & Menaghan, 1990b). The model we have developed here, however, provides an important foundation for this larger story.

ACKNOWLEDGMENTS

An earlier version of this chapter was circulated for discussion and critique at the Theory Construction and Research Methodology Workshop held in conjunction with the National Council on Family Relations Annual Meetings, Philadelphia, PA, November 11, 1988. We are grateful to our discussants, Patricia Voydanoff and Sharon Price, and to the workshop participants for their comments. We also acknowledge the assistance of Stacy Rogers and Martha Brown. Work on this manuscripts was partially supported by the National Institute of Child Health and Human Development (R01 HD23467).

REFERENCES

Ainsworth, M., Blehar, M., Waters, E., & Wall S. (1978). *Patterns of attachment*. Hillsdale, NJ: Lawrence Erlbaum Associates.

Alexander, K., & Eckland, B. K. (1975). Contextual effects in the high school attainment process. *American Sociological Review, 40*, 402–416.

Alexander, K., Fennessey, J., McDill, E. L., & D'Amico, R. J. (1979). School SES influences—Composition or context? *Sociology of Education, 52*, 222–237.

Anderson, C. W. (1980). Attachment in daily separations: Reconceptualizing day care and maternal employment issues. *Child Development, 51*, 242–245.

Andrisani, P. J. (1978). *Work attitudes and labor market experience*. New York: Praeger.

Averitt, R. T. (1968). *The dual economy*. New York: Norton.

Baron, J. N., & Bielby, W. T. (1980). Bringing the boss back in: Stratification, segmentation and the organization of work. *American Sociological Review, 45*, 737–765.

Beck, E. M., Horan, P., & Tolbert, C. (1978). Stratification in a dual economy: A sectoral model of earnings determination. *American Sociological Review, 43*, 704–720.

Becker, G. S. (1964). *Human capital*. New York: National Bureau of Economic Research.

Belsky, J. (1984a). The determinants of parenting: A process model. *Child Development, 555*, 83–96.

Belsky, J. (1984b). Two waves of day care research: Developmental effects and conditions of quality. In R. C. Ainslie (Ed.), *The child and the day care setting: Qualitative variations and development* (pp. 1-34). New York: Praeger.

Belsky, J. (1986). Infant day care: A case for concern? *Zero to three: Bulletin for the National Center of Clinical Infant Studies 6*, 1–7.

Benn, R. (1986). Factors promoting secure attachment relationships between employed mothers and their sons. *Child Development, 57*, 1224–1231.

Berg, I. (1970). *Education and jobs: The great training robbery*. New York: Praeger.

Blake, J. (1989). *Family size and achievement*. Berkeley CA: University of California Press.

Blau, P. M., & Duncan, O. D. (1967). *The American occupational structure*. New York: Wiley.

Blaug, M. (1976). The empirical status of human capital theory: A slightly jaundiced survey. *Journal of Economic Literature, 14*, 827–855.

Boissiere, M., Knight, J. B., & Sabot, R. H. (1985). Earnings, schooling, ability and cognitive skills. *American Economic Review 75*, 1016–1030.

Bowlby, J. (1969). *Attachment*. New York: Basic Books.

Bradley, R. B., & Caldwell, B. (1984). The relation of infants' home environments to achievement test performance in first grade: A follow-up study. *Child Development 55*, 803–809.

Bronfenbrenner, U., (1979). *The ecology of human development: Experiments by nature and design*. Cambridge: Harvard University Press.

Bronfenbrenner, U., & Crouter, A. C. (1982). Work and family through time and space. In S. Kamerman & C. Hayes (Eds.), *Families that work: Children in a changing world* (pp. 39-83). Washington, DC: National Academy of Science.

Bronfenbrenner, U., Alvarez, W. F., & Henderson, Jr., C. R. (1984). Working and watching: Maternal employment status and parents' perceptions of their 3-year-old children. *Child Development, 55*, 1362–1378.

Brown, J. N. (1989). Why do wages increase with tenure? On-the-job training and life cycle wage growth observed within firms. *American Economic Review, 79*, 971–991.

Clarke-Stewart, A. (1982). *Daycare*. Cambridge: Harvard University Press.

Clarke-Stewart, A. (1989). Infant day care: Maligned or malignant? *American Psychologist, 44*, 266–273.

Conger, R. D., McCarty, J. A., Yang, R. K., Lahey, B. B., & Kropp, J. P. (1984). Perceptions of child, child-rearing values, and emotional distress as mediating links between environmental stressors and observed maternal behavior. *Child Development, 55*, 2234–2247.

Crouter, A. C., Belsky, J., & Spanier, G. B. (1984). The family context of child development: Divorce and maternal employment. In G. J. Whitehurst (Ed.), *Annals of child development* (Vol. 1, pp. 201–238). Greenwich, CT: JAI Press.

Cyert, R. M., & Mowery, D. C. (Eds.). (1987). *Technology and employment: Innovation and growth in the U.S. economy*. Washington, DC: National Academy Press.

Doeringer, P. B., & Piore, M. J. (1971). *Internal labor markets and manpower analysis*. Lexington, MA: Heath.

Downey, G., & Moen, P. (1987). Personal efficacy, income, and family transitions: A longitudinal study of women heading households. *Journal of Health and Social Behavior, 28*, 320–333.

Duncan, G., & Hill, C. R. (1975). Modal choice in child care arrangements. In G. J. Duncan & J. N. Morgan (Eds.), *Five thousand American families: Patterns of economic progress* (Vol. 2, pp. 235–258). Ann Arbor, MI: Institute for Social Research.

Duncan, G., & Hill, C. R. (1977). The child care mode choice of working mothers. In G. J. Duncan & J. N. Morgan (Eds.), *Five thousand American families: Patterns of economic progress* (Vol. 5, pp. 379–388). Ann Arbor, MI: Institute for Social Research.

Duncan, G. J., & Liker, J. K. (1983). Disentangling the efficacy-earnings relationship among white men. In G. J. Duncan & J. N. Morgan (Eds.), *Five thousand families: Patterns of economic progress* (Vol. 10, pp. 218–248). Ann Arbor, MI: Institute for Social Research.

Duncan, G. J., & Morgan, J. W. (1980). Sense of efficacy and subsequent change in earnings: A replication. *Journal of Human Resources, 14*, 649–648.

Edwards, R. C. (1975). The social relations of production in the firm and labor market structure. In R. C. Edwards, R. Reich, & D. Gordon (Eds.), *Labor market segmentation* (pp. 1–26). Lexington, MA: D.C. Heath.

Edwards, R. C. (1979). *Contested terrain: The transformation of the workplace in the twentieth century*. New York: Basic Books, Inc.

Elder, Jr., G. H. (1974). *Children of the great depression*. Chicago: University of Chicago Press.

Estrada, P., Arsenio, W. F., Hess, R. D., & Holloway, S. D. (1987). Affective quality of the mother–child relationship: Longitudinal consequences for children's school-relevant cognitive functioning. *Developmental Psychology, 23*, 210–215.

Featherman, D. L (1976). Coser's 'In search of substance.' *The American Sociologist, 11*, 21–27.

Featherman, D. L., & Hauser, R. M. (1978). *Opportunity and change*. New York: Academic Press.

Furstenburg, Jr. F. F., (1985). Sociological ventures in child development. *Child Development, 56*, 281–288.

Furstenburg, Jr. F. F., & Nord, C. W. (1985). Parenting apart: patterns of childrearing after marital disruption. *Journal of Marriage and the Family, 50*, 893–904.

Furstenburg, Jr. F. F., & Seltzer, J. A. (1986). Divorce and child development. *Sociological Studies of Child Development, 1*, 137–160.

Gecas, V. (1979). The influence of social class on socialization. In W. C. Burr, R. Hill, F. I. Nye, & I. L. Reiss (Eds.), *Contemporary theories about the family* (Vol. 1, pp. 365–404). New York: The Free Press.

Gecas, V. (1981). Contexts of socialization. In M. Rosenberg & J. H. Turner (Eds.), *Social psychology* (pp. 165–199). New York: The Free Press.

Gecas, V., & Seff, M. (1989). Social class, occupational conditions, and self-esteem. *Sociological Perspectives, 32*(3), 356–365.

Grant, D. S. II, & Parcel, T. L. (1990). Revisiting metropolitan racial inequality: The case for a resource approach. *Social Forces, 68*(4), 1121–1142.

Hayes, C. D., Palmer, J. L. & Zaslow, M. J. (Eds.). (1990). *Who cares for America's children?* Washington, DC: National Academy Press.

Heckman, J. J. (1974). Effects of child-care programs on women's work-effort. *Journal of Political Economy, 82*(2), 136–163.

Hernandez, D. J., & Myers, D. E. (1988, April). *Family composition, parents' work, and the need for child care among preschool children.* Paper presented at the meeting of the Population Association of America, New Orleans, LA.

Hetherington, E. M., Cox, M., & Cox, R. (1978). The aftermath of divorce. In J. H. Stevens, Jr. & M. Matthews (Eds.), *Mother/child, father/child relationships* (pp. 149–176). Washington, DC: National Association for the Education of Young Children.

Hodson, R. (1983). *Workers' earnings and corporate economic structure.* New York: Academic Press.

Hodson, R. (1984). Companies, industries, and the measurement of economic segmentation. *American Sociological Review, 3*, 335–348.

Hodson, R. (1986). Modeling the effects of industrial structure on wages and benefits. *Work and Occupations, 13*, 488–510.

Hodson, R., & Kaufman, R. L. (1982). Economic dualism: A critical review. *American Sociological Review, 47*, 727–739.

Hoffman, L. W., & Nye, F. I. (1974). *Working mothers.* San Francisco: Jossey-Bass Publishers.

Hoffman, L. W. (1983). Increasing fathering: Effects on the mother. In E. Lamb & A. Sagi (Eds.), *Fatherhood and family policy* (pp. 167–90). Hillsdale, NJ: Lawrence Erlbaum Associates.

Hoffman, L. W. (1989). Effects of maternal employment in the two-parent family. *American Psychologist 44*, 283–292.

Horan, P. M. (1978). Is status attainment research atheoretical? *American Sociological Review, 43*, 534–541.

Howell, F. M., & McBroom, L. W. (1982). Social relations at home and at school: An analysis of the correspondence principle. *Sociology of Education 55*, 40–52.

Howes, C. (1988). Relations between early child care and schooling. *Developmental Psychology, 24*, 53–57.

Howes, C., & Stewart, P. (1987). Child's play with adults, toys, peers: An examination of family and child care influences. *Developmental Psychology, 23*, 423-430.

Jacobs, J. (1989). *Revolving doors: Sex segregation and women's careers*. Stanford, CA: Stanford University Press.

Kohn, M. L. (1963). Social class and parent-child relationships: An interpretation. *American Journal of Sociology 68*, 471-480.

Kohn, M. L. (1976). Comment on Wright and Wright: Social class and parental values. *American Sociological Review, 41*, 538-545.

Kohn, M. L. (1977). *Class and conformity: A study in values* (2nd ed.). Chicago: University of Chicago Press.

Kohn, M. L., & Schooler, C. (1973). Occupational experience and psychological functioning: An assessment of reciprocal effects. *American Sociological Review, 38*, 97-118.

Kohn, M. L., & Schooler, C. (1978). The reciprocal effects of the substantive complexity of work and intellectual flexibility: A longitudinal assessment. *American Journal of Sociology, 84*, 24-52.

Kohn, M. L., & Schooler, C. (1982). Job conditions and personality: A longitudinal assessment of their reciprocal effects. *American Journal of Sociology, 87*, 1257-1286.

Kohn, M. L., & Schooler, C. (1983). *Work and personality: An inquiry into the impact of social stratification*. Norwood: Ablex.

Kohn, M. L., Naoi, A., Schoenbach, C., Schooler, C., & Slomczynski, K. M. (1990). Position in the class structure and psychological functioning in the United States, Japan, and Poland. *American Journal of Sociology, 95*(4), 964-1008.

Lehrer, E. (1983). Determinants of child care mode choice: An economic perspective. *Social Science Research, 12*, 69-80.

Lehrer, E., & Kawasaki, S. (1985). Child care arrangements and fertility: An analysis of two-earner households. *Demography, 22*, 499-513.

Leibowitz, A., Waite, L. J., & Witsberger, C. (1988). Child care for preschoolers: Differences by child's age. *Demography, 25*, 205-220.

Lennon, M. C. (1987). Sex differences in distress: The impact of gender and work roles. *Journal of Health and Social Behavior, 28*, 290-305.

McCartney, K. (1984). The effect of quality of day care environment on children's language development. *Developmental Psychology, 21*, 244-260.

McCartney, K., Scarr, S., Phillips, D., Grajek, S., & Schwarz, J. C. (1982). Environmental differences among day care centers and their effects on children's development. In E. F. Zigler & E. W. Gordon (Eds.), *Day care: Scientific and social policy issues* (pp. 126-151). Boston: Auburn.

Menaghan, E. G. (1983). Individual coping efforts: Moderators of the relationship between life stress and mental health outcomes. In H. B. Kaplan (Ed.), *Psychosocial stress: Trends in theory and research* (pp. 157-191). New York: Academic Press.

Menaghan, E. G. (1990). Social stress and individual distress. In J. Greenley (Ed.), *Research community and mental health, Vol. 6: Mental disorder in social context* (pp. 235-272). Greenwich, CT: JAI Press.

Menaghan, E. G., & Merves, E. S. (1984). Coping with occupational problems: The limits of individual efforts. *Journal of Health and Social Behavior, 25*, 406-423.

Menaghan, E. G., & Parcel, T. L. (1989). *Parental occupations and child care effects on child outcomes*. Research grant funded by the National Institutes of Child Health and Human Development.

Menaghan, E. G., & Parcel, T. L. (1991). Determining children's home environments: The impact of maternal characteristics and current occupational family experiences. *Journal of Marriage and the Family, 53.*

Miller, J., Schooler, C., Kohn, M. L., & Miller, K. A. (1979). Women and work: The psychological effects of occupational conditions. *American Journal of Sociology, 85,* 66–94.

Miller, J., Slomczynski, K. M., & Kohn, M. L. (1985). Continuity of learning-generalization: The effect of job on men's intelligence process in the United States and Poland. *American Journal of Sociology, 91,* 593–615.

Mincer, J. (1974). *Schooling, experience and earnings.* New York: National Bureau of Economic Research.

Minturn, L., & Lambert, W. W. (1964). *Mothers of six cultures: Antecedents of child rearing.* New York: Wiley.

Mirowsky, J., & Ross, C. (1986). Social patterns of distress. *Annual Review of Sociology, 12,* 23–45.

Mortimer, J., & Borman, K. M. (Eds.). (1988). *Work experience and psychological development through the life span.* Boulder, CO: Westview Press.

Naoi, A., & Schooler, C. (1985). Occupational conditions and psychological functioning in Japan. *American Journal of Sociology, 90,* 729–752.

O'Connor, J. (1973). *The fiscal crisis of the state.* New York: St. Martin's Press.

Osterman, P. (Ed.). (1984). *Internal labor markets.* Cambridge: MIT Press.

Parcel, T. L. (1987). Theories of the labor market and the employment of youth. In R. Corwin (Ed.), *Research in the sociology of education and socialization* (pp. 29–55). Greenwood, CT: JAI Press.

Parcel, T. L., & Menaghan, E. G. (1988). *Linking maternal employment and child care arrangements to child development.* Research grant funded by the National Institutes of Child Health and Human Development.

Parcel, T. L., & Menaghan, E. G. (1989). *Child home environment as a mediating construct between SES and child outcomes.* Unpublished manuscript.

Parcel, T. L., & Menaghan, E. G. (1990a). Maternal working conditions and child verbal facility: Studying the intergenerational transmission of inequality from mothers to young children. *Social Psychology Quarterly, 53*(2), 132–147.

Parcel, T. L., & Menaghan, E. G. (1990b, July). *Mothers' careers and child development: Evidence from the NYS Youth.* Paper presented at the 12th World Congress of Sociology, Madrid, Spain.

Parcel, T. L., & Mueller, C. W. (1983). *Ascription and labor markets: Race and sex differences in earnings.* New York: Academic Press.

Parcel, T. L., & Sickmeier, M. (1988). One firm, two labor markets: The case of McDonald's in the fast food industry. *The Sociological Quarterly, 29,* 29–46.

Parke, R., MacDonald, K., Beitel, A., & Bhavnagri, N. (1988). The role of the family in the development of peer relationships. In R. D. Peters & R. J. McMahon (Eds.), *Social learning and systems approaches to marriage and the family* (pp. 17–44). New York: Brunner-Mazel.

Pearlin, L. I., & Kohn, M. L. (1966). Social class, occupation, and parental values: A cross-national study. *American Journal of Sociology 31,* 466–479.

Phillips, D., McCartney, K., & Scarr, S. (1987). Child-care quality and children's social development. *Developmental Psychology, 23,* 537–543.

Phillips, D., McCartney, K., Scarr, S., & Howes, C. (1987). Selective review of infant day care research: A cause for concern. *Zero to three: Bulletin of the National Center for Clinical Infant Studies 7*, 18-21.

Phillips, D., & Howes, C. (1989). *The national child care staffing study*. Child Care Employee Project: Oakland, CA.

Piotrkowski, C. S., & Katz, M. H. (1982). Indirect socialization of children: The effects of mothers' jobs on academic behaviors. *Child Development, 53*, 409-415.

Piotrkowski, C. S., Rapoport, R. N., & Rapoport, R. (1987). Families and work. In M. B. Sussman & S. K. Steinmetz (Eds.), *Handbook of marriage and the family* (pp. 251-283). New York: Plenum Press.

Plomin, R., & Daniels, D. (1987). Why are children in the same family so different from one another? *Behavioral and Brain Sciences 10*, 1-16.

Plomin, R., & DeFries, J. C. (1983). The Colorado adoption project. *Child Development, 54*, 276-289.

Presser, H. B. (1987). Shift work of full-time dual-career couples: Patterns and contrasts by sex of spouse. *Demography, 24*, 99-112.

Presser, H. B., & Baldwin, W. (1980). Child care as a constraint on employment: Prevalence, correlates, and bearing on the work and fertility nexus. *American Journal of Sociology, 85*, 1202-1213.

Ramey, C., Dorval, D., & Baker-Ward, L. (1981). Group day care and socially disadvantaged families: Effects on the child and the family. In S. Kilmer (Ed.), *Advances in early education and day care*. Greenwich, CT: JAI Press.

Repetti, R. L., & Crosby, F. (1984). Gender and depression: Exploring the adult-role explanation. *Journal of Social and Clinical Psychology 2*, 57-70.

Reskin, B. (Ed.) (1984). *Sex segregation in the workplace: Trends, explanations, remedies*. Washington, D.C.: National Academy Press.

Reskin, B., Roos, P. (1990). *Job queues, gender queues: Explaining women's inroads into male occupations*. Philadelphia, PA: Temple University Press.

Robins, P. K., & Spiegelman, R. G. (1978). An econometric model of the demand for child care. *Economic Inquiry, 41*, 83-94.

Rogers, S. J., Parcel, T. L., & Menaghan, E. G. (1991). The effects of maternal working conditions and mastery on child behavior problems: Studying the intergenerational transmission of social control. *Journal of Health and Social Behavior, 32*(2).

Ruopp, R., & Travers, J. (1982). Janus faces day care: Perspectives on quality and cost. In E. F. Zigler & E. W. Gordon (Eds.), *Day care: Scientific and social policy issues*. Boston: Auburn House.

Saenz, R., Goudy, W. J., & Lorenz, F. O. (1989). The effects of employment and marital relations on depression among Mexican American women. *Journal of Marriage and the Family 51*, 239-251.

Scarr, S. (1984). *Mother care/other care*. New York: Basic Books.

Scarr, S., & McCartney, K. (1983). How people make their own environments: A theory of genotype environment effects. *Child Development, 54*, 424-435.

Schervish, P. G. (1983). *The structural determinants of unemployment*. New York: Academic Press.

Schultz, H. (1962). Reflections on investment in man. *Journal of Political Economy 60*, (Supplement Part 2), 1-8.

Siegal, M. (1984). Economic deprivation and the quality of parent-child relations: A trickle-down framework. *Journal of Applied Developmental Psychology, 5*, 127-144.

Slomczynski, K. M., Miller, J., & Kohn, M. L. (1981). Stratification, work, and values: A Polish-United States comparison. *American Sociological Review, 46,* 720-744.

Smith, J. P. (1984). Race and human capital. *American Economic Review, 74,* 685-98.

Sorensen, A., & McLanahan, S. (1987). Married women's economic dependency. *American Journal of Sociology, 93,* 659-687.

Spenner, K. I. (1983). Deciphering Prometheus: Temporal change in the skill level of work. *American Sociological Review, 48,* 824-837.

Spenner, K. I., & Otto, L. B. (1985). Work and self-concept: Selection and socialization in the early career. In A. C. Kerckhoff (Ed.), *Research in sociology of education and socialization* (Vol. 5, pp. 197-235). Greenwich, CT: JAI Press.

Stolzenberg, R. M., & Waite, L. J. (1984). Local labor markets, children and labor force participation of wives. *Demography, 21,* 157-170.

U.S. Census, Current Population Reports, Series P-70, No. 10. (1987) *Male-female differences in work experience, occupation, and earnings: 1984.* Washington, DC: U. S. Government Printing Office.

Vaughn, B., Gove, F., & Egeland, B. (1980). The relationship between out-of-home care and the quality of infant-mother attachment in an economically disadvantaged population. *Child Development, 51,* 1203-1214.

Voydanoff, P. (1987). *Work and family life.* Beverly Hills, CA: Sage.

Voydanoff, P., & Donnelly, B. W. (1988). Economic distress, family coping, and quality of family life. In P. Voydanoff & L. C. Majka (Eds.), *Families and economic distress: Coping strategies and social policy* (pp. 97-116). Beverly Hills, CA: Sage.

Age-Group Relationships:
Generational Equity and Inequity

Vern L. Bengtson
Gerardo Marti
Robert E.L. Roberts
University of Southern California

Within the last 5 years a debate over "generational equity" concerns has emerged in industrial societies. The debate reflects a new and potentially explosive policy issue involving age groups and social stratification in the late 20th century: the distribution of tax-generated societal resources to different age groups, particularly the young and the old. Our purpose in this chapter is to explore three psychosocial-level issues—autonomy, solidarity, and affirmation—which we feel relate to this societal-level debate. These three psychosocial concepts have emerged from examination of families and their intergenerational relationships across the life span (Bengtson, Gatz, Roberts, & Richards, 1988). We suggest that these three issues are also relevant at the macrosocial level of public policy in the debate over inequalities and equities among age groups. Proposed connections between demographic, economic, and political conditions and family interactions over the life span with respect to autonomy, solidarity, and affirmation may serve as guideposts to policymakers and researchers in the controversy over the distribution of public resources across generations.

In this chapter we first review the demographic background of the current debate over age-group inequalities. Second, we outline some of the major arguments regarding the existence and resolution of generational inequity. Third, we shift attention to the microsocial level, describing the interplay between autonomy and dependency, solidarity and individuality, affirmation and conflict, as individuals of different ages negotiate the changes of aging. Finally, we suggest some implications for future policy and research agendas.

In addressing these topics, we are drawing on data from the University of Southern California Longitudinal Study of Three-Generation Families. This study, involving some 300 families, began in 1971 with 2,000 grandparents, parents, and youth; a second wave of data was gathered in 1985, and a third wave in 1988 (for details concerning sample characteristics see Richards, Bengtson, & Miller, 1989; Roberts & Bengtson, 1990). Two kinds of data have been gathered: survey responses to a structured questionnaire, and intensive interviews with a subsample of 100 family members conducted in 1987 (Mellins, Boyd, & Gatz, 1988).

DEMOGRAPHIC TRENDS OF THE 20TH CENTURY

Historically unique demographic trends in both mortality and fertility rates in the 20th century have created dramatic changes in the age structure of American society. It is useful to review these trends in population aging because they have special relevance to intergenerational interaction, both at the microlevel of the family and the macrolevel of industrialized societies (Bengtson, Rosenthal, & Burton, 1990).

With regard to American fertility patterns, the 20th century has witnessed three notable events. First, after relatively low fertility in the 1930s, a marked increase in the number of births occurred shortly after World War II. The birth rate of the population (total live births per 1,000) jumped from 20.4 in 1945 to 26.6 in 1947. Second, a high birth rate was sustained over the next two decades. Third, a marked decline in fertility was finally observed in the early 1960s, falling to 19.4 in 1965. Fertility has remained fairly stable at this low rate since that point.

Because increased numbers of people were introduced into the population so quickly (and so unexpectedly), a population "bulge" was created in the flow of birth cohorts that has forced its way through our educational systems, occupational structures, housing markets and—ever increasingly—into our nursing homes. These "Baby Boom" cohorts have already exerted a profound influence in industrialized societies and, as we shall see, will continue to do so on into the next century as these individuals pass through retirement and into old age. The decline in fertility after the Baby Boom translates into fewer workers left to support aging retirees. Indeed, it has been estimated by Soldo (1981) that, although the ratio of workers to "dependent" nonworking aged was 18.4 to 100 in 1980, by the year 2020 it will be 26.0 to 100, and in the year 2030 will be 31.8 to 100 (see also Longman, 1987).

With regard to mortality, this century has experienced an unprecedented expansion in life expectancy. In the United States, life expectancy for females has increased from 49 years in 1900 to 79 years in 1980. The population of those 65 and older is expected to grow more than four times as fast as the rest of the population from 1985 through 2050 (Siegel & Taeuber, 1986). What this means in family terms is that, for women born in 1920 who celebrated their 60th birthday in 1990, almost one in four had a mother who is still living. Much of the extension in overall life expectancy during this century, it should be noted, is due to significant decreases in infant mortality. Yet, changes in death rates at the upper ages are attributed to decreases in deaths due to infectious diseases along with notable advances in medical technology. These mortality declines are responsible for the much of the continued increase in the population of those 85 years and older (Rosenwaike, 1985).

Such marked changes in fertility and mortality resulted in the emergence of the Baby Boom, as well as ever-larger cohorts of those living past retirement age. At the family level these demographic trends have produced similarly dramatic changes in intergenerational patterns.

First, there has been an emergence of *multigeneration kinship patterns* unlike anything existing earlier (Crimmins, 1985). This has been called the *beanpole* family structure: more members of successive generations are alive at any given point in time, while there are fewer members within each generation (Bengtson, Rosenthal, & Burton, 1990). In one study of obituaries for elderly women in Pennsylvania, 20% of women who died after the age of 80 had great-great-great grandchildren, a five-generation family structure (Hagestad, 1986). For the first time in history, the typical child will have grown to maturity knowing not just grandparents, but great-grandparents as well.

Second, a longer life ensures that family members will spend more time occupying *intergenerational family roles* than ever before. For example, cohorts born in 1960 and 1980 spend more years both as parents and as children of aging parents than any earlier generations due to extensions in longevity (Watkins, Menken, & Bongaarts, 1987).

Third, there is an increased probability that family members will be involved in longer periods of *elder-caregiving* due to chronic health disorders associated with aging (Gatz, Bengtson, & Blum, 1990). Elder-caregiving has already become a normative life event for a majority of Americans (Brody, 1985). The "middle-generation squeeze," experienced by those caring for both dependent elderly as well as dependent children (and possibly grandchildren), will become a pattern for even more individuals in the next few decades. Also, greater number of elderly and longer lives of individuals will also contribute to the rise of "two-generation geriatric families" with children at the younger ages (65 +) caring for their parents (85 +) (Gelfand, Olsen, & Block, 1978). To the extent that these intergenerational relationships are negative, decades of conflict, guilt, disappointment, and stress may result.

Fourth, it should also be noted that emergence of multigenerational, beanpole structured families engenders several *positive benefits* to society and to families. For example, grandparents and great-grandparents serve as role models, maintaining ties to the past that have identity functions (Bengtson, 1986; Troll, 1985). The presence of family elders also augments "kin-keeping" activities and enhances ritual solidarity, even over long distances (Rosenthal, 1985).

Moreover, several generations of adults in one family represent a significant increment in the potential support available for dependent family members, whether young or old. Although longer lives may mean longer periods of chronic illness, longer lives also mean more years of access to collective family resources when support is needed—with fewer children and grandchildren to compete for them.

INTERGENERATIONAL EQUITY:
THE GROWING DEBATE

On the basis of age, society can be viewed as supporting two "dependent" (nonworking) populations: children and the elderly. The profound demographic shifts that reflect a remolding of the age structure of society have led to recent controversy concerning the distribution of public resources between these two dependent age groups. As Kingson (1988) has suggested, "The heart of the generational equity controversy concerns differences regarding what criteria should be used to guide difficult choices over the allocation of resources in the aging society" (p. 766).

Achenbaum (1989) and Quadagno (1990) provide useful summaries of the historical and political background to social policy and the generational equity debate. Beginning in the early 1980s, several movements to address issues of distribution of public resources among age groups in light of increased longevity arose in several industrialized societies. In the United States, Americans for Generational Equity (AGE) was formed in 1984 by Minnesota senator David Durenberger and former Minnesota representative James Jones. As Durenberger (1989) described it, AGE was formed to be the lobby for the future, pledged to advocate policies that obey Thomas Jefferson's exhortation "that each generation has a moral obligation to pass on to the next—opportunities and possibilities for life at least as good as it received from the generation before" (p. 5). Jones (1988) stated that "Americans for Generational Equity was founded as a research organization, a clearing house for ideas, and a vehicle for disseminating possible solutions to what in the next century could be a social conflict as great as any we have seen in this country since the Civil War" (p. 7). According to Durenberger (1987),

> We have entered an era in which the date of one's birth has become the prime determinate of one's prospects for realizing the American dream. Younger Americans—regardless of their class or ethnic origin—are in the grip of what seems like a permanent and compounding downward spiral. (p. 9)

Wisconsin Democratic Congressman Jim Moody (1986), AGE co-chairman said:

Many people receiving Social Security benefits are better off than those taxed to pay them. The federal deficit is out of control, and the young are too heavily taxed. Everyone must sacrifice; Social Security must be curbed. (p. 37)

In other nations with a more explicit welfare state orientation (e.g., New Zealand and Great Britain) groups with similar concerns have formed; Thomson (1988a) suggested that "the inability, or unwillingness to operate intergenerational exchanges fairly is now revealed on such a scale as to seriously endanger the continued consensus for collective welfare programs" (p. 2).

The essential points of the generational equity debate include: (a) the rise in the proportion of elderly vis-à-vis younger cohorts; (b) current social insurance mechanisms that benefit the elderly; and (c) societal responsibility to provide for the nation's elderly without harming the well-being of younger cohorts. The argument, in summary, is as follows. Because of changes in mortality and fertility rates in the last century, the United States, in consort with other industrialized societies, is faced with a profound public policy dilemma: We must fulfill promises made in the past to support the growing elderly population, while simultaneously providing adequate social resources to both the working and dependent young. In view of scarce societal resources, how is an equitable distribution of public welfare across age cohorts to be accomplished?

Four Approaches to the Generational Equity Debate

Our review of the literature suggests that four general positions have emerged so far in this debate. The first emphasizes that benefits to the elderly must be curtailed in some fashion, thus "freeing-up" resources for other age cohorts. This approach frames the problem in terms of intergenerational conflict, and assumes discord between generational strata due to differentials in resource allocations—with "greedy elders" as one of the causes of this conflict. A second position, rather than focusing on often arbitrary inequities based on age status, instead proposes that social policy address the growing inequity between rich and poor. The implicit goal is "distributive justice" both within and across age groups. A third approach asserts that the problem does not lie in either age group membership or social policy, but rather in our "moral values" regarding aging and age-related dependencies or resources. A solution to current generational equity problems from this perspective can ultimately be solved by significant change in cultural norms. A fourth approach suggests that generational inequities result from long-term as well as cross-sectional income differentials throughout the life course. From this perspective, the "generational equity" debate reflects misunderstandings of general labor market conditions in society differentially affecting age cohorts. We now explore each of these perspectives in the emerging generational equity debate.

Greedy Elders. Much of the intergenerational equity rhetoric has been framed as a struggle between "greedy elders" and "powerless children." These two age strata combat with one another in a battle for scarce resources. By virtue of self-interest and political clout, the elderly hoard whatever they can in an attempt not only to maintain but also supplement an affluent lifestyle to which they had become accustomed during their productive years. The increased well-being of the elderly in recent decades is associated with a decline in the economic condition of younger cohorts who receive only the political pennies that trickle down to them in their impoverished existence. This harsh tone of censoring elderly cohorts for their self-interest is a consistent theme in the emerging literature.

For example, in what might be considered the landmark scholarly paper regarding intergenerational equity, Preston (1984a, 1984b) argued that demographic changes in the age composition of society have resulted in an improvement of conditions for the elderly coupled with a deterioration of conditions for children. Assuming that children and the elderly compete for societal resources, Preston cited various inequalities between 1960 and 1984 in poverty levels, suicide rates, and public expenditures, along with demographic changes in the familial, political and industrial environment, to support his conclusion. These macrostructural changes point to a distribution of societal resources toward the elderly in the population. Moreover, he asserted that such a redistribution is a manifestation of an overall selfish, individualistic concern among societal members for their own individual futures.

Preston's moralistic tone ("Do we care?" is one of his concluding questions) condemns such private concerns and gives a rallying call for society to embrace altruistic concerns for our collective future. Preston asserted that current American government policies accept less responsibility for the young than for the old; consequently, the young are less protected from aberrations occurring in family structure. He advocated turning away from individual futures toward the collective future embodied in our children. He said we need to assume responsibility for our children collectively, rather than insisting that our faltering nuclear family can bear the responsibility alone.

Preston implied that resources reserved for children have been displaced to serve the needs of the aged. But, as Easterlin (1987) stated, "The juxtaposition of the experience of children and the elderly lends itself to the view that the gains of one have been at the expense of the other; more specifically, that expanded government programs underlying the improved status of the elderly have been purchased by sacrificing programs for the young" (p. 195). The assumptions hidden within such assertions pose a threat to the well-being of the elderly. Policymakers and the general public may cultivate and maintain prejudices toward the elderly, thereby threatening access to scarce resources. Claims to societal resources may be seen as illegitimate in comparison with the needs of other segments of the population. This perspective is mirrored by Fairlie (1988), who suggested that "Something is wrong with a society that is willing to drain itself to foster such an unproductive section of its population, one that does not even promise (as children do) one day to be productive" (p. 19). Moreover, Preston's argument coincides with a view of the aged as an impediment to societal development. As Treas and Logue (1986) noted, this perspective assumes that the aged absorb resources from both private and public sources to the detriment of other groups in society, because the elderly demand significant portions of societal resources for their survival.

Binstock (1983) discussed the underlying ageism of this perspective, in the sense that it treats the elderly as a homogeneous age group. In the past, the aged have been perceived as poor, frail, and deserving. Since 1978, in the midst of crises regarding social security, the aged have become characterized as affluent, self-interested, and politically powerful. For example, Senator Daniel Patrick Moynihan (1987) stated that "the United States has become the first society in history in which a person is more likely to be poor if young rather than old" (p. 112). This new stereotype is the foundation for the aged as a scapegoat for society. For Binstock (1983), "the aged are bearing the blame for a variety of economic and political frustrations" (p. 136). Scapegoating the elderly: (a) diverts attention away from deficiencies in political leadership and public policy, (b) engenders intergenerational conflict, and (c) diverts attention from issues of reform providing benefits to the aged.

Minkler (1986) and Quadagno (1988) offered a further challenge to Preston's claims. Although a majority of today's elderly as a group are financially comfortable (in contrast to the situation only a few years ago), only a small number are well-off and many are quite poor. Whereas the aged constitute a large block of participating voters, the elderly do not vote in a monolithic bloc pursuing their own vested interests. Although demographic changes will result in an increased number and proportion of elderly, the consequent cost to society will depend on our response to escalating costs for health care.

The basic argument made by "generational equity" advocates who emphasize "greedy elders" as the source of cohort-based inequities can be summarized as follows. First, in recent years there has been a growth of public resources directed toward elderly members of the population. This has come about in part because of previous levels of real poverty among the elderly, and in part because unprecedented growth of their numbers has translated into an effective political lobby on their behalf.

Second, this has led to substantial improvement in the economic status of the elderly and in their access to health care. In fact, the elderly are coming to be better off as a group than the non-aged population, especially children; and the proportion of federal funds directed to the oldest age group is increasing every year.

Third, at the same time the flow of resources to children and other dependent populations has decreased, proportionally. This reflects a decrease in tax-generated funds (the interest necessary to pay the federal debt has foreclosed discretionary programs).

Fourth, and in conclusion, to continue the flow of federal resources to the elderly is inequitable, and will be a source of intergenerational conflict. According to AGE co-founder James Jones (1987), "I personally believe that there is probably no greater social issue facing us over the next forty or fifty years than the potential for intergenerational conflict" (p. 61). As former Governor Lamm (1985) of Colorado has put it: "We have turned the Biblical account of the prodigal son on its head. Now we are faced with the prodigal father" (p. 118).

Each of these points is, of course, open to debate (see Kingson, Hirshorn, & Cornman, 1986). Overall, Preston and the AGE founders suggest an inverse relationship between the objective conditions of the two age groups (i.e., that any improvement in the condition of the aged results in a deterioration of the condition of children). In the sphere of public expenditures, an increase in the allocation of resources to the elderly results in a decrease in the allocation of resources to children. The elderly displace resources reserved for children. Four assumptions are particularly questionable: (a) there can be no increase in federal support for the young *except* by decreasing benefits to the old; (b) the majority of older people are well-off, and thus undeserving of public assistance; (c) the elders are "debtors" rather than donors in cross-generational transfers; (d) issues of "equity" are to be viewed as cross-sectional, rather than life-course or longitudinal. This assumption ignores shared needs that occur in everyone's life cycle.

Three additional perspectives on the generational equity debate relate to several of these issues.

Age-irrelevant distributive justice.   The distributive justice approach advocates a redistribution of social wealth such that it is not concentrated in a select few, but rather broadly diffused throughout society. In this context, aging is not the central focus, but rather an equitable distribution of resources regardless of age. In this respect, Minkler and Stone (1985) noted that elderly women are the fastest growing and the single poorest segment of American society. Although their argument is persuasive, aging seems to occupy a secondary role to female poverty. Kingson (1988) suggested that the real debate facing our national social policy agenda is the growing inequity between the rich and poor, not between the young and old.

From this viewpoint, inequality is not dependent on age. Achenbaum (1989) stated that "it must be emphasized that a persuasive case has not been made, on theoretical or empirical grounds, to sustain the proposition that 'age' is the most salient predictor of inequality in the US" (p. 129). In other words, inequality is not based on age status, but rather on a variety of economic, political, and historical factors. The American interest group political system allows certain groups to maintain power and influence over groups with access to fewer resources. Inequities are not shaped by generational interests, but rather by self-serving interest groups that are age heterogeneous.

Those who cling to the distributive justice perspective tend to advocate resolving inequities through need-based programs that are irrespective of age. In criticizing the "greedy elders" framework, Neugarten and Neugarten (1986) stated,

> It is undeniable that the increasing number of poor children is a disgrace to the affluent society, and that the implications are calamitous. But the problem is part of a larger and more complex one: what proportion of federal resources should go to social programs, and how should those resources be allocated to the various subgroups who need assistance? (p. 44)

They concluded (1986): "Is it more constructive for society to create policies designed for age groups, or instead, policies for persons who, irrespective of age, share a problem or a life condition that calls for intervention by a public or private agency?" (p. 45).

Achenbaum (1989) suggested that in reducing poverty, "The most efficacious strategy would adopt needs-based rather than age-based criteria" (p. 130). Generally, policymakers should avoid constructing programs based solely on age. However, Neugarten and Neugarten (1986) reminded us that "the policy issues are, in truth, more complex. In practice, they do not usually take the form of either/or decisions, but involve complicated combinations of age and need" (p. 47). Despite the complex interaction between age and need, Neugarten and Neugarten (1986) emphasized that "age is becoming a less relevant basis for assessing adult competencies and needs" (p. 45) requiring that we seek out alternative means beyond age status for determining both the type and the degree of need present.

Moral Revolution.   A third approach to the debate focuses on values regarding aging, dependency, productivity, and obligations over the life course. In light of dramatically increased longevity, industrialized societies need to revise previous moral standards regarding obligations toward the elderly and what the still-healthy elderly owe society. The most articulate exponent of this position is Callahan (1986, 1987a, 1987b). For Callahan, escalating health-care costs constitute the crux of the intergenerational struggle over public resources, a struggle that will become ever more acute as both the number and the proportion of the elderly increase. He argued that, given current levels of production and consumption, it is impossible to fulfill our promises dictated by moral obligations that characterized past cohorts: "A satisfactory general solution to the rising costs of health care for the elderly is unlikely to be reached without a fundamental reassessment of those values—moral, social, and cultural—that created the problems in the first place'' (1986, p. 333). In short, we are pushing our current resources to the limit. In light of these limits, we must revise our goals, and the standards that serve to meet these goals.

By far the most important change advocated by Callahan involves a reevaluation of the goal of medicine and the acceptance of death. Callahan (1987a, 1987b) viewed the advancement of medical technology as a mixed blessing. While extending longevity to an unprecedented level, medical advances represent an investment of resources toward fulfilling a continually elusive goal of perpetual health: ''No matter how much is spent, the ultimate problem will still remain: people will grow old and die'' (1987b, p. 126). Yet, the certainty and finality of death should not lead to a fatalistic response. Old age should be a meaningful stage of life as such, not an endless extension of middle age. As Cole (1989) suggested, ''In rebuilding the moral economy of an extended life course . . . we must also forge a new sense of the meanings and purposes of the last half of life'' (p. 381).

Callahan recommended that aging be accepted as part of the human condition. The return to a belief in a natural life span (he suggested the late 70s or early 80s) is essential to cost-containment; the goal of medicine would then be to prevent premature death (death prior to completion of the natural life span), rather than a needless extension of life. Because the elderly account for a large portion of health-care expenditures; and because health-care costs are directly associated with both the absolute number and relative proportion of elderly in the population, an emphasis on the extension of life only increases costs to society. According to Callahan, the rationing of health care for the elderly is already evident under Medicare and may be further extended to other areas of federal funding.

Callahan (1986) presented what appears to many observers some highly unrealistic recommendations:

> We would not be facing the problem of health-care costs at all, or be confronting an aging society, had not that commitment to individual welfare and medical progress been so powerful and so potently complementary to our desire to create a different kind of old age than the one previous human generations experienced. A full and genuine coping with the moral problems might require nothing less than a severe reduction in, or alteration of, that commitment; that in turn could require still broader changes in moral perspective of consequence to many other aspects of communal life as well. (p. 331)

Clearly, Callahan called for a radical revision of our moral standards. Yet, how easy is it for an entire society to change the norms and mores embedded within its culture regarding the value of life and the acceptance of death?

A Life-Course Perspective. Finally, Easterlin (1987) challenged Preston's assertions regarding the relative poverty rates of America's older and younger dependents in exploring the causes of a new age structure of poverty. According to Easterlin, there is no direct causal relation between improvement in the well-being of the elderly and the increased poverty rate among children. The elderly have *not* improved their well-being by stealing from children. He dismissed the assertion that gains for the elderly have been accrued at the expense of children. For Easterlin, the divergent trends in poverty rates are a result of two largely independent causes; a direct causal relation is erroneous.

The improved status of the elderly is attributed to government action in favor of the aged. In contrast, the increased poverty rate of children is attributed to adverse labor market conditions affecting younger adults at family-forming ages and female-headed families. Lower income for heads of families means lower overall household income. After all, the economic condition of children is dependent on the economic condition of their family. The high rate of poverty for children is asserted to be a transient phenomenon, and will decrease throughout the next two decades as labor market conditions improve. The present poverty rate differential between children and the elderly should diminish in the 1990s.

Smeeding, Torrey, and Rein (1986) made comparisons of the economic status of children and the aged in six industrial countries. Four possible explanations for the differences in economic statuses of children and the elderly are given: (a) relative size of the two age groups in the population, (b) differences in family structure over time (i.e., one vs. two-parent families), (c) income inequality within age cohorts, and (d) differences in income support systems. First, the data show insufficient support for the size of an age group as a predictor. Second, changes in family structure account for a re-shuffling of poverty rather than its increase. Thus, children's poverty rates cannot be adequately explained by either the relative number of children in the United States in general or the number of single-parent families in particular. Third, part of the explanation may come from income distributions that favor older families without dependent children over younger families with dependent children. Finally, no analysis is made of income support systems.

Smeeding et al. confirmed a life course approach incorporating shifts in income. The life-course approach predicts that income at the beginning and end of people's cycles are significantly lower than income in the middle periods. In general, adjustable disposable income are highest for households with heads age 55 to 60. Approaching retirement age, adjusted disposable income declines, and continues to do so.

A similar life-course approach incorporating stages of working and nonworking is advocated by Helco (1988). For instance, the economic well-being of a child depends mostly on his or her parents' employment history and access to public and private benefits. Moreover, the heterogeneous economic status of the elderly is a result of differential employment histories and retirement benefits. According to Helco (1988), ''it is in the generational interdependencies tied to the labor market—and not some media-hyped competition between young and old—that the real challenge of American politics lies" (p. 388).

Political leadership should emphasize the mutual dependence and obligation between the generations. Helco (1988) advocated a generational political perspective:

> [This perspective] asks us to think in terms broader than conventional, budget-like decisions of more for this group and less for that group at one moment in time. It invites us to think less about a time-slice distribution problem and more about time-flow distributions—choices for channeling resources among age groups that themselves age and that are in turn replaced. (p. 391)

In other words, age groups are not static entities, but are in constant flux as individuals move through time. Throughout the life course, an individual occupies several age strata, with varying degrees of dependence. Thus, members of society are mutually dependent on one another, sharing different degrees of obligation over time on the basis of age. Public policy should thereby target fulfillment of needs stemming from various stressors and pressures that change throughout the life course (see also Daniels, 1988).

The intergenerational debate is far from being settled. The arguments are varied, with the solutions to each almost completely incomparable. Indeed, what has come to be called the *intergenerational equity debate* is actually a confused, convoluted cacophony of generational rhetoric. The call to a solution to the equity debate is premature. Indeed, the first task is to define the problem.

Overall, we currently detect a lull in the debate. Other, more pressing concerns have pushed intergenerational politics to the side in Europe, as well as the United States. Helco (1988) suggested why policy choices may not, and should not, posit the children and the elderly as being in political conflict over scarce resources. Helco (1988) described four general barriers preventing development of a framework of conflicting generations. First, it is in the self-interest of elected politicians "to promise benefits and avoid discussion of unpleasant trade-offs" (p. 383). This is especially true when children and the elderly both enjoy immense public sympathy. Also, the difficulties in drawing comparisons between the two age groups make statements of relative well-being shaky and politically unwise. Second, competition existing among groups served by the elected official discourages discussion of trade-offs. Politicians and political organizations commonly face a "united front of silence" where it is understood that "you don't attack the worthiness of my cause, and I won't attack yours." Third, many political issues are absorbed within the categories of young and old. Helco stated "Policies for the elderly or children are, in fact, bundles of different programs, each with its own subsystem of politics" (p. 383). Finally, political structures tend to be class-based rather than age-based. That is to say, there are more compelling reasons for economic interest groups to coalesce, than age or cohort-based groups.

Conceptual Confusions

There are some basic confusions in conceptualization reflected in the "generational equity" debate that are unfortunate because they hinder adequate policy analysis of the "generational equity" arguments.

Cohorts, not Generations.   First, advocates blur and ignore the *distinction between generation and cohort*, between family and society, and between microsocial and macrosocial processes. We assert that the term *generation* should be reserved to represent role status within a family hierarchy. In contrast, the term *cohort* should be used only to represent a group of people born within a specified range of years who move together through time. It is often assumed that these individuals experience a series of developmental and historical events at approximately the same time. A generation is not synonymous with a cohort, and both researchers and policymakers must take care in using these terms (Bengtson, Cutler, Mangen, & Marshall, 1985). In current social science usage, we note that "generations" apply to families and microlevel interactions, whereas "cohorts" reflect societal and macrolevel dynamics.

Reciprocities, not Transfers.   Second, the position ignores existing *reciprocities among cohorts*. All age cohorts in society move together through time, and are mutually interdependent (Riley, 1985). As a whole, cohorts serve one another in multiple ways as individuals of all ages in society serve a variety of roles and functions through a division of labor (Durkheim, 1893/1984). No cohort is independent; cohorts are mutually beneficial to one another.

Incquitics, not Inequalities.   Third, the "generational equity" position actually refers to presumed *cohort inequalities*. Many social scientists have affirmed that differences among individuals in society are inevitable (e.g., Lenski, 1966; Weber, 1978). Moreover, due to variation in economic and historical conditions, entire aggregates of individuals (cohorts) may experience differential experiences and opportunities (see Elder, 1974; Elder & Liker, 1982).

Macro or Micro.   A final conceptual confusion between advocates and critics lies in the distinction between macrosocial dynamics of age groups, and their microsocial manifestations. We usually think of intergenerational relationships in conjunction with the family—a microsocial system of interacting personalities, norms of obligation and reciprocity, and direct exchanges of economic goods and nonmonetary services. This is the prototype of "generational" relations. Since the industrial revolution, the family has lost most of its economic functions, and cohorts (rather than generations) have become the most visible age differentiation in modern societies. However, these points should be emphasized: (a) families still function, and function well (Adams, 1986; Cherlin, 1981); (b) it is important to distinguish between macro- and microlevels of processes in working of age-group interactions; (c) there can be many points of similarity between the microlevel of generational interaction, as seen within the family and what we are most familiar with, and macrolevels of cohort interactions, which is the focus of the "generational equity" debate.

Our point in this analysis is not to debate any particular "generational equity" position. Rather, in the remainder of this chapter we wish to emphasize three points: (a) The debate is about *inequality*, real or perceived, between age cohorts. (b) These inequalities can be seen as arising from three *psychosocial* issues characterizing interactions between generations—autonomy, solidarity, and affirmation—which arise from the process of coping with change over the life-course. (c) These three polarities are most clearly seen at the *microsocial* levels of negotiating with change in multigeneration families; however, parallels can be drawn to the macrosocial level of age-group interactions of relevance to "generational equity." It is to these microsocial issues of generational interactions that we turn next, examining ways that families negotiate change and dependencies over the life course.

NEGOTIATING CHANGE BETWEEN GENERATIONS: INDIVIDUAL NEEDS AND MICROSOCIAL RELATIONSHIPS

Adult family members negotiate changes in personal competencies and interpersonal relationships, changes that inevitably occur with the passage of time and the aging of family members. The focus is on three psychosocial issues that characterize this negotiation in families: (a) the tension between autonomy and dependency, (b) the balance between family solidarity and individualism, (c) the interplay between conflict and affirmation. These issues represent not polarities, but dialectics of the developmental process.

Autonomy and Dependency

One of the basic issues involved in perceived "cohort inequalities" is the tension between autonomy and dependency in individuals of different ages. At the individual level, dependency needs are most obvious in childhood and old age; growing up and growing old reflect a change in the balance between dependency and autonomy. At the group and macrosocial levels, providing for dependent members' needs while maintaining autonomy of the nondependent members is a process requiring continual negotiation.

Strident discussion of the tension between autonomy and dependency at the cohort level of analysis is found in volume published by Longman (1987), one of the original AGE staff, entitled *Born to Pay: The New Politics of Aging in America*. Longman's thesis is that the baby boomers (of which he is a part) are being denied autonomy by the demands of older and younger generations, dependents for whom they must "pay" to the detriment of their own savings for old age.

One of the things that has impressed us in viewing data from a our longitudinal study of three-generation families is the amount of change in families over 17 years, and how often that change involves alterations in levels of dependency. For example, in response to the question, "How have things changed between you and your parents in the last few years?", a 57-year-old daughter answered: "My parents' health has deteriorated and I am beginning to assume a parenting role in caring for them—a true role reversal!"

At the same time, other respondents emphasize continuity and the maintenance of autonomy into old age. A 61-year-old son chose to emphasize this: "My mother is the steadying influence in all our lives—compassionate, humble, yet firm in her convictions. She will be forever young and abreast of the times."

Our grandparent-generation respondents frequently mention concerns about being dependent on others, and their wish to maintain autonomy. A 75-year-old grandmother said: "(I worry about) . . . being a burden to my family if I can't take care of myself." And a 72-year-old added: "(I look forward to) . . . living life to the fullest in good health and not be a burden to my children."

However, despite the older generations' frequent concern about age-related dependency, at least some of their children find positive benefits to it. One son, age 59, said:

I feel I've become closer to my mother since my father's death because of her increased needs. She doesn't drive and never handled money matters before. My realization that she won't always be there, and because of what we went through together [during his father's death], has led to this closeness.

The tension between autonomy and dependency in individuals, as well as families, as both age can be seen at many stages of psychosocial development throughout the life course (Baltes, 1987; Erikson, 1950; Havighurst, 1954, 1957). The family is a primary context for the negotiating of each. For instance, one clearly sees in adolescence the conflict between autonomy and dependency (both parents and teenagers may feel the demand for autonomy, and then the denial of responsibilities associated with it). Erikson (1950) long ago characterized this as reflecting a developmental crisis of identity versus role diffusion. He noted that this is a recurrent issue throughout the life cycle, never completely resolved once and for all, involving continual negotiation as crises are encountered throughout development.

Transitions to old age manifest the tension between autonomy and dependency as previously independent adults encounter age-related dependency in various guises, like role transitions brought on by retirement, widowhood, or sickness. Often, these transitions involve a new dependency on external valuations, affirmations, and expectations (Bengtson & Kuypers, 1974). The previous balance needs to be adjudicated due to age-related changes. This requires negotiation.

The challenge for different generations involves coping with the new dependencies of the older member and enhancing what autonomy is present. For families involved in caretaking for a suddenly dependent parent, the task is to work out some accommodation between autonomy and dependency for the elder and for the ongoing family unit.

At the macrosocial level, the same process is evident. A population of increasingly aged individuals faces increasing dependencies, but wishes to retain some degree of autonomy. As Cole (1989) asserted, "We need policies that eliminate the surplus dependency imposed on older people, policies that strengthen their ability to solve their own problems and contribute to their communities" (p. 382). Public policy must attempt to alleviate dependency, fostering the autonomy of elderly individuals that will enable continuing contributions to the surrounding social environment.

Solidarity and Individualism

Solidarity is a second conceptual issue relevant to issues of intercohort inequities. By solidarity we mean the cohesion of a group: the way it draws from (and gives to) individuals that comprise it, and the ways it is distinguished from other groups as a result. Hechter (1986) suggested a general proposition to explain variations in solidarity: "The higher the level of individual resources which are committed to collective activity, the higher the solidarity of the group" (p. 126). There is an inherent tension here in the potential conflict between individual needs and identities, and those of the group. It is a tension that has relevance for the struggle for autonomy, and, as we will see later, for issues of affirmation and conflict.

Solidarity can be seen in two ways. First and most obvious are its microsocial dimensions in the interactions between family members of different generations, as individual needs and wishes confront family needs and expectations. This tension and its resolution results in differing levels of cohesion, or "solidarity," among dyads within the family, and between one family as compared to another. At the microsocial level, generational solidarity is evident, because we reserve the term *generation* to refer to role status within the family hierarchy.

Second, solidarity can be seen as a mechanism in intercohort, as well as intracohort, interactions at the macrosocial level. One manifestation of this is the concern that, individually and collectively, too many resources are being demanded by another cohort (the concern of Longman in *Born to Pay*, and a theme of many "generational equity" advocates). Another is the presumed greater "solidarity" among the aged as a cohort, compared to other cohorts, seen in the "old age lobby" of AARP and NCOA being more well-organized than those of the "children's lobby." A third component is related to stereotypes about cohorts: the "Greedy Geezers" portrayed in some "generational equity" accounts, and the "me first" orientations of Yuppies and baby boomers (a theme subtly defended by Philip Longman). These reflect beliefs about cohort inequalities being caused by overweening individualism, or selfishness. At the macrosocial level, intercohort and intracohort solidarity are both assumed in many analyses, and only sometimes actually observed empirically.

There are obvious differences between the micro- and macrosocial dynamics of generational and cohort solidarity. Yet it is instructive to examine the parameters of intergenerational solidarity at the small group level, as it is here the tensions between group solidarity and individualistic orientations can be most clearly seen.

Conflicts between individual needs and expectations about family solidarity were expressed by many members of our study sample: "My father feels that I don't have him to visit in our home enough. With our office at home and three late-teenagers, he demands that I give him a great deal of attention, which I can't" said a 56-year-old son. Another middle-aged child, a 46-year-old daughter, was concerned about the lack of family solidarity exhibited by her parents: "They are always complaining or not speaking to some members of the family, instead of looking for harmony. They pit members against each other instead of looking for harmony. When they have achieved their purpose, they sit back and ask why we can't get along together."

Our research team has attempted to specify the components of family intergenerational solidarity, to delineate their underlying components, and examine how they may be measured in survey research (Mangen, Bengtson, & Landry, 1988). First, we have come to believe that there are at least six conceptual dimensions of family solidarity (affect, association, consensus, exchanges, norms, and structure). Second, we have demonstrated that these are somewhat independent dimensions, and that their interrelationships are far more complex than we had earlier hypothesized (Roberts & Bengtson, 1990). Third, we are coming to see the crucial role that familistic norms about solidarity play, in terms of the highly predictable structure of kinship obligations (a point convincingly made by Rossi & Rossi, 1990) and as predictors of affect and association (Bengtson & Roberts, 1988). Fourth, we are finding that dimensions of solidarity remain remarkably stable over time—even, for example, in grandparent-grandchild relationships, where change might be the most expected (Miller, 1989).

The results of these microlevel explorations point to the tension between solidarity and individuality between generations within the family. On the one hand there is unmistakable evidence of family-level cohesion, interaction, and specific expectations that suggest high levels of support in many multigenerational networks. On the other hand there are concerns over unmet expectations, or too many expectations, leading to feelings of "burden," alienation, and guilt.

Particularly with regard to caregiving demands for a dependent elder, the negotiation of solidarity versus individuation is a difficult task for the families of aging individuals. The task, as in balancing autonomy and dependency needs, is in working out a balance of each, over time. The relevant variables in this process include: (a) objective resources (e.g., family structure and proximity, (b) previous levels of solidarity and involvement, (c) normative expectations regarding filial and paternal responsibilities, (d) subjective resources (e.g., the sense of competing demands, (e) the demand load of elder-caregiving, (f) guilt. An agenda for future research involves assessing the levels and relationships of these variables as they become part of the family intergenerational process of caregiving for dependent members, especially elders.

Affirmation and Conflict

By *affirmation* we mean behaviors that tend to confirm, give agreement to, and reinforce the acts of others. By *conflict* we mean opposition, disagreement, and negative reinforcement to others' behaviors.

Two things should be emphasized. First, conflict is part and parcel of any relational behavior, whether at the macrosocial level of interest groups or the microsocial level of families. Conflict is rarely acknowledged as part of "normal" family functioning (for an excellent exception, see Sprey, 1969, 1979). Second, affirmation and conflict are not necessarily contradictory (it is the duty of the "loyal opposition" to criticize policies of the party in power, while affirming the values of parliamentary process), although this is most often found in impersonal role relationships (such as between defense and prosecuting attorney). The greater the intimacy of parties in conflict, the greater their differences may be perceived as an erosion of affirmation.

A major source of conflict is social inequality, or its perception, which is usually called *inequity* in light of norms that say parties *should* be equal (e.g., examine the entire corpus of the adamant revolutionary, Karl Marx, in Tucker, 1978). Inequalities are, of course, one of the most usual aspects in intergenerational interaction, at least until the child is grown, with issues of control (and autonomy) being negotiated as both generations face each other as adults. Frequently parents are unwilling or unable to give up control; norms of equity having been violated (from the adult child's perspective), and the result is conflict, and feelings of a lack of affirmation.

Our respondents give many examples of perceived intergenerational inequities leading to conflict. A 56-year-old daughter said: "My mother has always tried to run my life—control everything I did; control my children, telling me what not to do, and what to do with my children—My mother still checks up on my children, asks them too many questions as she did me over the years, and my children object very much.'' Other respondents commented on their wishes for more affirmation from the other generation. This 87-year-old man perceived inequities in the way his children treat him:

> (I worry about) . . . loneliness and lack of respect from my children, who always got what they wanted from my wife and me. We put them in a very high standard of living and respect. Why did I have to end my twilight years like this? I never asked them for anything for us. Not one of them gave us anything. All we ask for and expect is a little respect . . . Maybe I have too big an estate and we don't die soon enough.

The maintenance of affirmation is difficult, especially in light of inequalities between groups, which may lead to conflict. Whether at the family level or the society level, these issues require negotiation as the passage of time brings changes in the balance among autonomy and dependency, solidarity and individuality, affirmation and conflict.

CONCLUSION

Generational Equity and Parent–Child Relations

In summary, unique demographic trends in both mortality and fertility rates account for dramatic changes in the age structure of American society in the 20th century. An increase in the birth rate following World War II (sustained for nearly two decades) followed by a gradual decline in the 1960s produced a population "bulge" in the flow of birth cohorts. The occurrence of this Baby Boom, combined with an unprecedented expansion of longevity, have remolded the age structure of society.

In the context of these demographic shifts, a controversy is emerging concerning the distribution of public resources between the elderly and other age groups in the population. *Generational equity* is the phrase most often used to summarize the controversy, although as we have argued neither *generational* or *equity* are the correct terms to use. The essential elements of this debate involve the rise in the proportion of elderly in the population, various social policies directing federal funds that benefit the elderly, and the perceived societal responsibility in providing for the elderly without harming younger age groups.

We have discussed four general approaches that have emerged in the 1980s in the debate. The "Greedy Elders" perspective, frequently reflected in mass media accounts, assumes an imminant conflict between the aged and younger age groups, stressing that benefits to the aged must not be allowed to expand,

and perhaps should be cut back. The "Distributive Justice" approach, instead of focusing on age-status, inequities, proposes social policy directed toward the growing inequity between rich and poor. The "Moral Revolution" approach asserts that our moral values about aging and retirement as well as chronic or custodial care must change. Generational inequity is ultimately solved by a change in cultural norms. Finally, the "Life Course" approach suggests that inequities result from income differentials throughout the life course. The debate involves a misunderstanding of general labor market conditions that affect age cohorts differently. As noted earlier, this debate is far from being resolved.

We also have examined some of the microsocial or social/psychological dimensions of the debate noting that both microsocial and macrosocial dimensions of age-group interactions over them involve negotiations regarding autonomy, solidarity, and affirmation between generations. We emphasized three points: (a) The debate is about *inequality*, real or perceived, between age cohorts. (b) These inequalities can be seen as arising from three *social-psychological issues* characterizing interactions between generations—autonomy, solidarity, and affirmation—which arise from the process of coping with change over the life course. (c) These three polarities are most clearly seen at the *microsocial levels* of negotiating with change in multi-generation families; however, parallels can be drawn to the macrosocial level of age-group interactions of relevance to generational equity.

Our central arguments can be summarized as follows. First, the generational equity debate is about *inequality* between cohorts, real or imagined: the unequal distribution of resources between individuals of different ages. Second, we have suggested that this debate is rooted in life-course processes involving, (a) the changing needs of cohorts—individuals of similar ages—as they grow and age through time, and (b) norms of equity and reciprocity involving the succession of generations. The norm of reciprocity (Gouldner, 1960) is strong in intergenerational relationships and works both ways. At the microsocial level the implied contract of generations calls for the parents to invest a major portion of their resources throughout their adult years in the rearing of children; in old age, the caregiving is expected to be reversed. Third, we have argued that, in both of these processes, issues of autonomy, solidarity, and affirmation require negotiation—both at the microsocial level of face-to-face interaction, especially within families, and at the macrosocial level of policies reflecting cohorts. We should not confuse the two, nor should we ignore similar or parallel processes in negotiating change and dependency with the passage of time.

Policy Recommendations

It is clear to us that the "Greedy Elders" framework is unsuitable. We must recognize other ways of conceptualizing the debate. This chapter is an effort to make explicit some of these alternative approaches.

In agreement with Gould and Palmer (1988), we feel that the current rhetoric of generational equity is not constructive. It constitutes a hinderance to the conceptualization and explanation of the problem. As Kingson, Hirshorn, and Cornman (1986) stated:

> At best, the framing of issues in terms of competition and conflict between generations is based on a misunderstanding of relations between generations and distracts attention from more useful ways of examining social problems. At worst, it is a cynical and purposely divisive strategy put forth to justify and build political support for attacks on policies and reductions in programs that benefit all age groups. (pp. 13-14)

The current "generational equity vocabulary" is ineffective in guiding toward solutions. Moreover, we should not allow our words to carry our debate.

The message to policymakers is quite simple: We must be prepared for the aging of the Baby Boom. In the next two decades, our government must have clear standards regarding: (a) what type of obligation is owed to retirees in terms of the benefits collectively committed to the nation's elderly, and (b) the scope, or extent of the benefits that have been allotted. Apart from dealing with the Baby Boom cohorts, we must deal with the more general moral questions of our obligation to the elderly in the future. As a society, what do we owe elderly cohorts? And, how much do we give?

In approaching these questions, we sense the need for a historically grounded perspective to the debate, and the problem of cohort inequality. As Achenbaum (1989) asserted, "a historical perspective is required to leaven what too often has been a static policy discussion. The US generational equity debate surprisingly neglects differences in experiences and opportunities that are bound to exist among separate birth cohorts who live(d) in real time" (p. 131). Again, Achenbaum (1989) stated that "A fairer comparison requires examining cohorts' cumulative experiences in their proper historical context" (p. 132). Specifically, researchers and policymakers need to be conscious of both period and cohort effects in determining the sources of cohort inequality. A historically informed life-course approach seems prudent. Such an approach is suggested by both Easterlin (1987) and Helco (1988). Easterlin accounted for differential rates in poverty by linking macrolevel labor market conditions with their effect on families at family-forming ages. Similarly, Helco proposed a life-course approach that explicitly incorporates working and nonworking stages of individuals, acknowledging differential employment histories of individuals and differential employment opportunities of cohorts, to explain the economic wellbeing of different age groups.

Moreover, policymakers must make efforts to facilitate the microlevel negotiations occurring between family members as individuals age over time. This must begin with recognizing the reality of such negotiations, and then encouraging programs that target such processes. A population of increasingly aged individuals faces increasing dependencies, but wishes to retain some degree of autonomy. The challenge for different generations involves coping with the new dependencies of the elder member and enhancing what autonomy is present. We must recognize the tension and potential conflict between individual needs, and those of the collectivity as a whole. The resulting negotiation of solidarity versus individuation is a difficult task for the families of aging individuals. The maintenance of affirmation is difficult, especially in light of inequalities between groups, that lead to conflict.

Research Recommendations

Even before we can address policy issues related to generations, we need more knowledge about cross-age linkages, exchange, and reciprocities. Data need to be presented that relate to the following issues:

1. We need a better understanding of the "ties that bind" (i.e., the linkages that occur between generations and cohorts). Specifically, what are the reciprocities, exchanges, and obligations existing with respect to: (a) intrafamily interactions between generation; (b) individuals within and between cohorts; (c) aggregate levels between cohorts?

2. We need to understand the influences that shape norms of reciprocity, exchange, and obligation. For example: What are the mechanisms of value transmission regarding age group membership and duty? In the evolution (and revolution) of moral values, what is the impact of the changing demographic context, such as the impact of changing cohort flows, over time? What is the influence of the reigning political climate? And what are the consequences of the economic environment, especially in terms of levels of inflation, shifting labor conditions, advances in technology, global competition, and concerns overs the national budget?

3. We need a more comprehensive understanding of the distribution of public and private resources between generations and cohorts. What is the nature and extent of resource distribution for individuals across the life course, for example? or between generations within the family? or between cohorts within society?

4. An understanding of the politics of age groups is essential because intergenerational obligations are generalized at the societal level in becoming institutionalized by law. It is important we expand our understanding of (a) influences determining age-group perceptions of policymakers; (b) influences on age-group perceptions of voters and lobbyists; (c) the impact of age-group advocates on the decision-making process.

5. Finally, we need to expand our conclusions with cross-cultural comparisons of reciprocity, exchange, and obligation. For example, what are the most

salient historical, political, and economic variables in determining: (a) types of obligation, (b) methods of resource distribution, and (c) the extent of exchanges existing within a society?

Also, cross-cultural comparison of political systems would be fruitful. We need to better articulate: (a) the nature and implication of alternative political systems on intergenerational and intercohort interactions, (b) the differing political processes used to facilitate and/or enforce intergenerational and intercohort obligations, (c) the nature of the welfare state and the future of welfare programs for both the young and the old in the face of competing programs such as defense spending.

The central question is this: How can we alleviate generational tensions and inequalities arising from age-related struggles regarding autonomy, solidarity, and affirmation? This question will, we feel, represent a major part of the social policy agenda for the 1990's and beyond, just as it will be the focus of most families for the 21st century.

REFERENCES

Achenbaum, A. (1989). Public pensions as intergenerational transfers in the United States. In P. Johnson, C. Conrad, & D. Thomson (Eds.), *Workers versus pensioners: Intergenerational justice in an aging world* (pp. 121–136). Manchester: Manchester University Press.

Adams, B. N. (1986). *The family in transition.* Homewood, IL: Dorsey Press.

Baltes, P. B. (1987). Theoretical propositions of life-span developmental psychology: On the dynamics between growth and decline. *Developmental Psychology, 23,* 611–626.

Bengtson, V. L. (1986). Sociological perspectives on aging, families, and the future. In M. Bergener (Ed.), *Perspectives on aging: The 1986 Sandoz lectures in gerontology* (pp. 237–263). New York & London: Academic Press.

Bengtson, V. L., Cutler, N. E., Mangen, D. J., & Marshall, V. W. (1985). Generations, cohorts, and relations between age groups. In R. Binstock & E. Shanas (Eds.), *Handbook of aging and the social sciences* (Vol. 2, pp. 304–338). New York: Van Nostrand Reinhold.

Bengtson, V. L., Gatz, M., Roberts, R. E. L., & Richards, L. (1988, November). *Notes on autonomy, solidarity, and affirmation in aging families.* Paper presented as part of the Symposium: New Perspectives on Autonomy and Aging, at the annual meeting of the Gerontological Society of America, San Francisco.

Bengtson, V. L., & Kuypers, J. A. (1974). Toward competence in the older family. In T. H. Brubaker (Ed.), *Family relationships in later life* (pp. 211–228). Beverly Hills, CA: Sage.

Bengtson, V. L., & Roberts, R. E. L. (1988, November). *On the utility of intergenerational solidarity: Replication and reconceptualization.* Paper presented at the Annual Meeting of the National Council on Family Relations, Pre-conference Theory and Methodology Workshop, Philadelphia, PA.

Bengston, V. L., Rosenthal, C., & Burton, L. (1990). Families and aging: Diversity and heterogeneity. In R Binstock & K. George (Eds.), *Handbook of Aging and the Social Sciences* (3rd ed., pp. 263–287). San Diego: Academic Press.

Binstock, R. H. (1983). The aged as scapegoat. *The Gerontologist, 23*, 136–143.

Brody, E. M. (1985). Parent care as a normative family stress. *The Gerontologist, 25*, 19–29.

Callahan, D. (1986). Health care in the aging society: A moral dilemma. In A. Pifer & L. Bronte (Eds.), *Our aging society*, (pp. 319–339). New York: Norton.

Callahan, D. (1987a). *Setting limits.* New York: Simon & Schuster.

Callahan, D. (1987b, August). "What's a 'good age'?" Limiting health care for the old. *The Nation, 22*(1), 125–127.

Cherlin, A. J. (1981). *Marriage, divorce, remarriage.* Cambridge: Harvard University Press.

Cole, T. R. (1989). Generational equity in America: A cultural historian's perspective. *Social Science Medicine, 29*, 377–383.

Crimmins, E. M. (1985). The social impact of recent and prospective mortality declines among older Americans. *Social Science Review, 70*, 192–198.

Daniels, N. (1988). *Am I my parents' keeper?* New York: Oxford University Press.

Durenberger, D. (1987, January). [Remarks made by Senator Dave Durenberger to the conference on "An agenda for the aging society," Minneapolis, MN].

Durenberger, D. (1989). Education and the contract between the generations. *The Generational Journal, 2*(1), 5–8.

Durkheim, E. (1984). *The division of labor in society.* New York: The Free Press. (Original work published 1893)

Easterlin, R. A. (1987). The new age structure of poverty in America: Permanent or transient? *Population and Development Review, 13*, 195–208.

Elder, G. H., Jr. (1974). *Children of the great depression.* Chicago: University of Chicago Press.

Elder, G. H., Jr., & Liker, J. K. (1982). Hard times in women's lives: Historical infuences across forty years. *American Journal of Sociology, 88*, 241–269.

Erikson, R. (1950). *Childhood and society.* New York: Norton.

Fairlie, H. (1988, March 28). Talkin' bout my generation. *The New Republic*, p. 19.

Gatz, M., Bengston, V. L., & Blum, M. J. (1990). Caregiving families. In J. E. Birren & K. W. Schaie (Eds.), *Handbook of the psychology of aging* (3rd ed., pp. 561–589). San Diego, CA: Academic Press.

Gelfand, D. E., Olsen, J. K., & Block, M. R. (1978). Two generations of elderly in the changing American family: Implications for family services. *The Family Coordinator, 27*, 395–403.

Gould, S., & Palmer, J. (1988). Outcomes, interpretations, and policy implications. In J. Palmer, T. Smeeding, & B. Torrey (Eds.), *The vulnerable* (pp. 413–441). Washington, DC: The Urban Institute.

Gouldner, A. W. (1960). The norm of reciprocity. *American Sociological Review, 25*, 161–178.

Hagestad, G. O. (1986). The aging society as a context for family life. *Daedalus, 115*, 119–139.

Havighurst, R. J. (1954). *Education and society.* New York: Allyn & Bacon.

Havighurst, R. J. (1957). The social competence of middle-aged people. *Genetic Psychology Monograph, 56*, 297–375.

Hechter, M. (1986). *Principles of group solidarity.* Berkeley, CA: University of California Press.

Helco, H. (1988). Generational politics. In J. Palmer, T. Smeeding, & B. Torrey (Eds.), *The vulnerable* (pp. 381–411). Washington, DC: The Urban Institute.

Jones, J. (1988, July). *Proceedings from the National Conference on "Retiree Health Benefits: The Generational Equity Perspective."* Sixth National Conference of Americans for Generational Equity, Washington, DC.

Jones, J. (1987, September). *Proceedings from the National Conference on "Ties that Bind: Debts, Deficits, Demographics."* Sixth national conference of Americans for Generational Equity, Washington, DC.

Kingson, E. R. (1988). Generational equity: An unexpected opportunity to broaden the politics of aging. *The Gerontologist, 28,* 765–772.

Kingson, E. R., Hirshorn, B. A., & Cornman, J. M. (1986). *Ties that bind: The interdependence of generations.* Washington, DC: Seven Locks Press.

Lamm, R. D. (1985). *Megatraumas: America in the year 2000.* Boston, MA: Houghton Mifflin.

Lenski, G. (1966). *Power and privilege: A theory of social stratification.* New York: McGraw-Hill.

Longman, P. (1987). *Born to pay: The new politics of aging in America.* Boston: Houghton Mifflin Company.

Mangen, D. J., Bengtson, V. L., & Landry, P. (Eds.). (1988). *The measurement of intergenerational relations.* Beverly Hills: Sage.

Mellins, C. A., Boyd S. L., & Gatz, M. (1988, November). *Caregiving as a family network event.* Paper presented at the annual meeting of the Gerontological Society of America, San Francisco.

Miller, R. B. (1989). *Role transitions and grandparent-grandchild solidarity: A longitudinal analysis.* Unpublished doctoral dissertation, University of Southern California, Los Angeles.

Minkler, M. (1986). "Generational equity" and the new victim blaming: An emerging public policy issue. *International Journal of Health, 16,* 539–551.

Minkler, M., & Stone, R. (1985). The feminization of poverty and older women. *The Gerontologist, 25,* 351–357.

Moynihan, D. P. (1987). *Family and nation.* New York: Harcourt, Brace, Jovanovich.

Neugarten, B. L., & Neugarten, D. A. (1986). Changing meanings of age in the aging society. In A. Pifer & L. Bronte (Eds.), *Our aging society* (pp. 33–51). New York: W. W. Norton.

Preston, S. H. (1984a). Children and elderly: Divergent paths for America's dependents. *Demography, 21,* 435–437.

Preston, S. H. (1984b). Children and the elderly in the U.S. *Scientific American, 251,* 44–49.

Quadagno, J. (1988). *The transformation of old age security: Class and politics in the American welfare state.* Chicago, IL: University of Chicago Press.

Quadagno, J. (1990). Generational equity and the politics of the welfare state. *Politics and Society.*

Richards, L. N., Bengtson, V. L., & Miller, R. (1989). The "generation in the middle." Perceptions of adults' intergenerational relationships. In K. Kreppner & R. Lerner (Eds.), *Family systems and life-span development* (pp. 341–366). Hillsdale, NJ: Lawrence Erlbaum Associates.

Riley, M. W. (1985). Age strata in social systems. In R. H. Binstock & E. E. Shanas (Eds.), *Handbook of aging and the social sciences* (2nd ed., pp. 369–411). New York: Van Nostrand Reinhold.

Roberts, R. E. L., & Bengtson, V. L. (1990). Is family solidarity a unidimensional construct? A second test of a formal model. *Journal of Gerontology, 45*, S12–S20.

Rosenthal, C. J. (1985). Kinkeeping in the familial division of labor. *Journal of Marriage and the Family, 47*, 965–974.

Rosenwaike, I. (1985). A demographic portrait of the oldest old. *Milbank Memorial Fund Quarterly/Health and Society, 63*, 187–205.

Rossi, A., & Rossi, P. (1990). *Of human bonding: Parent–child relationships across the life course.* Hawthorne, NY: Aldine & Gruyter.

Siegel, J. S., & Taeuber, C. (1986, Winter). Demographic perspectives on the long-lived society. *Daedalus.*

Smeeding, T., Torrey, B. B., & Rein, M. (1986, May). *The economic status of the young and the old.* Paper presented at the annual meeting of the American Association for the Advancement of Science, Philadelphia.

Soldo, B. (1981). America's elderly in the 1980s. *Population Bulletin, 35*,

Sprey, J. (1969). The family as a system in conflict. *Journal of Marriage and the Family, 31*, 699–706.

Sprey, J. (1979). Conflict theory and the study of marriage and the family. In W. R. Burr, R. Hill, F. I. Nye, & I. L. Reiss (Eds.), *Contemporary theories about the family* (Vol. 2, pp. 130–159). New York: The Free Press.

Thomson, D. (1988, July). *The welfare state and generation conflict.* Paper presented at the Conference on Work, Retirement, and Intergenerational Equity, St. Johns College, Cambridge, MA.

Treas, J., & Logue, B. (1986). Economic development and the older population. *Population and Development Review, 12*, 645–673.

Troll, L. E. (1985). The contingencies of grandparenting. In V. L. Bengtson & J. F. Robertson (Eds.), *Grandparenthood.* Beverly Hills, CA: Sage.

Tucker, R. C. (1978). *The Marx-Engels reader* (2nd ed.). New York: W. W. Norton.

Watkins. S. C., Menken, J. A., & Bongaarts, J. (1987). Demographic foundations of family change. *American Sociological Review, 52*, 346–358.

Weber, M. (1978). In G. Roth & C. Wittich (Eds.), *Economy and society* (pp.). Berkeley, CA: University of California Press. (Original work published 1922)

Author Index

Subject Index